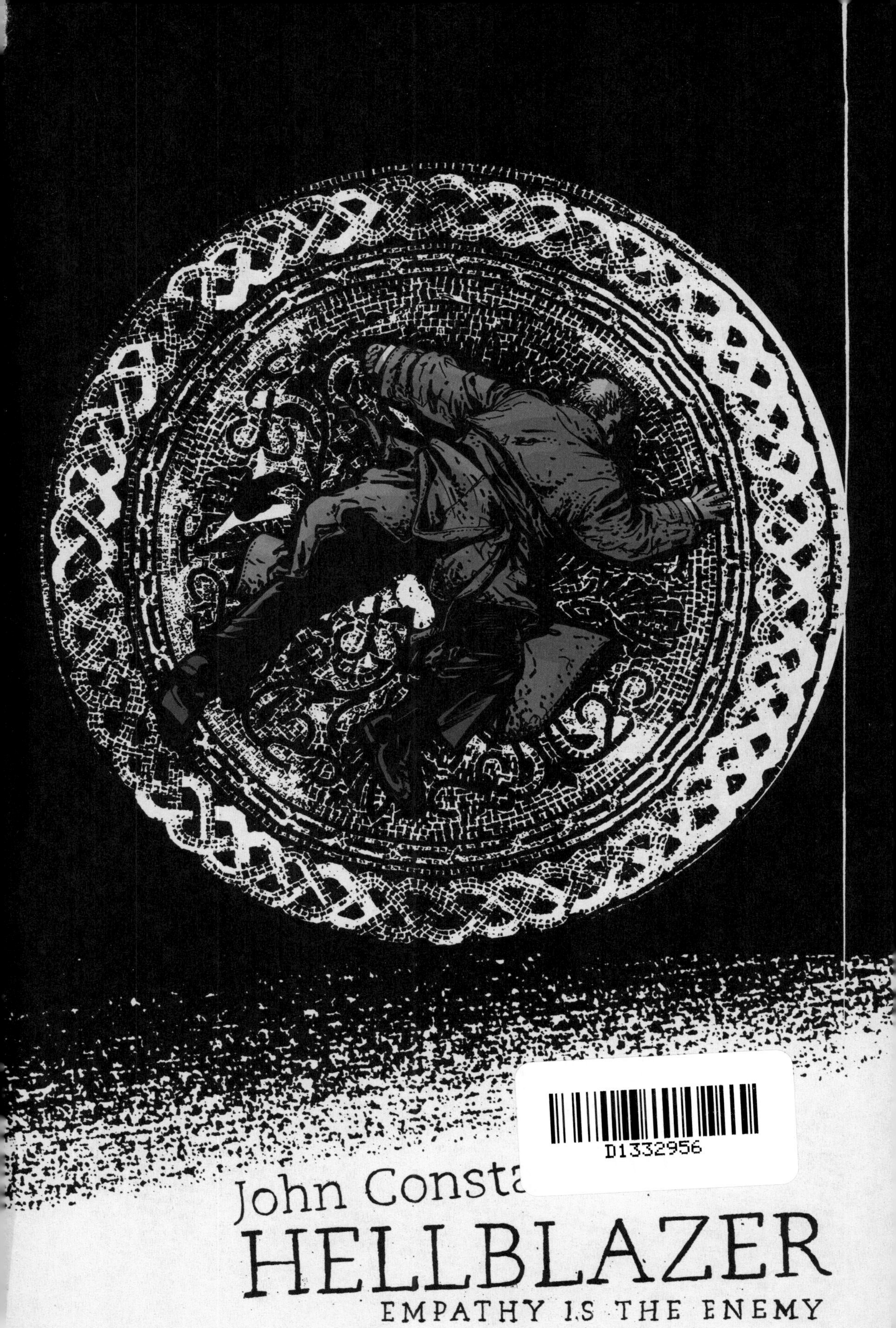

John Consta

HELLBLAZER

EMPATHY IS THE ENEMY

John Constantine
HELLBL

EMPATHY IS THE ENEMY

Denise Mina-writer

Leonardo Manco-artist

Lee Loughridge-colorist

Jared K. Fletcher-letterer

**Greg Lauren, Lee Bermejo
and Leonardo Manco**
-Original Series Covers

Karen Berger, Senior VP-Executive Editor   Jonathan Vankin, Editor-original series   Casey Seijas, Assistant Editor-original series
Bob Harras, Group Editor-collected edition   Robbin Brosterman, Senior Art Director   Louis Prandi, Art Director
Paul Levitz, President & Publisher   Georg Brewer, VP-Design & DC Direct Creative   Richard Bruning, Senior VP-Creative Director
Patrick Caldon, Executive VP-Finance & Operations   Chris Caramalis, VP-Finance   John Cunningham, VP-Marketing
Terri Cunningham, VP-Managing Editor   Stephanie Fierman, Senior VP-Sales & Marketing   Alison Gill, VP-Manufacturing
Hank Kanalz, VP-General Manager, WildStorm   Lillian Laserson, Senior VP & General Counsel   Jim Lee, Editorial Director-WildStorm
Paula Lowitt, Senior VP-Business & Legal Affairs   David McKillips, VP-Advertising & Custom Publishing
John Nee, VP-Business Development   Gregory Noveck, Senior VP-Creative Affairs   Cheryl Rubin, Senior VP-Brand Management
Jeff Trojan, VP-Business Development, DC Direct   Bob Wayne, VP-Sales

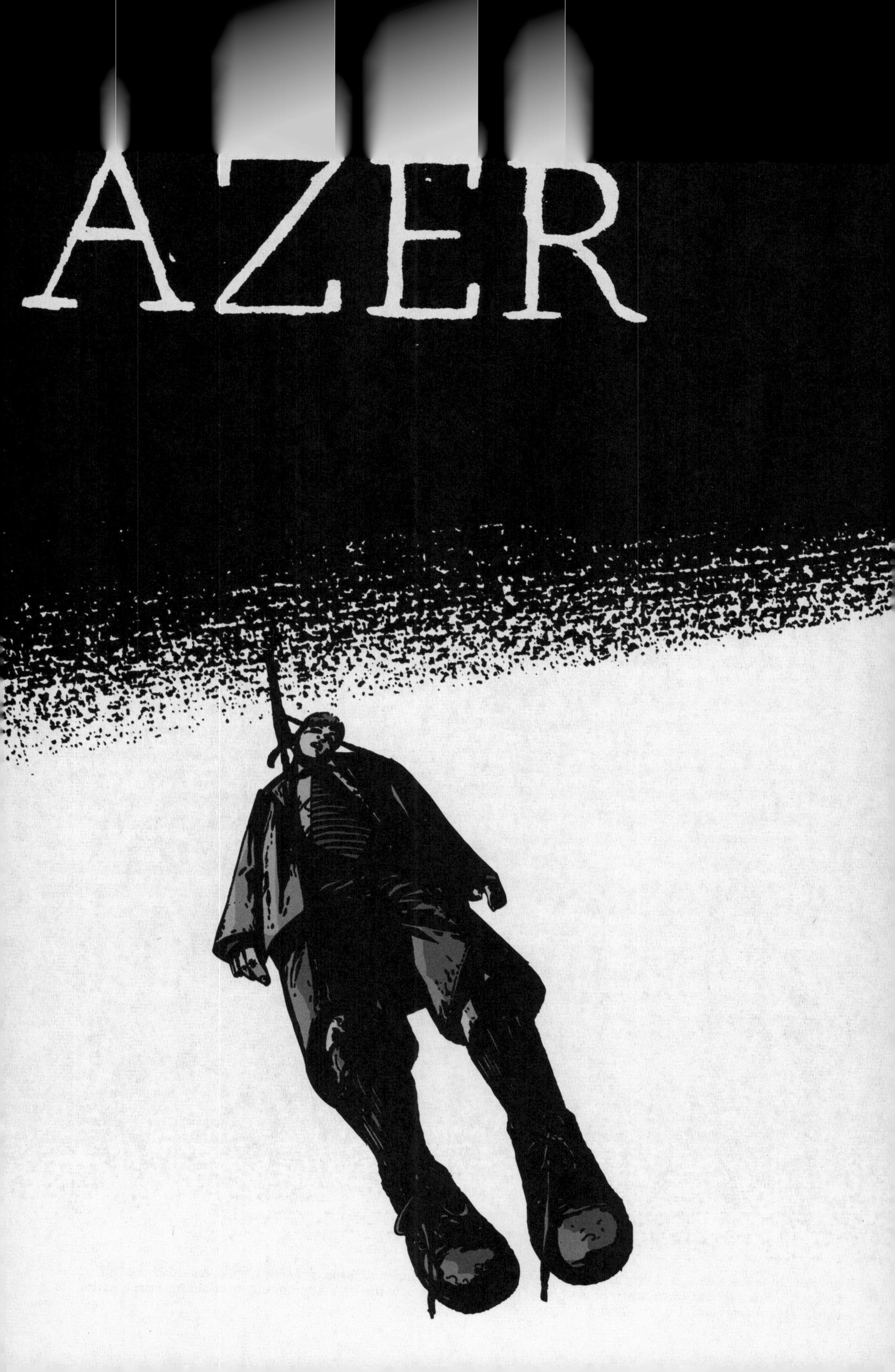
AZER

An Appreciation by Ian Rankin

Welcome to Scotland.

Not the Scotland you think you know, but a place riven by superstition and belief, a land dark with mischief and whispered terror.

The poet James Thomson lived most of his life away from Scotland, but was born in Port Glasgow. In 1874 he produced his masterpiece, "The City of Dreadful Night," a long surreal nightmare portraying an unnamed city. Thomson had lived in London, Colorado and Spain — his city could be anywhere at any point in history.

But I like to think he might have been commemorating his native Glasgow.

I also think John Constantine would love the writing's elegiac bleakness, though he might find it hard to agree with some of Thomson's beliefs:

The world rolls round for ever like a mill;
It grinds out death and life and good and ill;
It has no purpose, heart or mind or will.

Constantine knows differently. He's seen things that would send most of us scurrying to the asylum or slouching to the bottle (as Thomson himself eventually did). In "Empathy is the Enemy," Denise Mina takes Constantine to the city she knows best, a city she has made her own through her series of contemporary crime novels.

Glasgow may well prove to be the death of him.

But hey, it's not all grim up north — Mina brings plenty of humour with her, along with a few in-jokes (I had to smile at "Put that torch out!") and cultural references (the Rezillos were, for a brief moment, Scotland's premier punk act).

Above all, however, Mina is an extraordinary purveyor of shadow. As in her novels, we readers know that things are lurking just beyond our view: human predators, ghouls, psychosis and endgame. She also realises that religious zeal can beget cults, and by choosing to locate this story's beginning in Iona she is cutting to the quick of religious experience in Scotland. Iona was home to Scotland's first Christian community: the Word disseminated from that spot, and led, among other things, to bigotry, intolerance, murder and feuding... some of it still apparent on the streets of Glasgow.

There's another line I want to share with you from Thomson's poem: "No hope could have no fear." In other words, a man without any hope of betterment or salvation need have no fear of anything. To me, this says much about the character of John Constantine. Weary and cynical, his soul threadbare, he goes on fighting, prevails despite his dourest intentions. This makes him wonderfully human and supremely fitted for the path he continues to take. He fights the demons (both physical and emotional) because he can find no reason not to. Denise Mina leads him into trap after trap, and he goes willingly, knowing they are waiting. "Empathy is the Enemy" crackles with wit and horror, chills like a gust on a midnight street, and takes Constantine to new and overwhelming places.

Classic Hellblazer.

Classic Mina.

Welcome to Scotland... and haste ye back.

Ian Rankin is the award-winning author of the internationally renowned *Inspector Rebus* novels. Awarded the OBE in the Queen's Golden Jubilee Birthday Honours List in June 2002, he is now the UK's number one best-selling crime writer. He lives in Edinburgh with his wife and two sons.

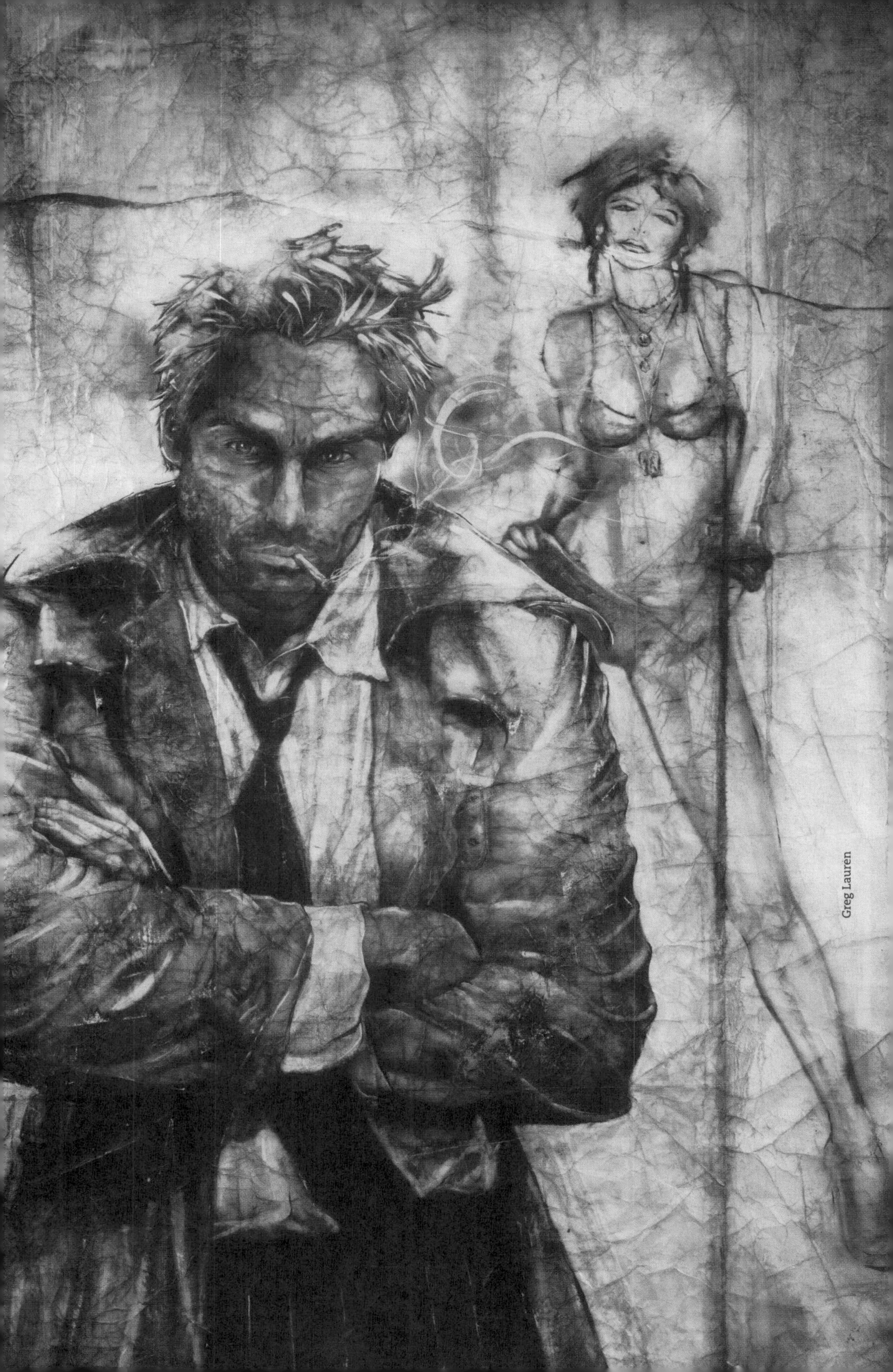
Greg Lauren

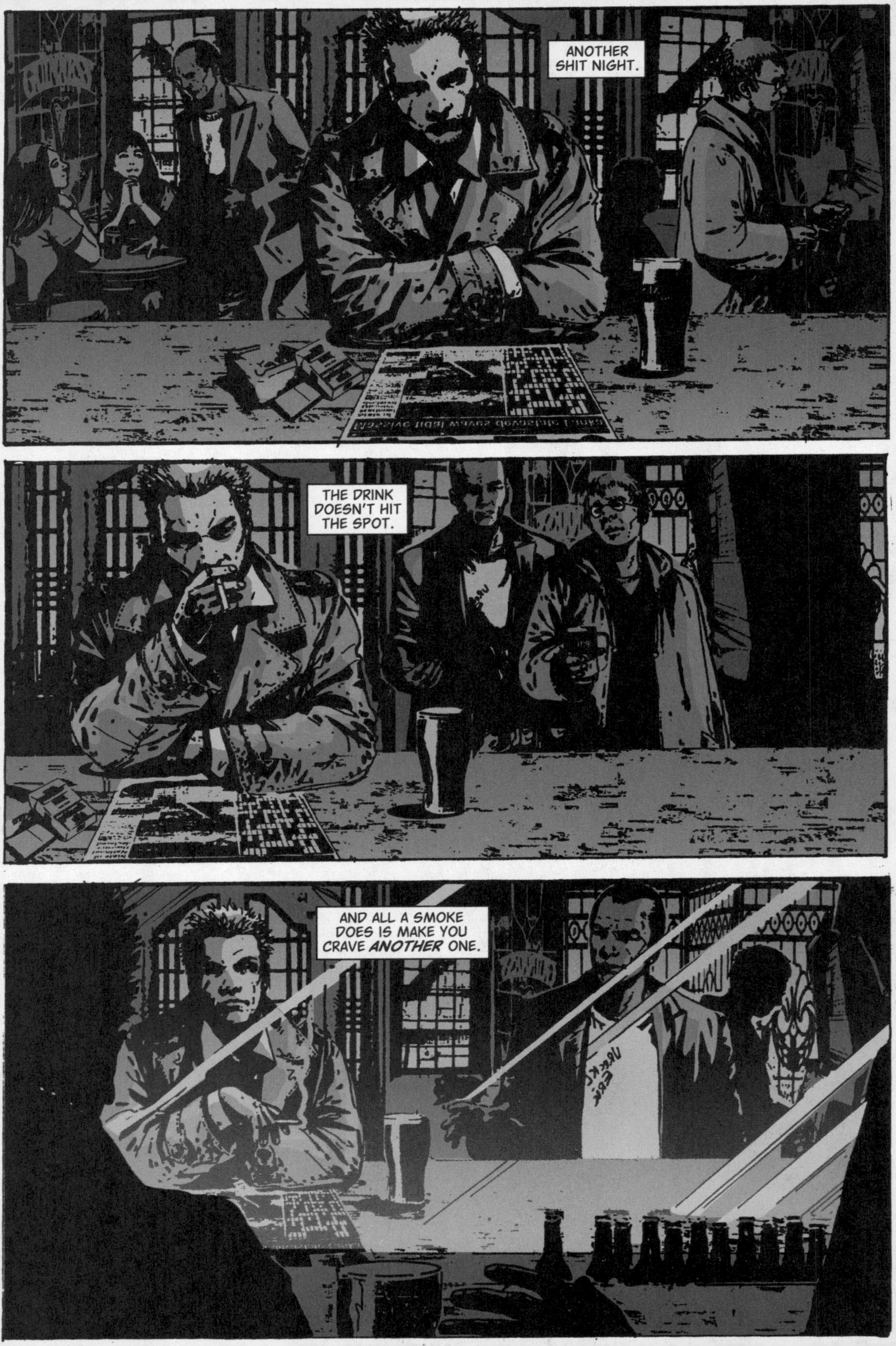
ANOTHER SHIT NIGHT.
THE DRINK DOESN'T HIT THE SPOT.
AND ALL A SMOKE DOES IS MAKE YOU CRAVE *ANOTHER* ONE.

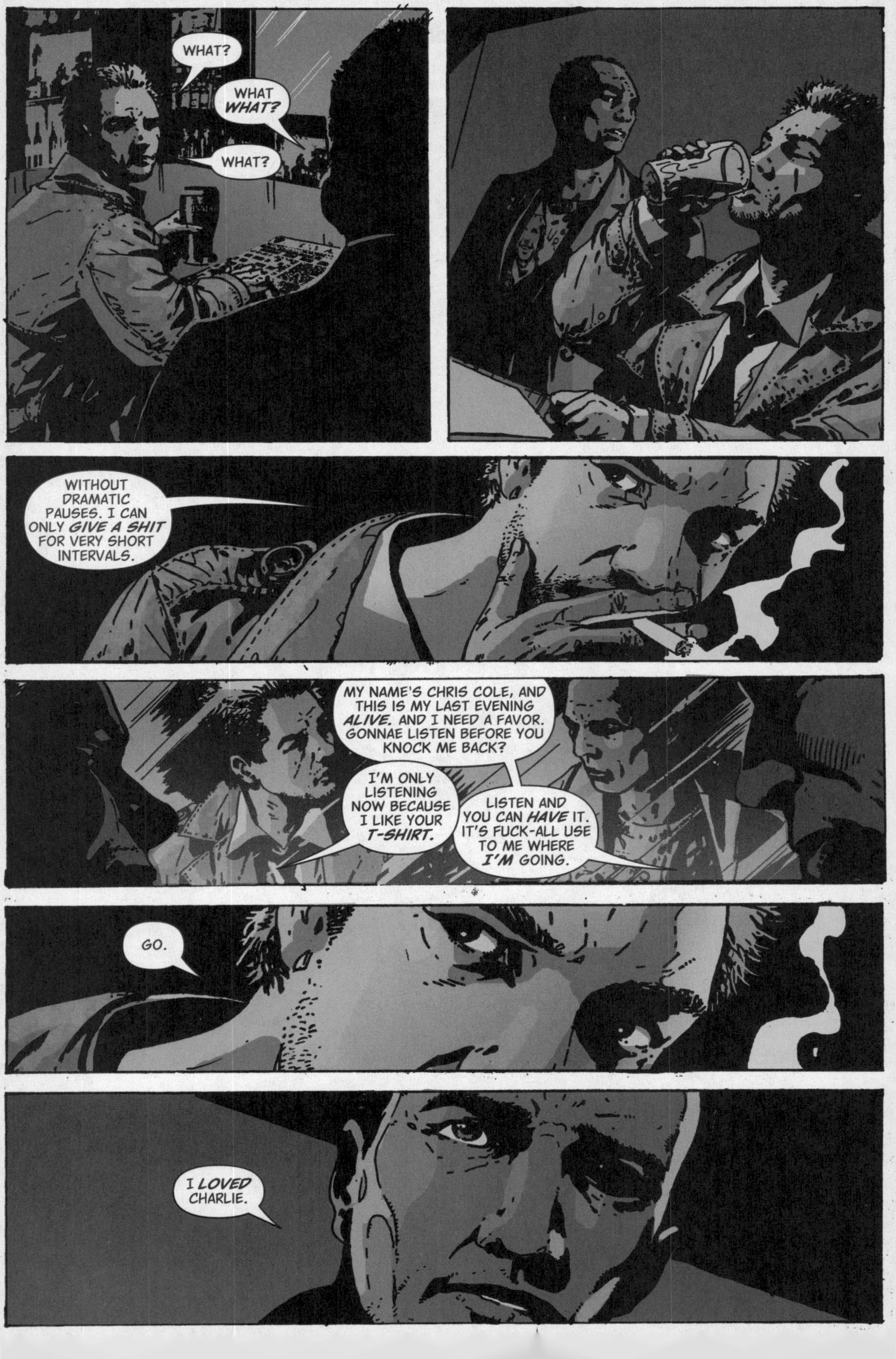
WHAT?
WHAT *WHAT?*
WHAT?
WITHOUT DRAMATIC PAUSES. I CAN ONLY *GIVE A SHIT* FOR VERY SHORT INTERVALS.
MY NAME'S CHRIS COLE, AND THIS IS MY LAST EVENING *ALIVE.* AND I NEED A FAVOR. GONNAE LISTEN BEFORE YOU KNOCK ME BACK?
I'M ONLY LISTENING NOW BECAUSE I LIKE YOUR *T-SHIRT.*
LISTEN AND YOU CAN *HAVE* IT. IT'S FUCK-ALL USE TO ME WHERE *I'M* GOING.
GO.
I *LOVED* CHARLIE.

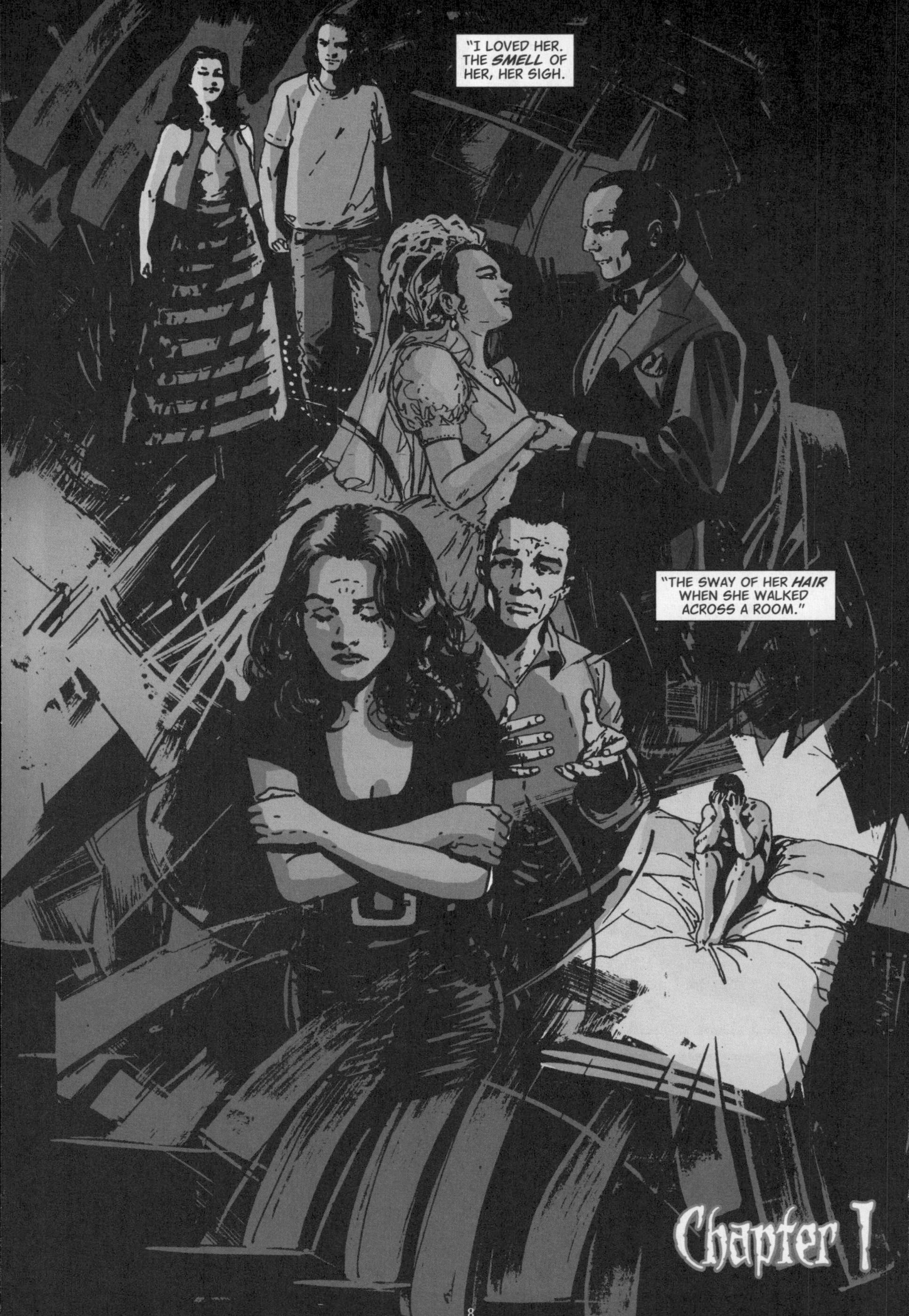
"I LOVED HER. THE SMELL OF HER, HER SIGH.
"THE SWAY OF HER HAIR WHEN SHE WALKED ACROSS A ROOM."
Chapter I

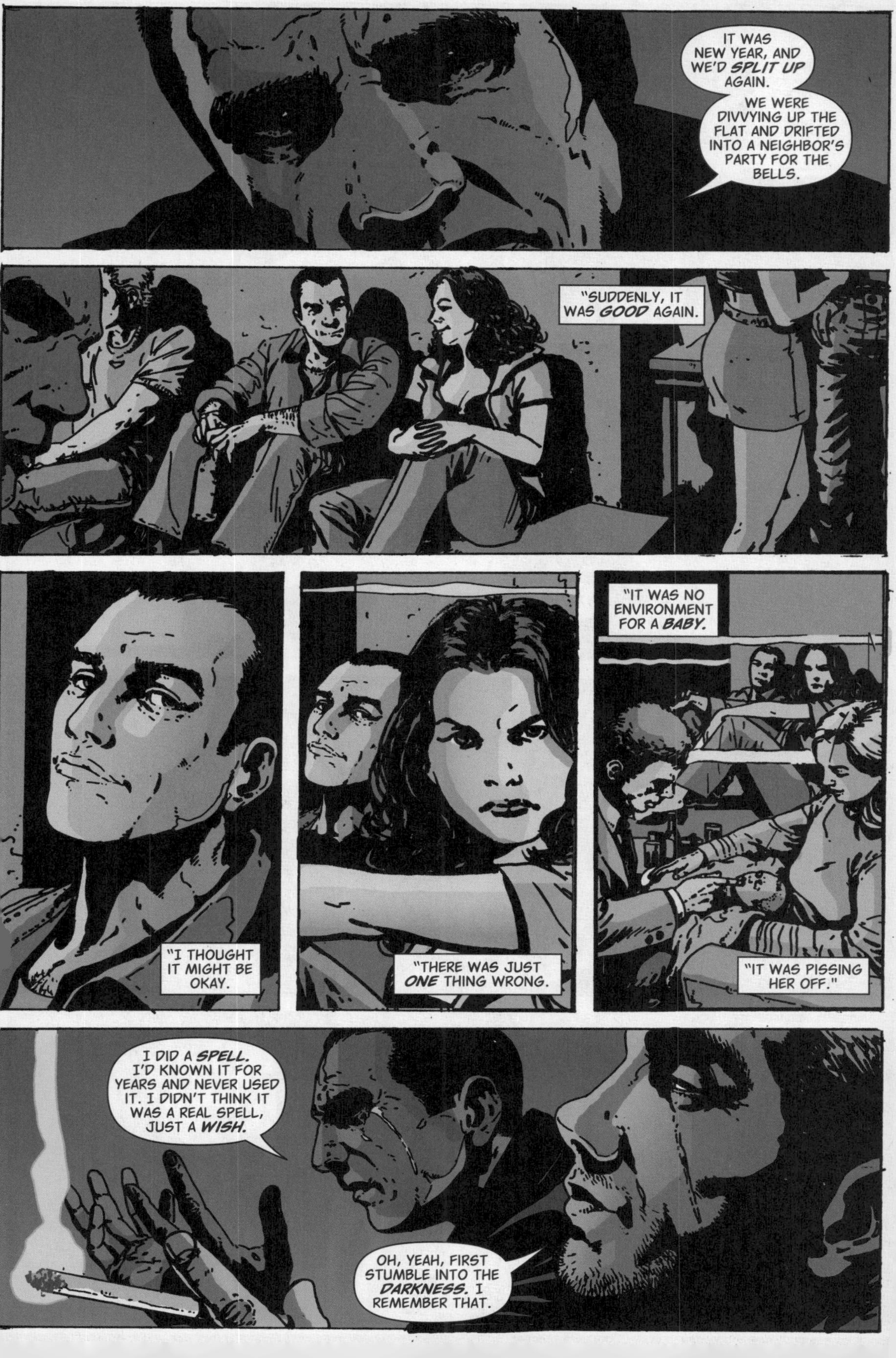
IT WAS NEW YEAR, AND WE'D SPLIT UP AGAIN.
WE WERE DIVVYING UP THE FLAT AND DRIFTED INTO A NEIGHBOR'S PARTY FOR THE BELLS.
"SUDDENLY, IT WAS GOOD AGAIN.
"I THOUGHT IT MIGHT BE OKAY.
"THERE WAS JUST ONE THING WRONG.
"IT WAS NO ENVIRONMENT FOR A BABY.
"IT WAS PISSING HER OFF."
I DID A SPELL. I'D KNOWN IT FOR YEARS AND NEVER USED IT. I DIDN'T THINK IT WAS A REAL SPELL, JUST A WISH.
OH, YEAH, FIRST STUMBLE INTO THE DARKNESS. I REMEMBER THAT.

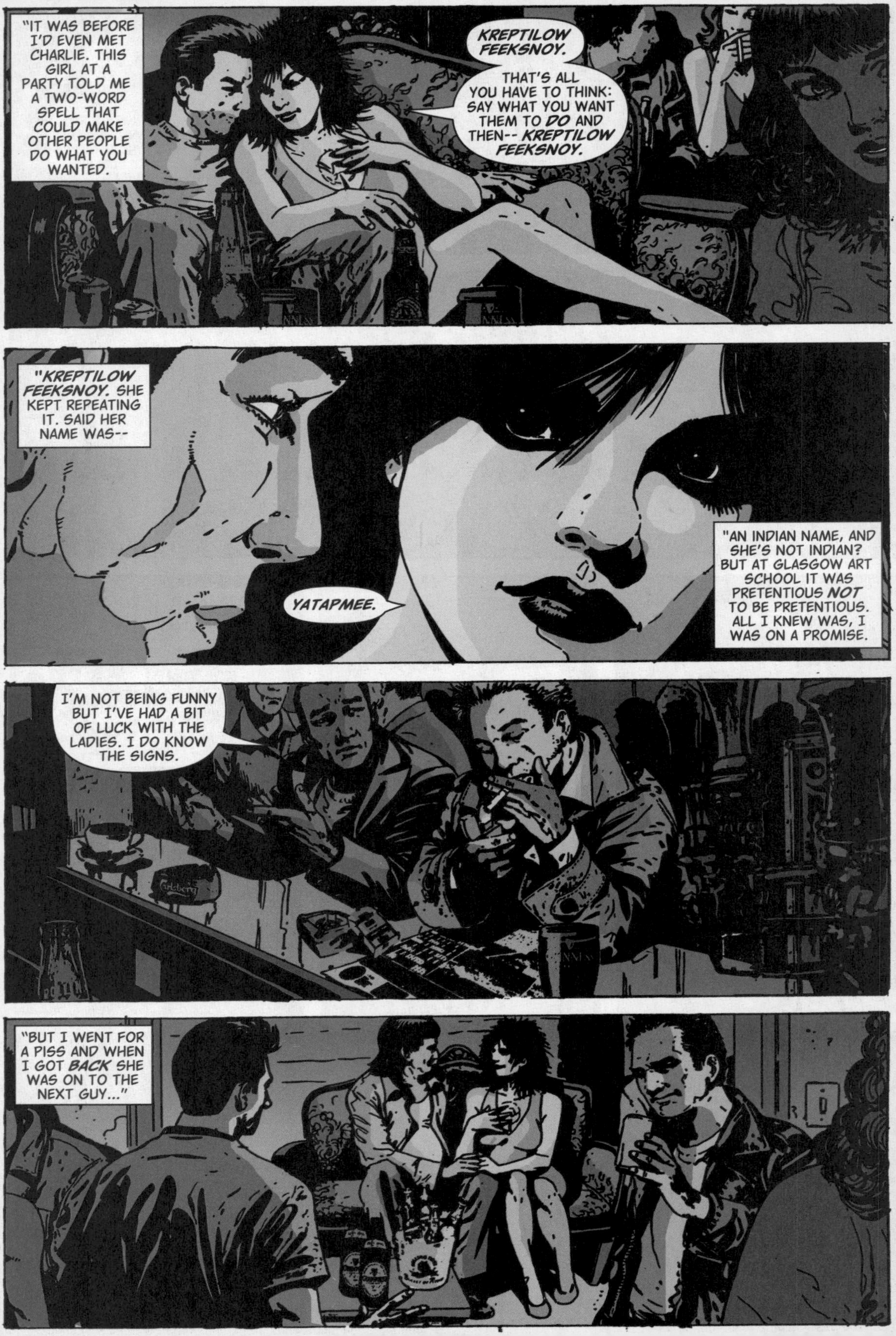
"IT WAS BEFORE I'D EVEN MET CHARLIE. THIS GIRL AT A PARTY TOLD ME A TWO-WORD SPELL THAT COULD MAKE OTHER PEOPLE DO WHAT YOU WANTED.
KREPTILOW FEEKSNOY.
THAT'S ALL YOU HAVE TO THINK: SAY WHAT YOU WANT THEM TO *DO* AND THEN-- *KREPTILOW FEEKSNOY.*
"*KREPTILOW FEEKSNOY.* SHE KEPT REPEATING IT. SAID HER NAME WAS--
YATAPMEE.
"AN INDIAN NAME, AND SHE'S NOT INDIAN? BUT AT GLASGOW ART SCHOOL IT WAS PRETENTIOUS *NOT* TO BE PRETENTIOUS. ALL I KNEW WAS, I WAS ON A PROMISE.
I'M NOT BEING FUNNY BUT I'VE HAD A BIT OF LUCK WITH THE LADIES. I DO KNOW THE SIGNS.
"BUT I WENT FOR A PISS AND WHEN I GOT *BACK* SHE WAS ON TO THE NEXT GUY..."

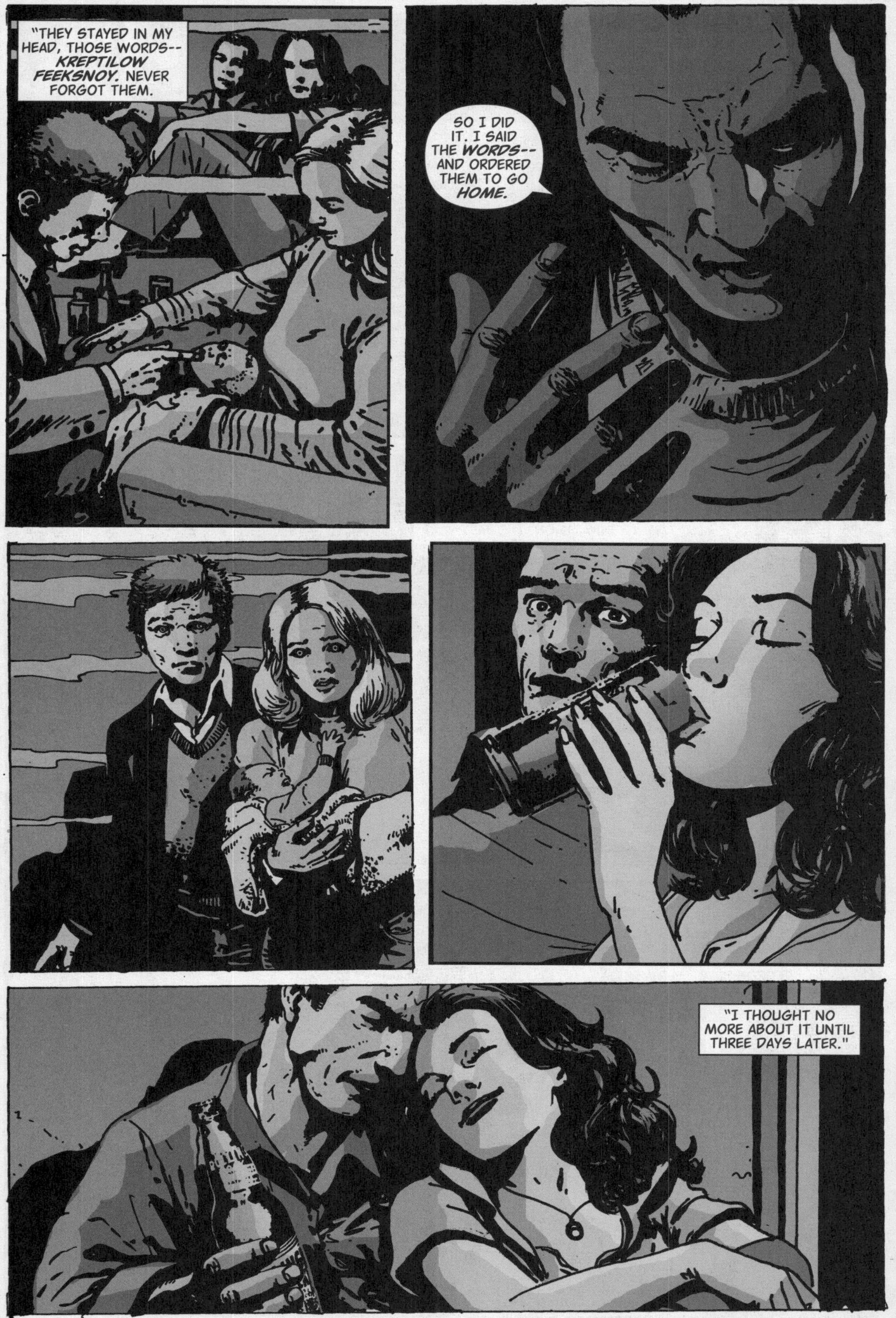
"THEY STAYED IN MY HEAD, THOSE WORDS-- KREPTILOW FEEKSNOY. NEVER FORGOT THEM.
SO I DID IT. I SAID THE WORDS-- AND ORDERED THEM TO GO HOME.
"I THOUGHT NO MORE ABOUT IT UNTIL THREE DAYS LATER."

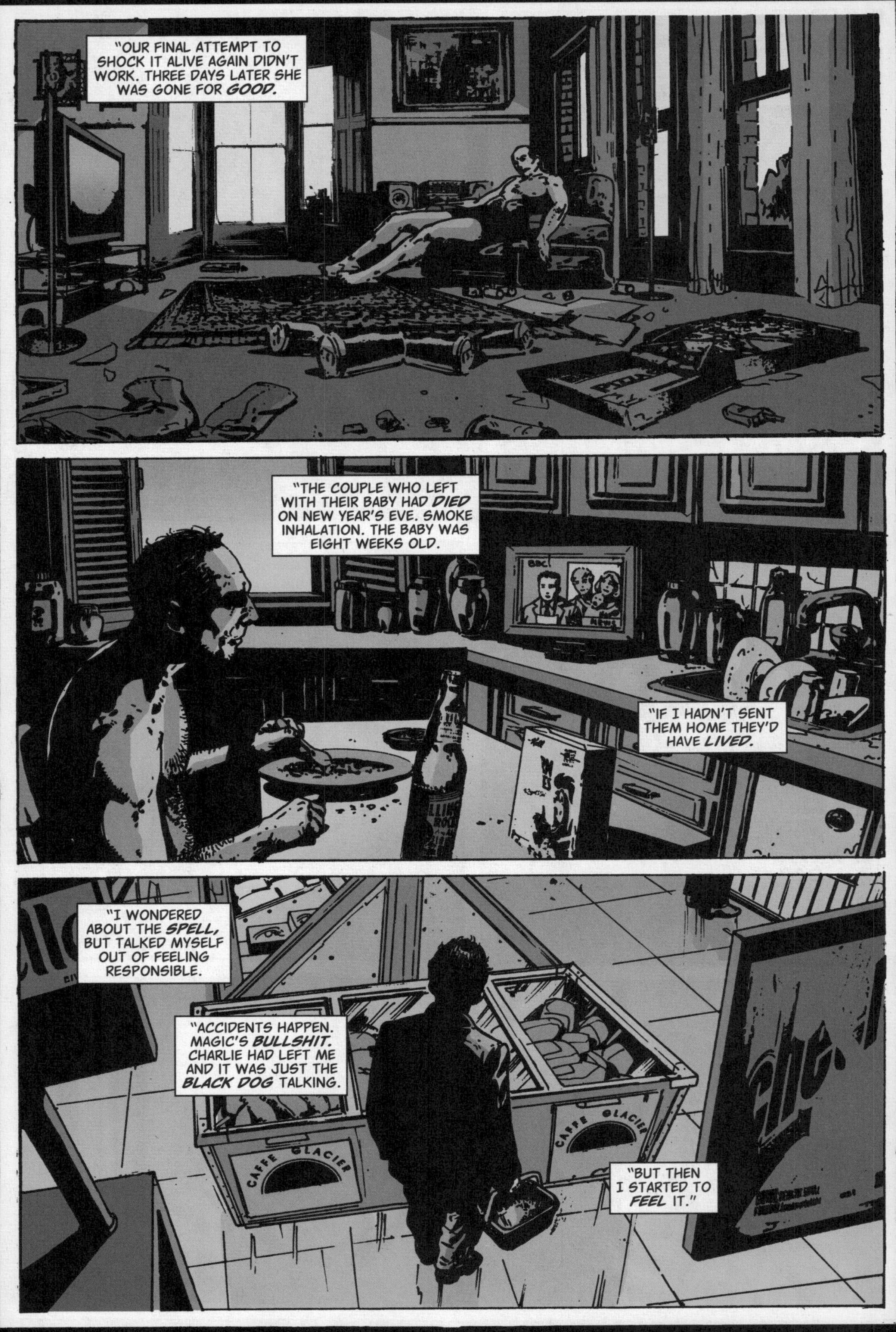
"OUR FINAL ATTEMPT TO SHOCK IT ALIVE AGAIN DIDN'T WORK. THREE DAYS LATER SHE WAS GONE FOR GOOD.
"THE COUPLE WHO LEFT WITH THEIR BABY HAD DIED ON NEW YEAR'S EVE. SMOKE INHALATION. THE BABY WAS EIGHT WEEKS OLD.
"IF I HADN'T SENT THEM HOME THEY'D HAVE LIVED.
"I WONDERED ABOUT THE SPELL, BUT TALKED MYSELF OUT OF FEELING RESPONSIBLE.
"ACCIDENTS HAPPEN. MAGIC'S BULLSHIT. CHARLIE HAD LEFT ME AND IT WAS JUST THE BLACK DOG TALKING.
CAFFE GLACIER
CAFFE GLACIER
"BUT THEN I STARTED TO FEEL IT."

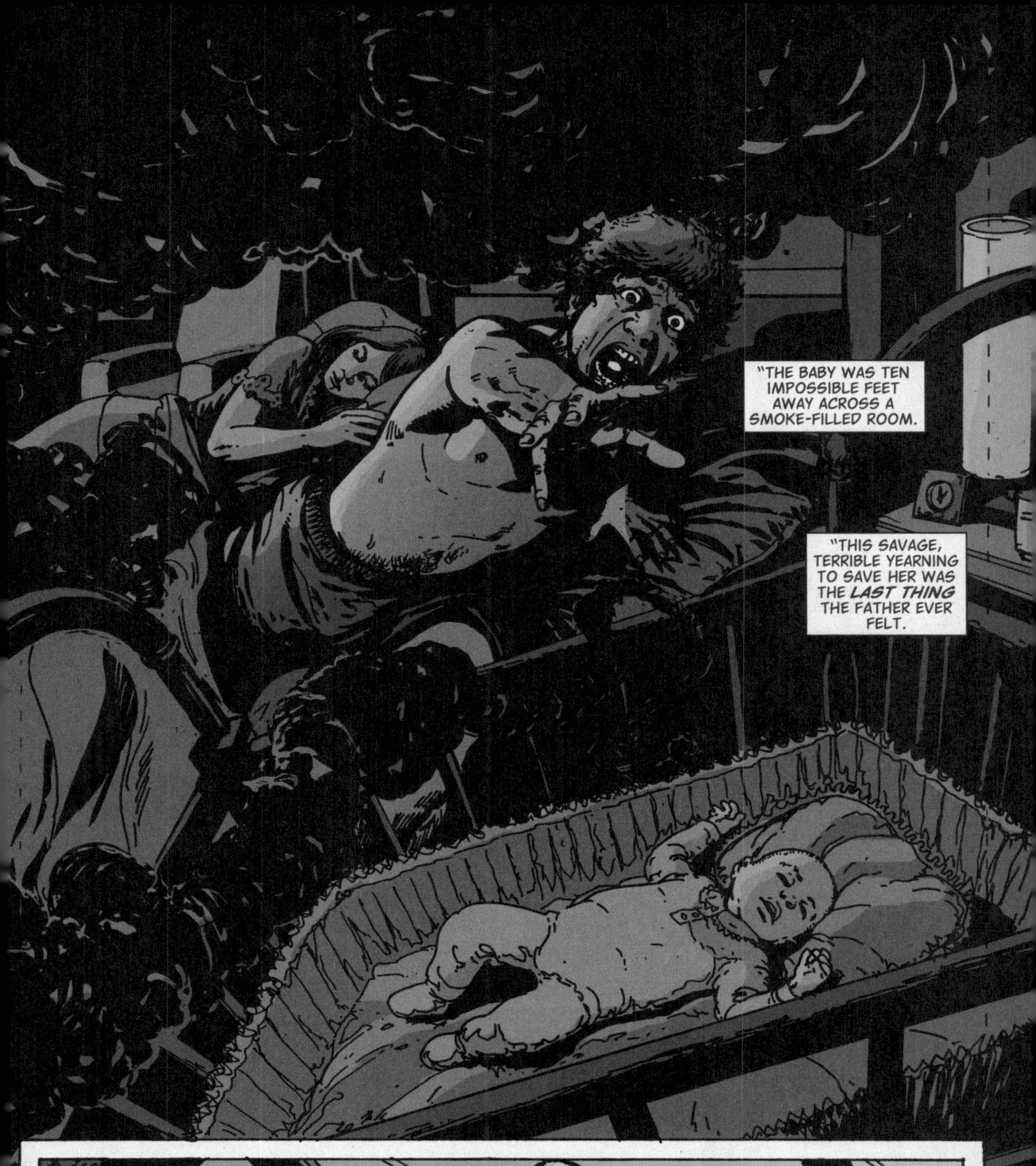
"THE BABY WAS TEN IMPOSSIBLE FEET AWAY ACROSS A SMOKE-FILLED ROOM.
"THIS SAVAGE, TERRIBLE YEARNING TO SAVE HER WAS THE *LAST THING* THE FATHER EVER FELT.

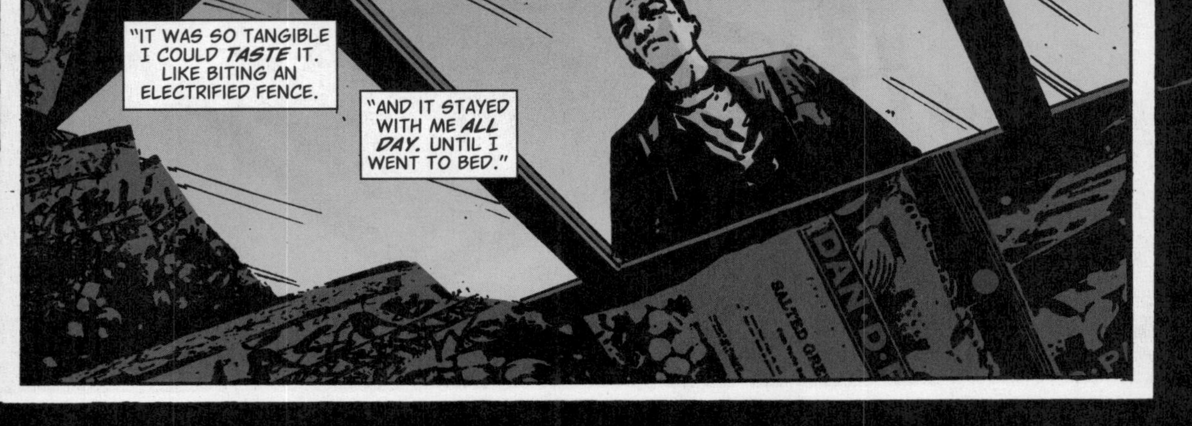
"IT WAS SO TANGIBLE I COULD *TASTE* IT. LIKE BITING AN ELECTRIFIED FENCE.
"AND IT STAYED WITH ME *ALL DAY.* UNTIL I WENT TO BED."

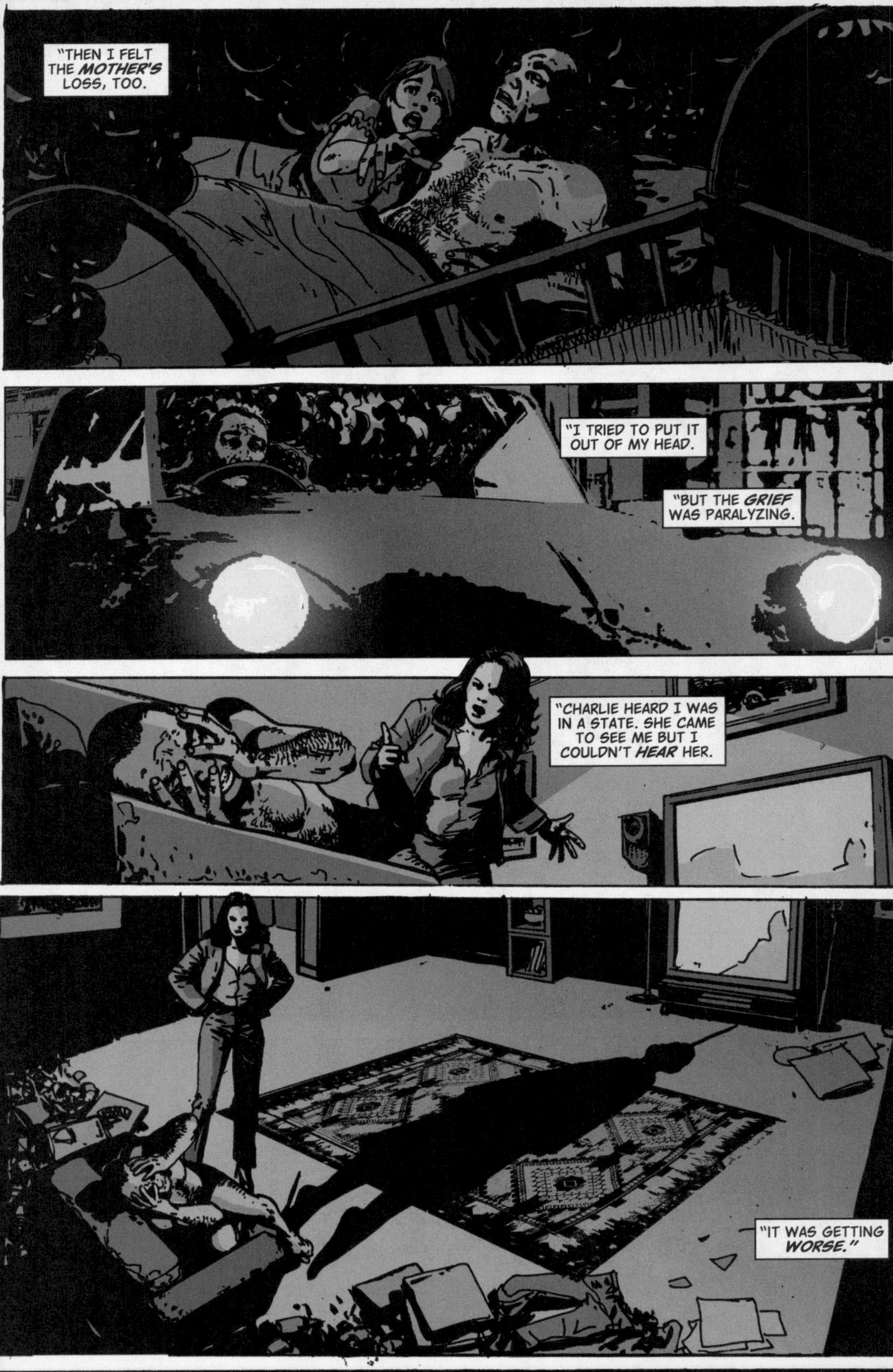
"THEN I FELT THE MOTHER'S LOSS, TOO.
"I TRIED TO PUT IT OUT OF MY HEAD.
"BUT THE GRIEF WAS PARALYZING.
"CHARLIE HEARD I WAS IN A STATE. SHE CAME TO SEE ME BUT I COULDN'T HEAR HER.
"IT WAS GETTING WORSE."

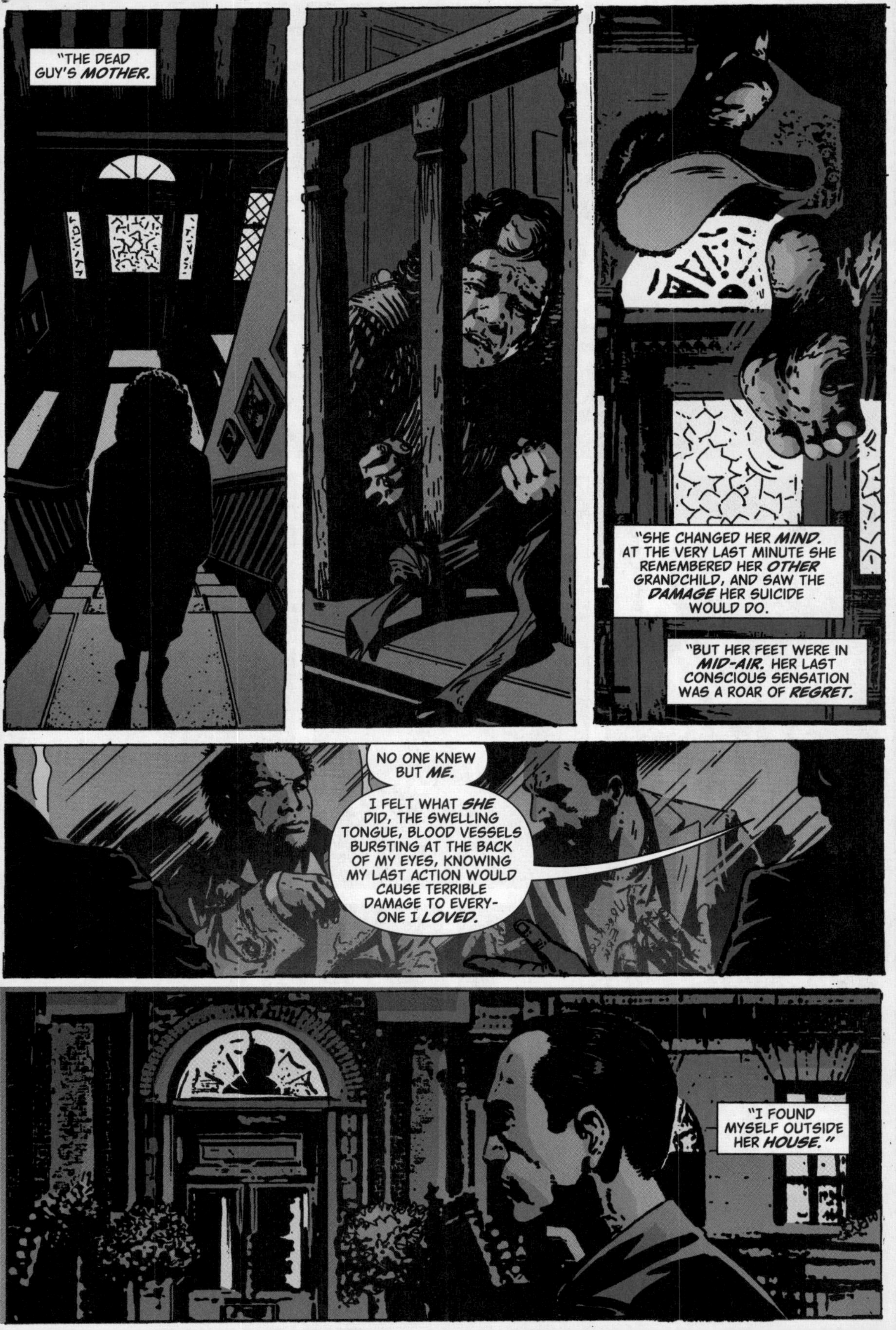
"THE DEAD GUY'S **MOTHER.**
"SHE CHANGED HER **MIND.** AT THE VERY LAST MINUTE SHE REMEMBERED HER **OTHER** GRANDCHILD, AND SAW THE **DAMAGE** HER SUICIDE WOULD DO.
"BUT HER FEET WERE IN **MID-AIR.** HER LAST CONSCIOUS SENSATION WAS A ROAR OF **REGRET.**
NO ONE KNEW BUT **ME.**
I FELT WHAT **SHE** DID, THE SWELLING TONGUE, BLOOD VESSELS BURSTING AT THE BACK OF MY EYES, KNOWING MY LAST ACTION WOULD CAUSE TERRIBLE DAMAGE TO EVERY-ONE I **LOVED.**
"I FOUND MYSELF OUTSIDE HER **HOUSE.**"

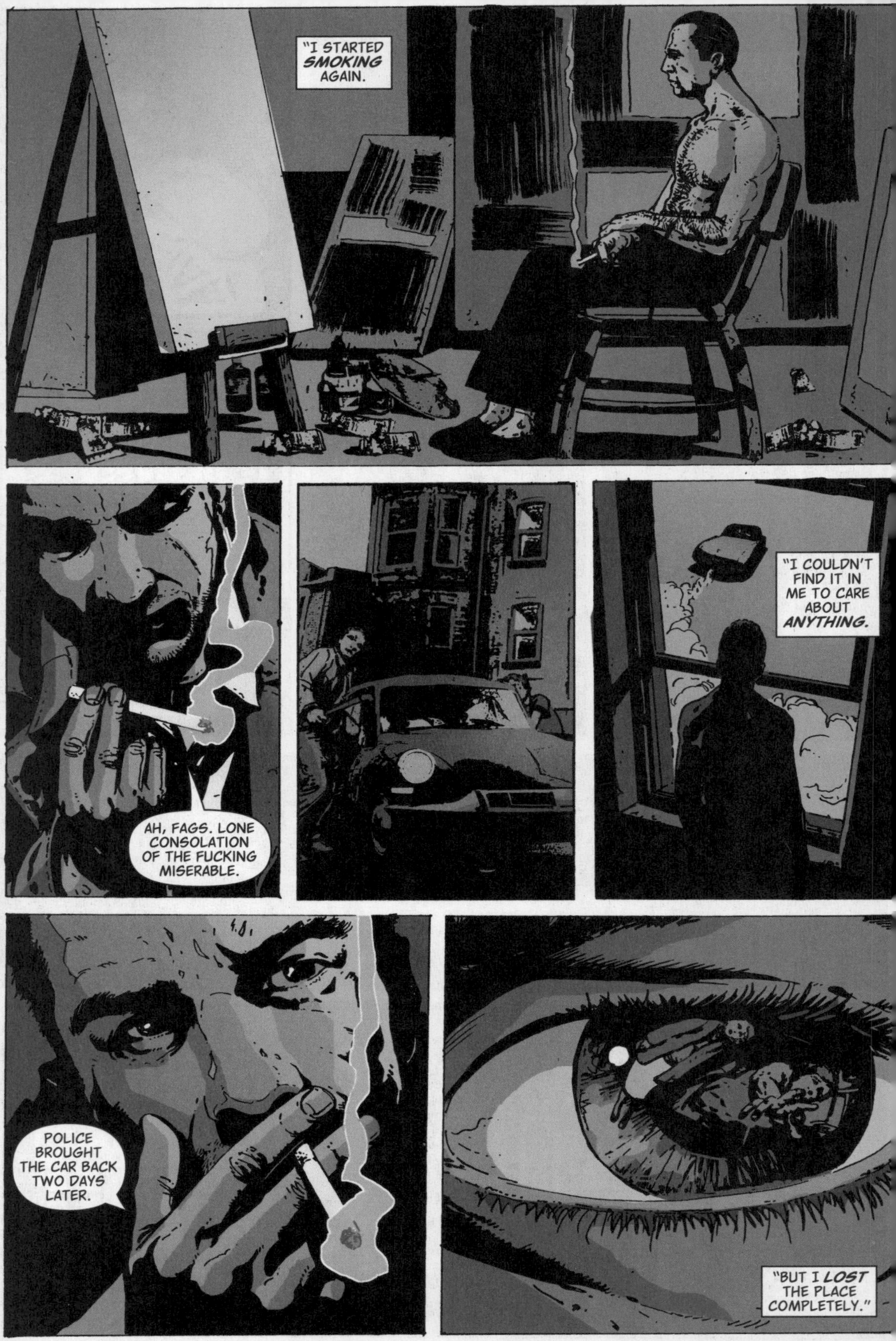
"I STARTED SMOKING AGAIN.
AH, FAGS. LONE CONSOLATION OF THE FUCKING MISERABLE.
"I COULDN'T FIND IT IN ME TO CARE ABOUT ANYTHING.
POLICE BROUGHT THE CAR BACK TWO DAYS LATER.
"BUT I LOST THE PLACE COMPLETELY."

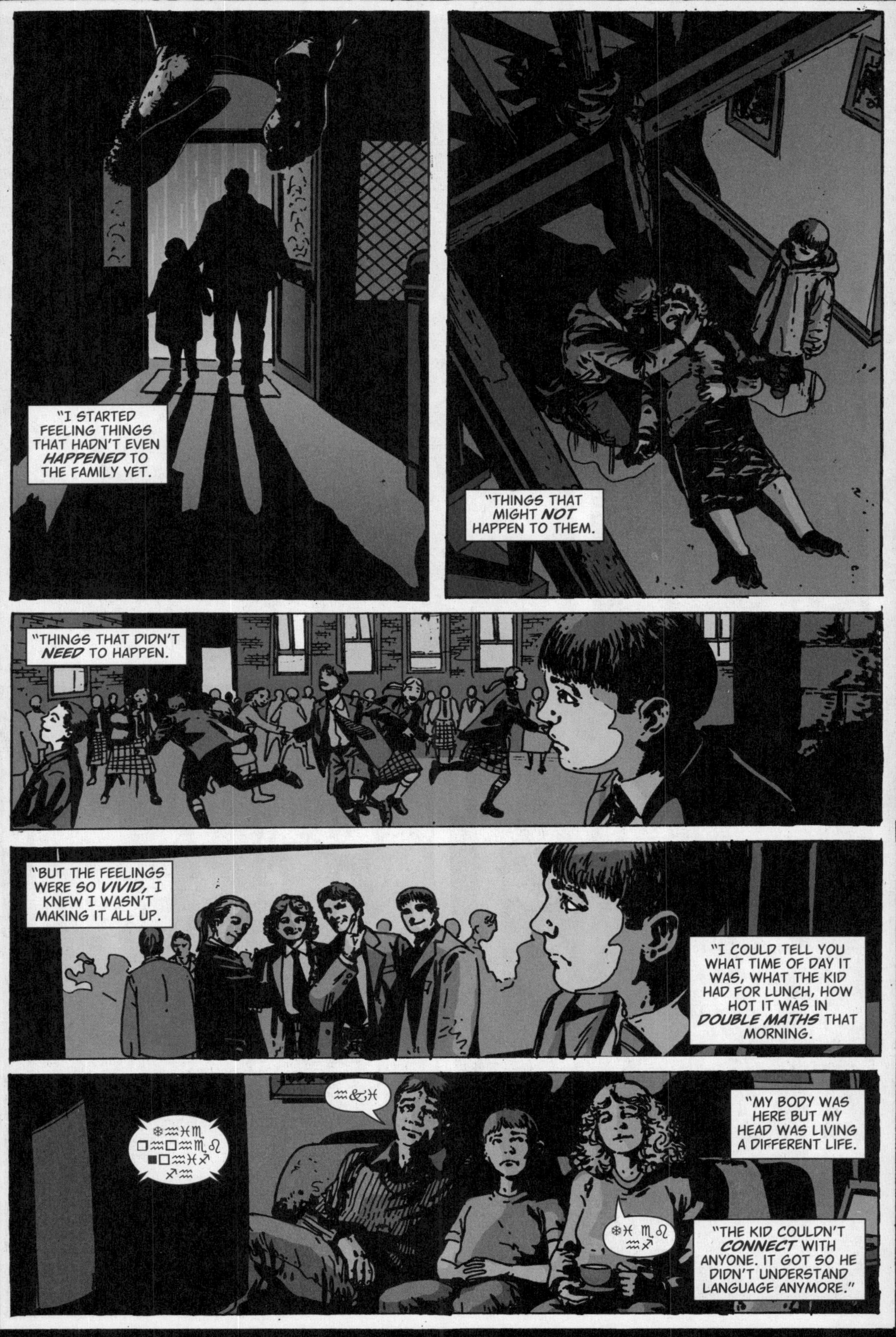
"I STARTED FEELING THINGS THAT HADN'T EVEN *HAPPENED* TO THE FAMILY YET.
"THINGS THAT MIGHT *NOT* HAPPEN TO THEM.
"THINGS THAT DIDN'T *NEED* TO HAPPEN.
"BUT THE FEELINGS WERE SO *VIVID,* I KNEW I WASN'T MAKING IT ALL UP.
"I COULD TELL YOU WHAT TIME OF DAY IT WAS, WHAT THE KID HAD FOR LUNCH, HOW HOT IT WAS IN *DOUBLE MATHS* THAT MORNING.
"MY BODY WAS HERE BUT MY HEAD WAS LIVING A DIFFERENT LIFE.
"THE KID COULDN'T *CONNECT* WITH ANYONE. IT GOT SO HE DIDN'T UNDERSTAND LANGUAGE ANYMORE."

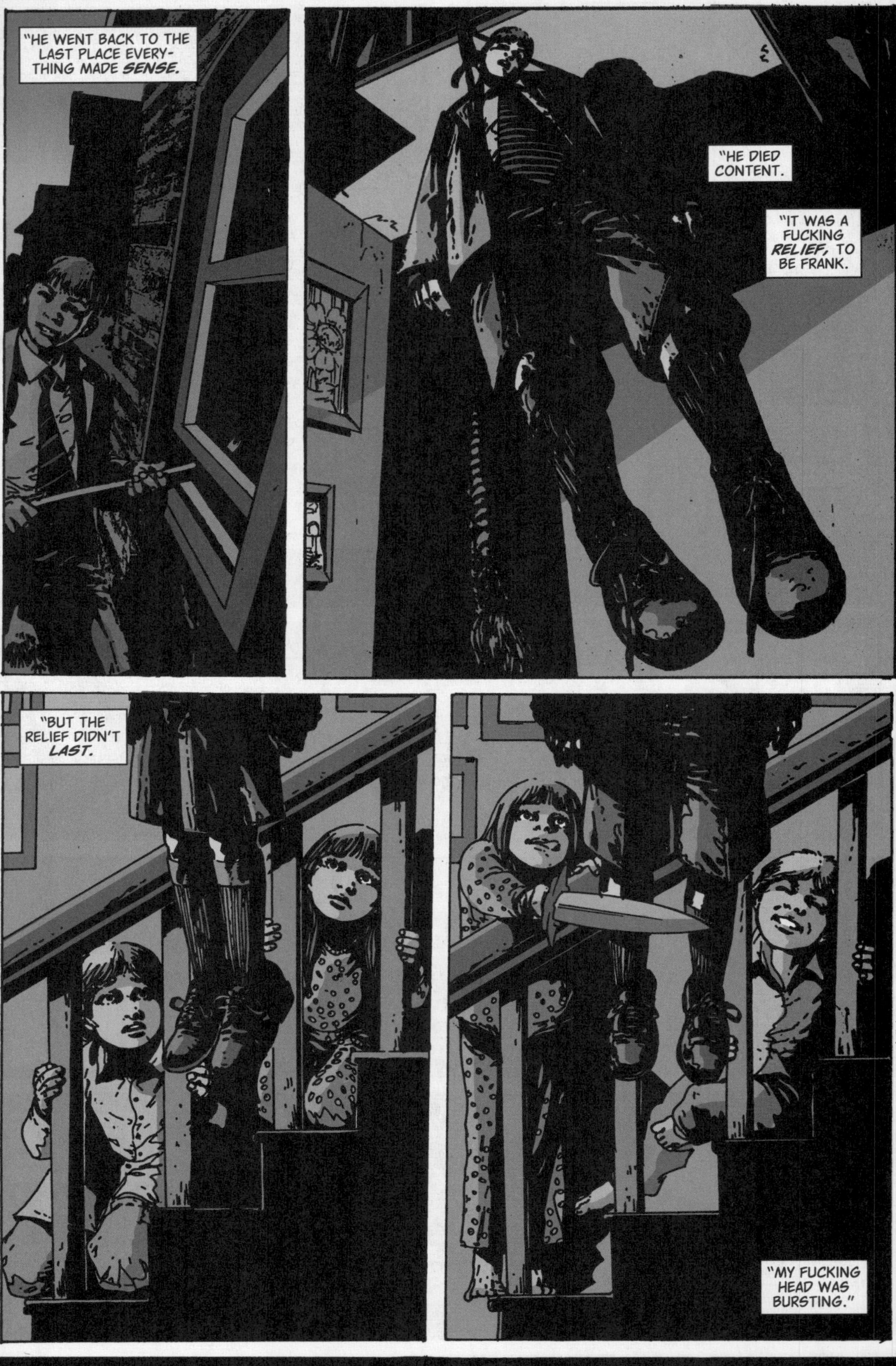
"HE WENT BACK TO THE LAST PLACE EVERY-THING MADE SENSE.
"HE DIED CONTENT.
"IT WAS A FUCKING RELIEF, TO BE FRANK.
"BUT THE RELIEF DIDN'T LAST.
"MY FUCKING HEAD WAS BURSTING."

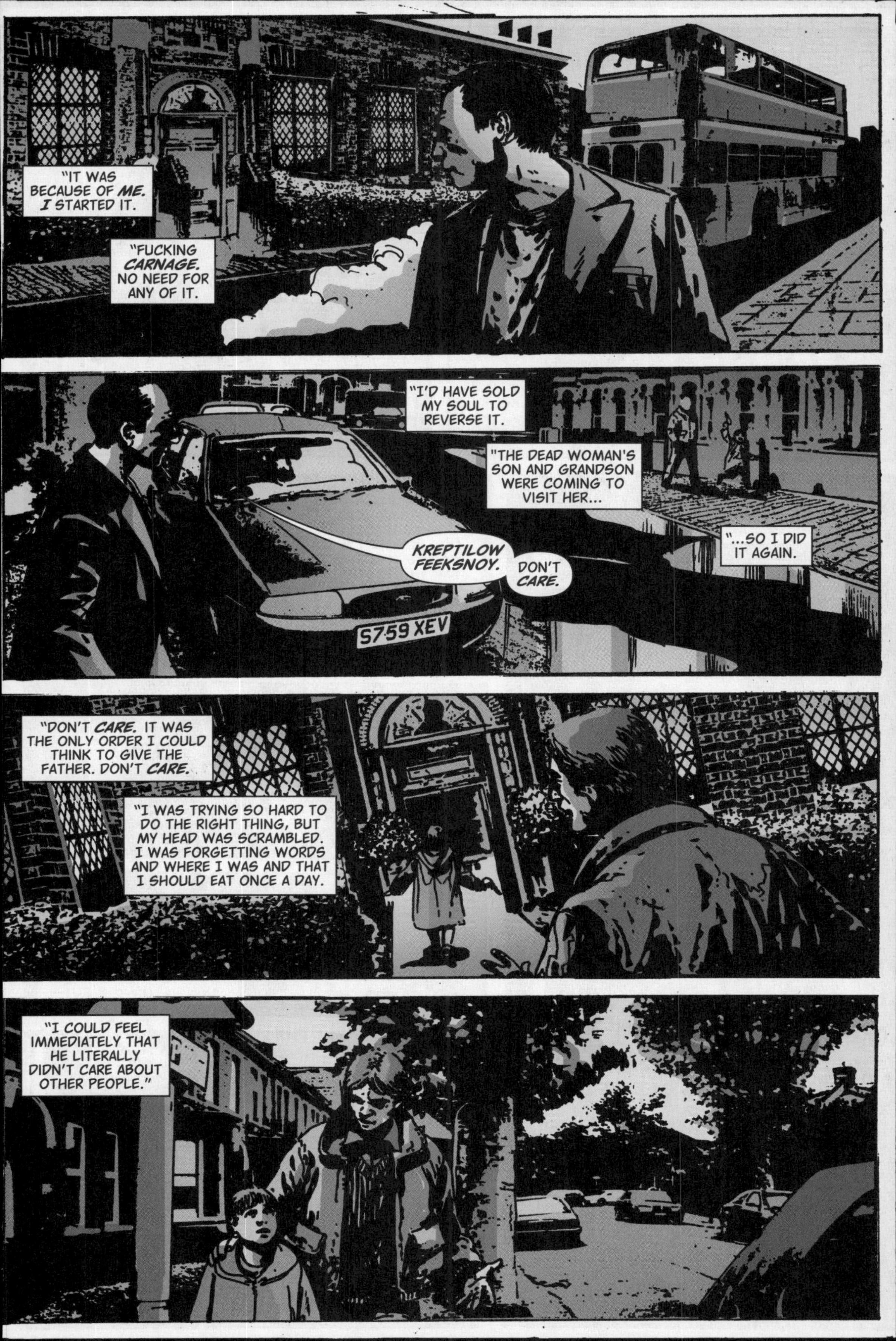
"IT WAS BECAUSE OF *ME.* *I* STARTED IT.
"FUCKING *CARNAGE.* NO NEED FOR ANY OF IT.
"I'D HAVE SOLD MY SOUL TO REVERSE IT.
"THE DEAD WOMAN'S SON AND GRANDSON WERE COMING TO VISIT HER...
KREPTILOW FEEKSNOY.
DON'T *CARE.*
"...SO I DID IT AGAIN.
S759 XEV
"DON'T *CARE.* IT WAS THE ONLY ORDER I COULD THINK TO GIVE THE FATHER. DON'T *CARE.*
"I WAS TRYING SO HARD TO DO THE RIGHT THING, BUT MY HEAD WAS SCRAMBLED. I WAS FORGETTING WORDS AND WHERE I WAS AND THAT I SHOULD EAT ONCE A DAY.
"I COULD FEEL IMMEDIATELY THAT HE LITERALLY DIDN'T CARE ABOUT OTHER PEOPLE."

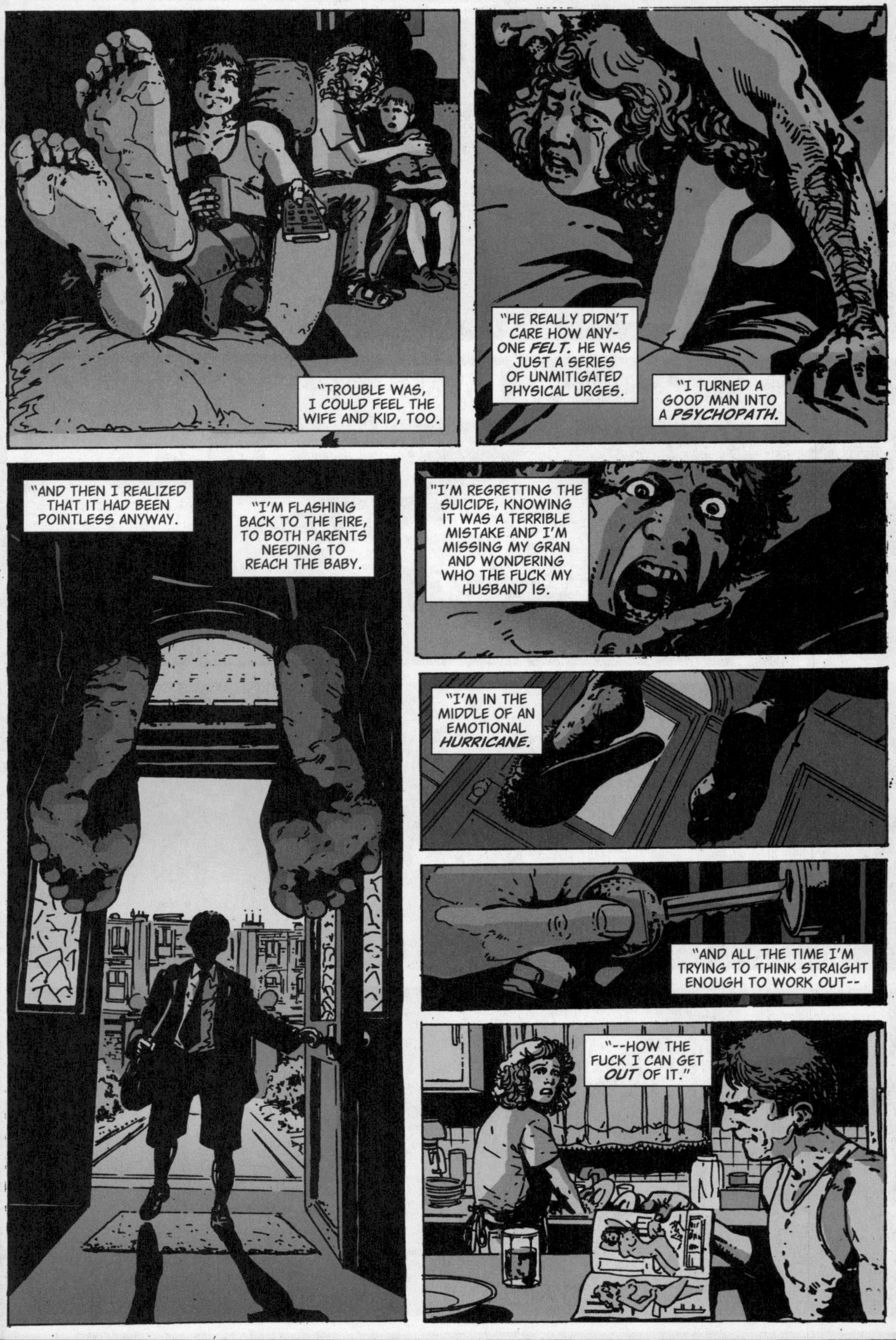
"TROUBLE WAS, I COULD FEEL THE WIFE AND KID, TOO.
"HE REALLY DIDN'T CARE HOW ANY-ONE FELT. HE WAS JUST A SERIES OF UNMITIGATED PHYSICAL URGES.
"I TURNED A GOOD MAN INTO A PSYCHOPATH.
"AND THEN I REALIZED THAT IT HAD BEEN POINTLESS ANYWAY.
"I'M FLASHING BACK TO THE FIRE, TO BOTH PARENTS NEEDING TO REACH THE BABY.
"I'M REGRETTING THE SUICIDE, KNOWING IT WAS A TERRIBLE MISTAKE AND I'M MISSING MY GRAN AND WONDERING WHO THE FUCK MY HUSBAND IS.
"I'M IN THE MIDDLE OF AN EMOTIONAL HURRICANE.
"AND ALL THE TIME I'M TRYING TO THINK STRAIGHT ENOUGH TO WORK OUT--
"--HOW THE FUCK I CAN GET OUT OF IT."

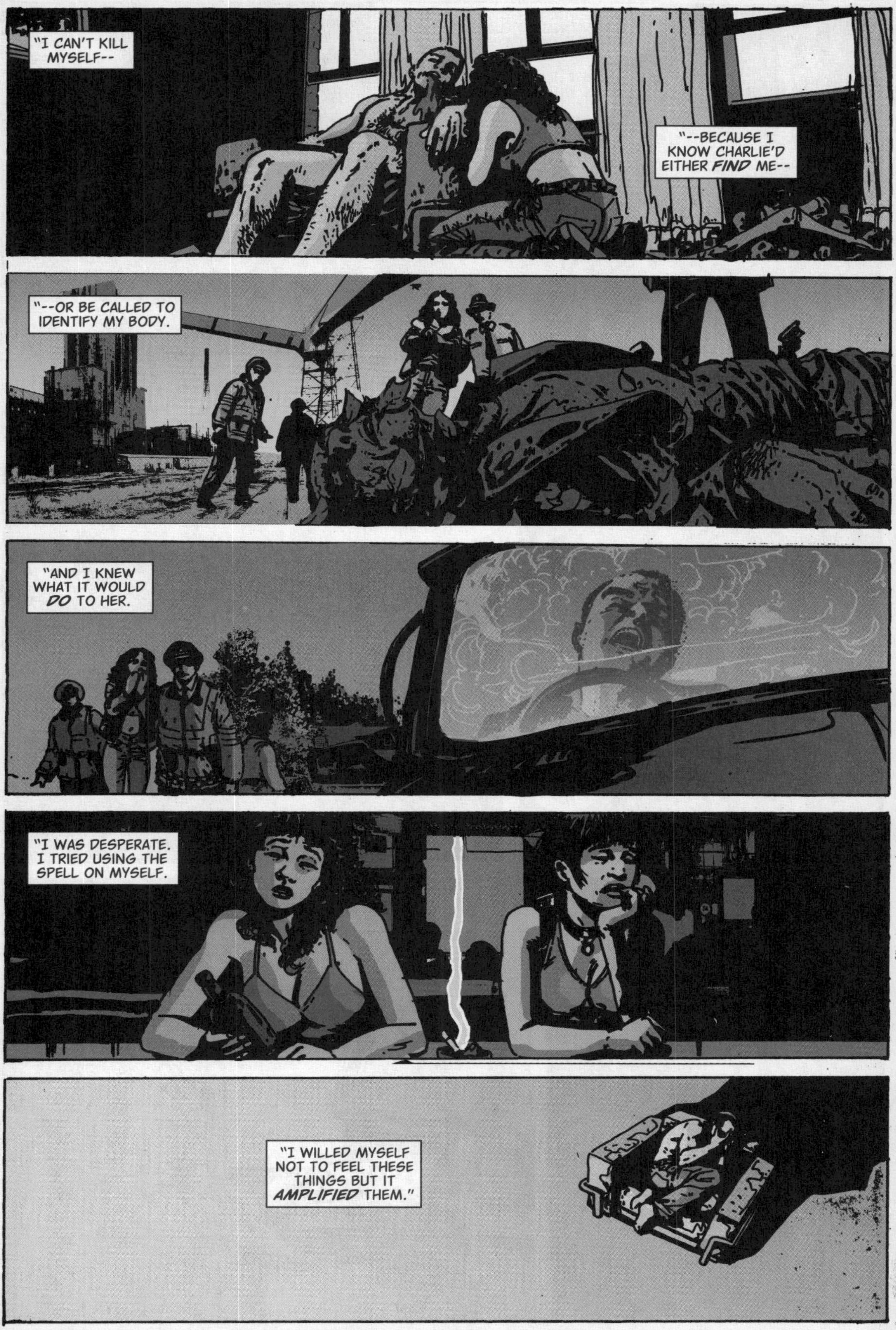
"I CAN'T KILL MYSELF--
"--BECAUSE I KNOW CHARLIE'D EITHER FIND ME--
"--OR BE CALLED TO IDENTIFY MY BODY.
"AND I KNEW WHAT IT WOULD DO TO HER.
"I WAS DESPERATE. I TRIED USING THE SPELL ON MYSELF.
"I WILLED MYSELF NOT TO FEEL THESE THINGS BUT IT AMPLIFIED THEM."

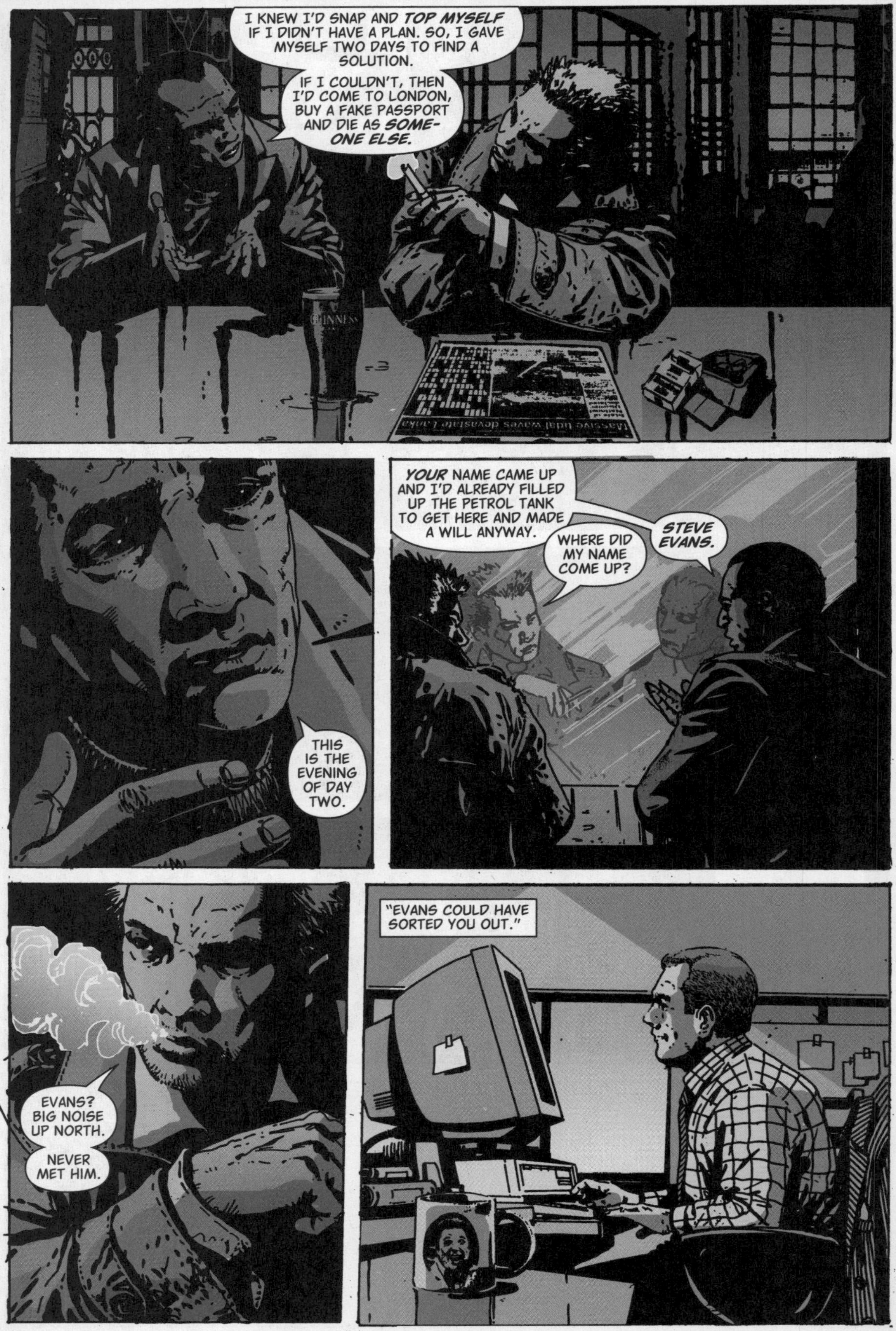
I KNEW I'D SNAP AND TOP MYSELF IF I DIDN'T HAVE A PLAN. SO, I GAVE MYSELF TWO DAYS TO FIND A SOLUTION.
IF I COULDN'T, THEN I'D COME TO LONDON, BUY A FAKE PASSPORT AND DIE AS SOME-ONE ELSE.
THIS IS THE EVENING OF DAY TWO.
YOUR NAME CAME UP AND I'D ALREADY FILLED UP THE PETROL TANK TO GET HERE AND MADE A WILL ANYWAY.
WHERE DID MY NAME COME UP?
STEVE EVANS.
EVANS? BIG NOISE UP NORTH.
NEVER MET HIM.
"EVANS COULD HAVE SORTED YOU OUT."

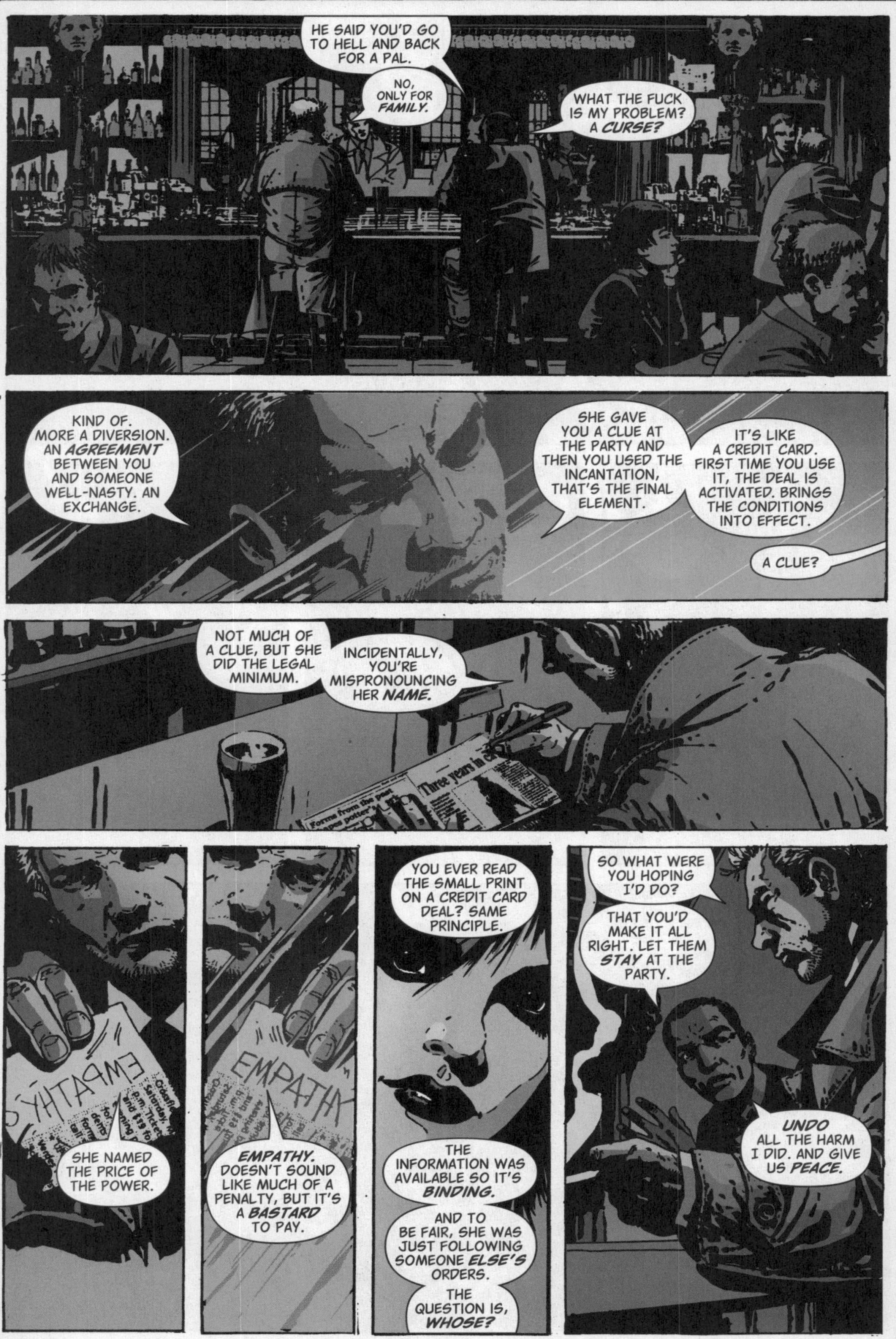
HE SAID YOU'D GO TO HELL AND BACK FOR A PAL.
NO, ONLY FOR FAMILY.
WHAT THE FUCK IS MY PROBLEM? A CURSE?
KIND OF. MORE A DIVERSION. AN AGREEMENT BETWEEN YOU AND SOMEONE WELL-NASTY. AN EXCHANGE.
SHE GAVE YOU A CLUE AT THE PARTY AND THEN YOU USED THE INCANTATION, THAT'S THE FINAL ELEMENT.
IT'S LIKE A CREDIT CARD. FIRST TIME YOU USE IT, THE DEAL IS ACTIVATED. BRINGS THE CONDITIONS INTO EFFECT.
A CLUE?
NOT MUCH OF A CLUE, BUT SHE DID THE LEGAL MINIMUM.
INCIDENTALLY, YOU'RE MISPRONOUNCING HER NAME.
Three years in
EMPATHY
SHE NAMED THE PRICE OF THE POWER.
EMPATHY
EMPATHY. DOESN'T SOUND LIKE MUCH OF A PENALTY, BUT IT'S A BASTARD TO PAY.
YOU EVER READ THE SMALL PRINT ON A CREDIT CARD DEAL? SAME PRINCIPLE.
THE INFORMATION WAS AVAILABLE SO IT'S BINDING.
AND TO BE FAIR, SHE WAS JUST FOLLOWING SOMEONE ELSE'S ORDERS.
THE QUESTION IS, WHOSE?
SO WHAT WERE YOU HOPING I'D DO?
THAT YOU'D MAKE IT ALL RIGHT. LET THEM STAY AT THE PARTY.
UNDO ALL THE HARM I DID. AND GIVE US PEACE.

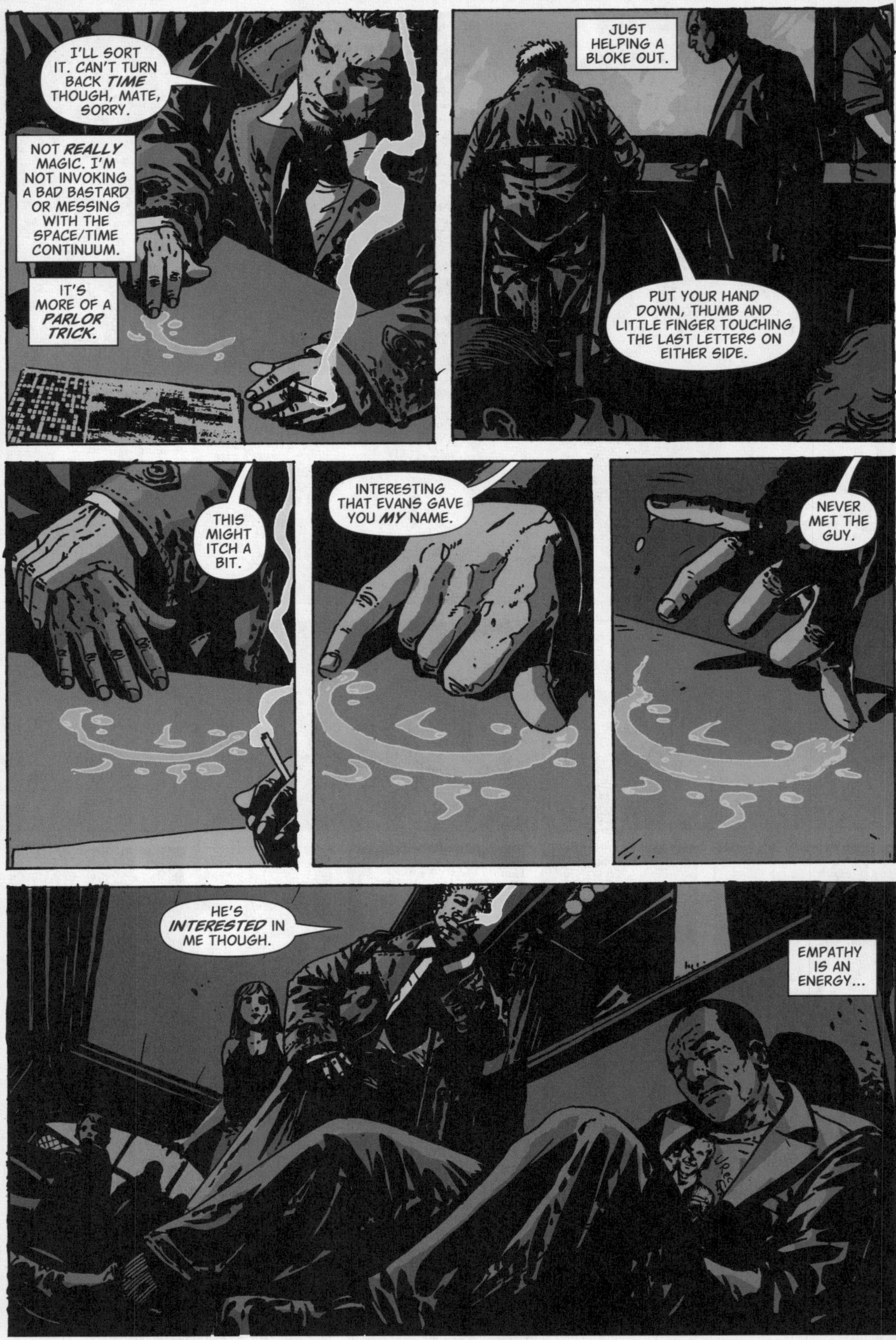
I'LL SORT IT. CAN'T TURN BACK TIME THOUGH, MATE, SORRY.
NOT REALLY MAGIC. I'M NOT INVOKING A BAD BASTARD OR MESSING WITH THE SPACE/TIME CONTINUUM.
IT'S MORE OF A PARLOR TRICK.
JUST HELPING A BLOKE OUT.
PUT YOUR HAND DOWN, THUMB AND LITTLE FINGER TOUCHING THE LAST LETTERS ON EITHER SIDE.
THIS MIGHT ITCH A BIT.
INTERESTING THAT EVANS GAVE YOU MY NAME.
NEVER MET THE GUY.
HE'S INTERESTED IN ME THOUGH.
EMPATHY IS AN ENERGY...

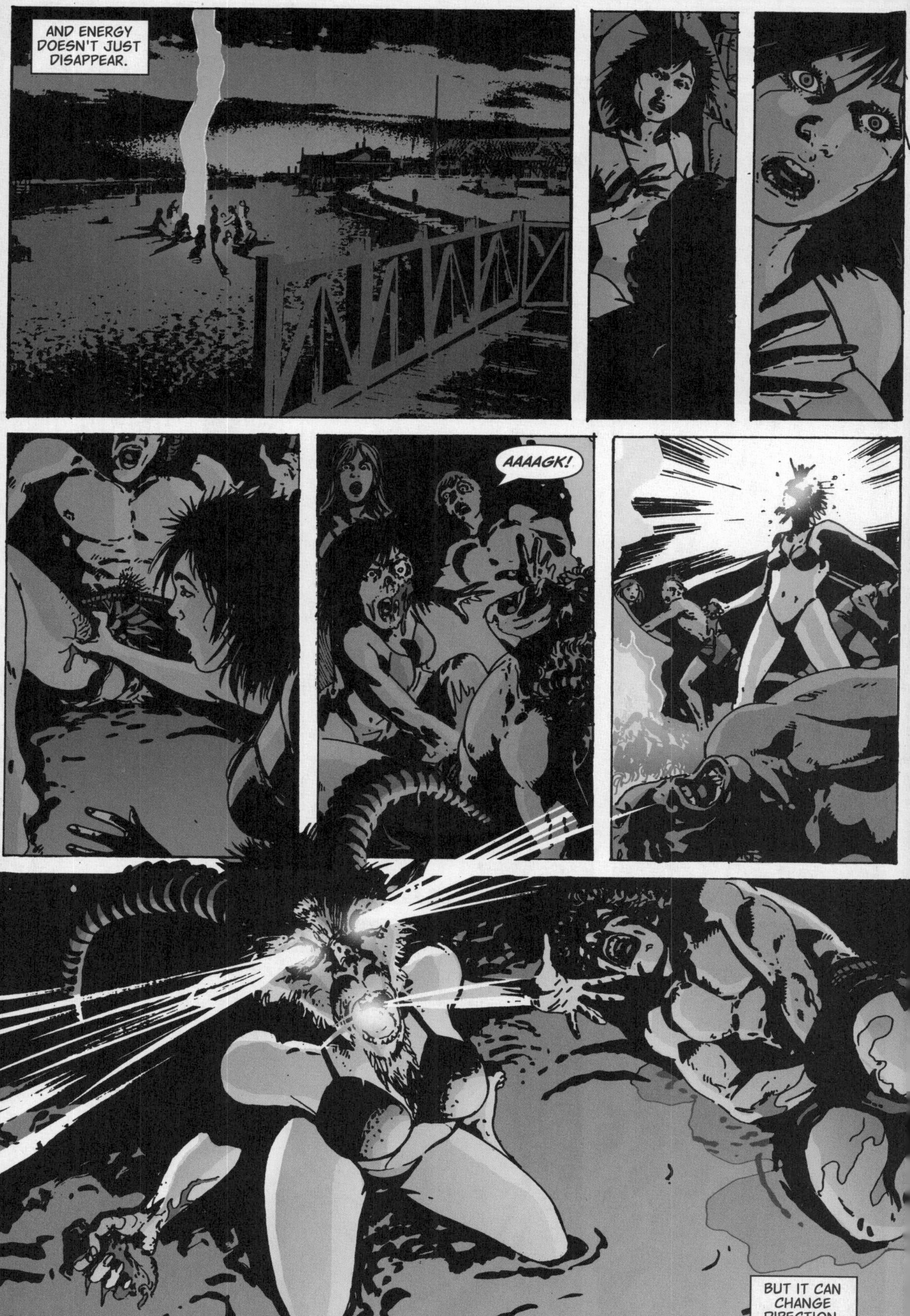
AND ENERGY DOESN'T JUST DISAPPEAR.
AAAAGK!
BUT IT CAN CHANGE DIRECTION.

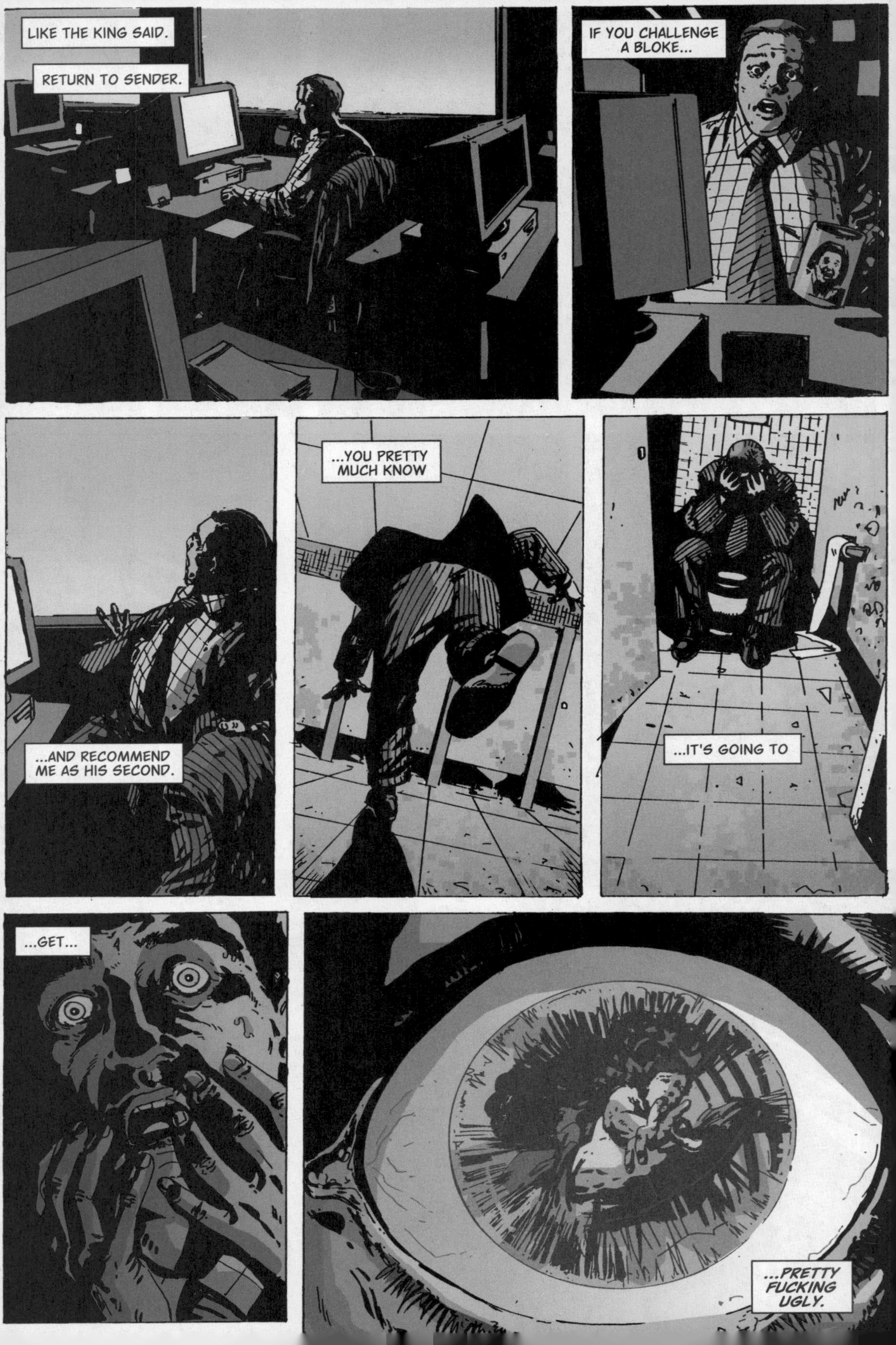
LIKE THE KING SAID.
RETURN TO SENDER.
IF YOU CHALLENGE A BLOKE...
...AND RECOMMEND ME AS HIS SECOND.
...YOU PRETTY MUCH KNOW
...IT'S GOING TO
...GET...
...PRETTY FUCKING UGLY.

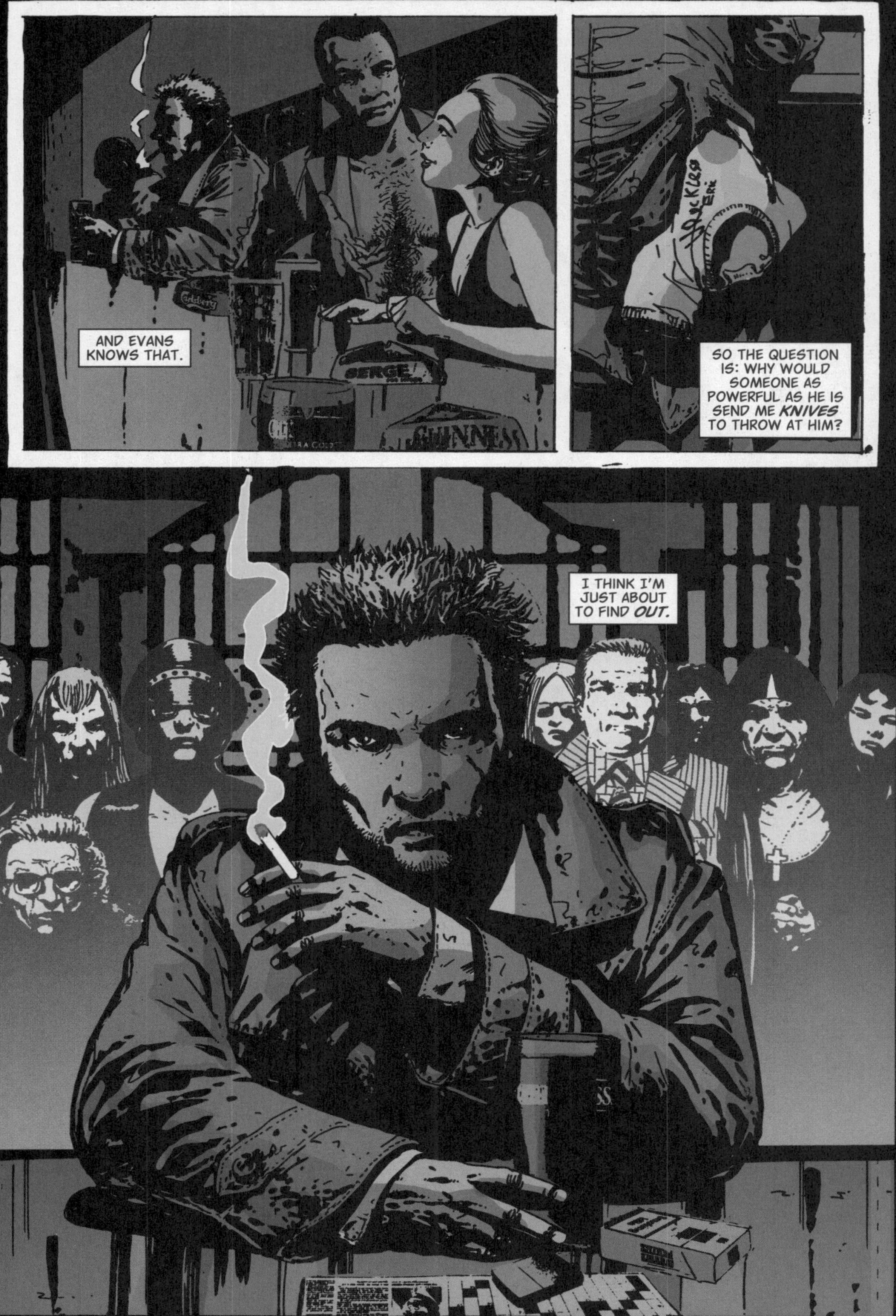
AND EVANS KNOWS THAT.
Carlsberg
SERGE
GUINNESS
SO THE QUESTION IS: WHY WOULD SOMEONE AS POWERFUL AS HE IS SEND ME *KNIVES* TO THROW AT HIM?
I THINK I'M JUST ABOUT TO FIND *OUT.*

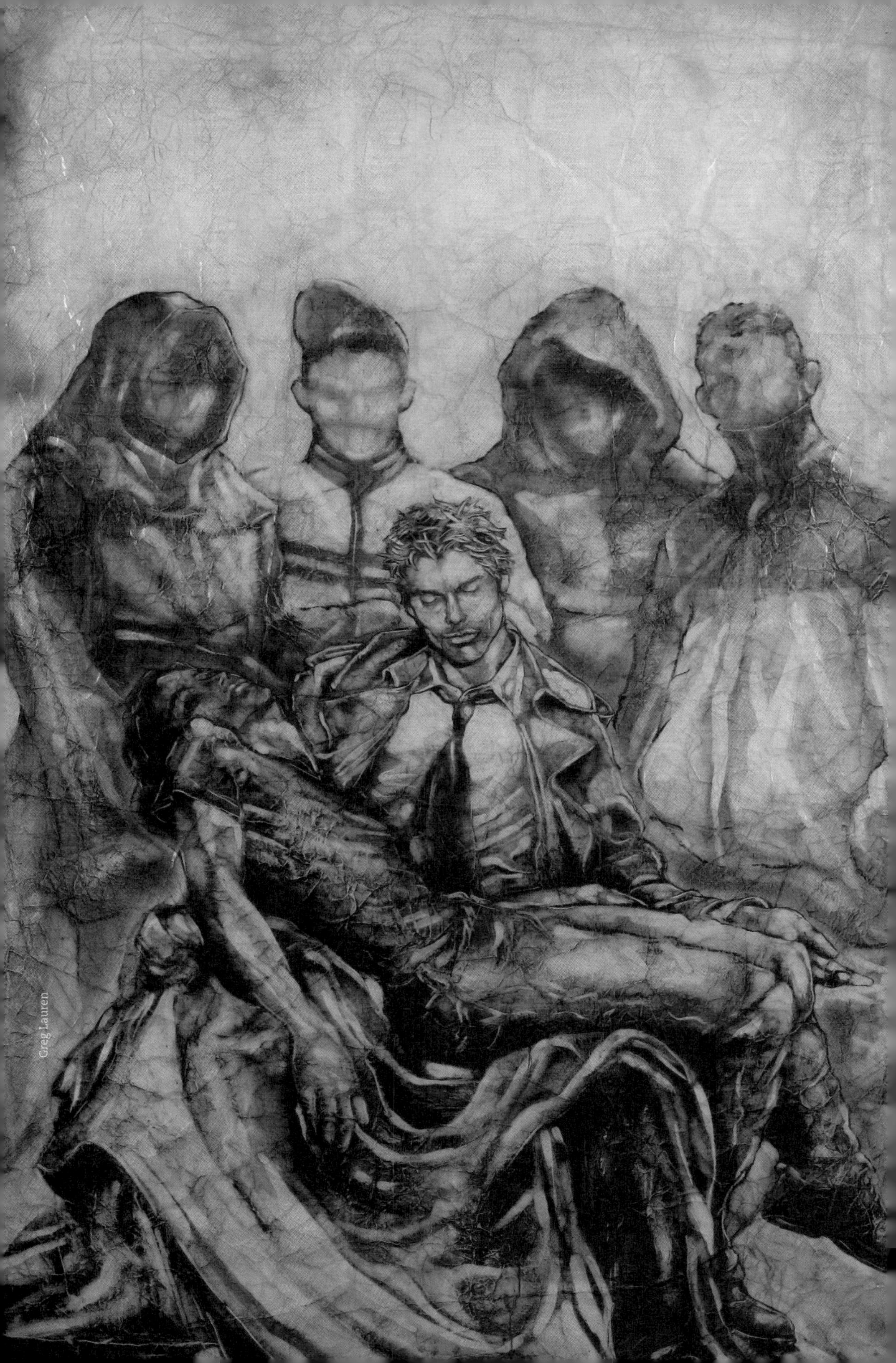
Greg Lauren

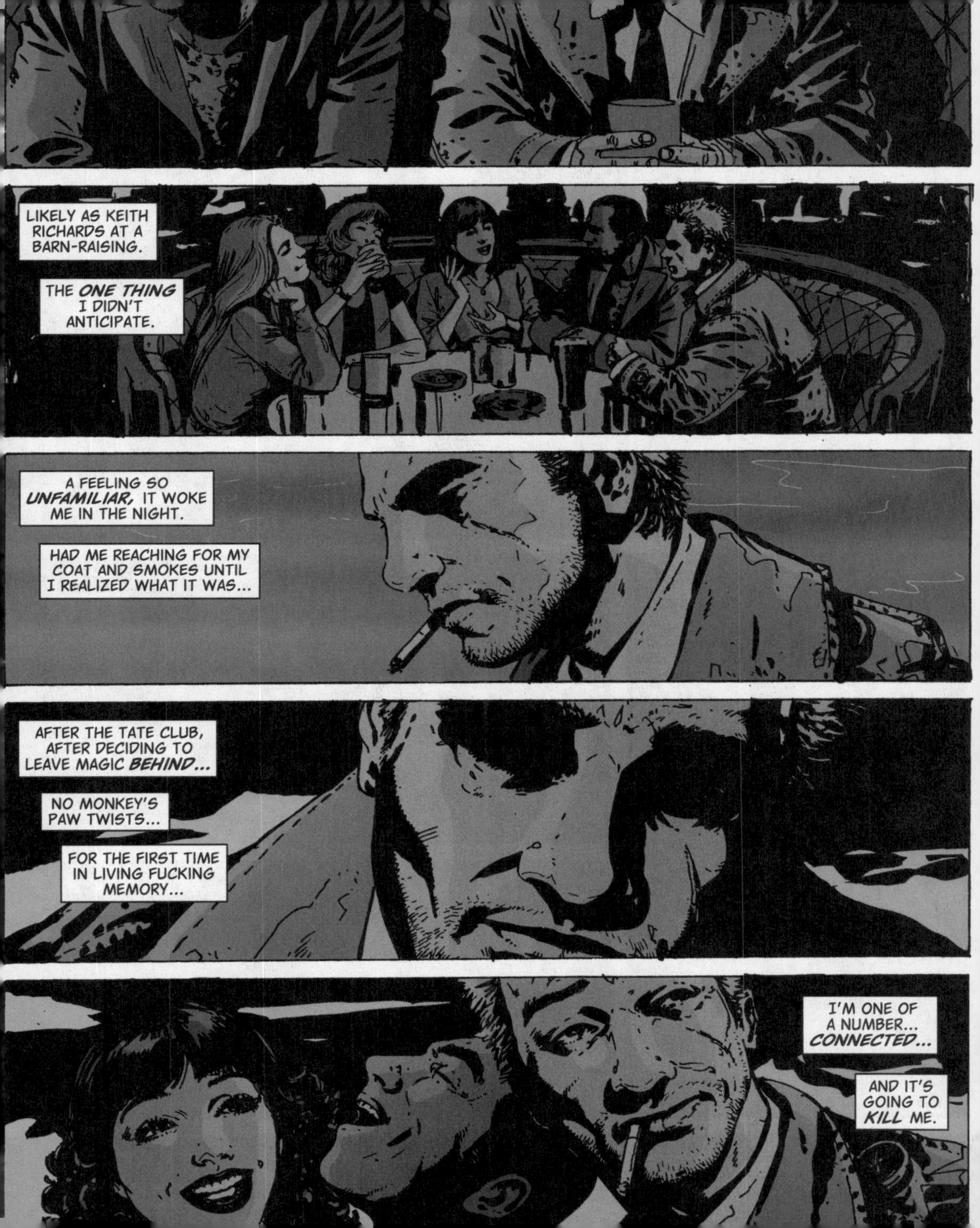
LIKELY AS KEITH RICHARDS AT A BARN-RAISING.
THE *ONE THING* I DIDN'T ANTICIPATE.
A FEELING SO *UNFAMILIAR,* IT WOKE ME IN THE NIGHT.
HAD ME REACHING FOR MY COAT AND SMOKES UNTIL I REALIZED WHAT IT WAS...
AFTER THE TATE CLUB, AFTER DECIDING TO LEAVE MAGIC *BEHIND...*
NO MONKEY'S PAW TWISTS...
FOR THE FIRST TIME IN LIVING FUCKING MEMORY...
I'M ONE OF A NUMBER... *CONNECTED...*
AND IT'S GOING TO *KILL* ME.

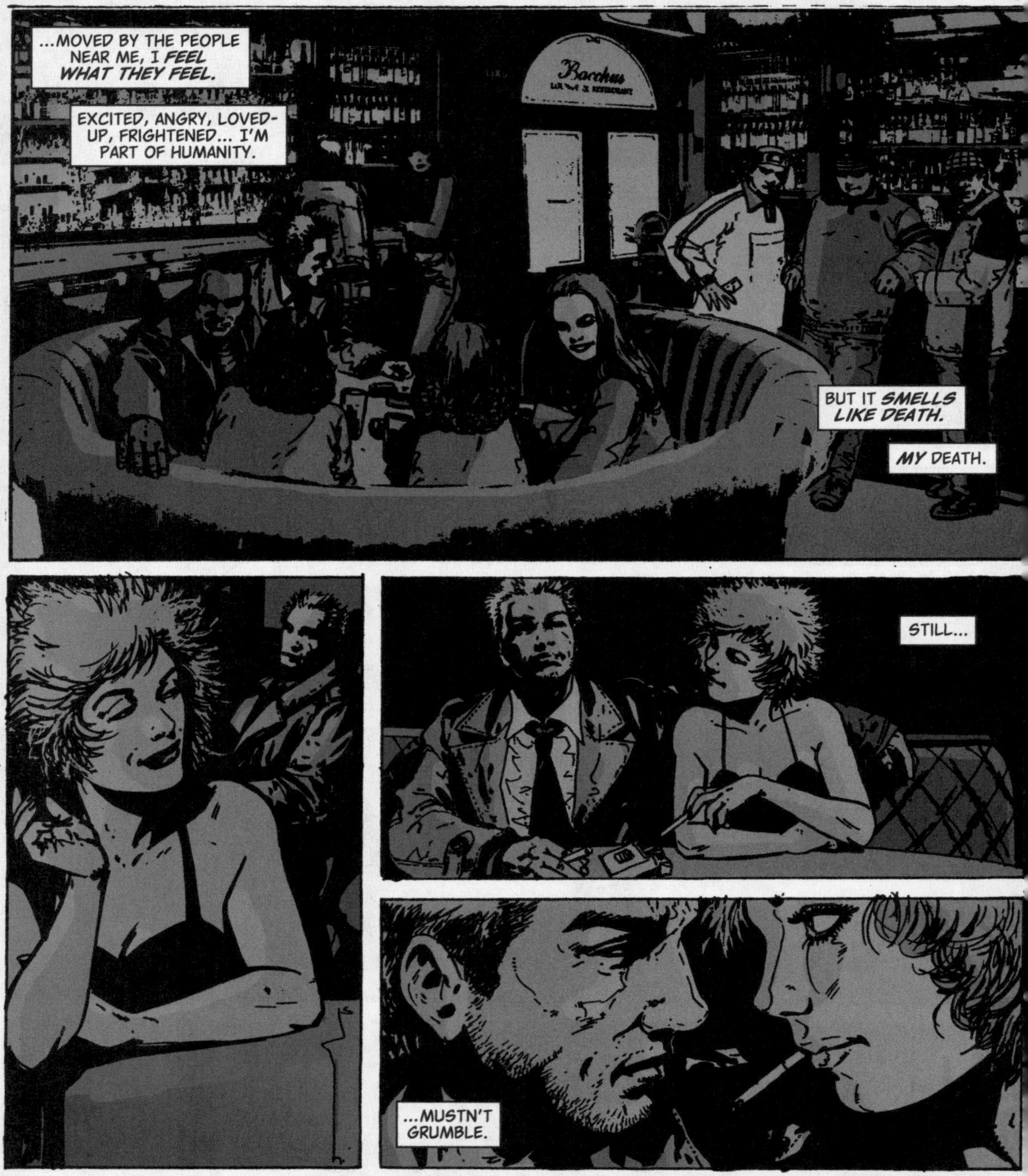
...MOVED BY THE PEOPLE NEAR ME, I *FEEL WHAT THEY FEEL.*
EXCITED, ANGRY, LOVED-UP, FRIGHTENED... I'M PART OF HUMANITY.
Bacchus
BUT IT *SMELLS LIKE DEATH.*
MY DEATH.
STILL...
...MUSTN'T GRUMBLE.

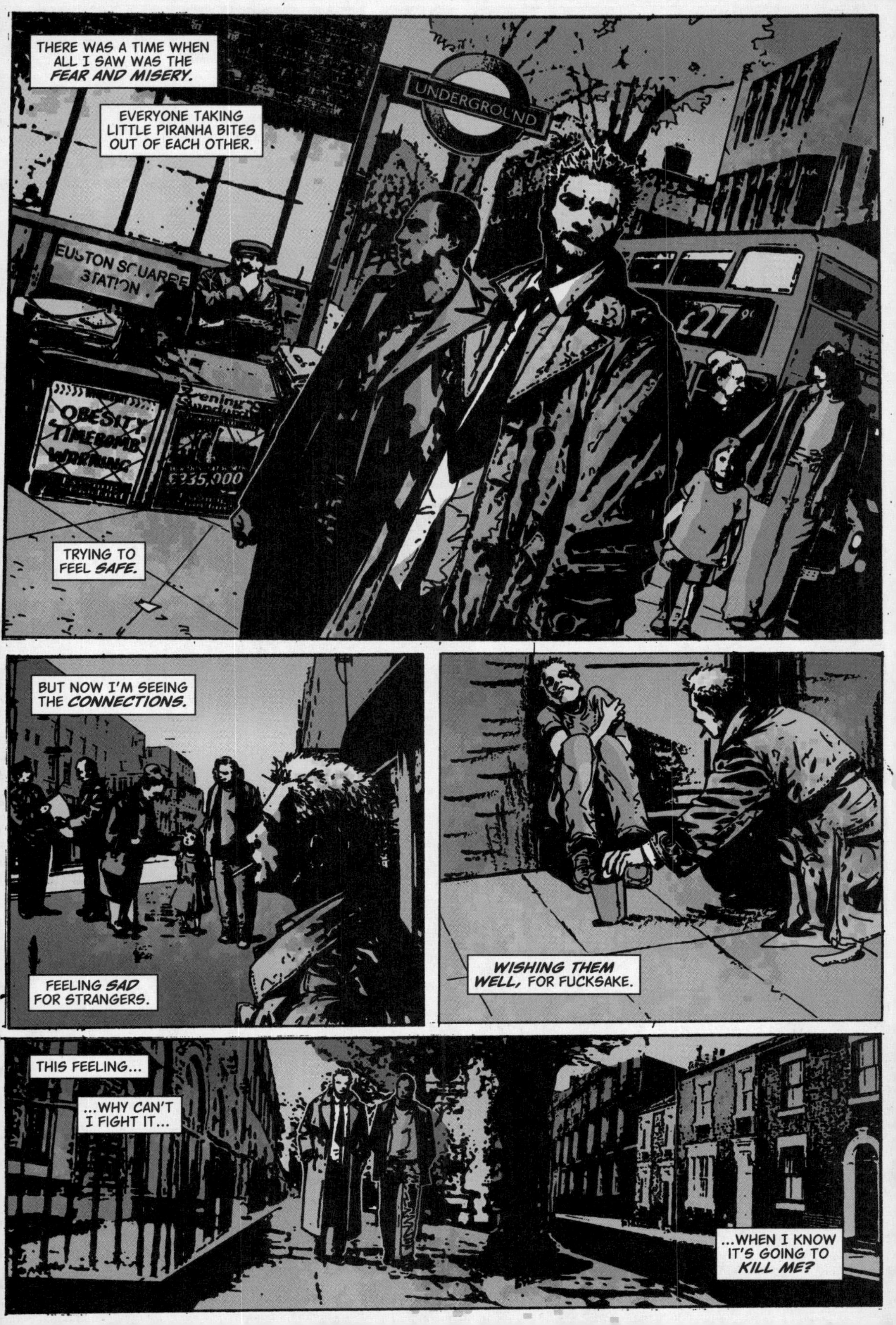

THERE WAS A TIME WHEN ALL I SAW WAS THE *FEAR AND MISERY.*
UNDERGROUND
EVERYONE TAKING LITTLE PIRANHA BITES OUT OF EACH OTHER.
EUSTON SQUARE STATION
OBESITY 'TIMEBOMB' WARNING
£335,000
27
TRYING TO FEEL *SAFE.*
BUT NOW I'M SEEING THE *CONNECTIONS.*
FEELING *SAD* FOR STRANGERS.
WISHING THEM WELL, FOR FUCKSAKE.
THIS FEELING...
...WHY CAN'T I FIGHT IT...
...WHEN I KNOW IT'S GOING TO *KILL ME?*

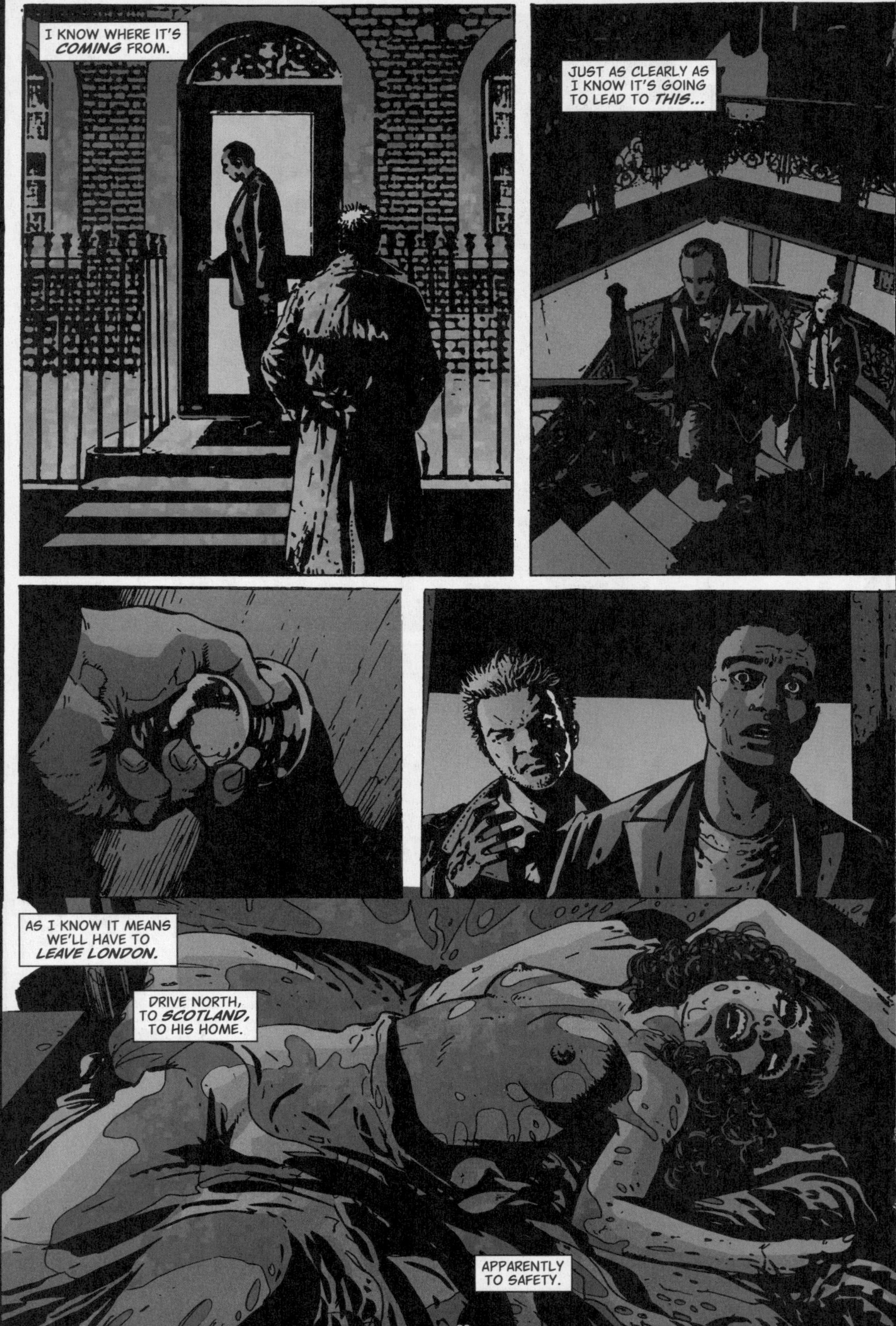
I KNOW WHERE IT'S *COMING* FROM.
JUST AS CLEARLY AS I KNOW IT'S GOING TO LEAD TO *THIS...*
AS I KNOW IT MEANS WE'LL HAVE TO *LEAVE LONDON.*
DRIVE NORTH, TO *SCOTLAND,* TO HIS HOME.
APPARENTLY TO SAFETY.

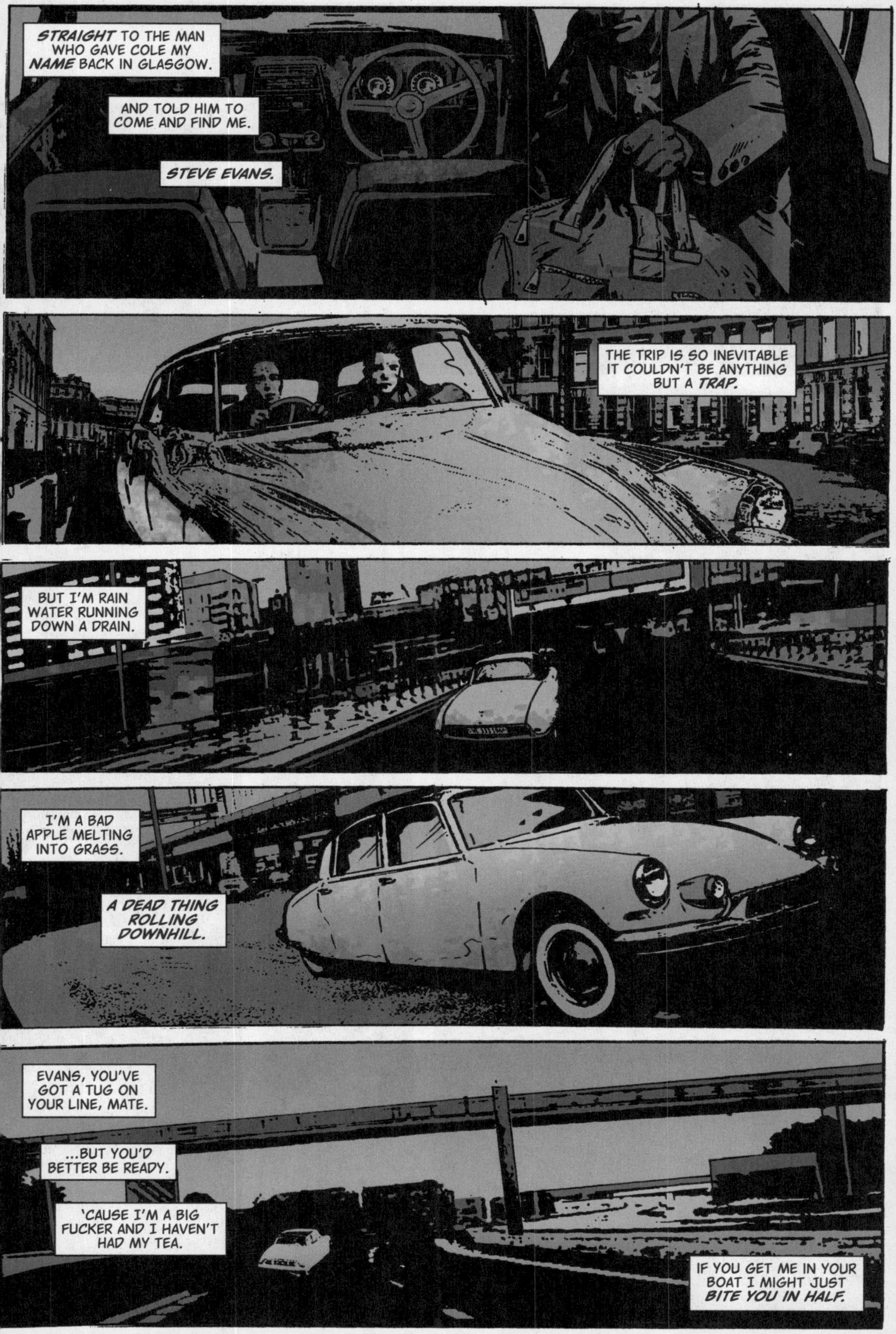
STRAIGHT TO THE MAN WHO GAVE COLE MY NAME BACK IN GLASGOW.
AND TOLD HIM TO COME AND FIND ME.
STEVE EVANS.
THE TRIP IS SO INEVITABLE IT COULDN'T BE ANYTHING BUT A TRAP.
BUT I'M RAIN WATER RUNNING DOWN A DRAIN.
I'M A BAD APPLE MELTING INTO GRASS.
A DEAD THING ROLLING DOWNHILL.
EVANS, YOU'VE GOT A TUG ON YOUR LINE, MATE.
...BUT YOU'D BETTER BE READY.
'CAUSE I'M A BIG FUCKER AND I HAVEN'T HAD MY TEA.
IF YOU GET ME IN YOUR BOAT I MIGHT JUST BITE YOU IN HALF.

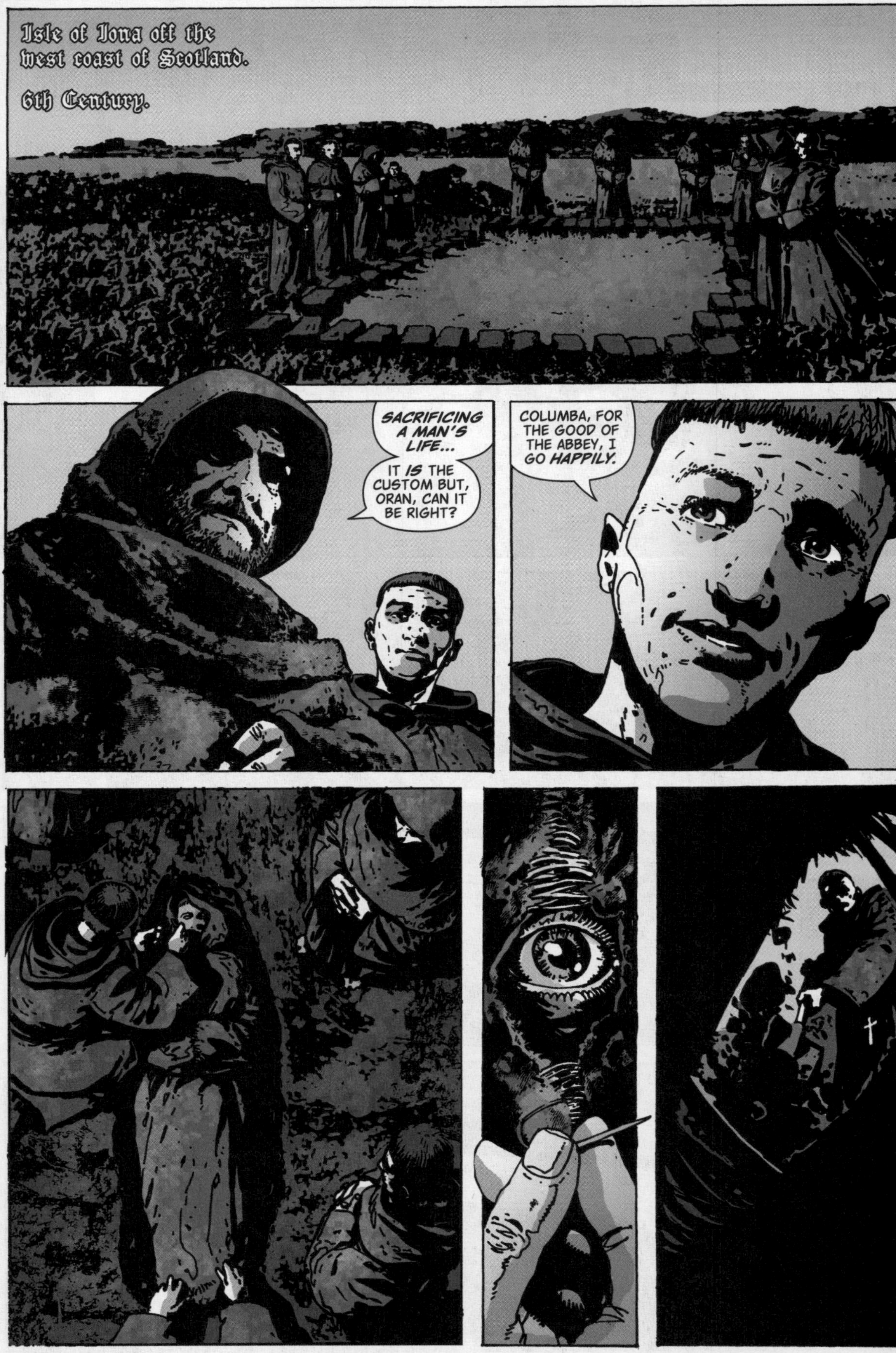
Isle of Iona off the west coast of Scotland.
6th Century.
SACRIFICING A MAN'S LIFE...
IT IS THE CUSTOM BUT, ORAN, CAN IT BE RIGHT?
COLUMBA, FOR THE GOOD OF THE ABBEY, I GO HAPPILY.

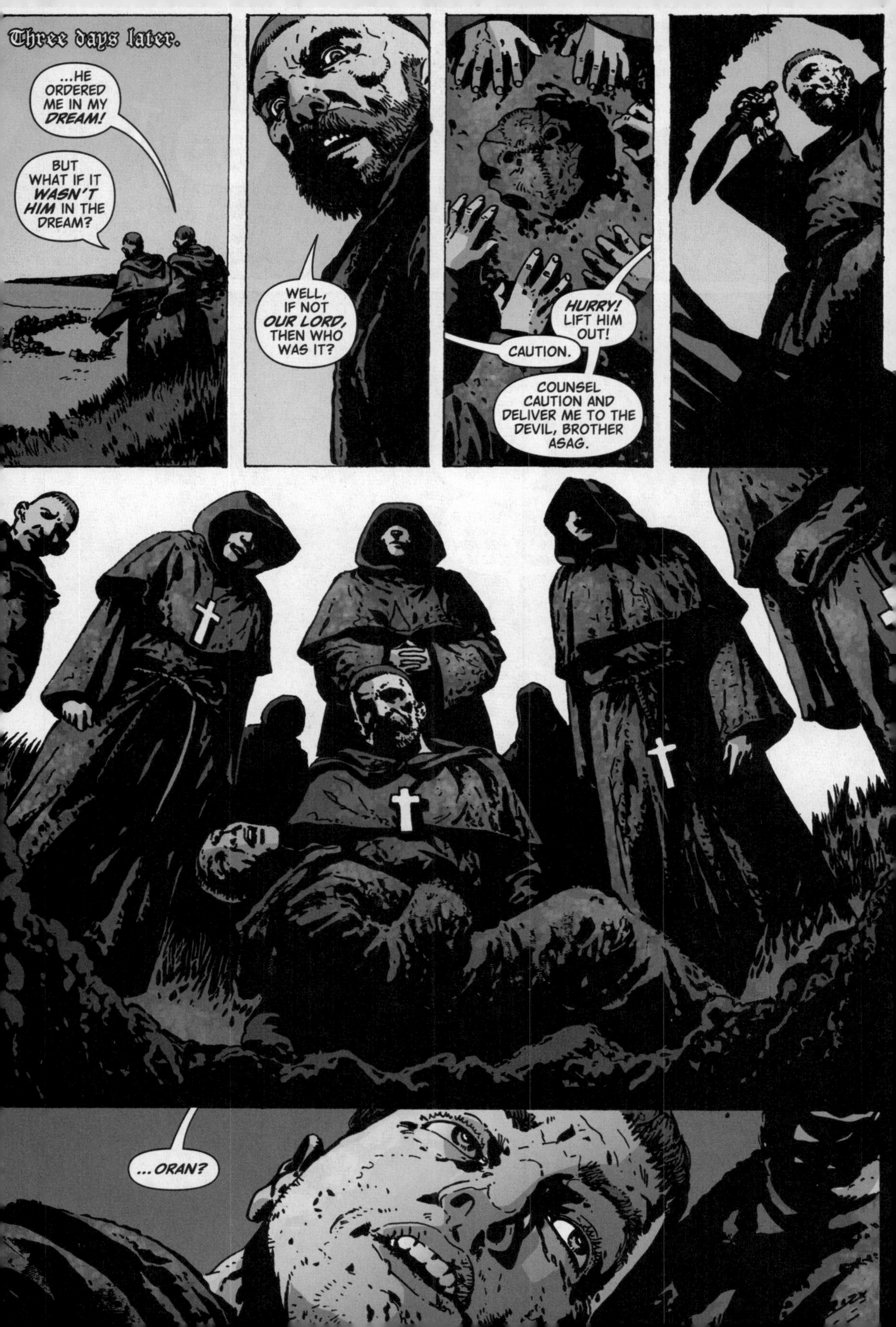
Three days later.
...HE ORDERED ME IN MY DREAM!
BUT WHAT IF IT WASN'T HIM IN THE DREAM?
WELL, IF NOT OUR LORD, THEN WHO WAS IT?
HURRY! LIFT HIM OUT!
CAUTION.
COUNSEL CAUTION AND DELIVER ME TO THE DEVIL, BROTHER ASAG.
...ORAN?

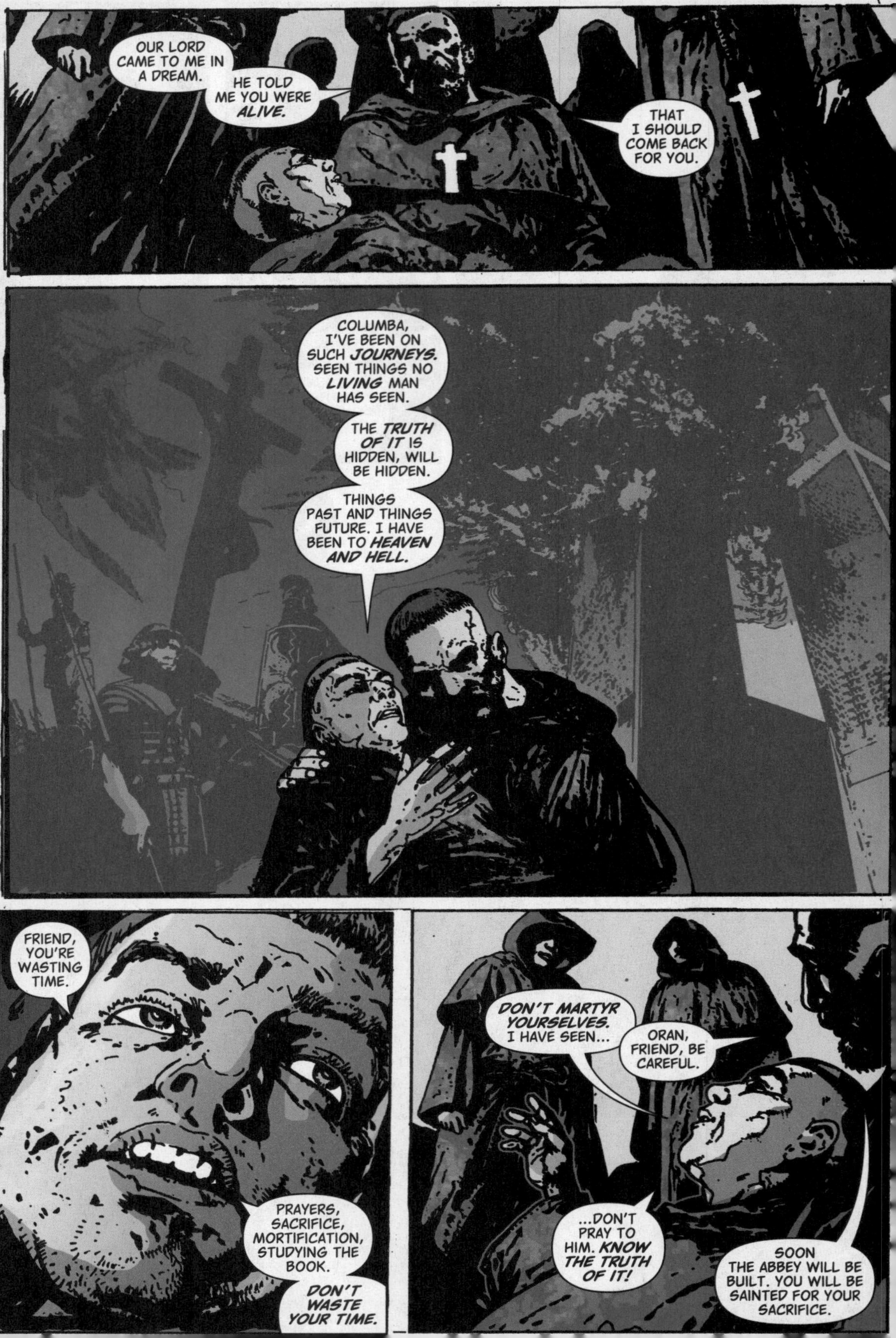
OUR LORD CAME TO ME IN A DREAM.
HE TOLD ME YOU WERE *ALIVE.*
THAT I SHOULD COME BACK FOR YOU.
COLUMBA, I'VE BEEN ON SUCH *JOURNEYS.* SEEN THINGS NO *LIVING* MAN HAS SEEN.
THE *TRUTH OF IT* IS HIDDEN, WILL BE HIDDEN.
THINGS PAST AND THINGS FUTURE. I HAVE BEEN TO *HEAVEN AND HELL.*
FRIEND, YOU'RE WASTING TIME.
PRAYERS, SACRIFICE, MORTIFICATION, STUDYING THE BOOK.
DON'T WASTE YOUR TIME.
DON'T MARTYR YOURSELVES. I HAVE SEEN...
ORAN, FRIEND, BE CAREFUL.
...DON'T PRAY TO HIM. *KNOW THE TRUTH OF IT!*
SOON THE ABBEY WILL BE BUILT. YOU WILL BE SAINTED FOR YOUR SACRIFICE.

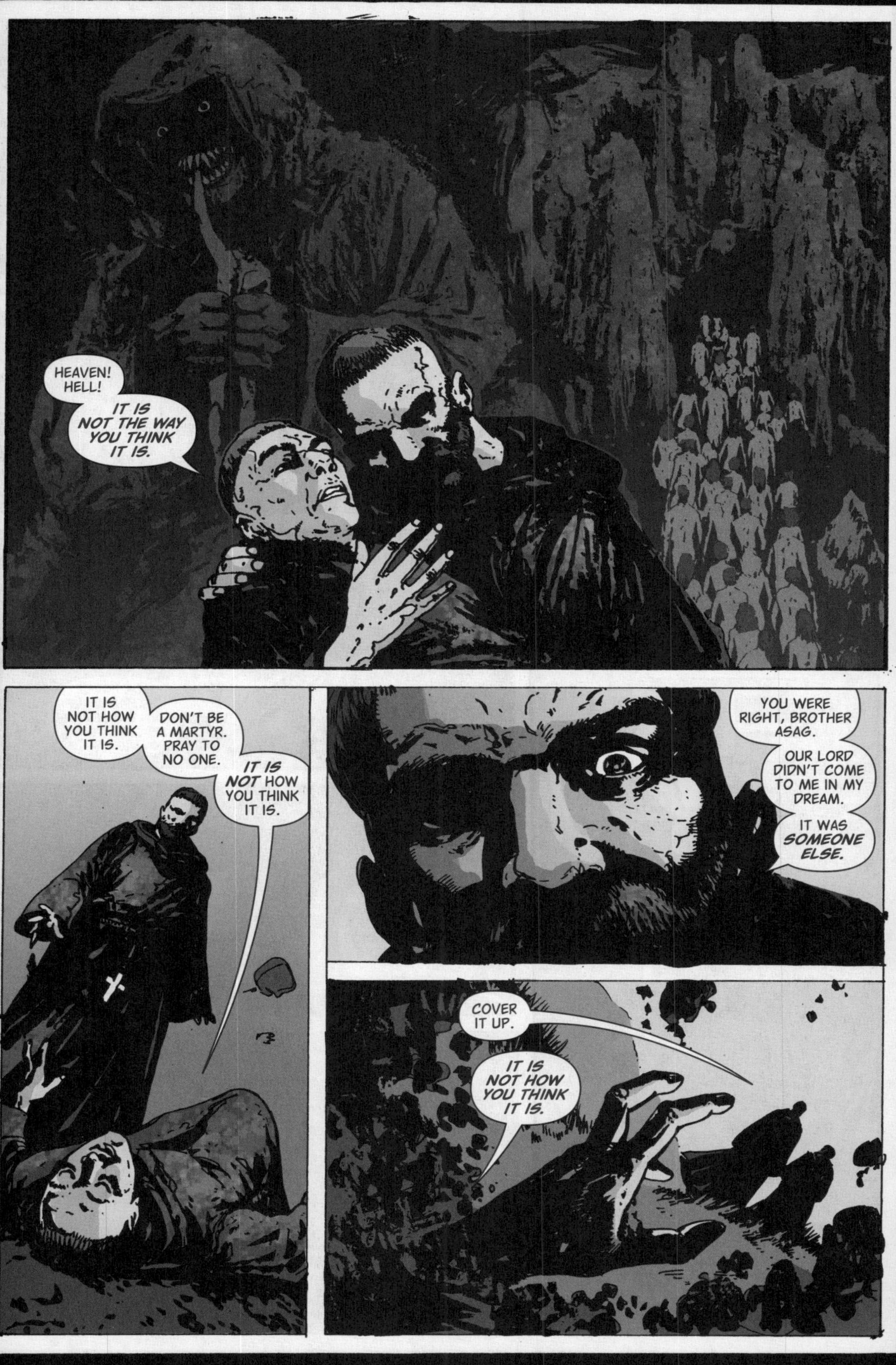
HEAVEN! HELL!
IT IS NOT THE WAY YOU THINK IT IS.
IT IS NOT HOW YOU THINK IT IS.
DON'T BE A MARTYR. PRAY TO NO ONE.
IT IS NOT HOW YOU THINK IT IS.
YOU WERE RIGHT, BROTHER ASAG.
OUR LORD DIDN'T COME TO ME IN MY DREAM.
IT WAS SOMEONE ELSE.
COVER IT UP.
IT IS NOT HOW YOU THINK IT IS.

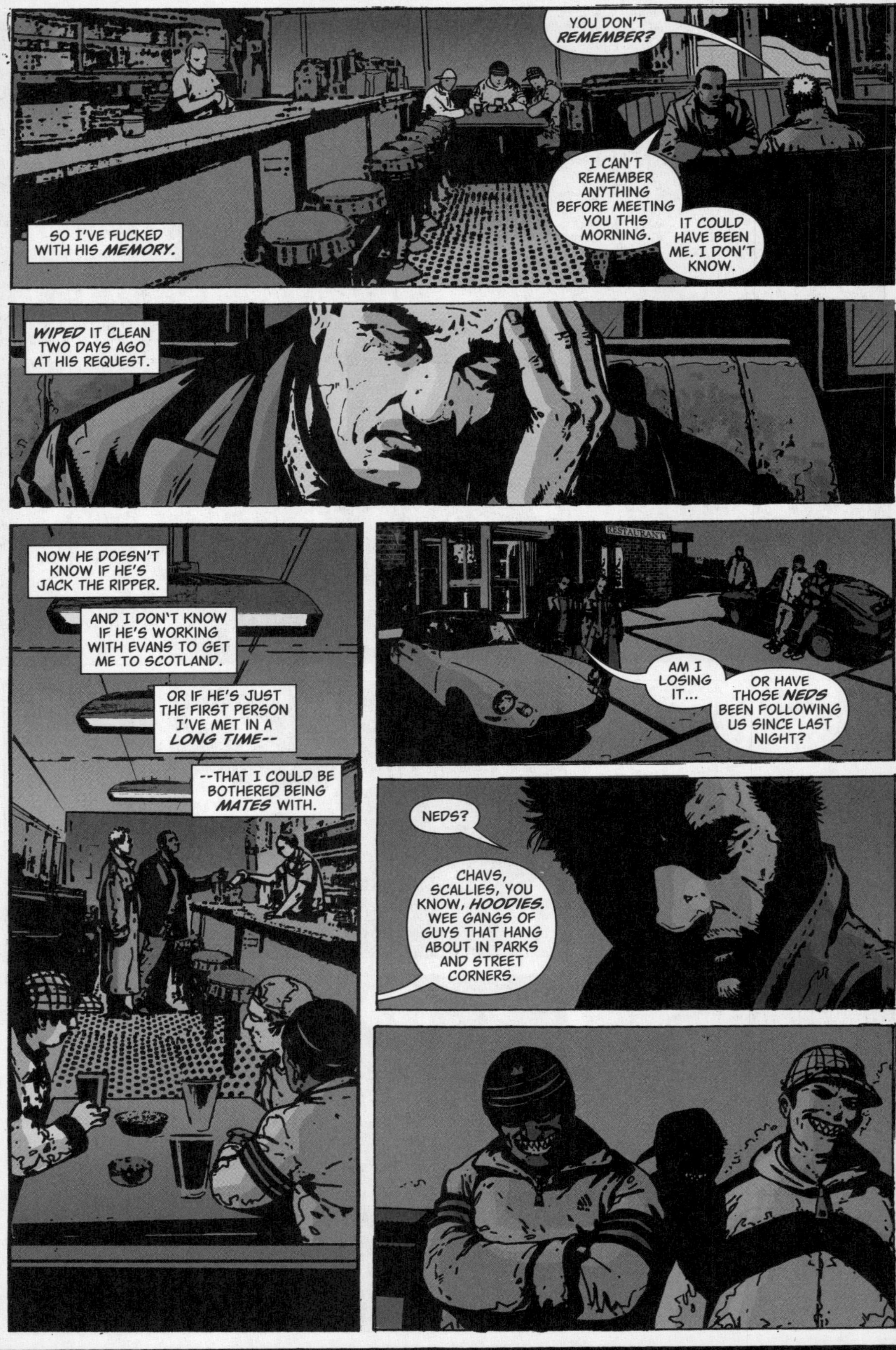
YOU DON'T REMEMBER?
I CAN'T REMEMBER ANYTHING BEFORE MEETING YOU THIS MORNING.
IT COULD HAVE BEEN ME. I DON'T KNOW.
SO I'VE FUCKED WITH HIS MEMORY.
WIPED IT CLEAN TWO DAYS AGO AT HIS REQUEST.
NOW HE DOESN'T KNOW IF HE'S JACK THE RIPPER.
AND I DON'T KNOW IF HE'S WORKING WITH EVANS TO GET ME TO SCOTLAND.
OR IF HE'S JUST THE FIRST PERSON I'VE MET IN A LONG TIME--
--THAT I COULD BE BOTHERED BEING MATES WITH.
RESTAURANT
AM I LOSING IT...
OR HAVE THOSE NEDS BEEN FOLLOWING US SINCE LAST NIGHT?
NEDS?
CHAVS, SCALLIES, YOU KNOW, HOODIES. WEE GANGS OF GUYS THAT HANG ABOUT IN PARKS AND STREET CORNERS.

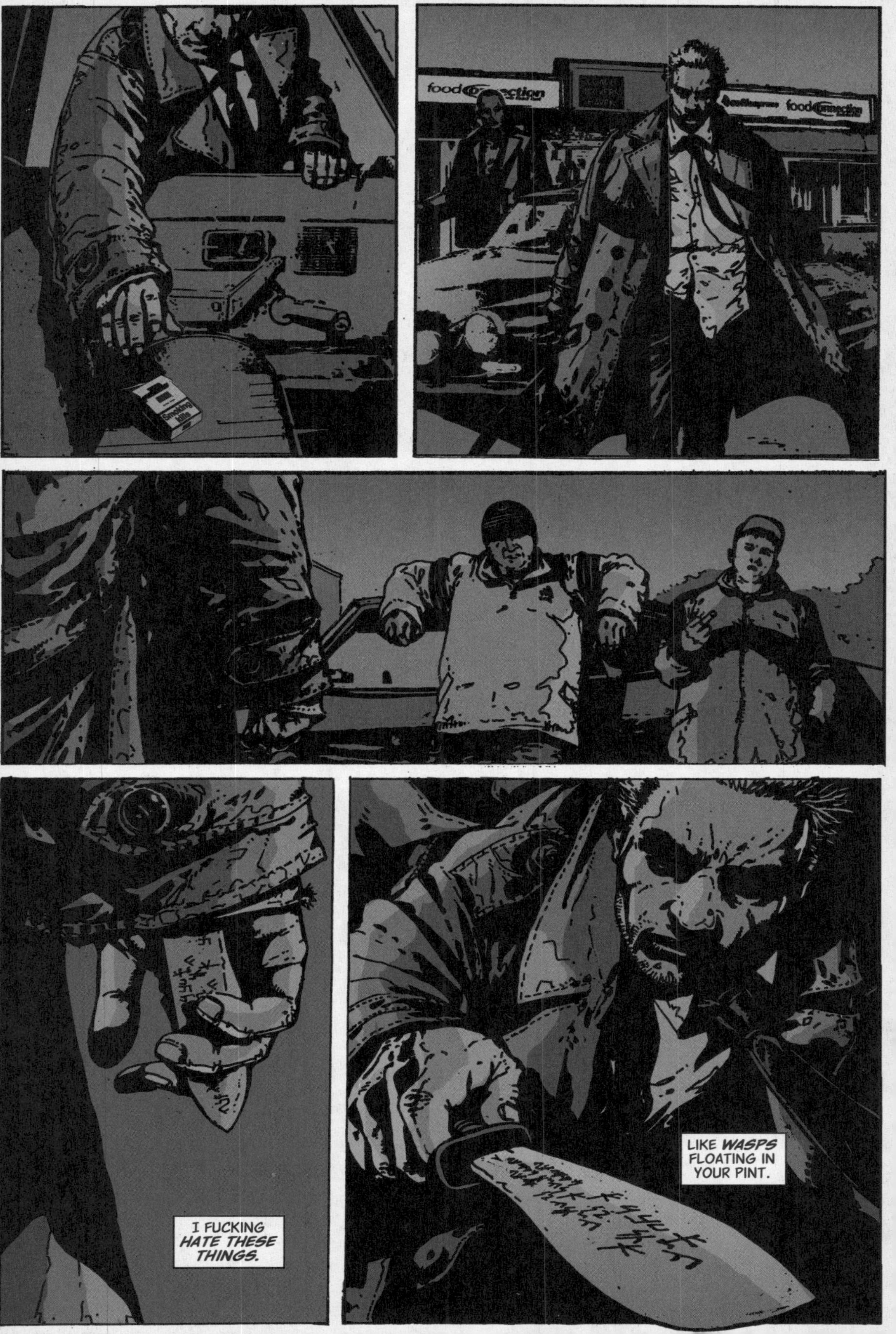
Smoking kills
food connection
food connection
I FUCKING
HATE THESE
THINGS.
LIKE WASPS
FLOATING IN
YOUR PINT.

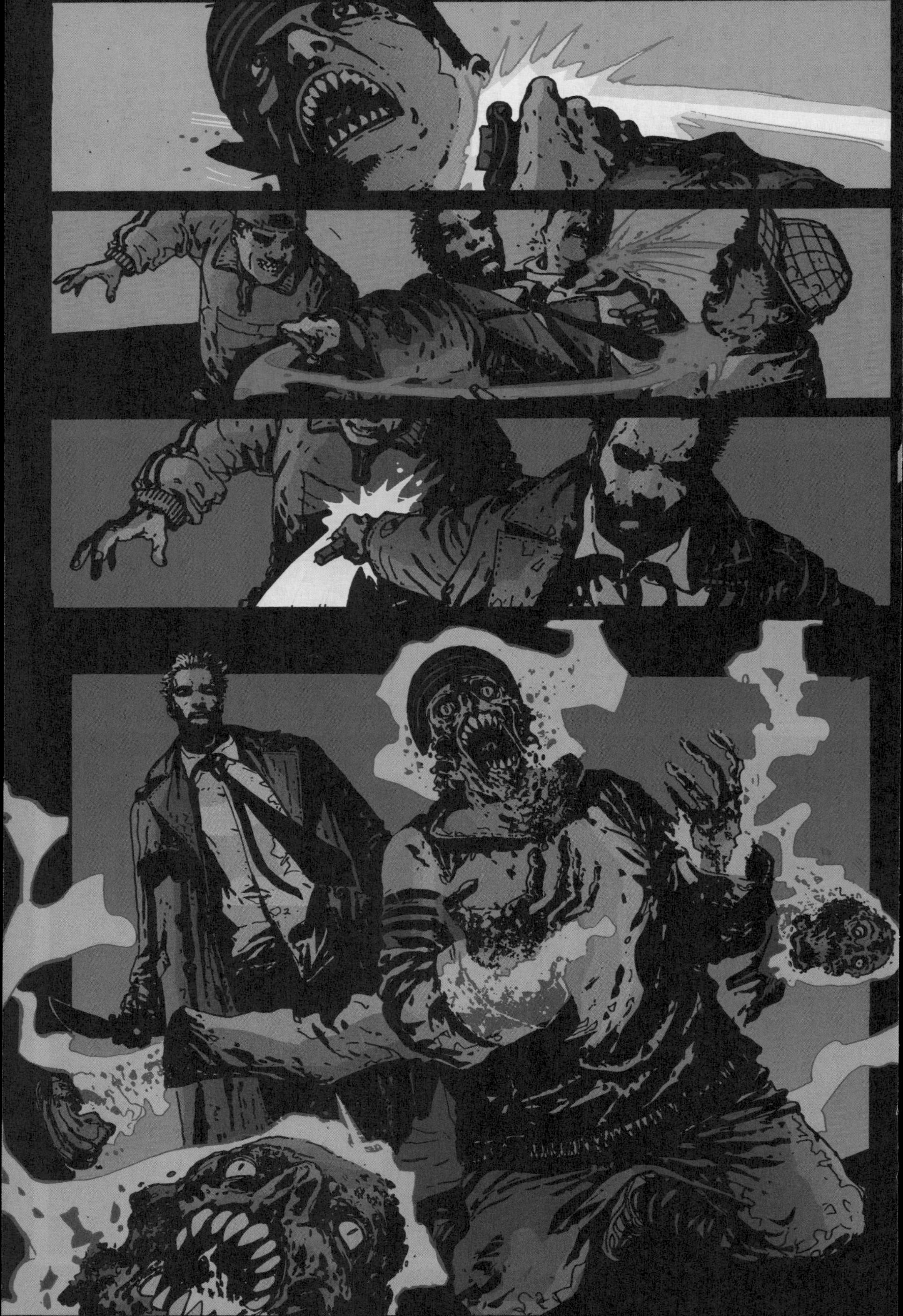

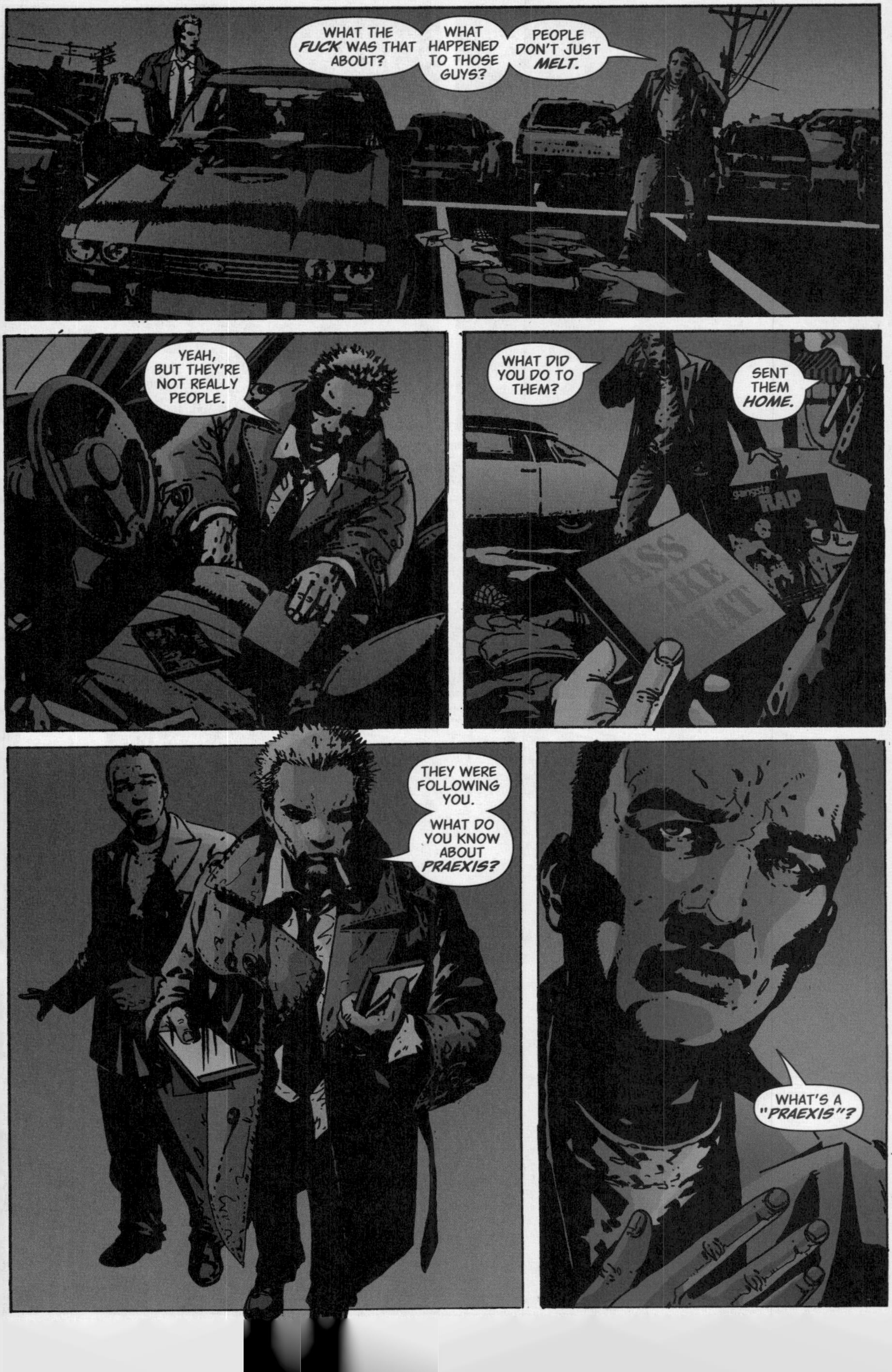
WHAT THE *FUCK* WAS THAT ABOUT?
WHAT HAPPENED TO THOSE GUYS?
PEOPLE DON'T JUST *MELT.*
YEAH, BUT THEY'RE NOT REALLY PEOPLE.
WHAT DID YOU DO TO THEM?
SENT THEM *HOME.*
THEY WERE FOLLOWING YOU.
WHAT DO YOU KNOW ABOUT *PRAEXIS?*
WHAT'S A *"PRAEXIS"?*

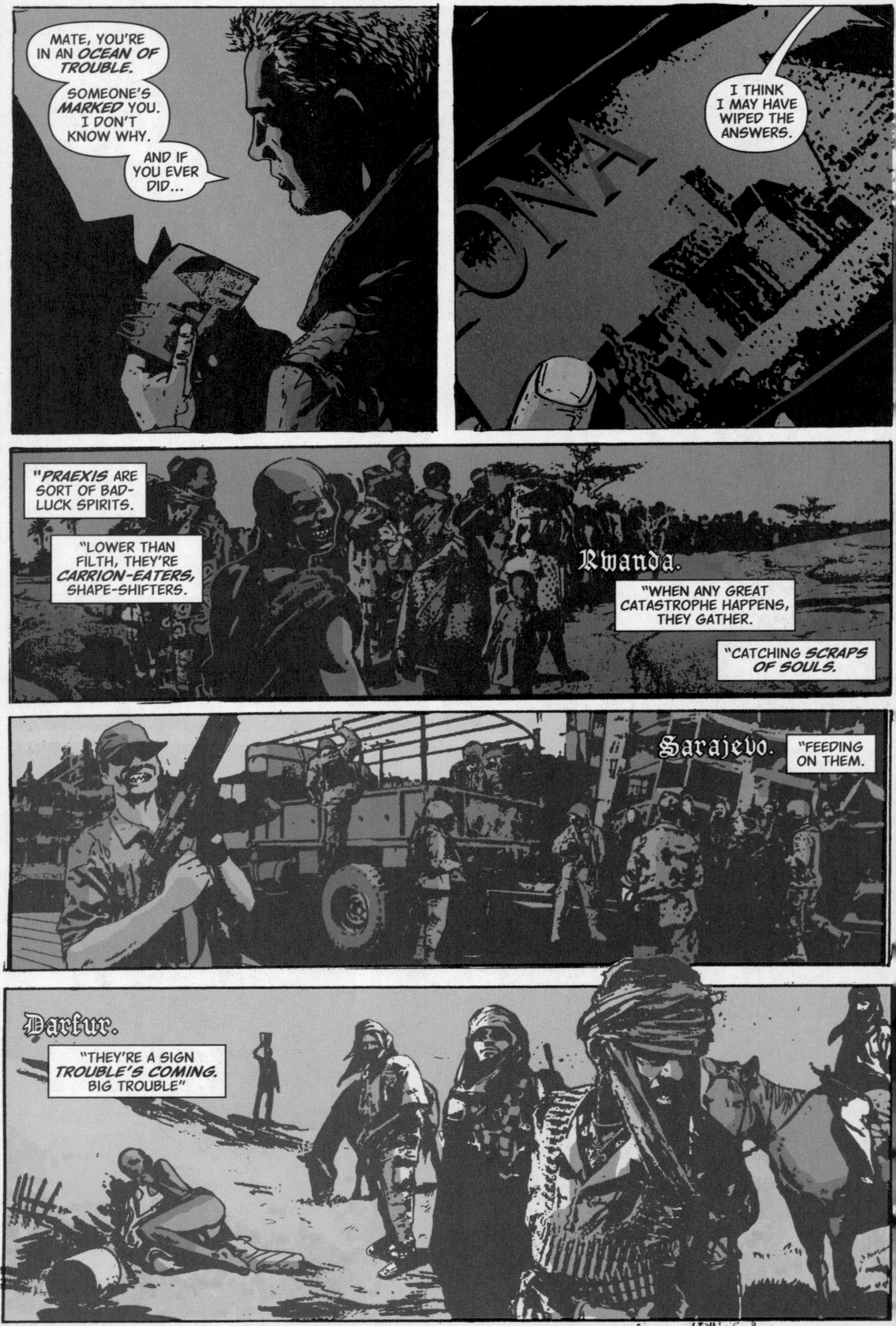

MATE, YOU'RE IN AN *OCEAN OF TROUBLE.*
SOMEONE'S *MARKED* YOU. I DON'T KNOW WHY.
AND IF YOU EVER DID...
I THINK I MAY HAVE WIPED THE ANSWERS.
"*PRAEXIS* ARE SORT OF BAD-LUCK SPIRITS.
"LOWER THAN FILTH, THEY'RE *CARRION-EATERS,* SHAPE-SHIFTERS.
Rwanda.
"WHEN ANY GREAT CATASTROPHE HAPPENS, THEY GATHER.
"CATCHING *SCRAPS OF SOULS.*
Sarajevo.
"FEEDING ON THEM.
Darfur.
"THEY'RE A SIGN *TROUBLE'S COMING.* BIG TROUBLE"

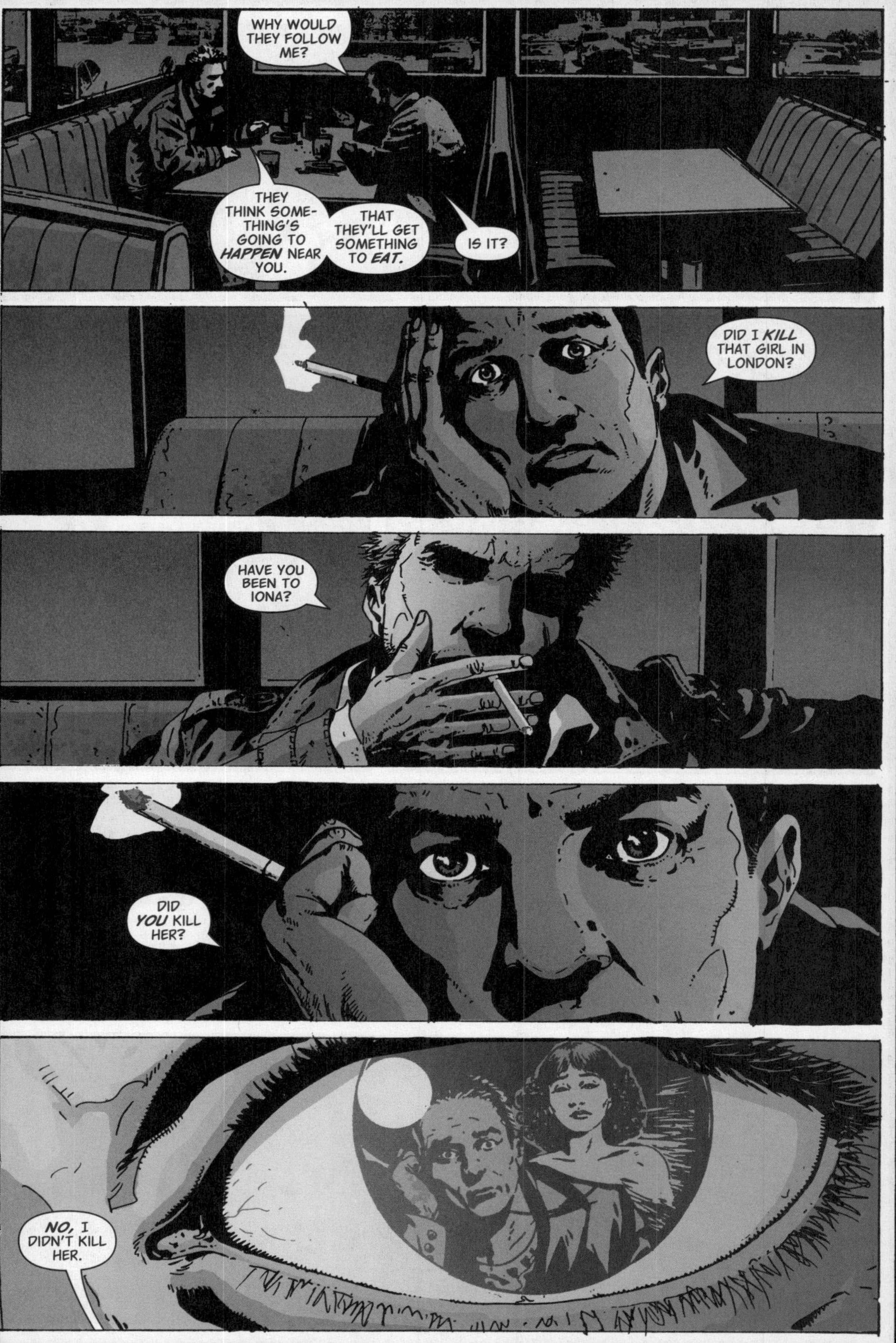
WHY WOULD THEY FOLLOW ME?
THEY THINK SOMETHING'S GOING TO *HAPPEN* NEAR YOU.
THAT THEY'LL GET SOMETHING TO *EAT.*
IS IT?
DID I *KILL* THAT GIRL IN LONDON?
HAVE YOU BEEN TO IONA?
DID *YOU* KILL HER?
NO, I DIDN'T KILL HER.

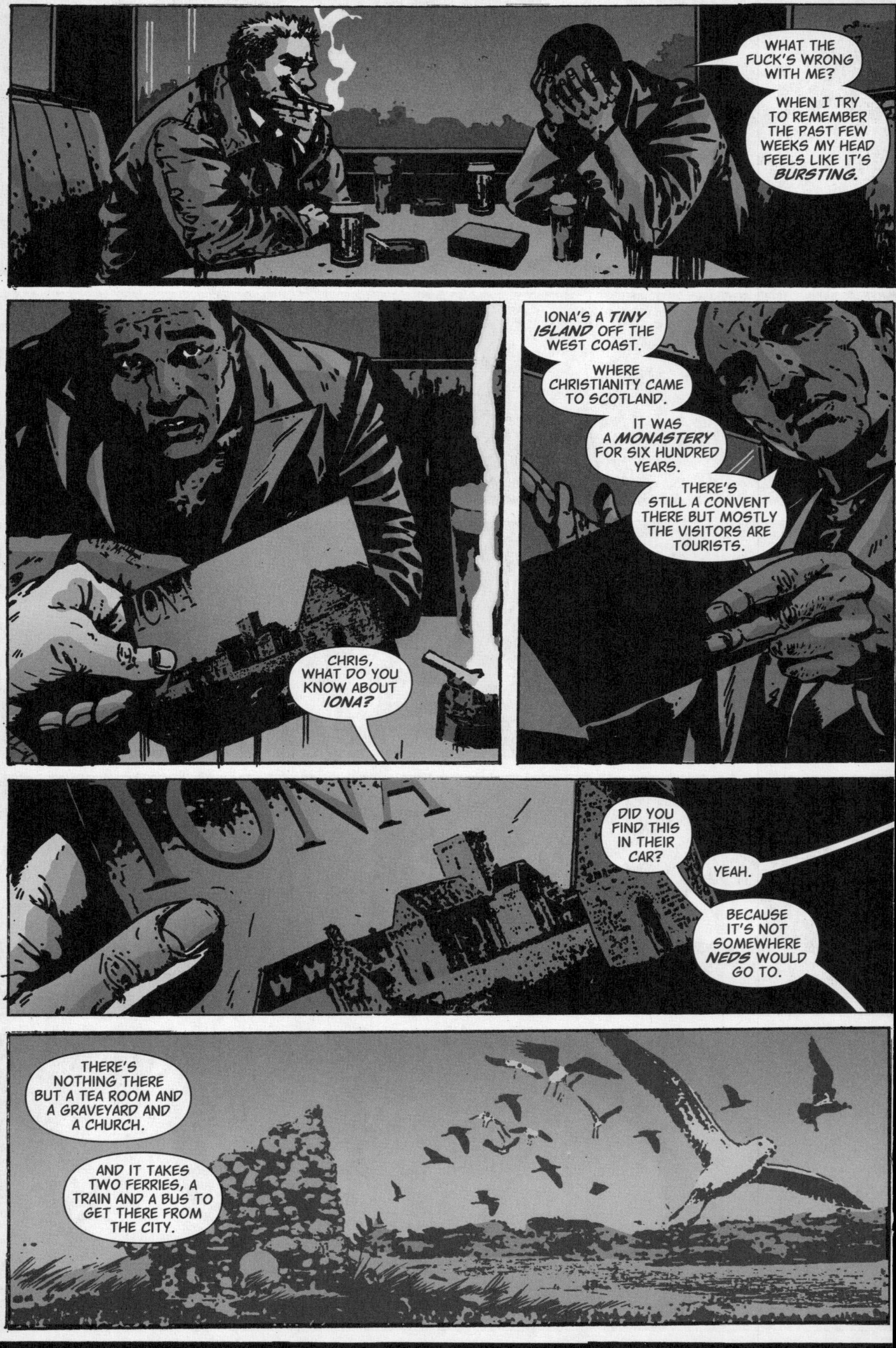
WHAT THE FUCK'S WRONG WITH ME?
WHEN I TRY TO REMEMBER THE PAST FEW WEEKS MY HEAD FEELS LIKE IT'S BURSTING.
IONA
CHRIS, WHAT DO YOU KNOW ABOUT IONA?
IONA'S A TINY ISLAND OFF THE WEST COAST.
WHERE CHRISTIANITY CAME TO SCOTLAND.
IT WAS A MONASTERY FOR SIX HUNDRED YEARS.
THERE'S STILL A CONVENT THERE BUT MOSTLY THE VISITORS ARE TOURISTS.
IONA
DID YOU FIND THIS IN THEIR CAR?
YEAH.
BECAUSE IT'S NOT SOMEWHERE NEDS WOULD GO TO.
THERE'S NOTHING THERE BUT A TEA ROOM AND A GRAVEYARD AND A CHURCH.
AND IT TAKES TWO FERRIES, A TRAIN AND A BUS TO GET THERE FROM THE CITY.

YOU KNOW ENOUGH ABOUT IT.

MY *PARENTS* WERE MEMBERS OF THE IONA COMMUNITY.

THAT MUST BE WHERE YOU GET YOUR *EDGE.*

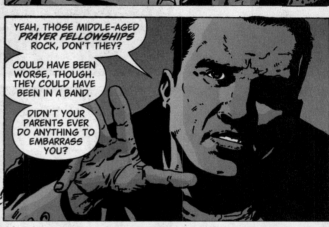

YEAH, THOSE MIDDLE-AGED *PRAYER FELLOWSHIPS* ROCK, DON'T THEY?

COULD HAVE BEEN WORSE, THOUGH. THEY COULD HAVE BEEN IN A BAND.

DIDN'T YOUR PARENTS EVER DO ANYTHING TO EMBARRASS YOU?

YEAH. THEY FUCK YOU UP, YOUR *MUM* AND *DAD.*

I CAN REMEMBER ALL THIS STUFF.

WHY CAN'T I REMEMBER DRIVING TO LONDON *THREE DAYS AGO?*

YOU WERE IN TROUBLE.

YOU CAME LOOKING FOR ME.

AND I *WIPED* YOUR MEMORY.

I CAME LOOKING FOR YOU?

WHAT DOES THE NAME *STEVE EVANS* MEAN TO YOU?

FUCK ALL.

HE'S THE GUY WHO *SENT* YOU TO LOOK FOR ME.

EITHER YOU MET HIM IN THE LAST TWO WEEKS, LIKE YOU SAID YOU DID.

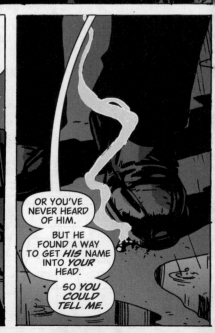

OR YOU'VE NEVER HEARD OF HIM.

BUT HE FOUND A WAY TO GET *HIS* NAME INTO *YOUR* HEAD.

SO *YOU* COULD TELL ME.

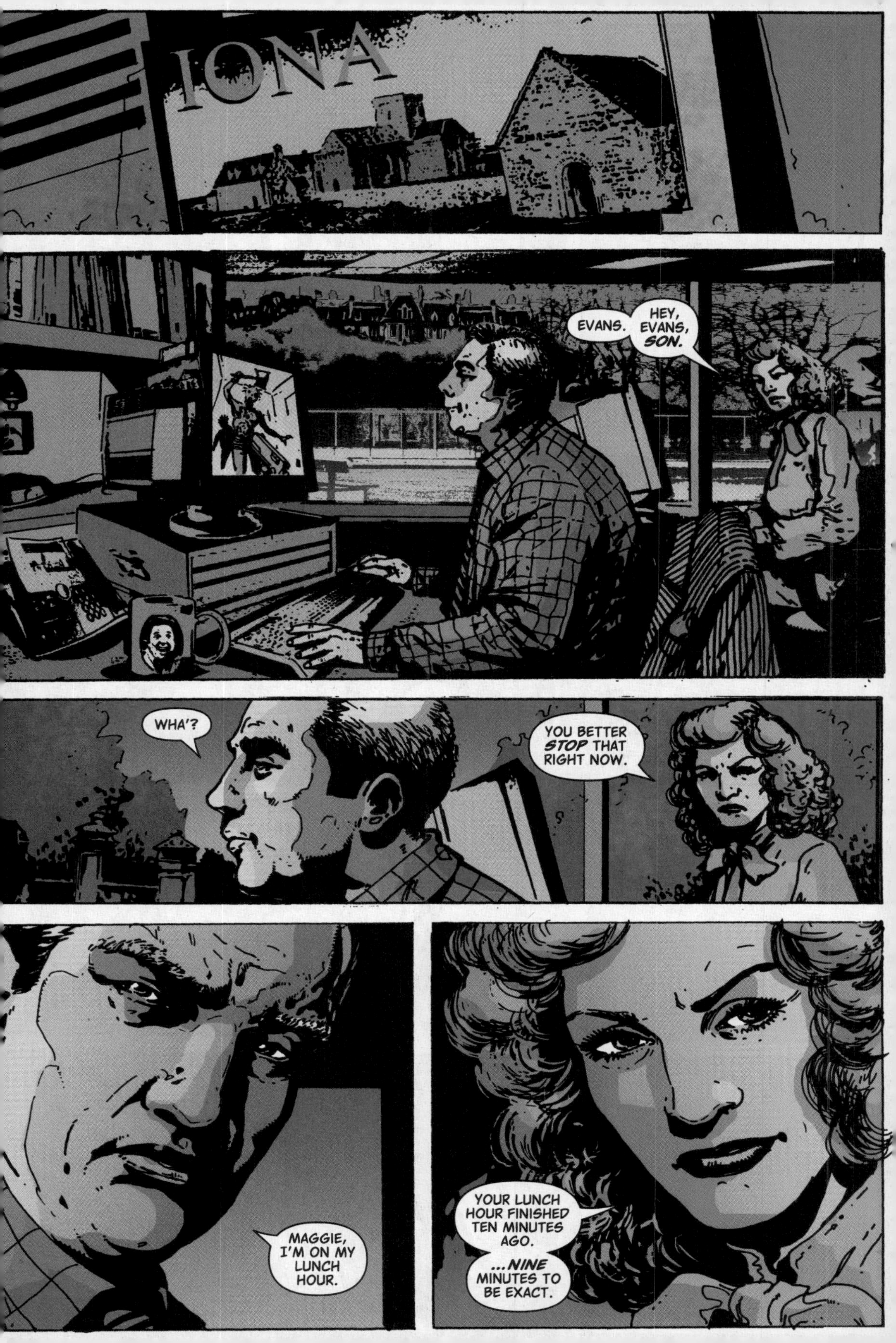
IONA
EVANS.
HEY, EVANS, SON.
WHA'?
YOU BETTER STOP THAT RIGHT NOW.
MAGGIE, I'M ON MY LUNCH HOUR.
YOUR LUNCH HOUR FINISHED TEN MINUTES AGO.
...NINE MINUTES TO BE EXACT.

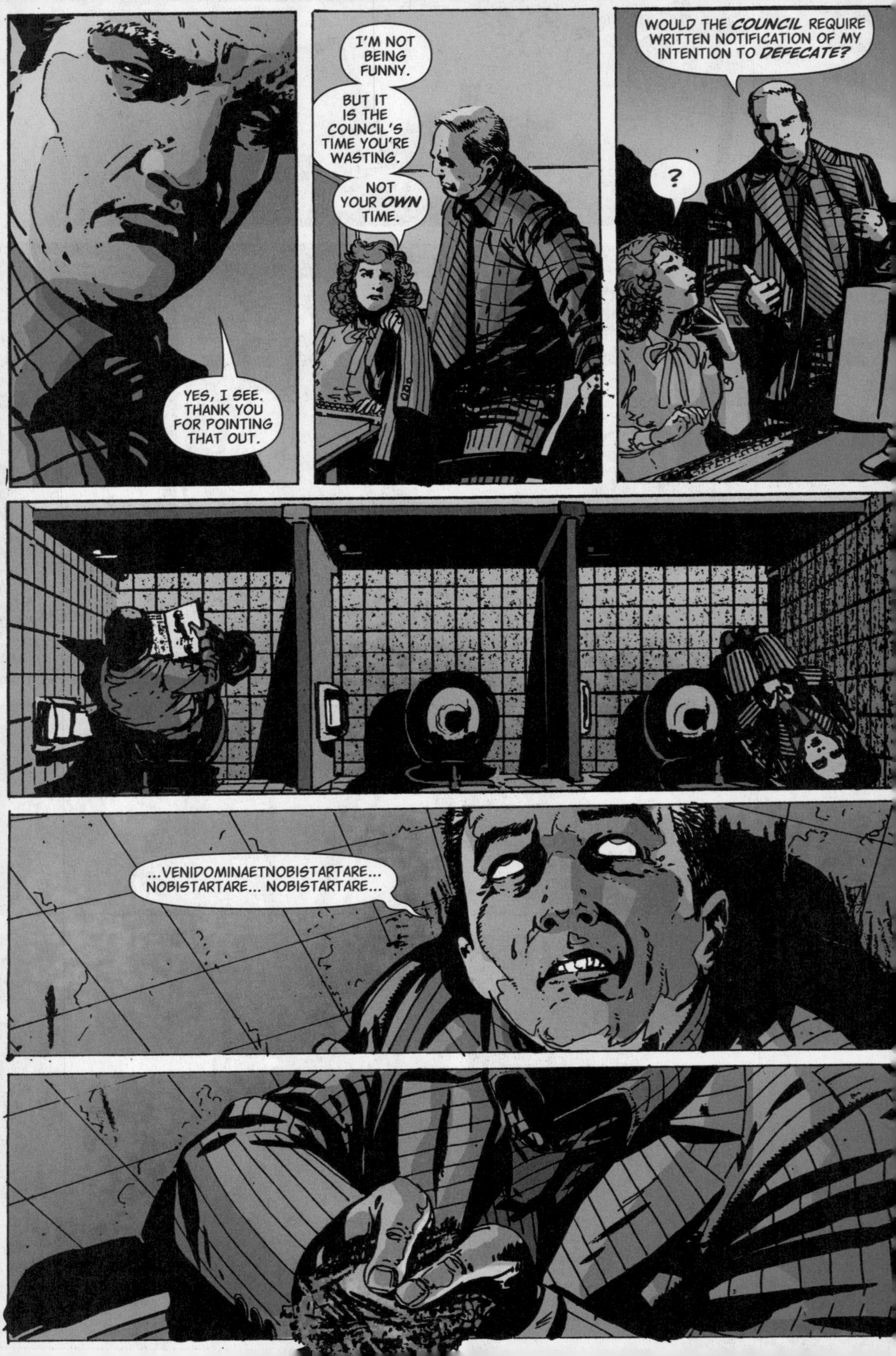
YES, I SEE. THANK YOU FOR POINTING THAT OUT.
I'M NOT BEING FUNNY.
BUT IT IS THE COUNCIL'S TIME YOU'RE WASTING.
NOT YOUR OWN TIME.
WOULD THE COUNCIL REQUIRE WRITTEN NOTIFICATION OF MY INTENTION TO DEFECATE?
?
...VENIDOMINAETNOBISTARTARE... NOBISTARTARE... NOBISTARTARE...

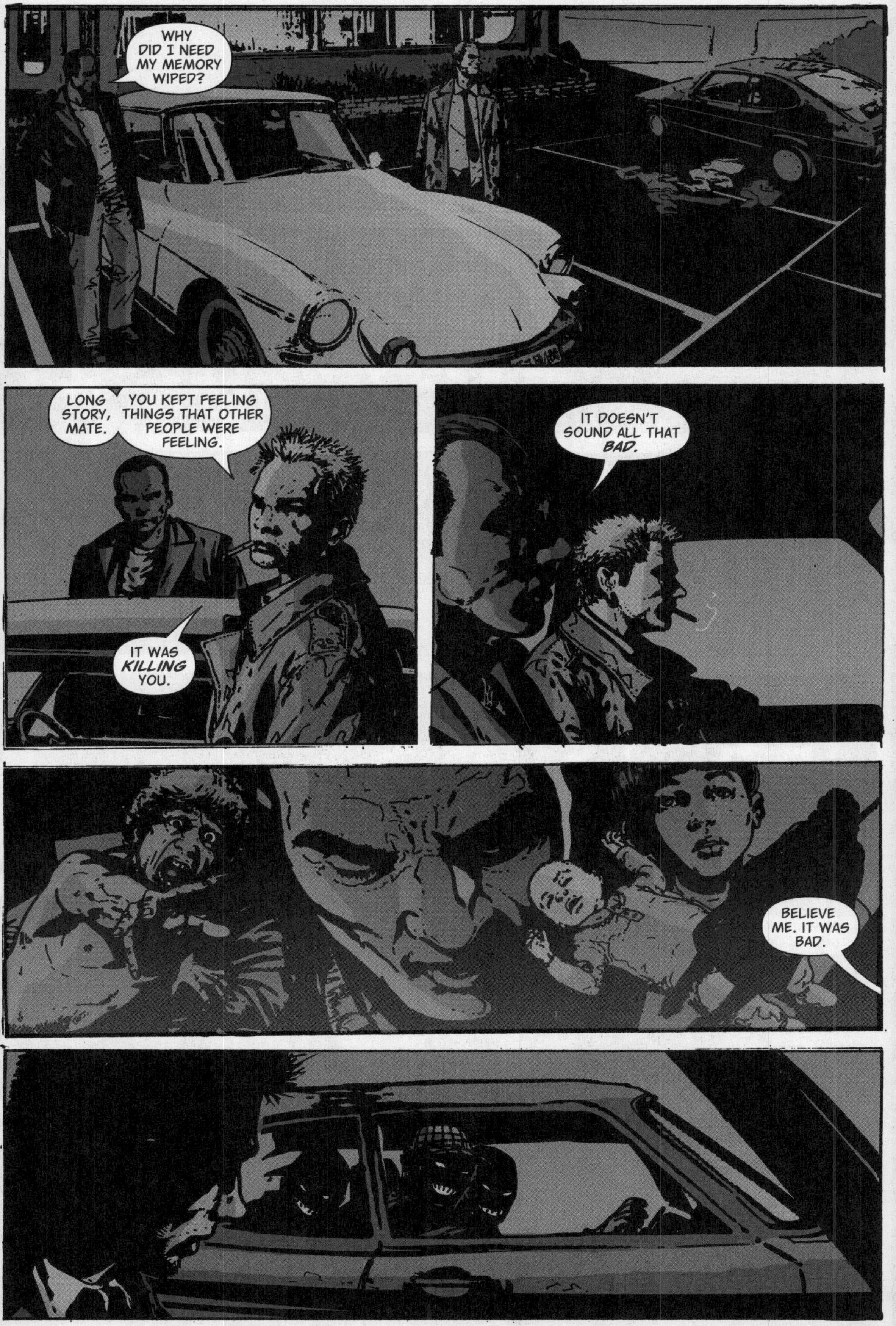
WHY DID I NEED MY MEMORY WIPED?
LONG STORY, MATE.
YOU KEPT FEELING THINGS THAT OTHER PEOPLE WERE FEELING.
IT WAS *KILLING* YOU.
IT DOESN'T SOUND ALL THAT *BAD.*
BELIEVE ME. IT WAS BAD.

REMEMBERING MY OLD MAN BACK THERE, FOR THE FIRST TIME EVER..

I FELT HIS DESOLATION. FELT HIM MISSING MUM.

SEEING THE FEAR IN HIS KIDS' EYES, KNOWING *HE PUT IT THERE.*

EMPATHY.

IT'S STRANGLING ME. SUFFOCATING...

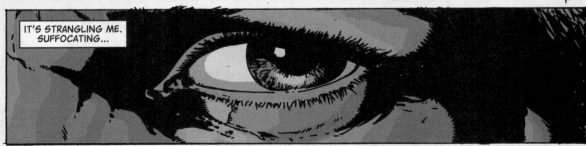

AND HERE I AM...
...DRIVING TOWARDS THE *SOURCE.*

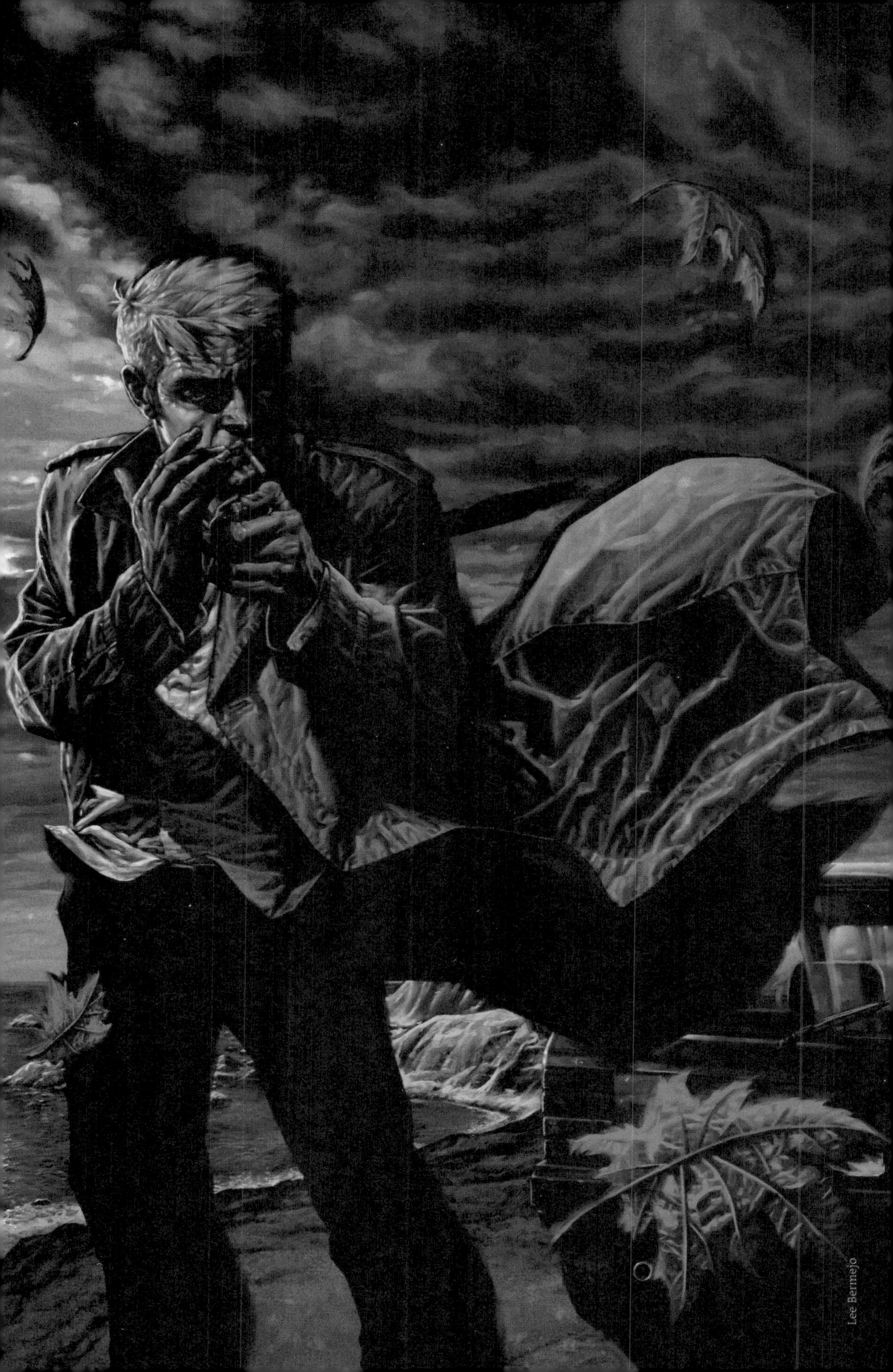
Lee Bermejo

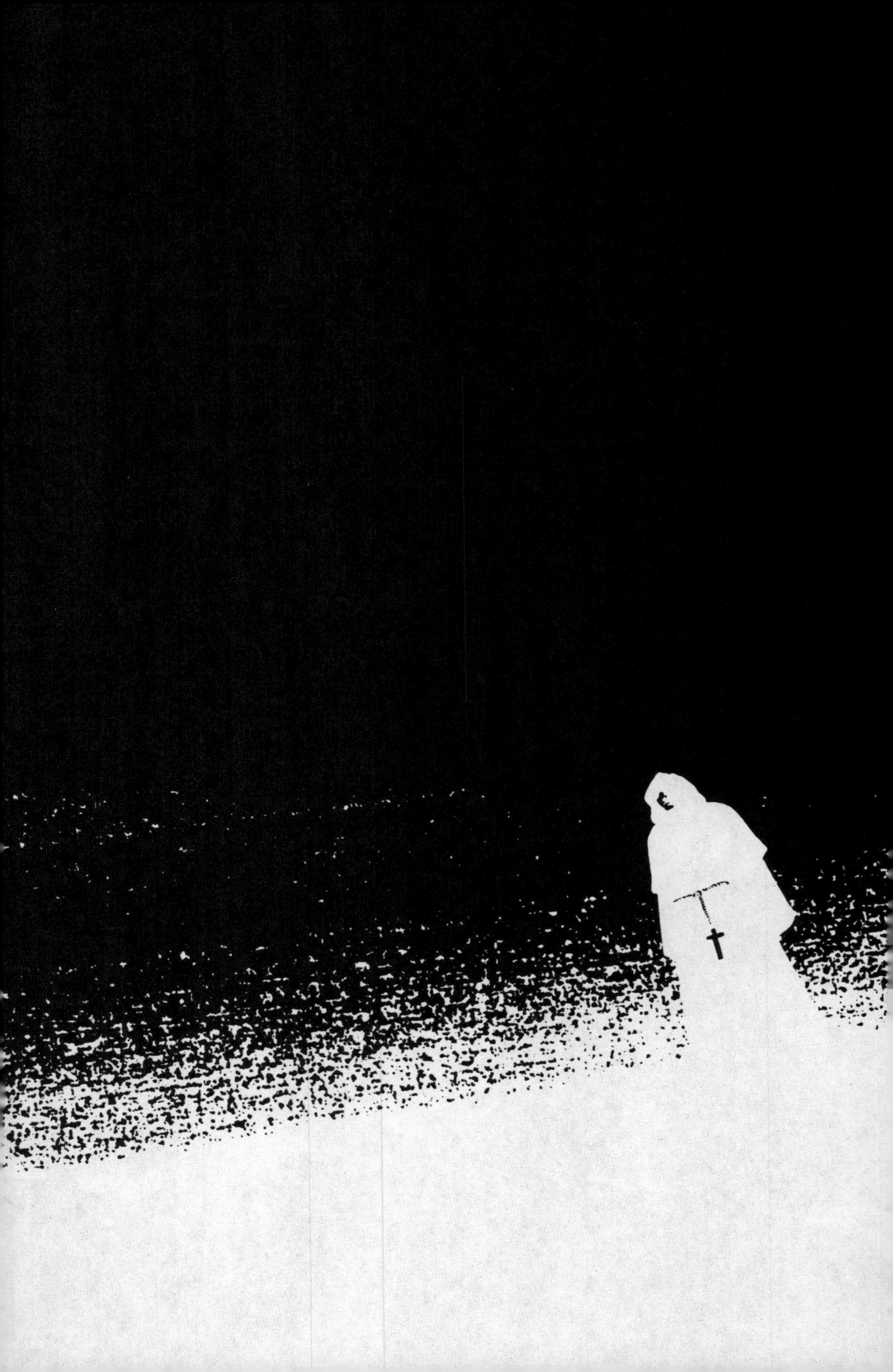

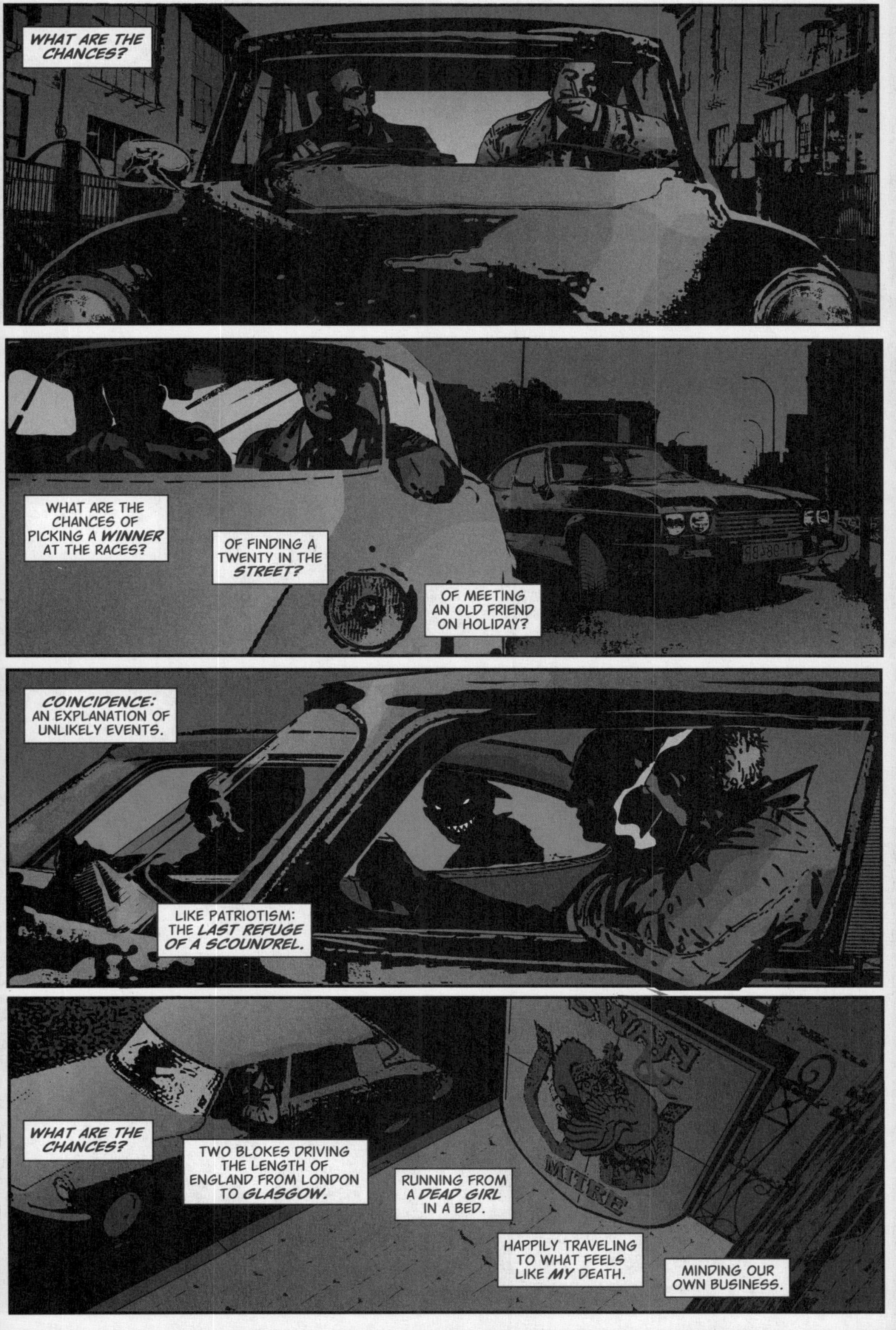
WHAT ARE THE CHANCES?
WHAT ARE THE CHANCES OF PICKING A WINNER AT THE RACES?
OF FINDING A TWENTY IN THE STREET?
OF MEETING AN OLD FRIEND ON HOLIDAY?
COINCIDENCE: AN EXPLANATION OF UNLIKELY EVENTS.
LIKE PATRIOTISM: THE LAST REFUGE OF A SCOUNDREL.
WHAT ARE THE CHANCES?
TWO BLOKES DRIVING THE LENGTH OF ENGLAND FROM LONDON TO GLASGOW.
RUNNING FROM A DEAD GIRL IN A BED.
HAPPILY TRAVELING TO WHAT FEELS LIKE MY DEATH.
MINDING OUR OWN BUSINESS.
MITRE

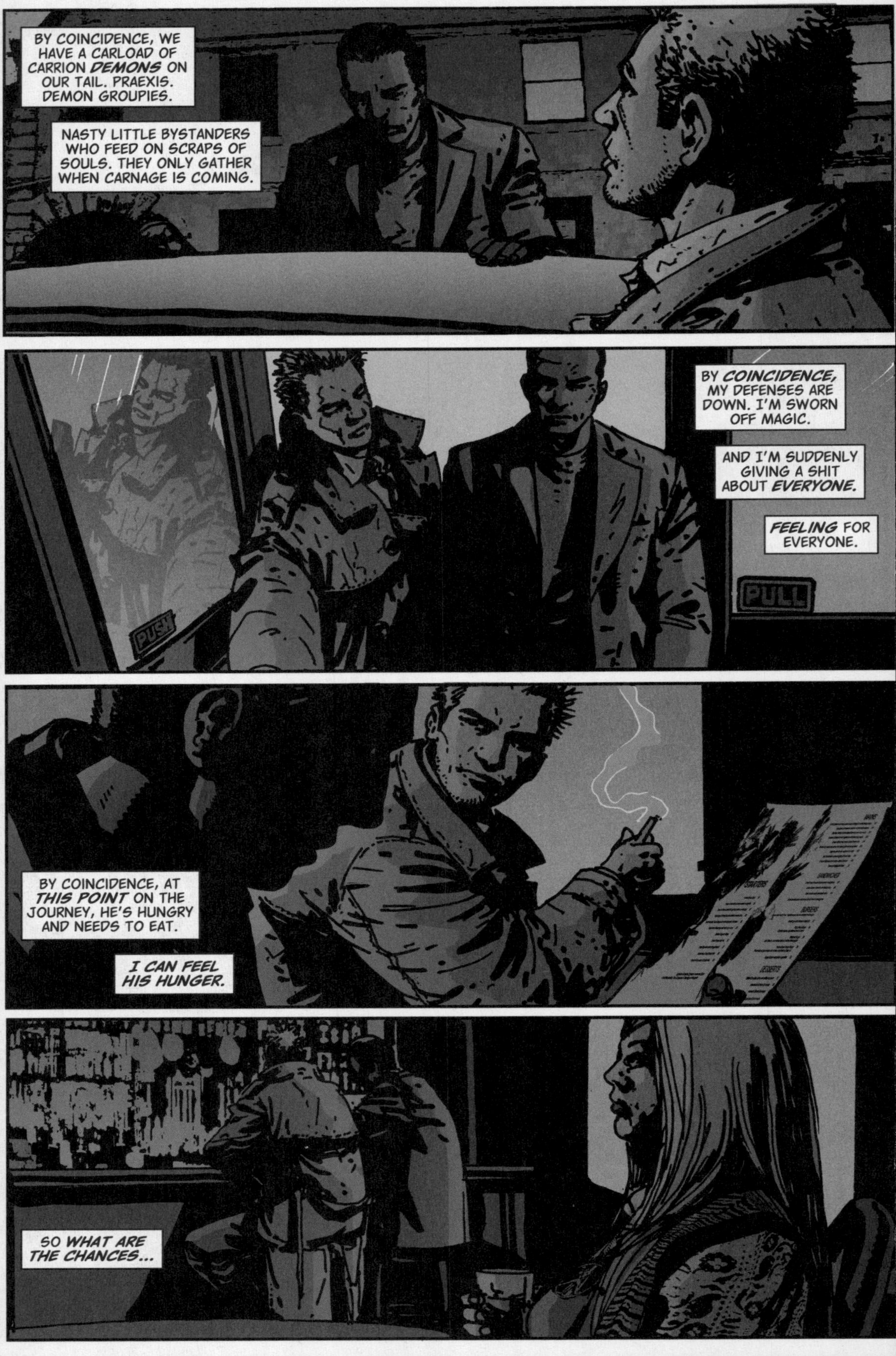
BY COINCIDENCE, WE HAVE A CARLOAD OF CARRION DEMONS ON OUR TAIL. PRAEXIS. DEMON GROUPIES.
NASTY LITTLE BYSTANDERS WHO FEED ON SCRAPS OF SOULS. THEY ONLY GATHER WHEN CARNAGE IS COMING.
BY COINCIDENCE, MY DEFENSES ARE DOWN. I'M SWORN OFF MAGIC.
AND I'M SUDDENLY GIVING A SHIT ABOUT EVERYONE.
FEELING FOR EVERYONE.
PUSH
PULL
BY COINCIDENCE, AT THIS POINT ON THE JOURNEY, HE'S HUNGRY AND NEEDS TO EAT.
I CAN FEEL HIS HUNGER.
SO WHAT ARE THE CHANCES...

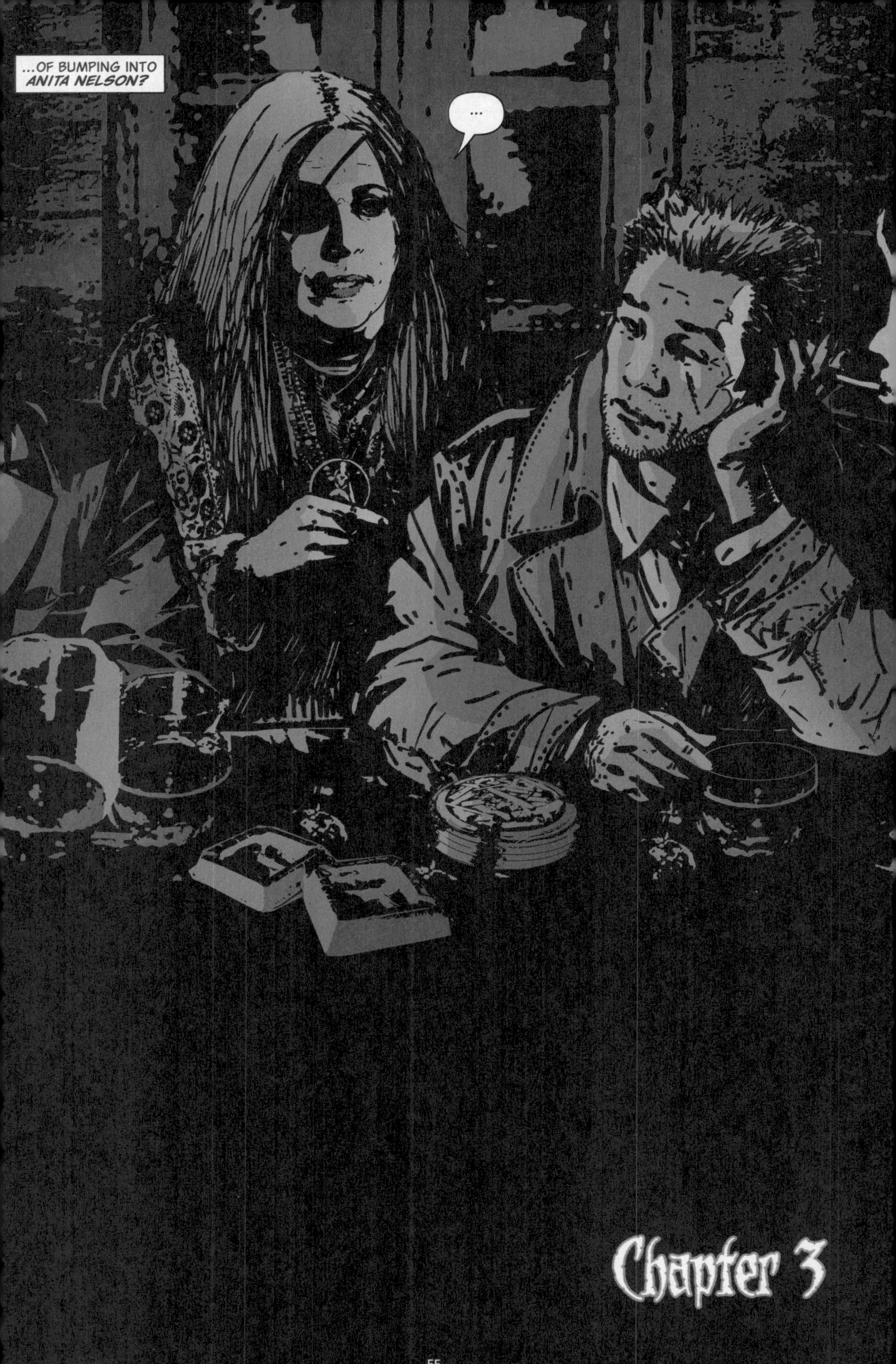
...OF BUMPING INTO *ANITA NELSON?*
...
Chapter 3

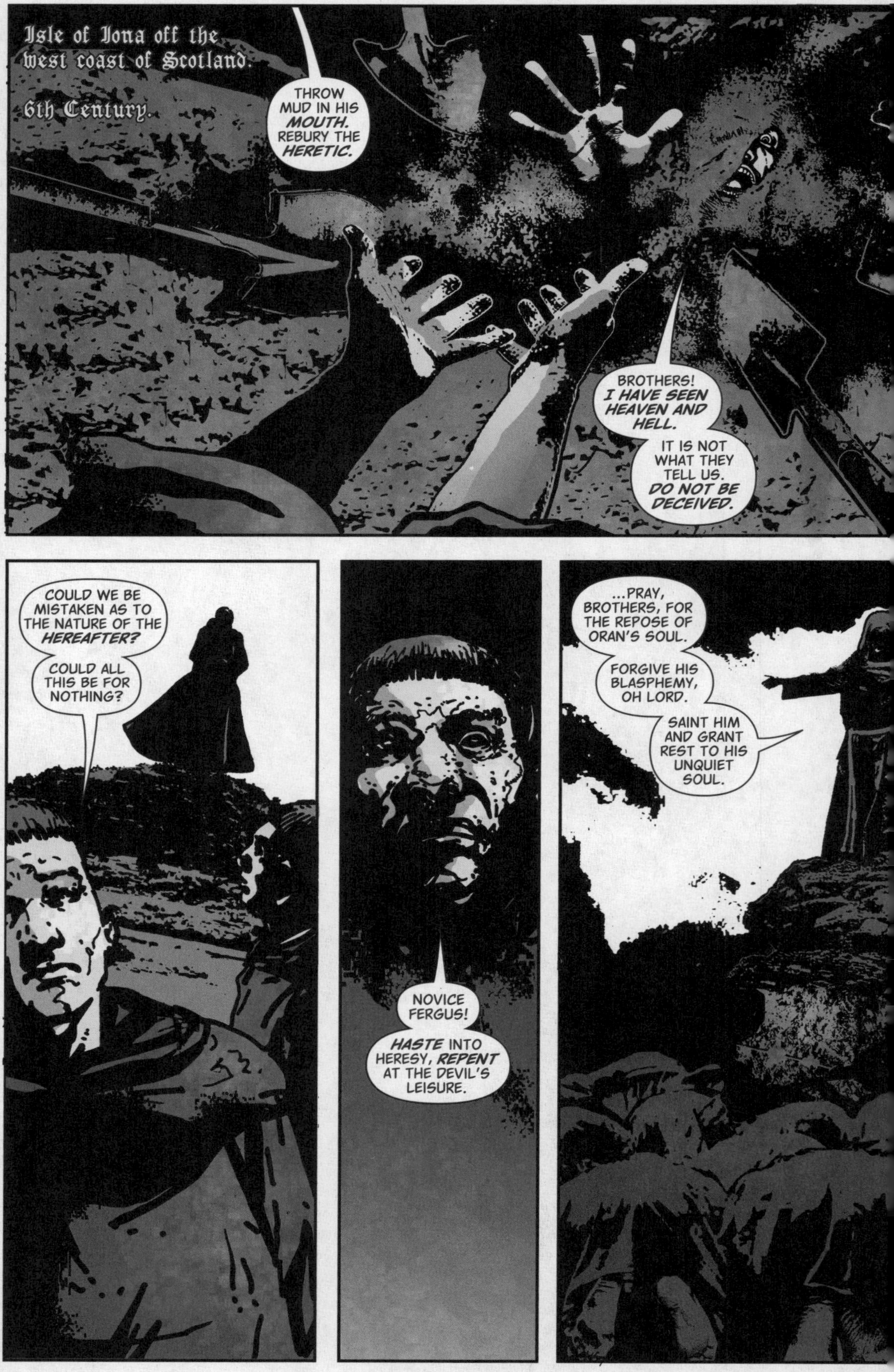

Isle of Iona off the west coast of Scotland.
6th Century.
THROW MUD IN HIS *MOUTH.* REBURY THE *HERETIC.*
BROTHERS! *I HAVE SEEN HEAVEN AND HELL.*
IT IS NOT WHAT THEY TELL US. *DO NOT BE DECEIVED.*
COULD WE BE MISTAKEN AS TO THE NATURE OF THE *HEREAFTER?*
COULD ALL THIS BE FOR NOTHING?
NOVICE FERGUS!
HASTE INTO HERESY, *REPENT* AT THE DEVIL'S LEISURE.
...PRAY, BROTHERS, FOR THE REPOSE OF ORAN'S SOUL.
FORGIVE HIS BLASPHEMY, OH LORD.
SAINT HIM AND GRANT REST TO HIS UNQUIET SOUL.

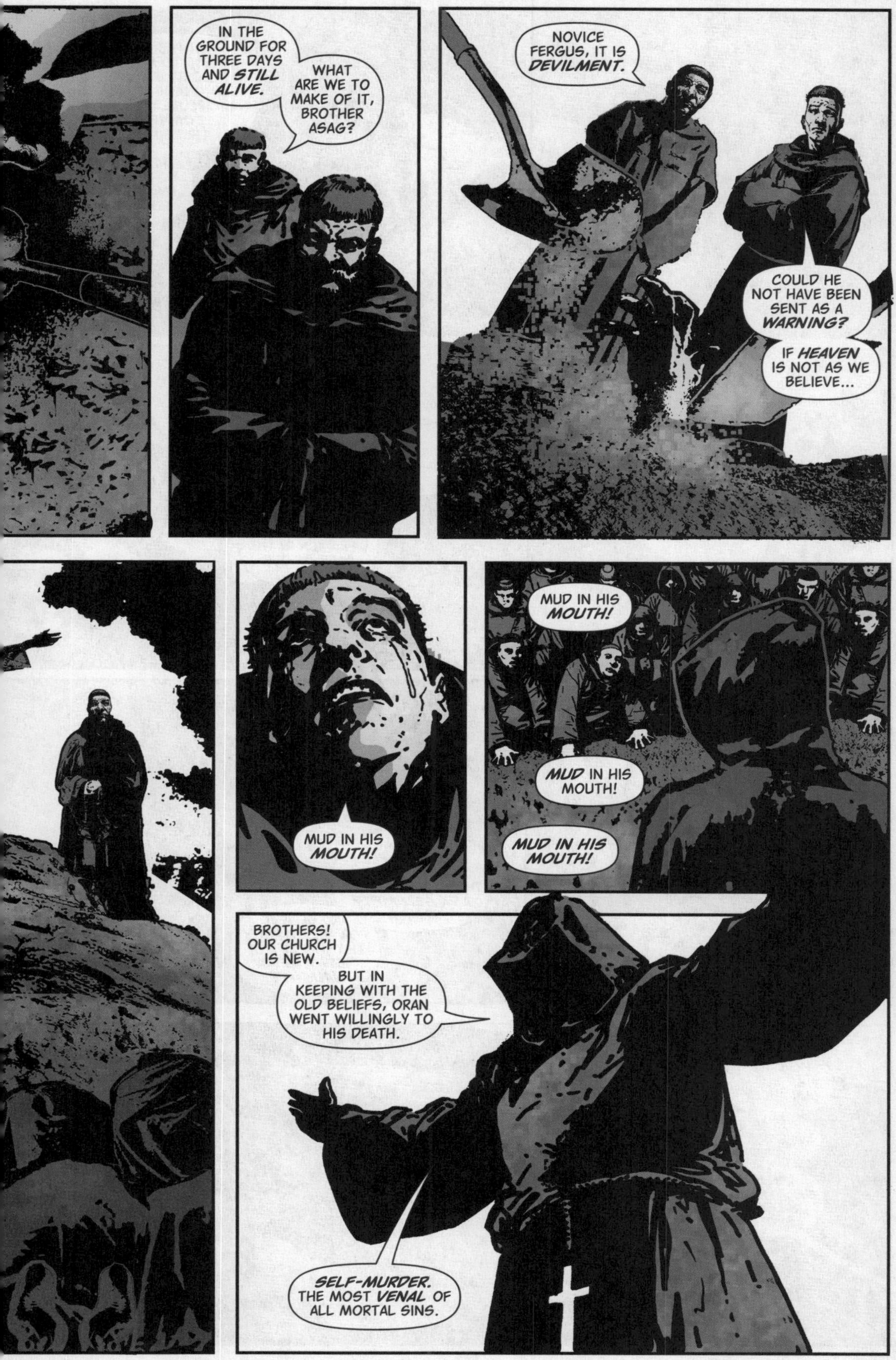
IN THE GROUND FOR THREE DAYS AND STILL ALIVE.
WHAT ARE WE TO MAKE OF IT, BROTHER ASAG?
NOVICE FERGUS, IT IS DEVILMENT.
COULD HE NOT HAVE BEEN SENT AS A WARNING?
IF HEAVEN IS NOT AS WE BELIEVE...
MUD IN HIS MOUTH!
MUD IN HIS MOUTH!
MUD IN HIS MOUTH!
MUD IN HIS MOUTH!
BROTHERS! OUR CHURCH IS NEW.
BUT IN KEEPING WITH THE OLD BELIEFS, ORAN WENT WILLINGLY TO HIS DEATH.
SELF-MURDER. THE MOST VENAL OF ALL MORTAL SINS.

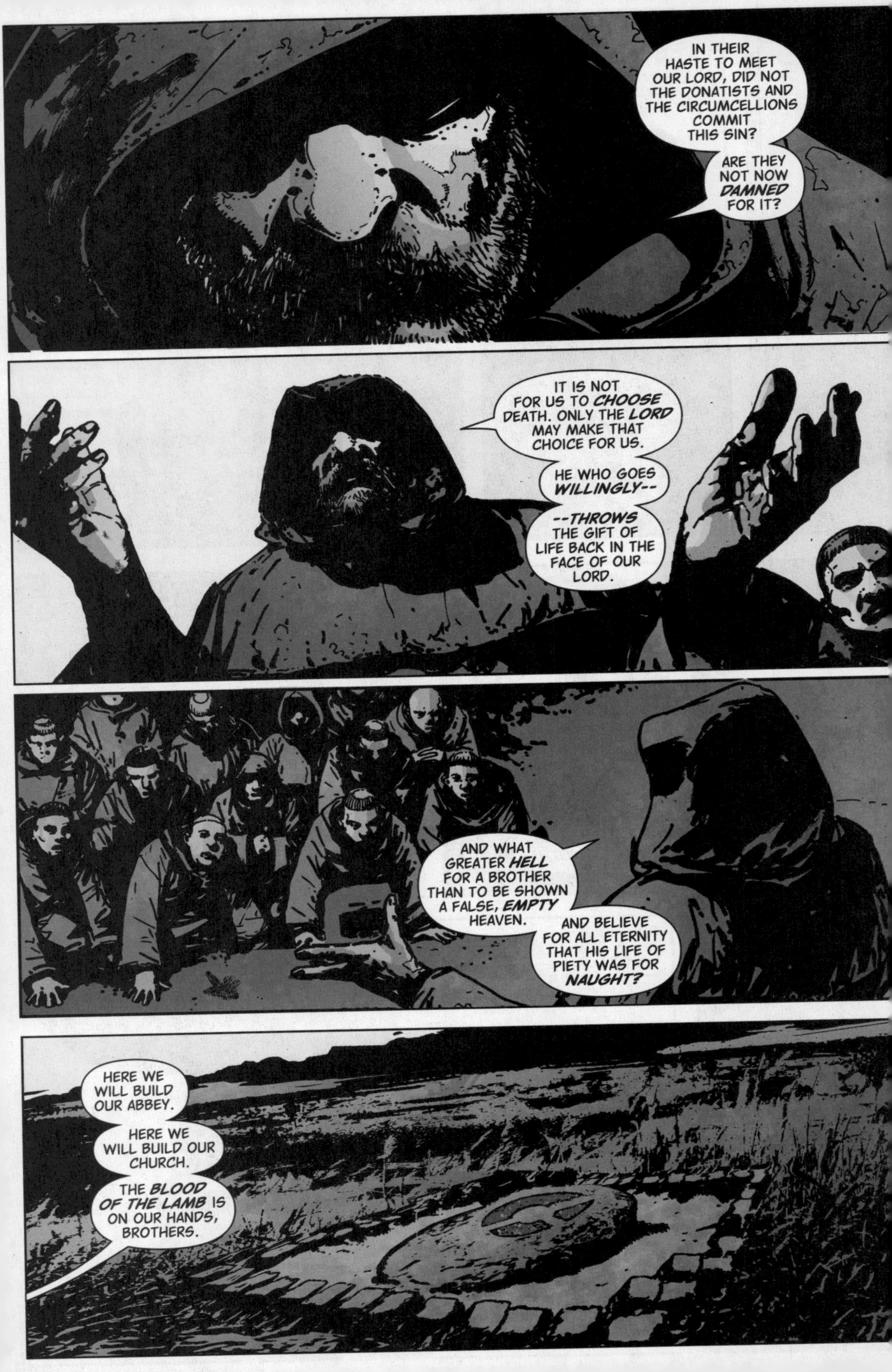
IN THEIR HASTE TO MEET OUR LORD, DID NOT THE DONATISTS AND THE CIRCUMCELLIONS COMMIT THIS SIN?
ARE THEY NOT NOW DAMNED FOR IT?
IT IS NOT FOR US TO CHOOSE DEATH. ONLY THE LORD MAY MAKE THAT CHOICE FOR US.
HE WHO GOES WILLINGLY--
--THROWS THE GIFT OF LIFE BACK IN THE FACE OF OUR LORD.
AND WHAT GREATER HELL FOR A BROTHER THAN TO BE SHOWN A FALSE, EMPTY HEAVEN.
AND BELIEVE FOR ALL ETERNITY THAT HIS LIFE OF PIETY WAS FOR NAUGHT?
HERE WE WILL BUILD OUR ABBEY.
HERE WE WILL BUILD OUR CHURCH.
THE BLOOD OF THE LAMB IS ON OUR HANDS, BROTHERS.

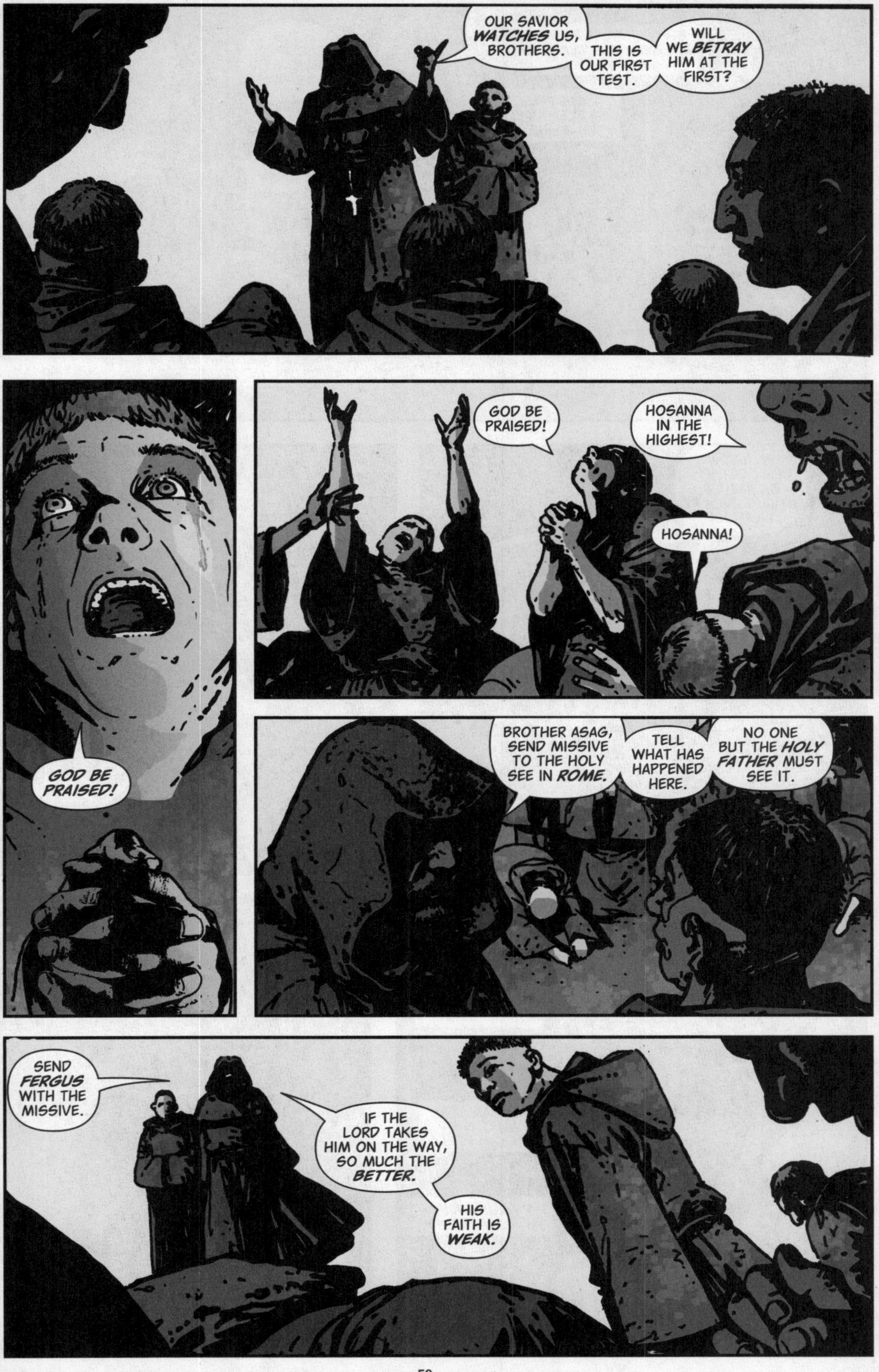
OUR SAVIOR WATCHES US, BROTHERS.
THIS IS OUR FIRST TEST.
WILL WE BETRAY HIM AT THE FIRST?
GOD BE PRAISED!
GOD BE PRAISED!
HOSANNA IN THE HIGHEST!
HOSANNA!
BROTHER ASAG, SEND MISSIVE TO THE HOLY SEE IN ROME.
TELL WHAT HAS HAPPENED HERE.
NO ONE BUT THE HOLY FATHER MUST SEE IT.
SEND FERGUS WITH THE MISSIVE.
IF THE LORD TAKES HIM ON THE WAY, SO MUCH THE BETTER.
HIS FAITH IS WEAK.

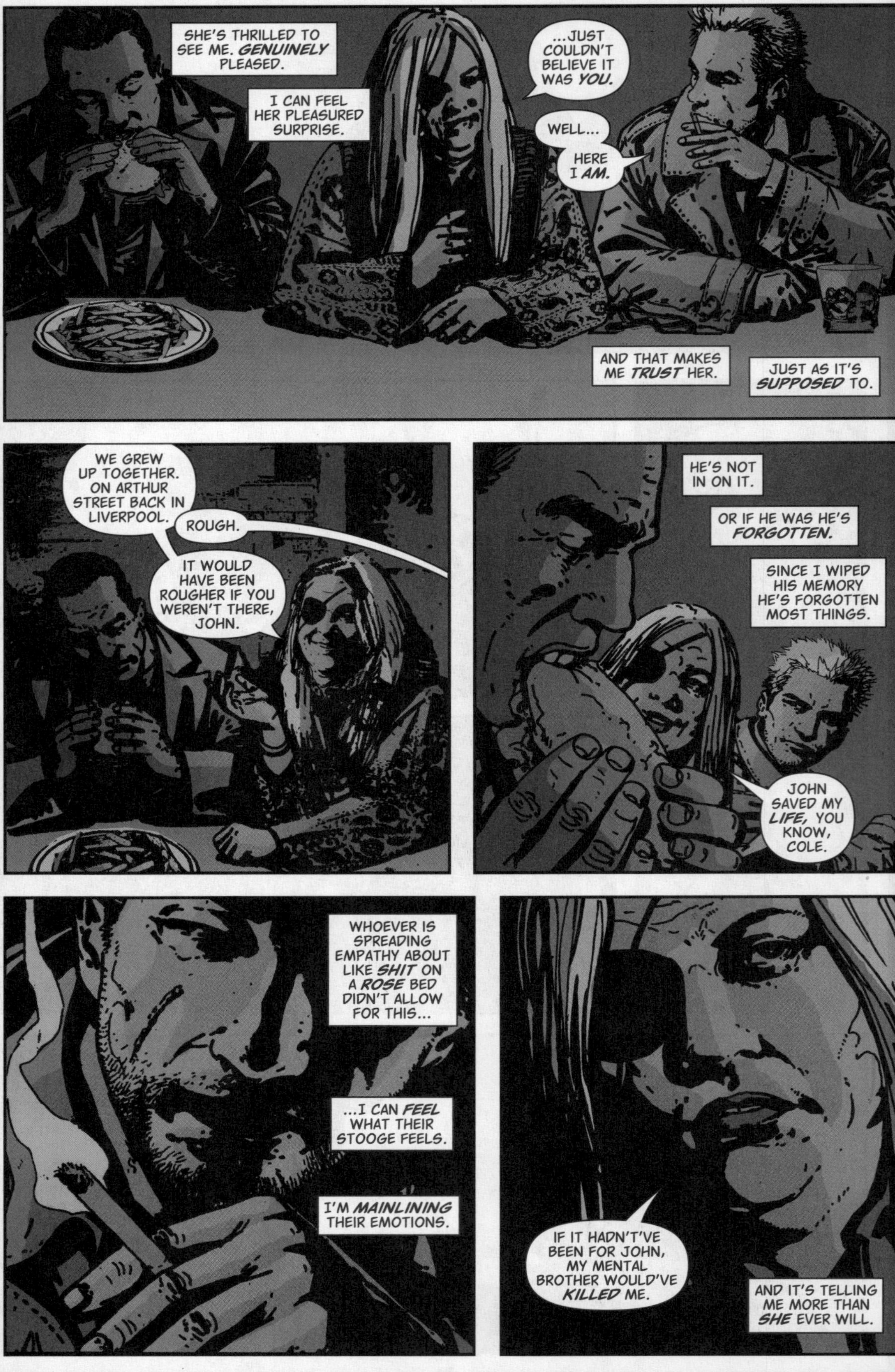

SHE'S THRILLED TO SEE ME. GENUINELY PLEASED.
I CAN FEEL HER PLEASURED SURPRISE.
...JUST COULDN'T BELIEVE IT WAS YOU.
WELL...
HERE I AM.
AND THAT MAKES ME TRUST HER.
JUST AS IT'S SUPPOSED TO.
WE GREW UP TOGETHER. ON ARTHUR STREET BACK IN LIVERPOOL.
ROUGH.
IT WOULD HAVE BEEN ROUGHER IF YOU WEREN'T THERE, JOHN.
HE'S NOT IN ON IT.
OR IF HE WAS HE'S FORGOTTEN.
SINCE I WIPED HIS MEMORY HE'S FORGOTTEN MOST THINGS.
JOHN SAVED MY LIFE, YOU KNOW, COLE.
WHOEVER IS SPREADING EMPATHY ABOUT LIKE SHIT ON A ROSE BED DIDN'T ALLOW FOR THIS...
...I CAN FEEL WHAT THEIR STOOGE FEELS.
I'M MAINLINING THEIR EMOTIONS.
IF IT HADN'T'VE BEEN FOR JOHN, MY MENTAL BROTHER WOULD'VE KILLED ME.
AND IT'S TELLING ME MORE THAN SHE EVER WILL.

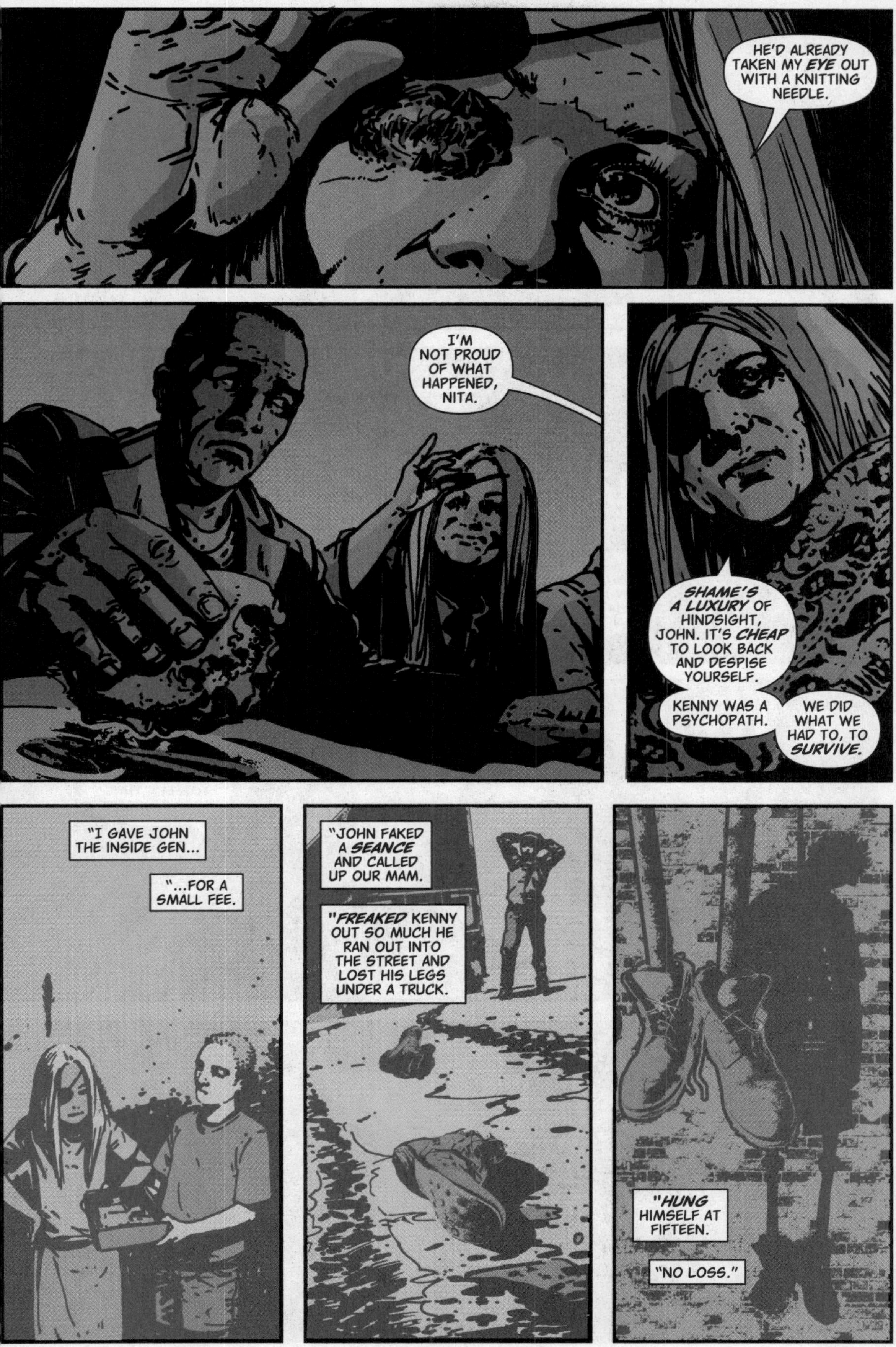
HE'D ALREADY TAKEN MY *EYE* OUT WITH A KNITTING NEEDLE.
I'M NOT PROUD OF WHAT HAPPENED, NITA.
SHAME'S A LUXURY OF HINDSIGHT, JOHN. IT'S *CHEAP* TO LOOK BACK AND DESPISE YOURSELF.
KENNY WAS A PSYCHOPATH.
WE DID WHAT WE HAD TO, TO *SURVIVE*.
"I GAVE JOHN THE INSIDE GEN...
"...FOR A SMALL FEE.
"JOHN FAKED A *SEANCE* AND CALLED UP OUR MAM.
"*FREAKED* KENNY OUT SO MUCH HE RAN OUT INTO THE STREET AND LOST HIS LEGS UNDER A TRUCK.
"*HUNG* HIMSELF AT FIFTEEN.
"NO LOSS."

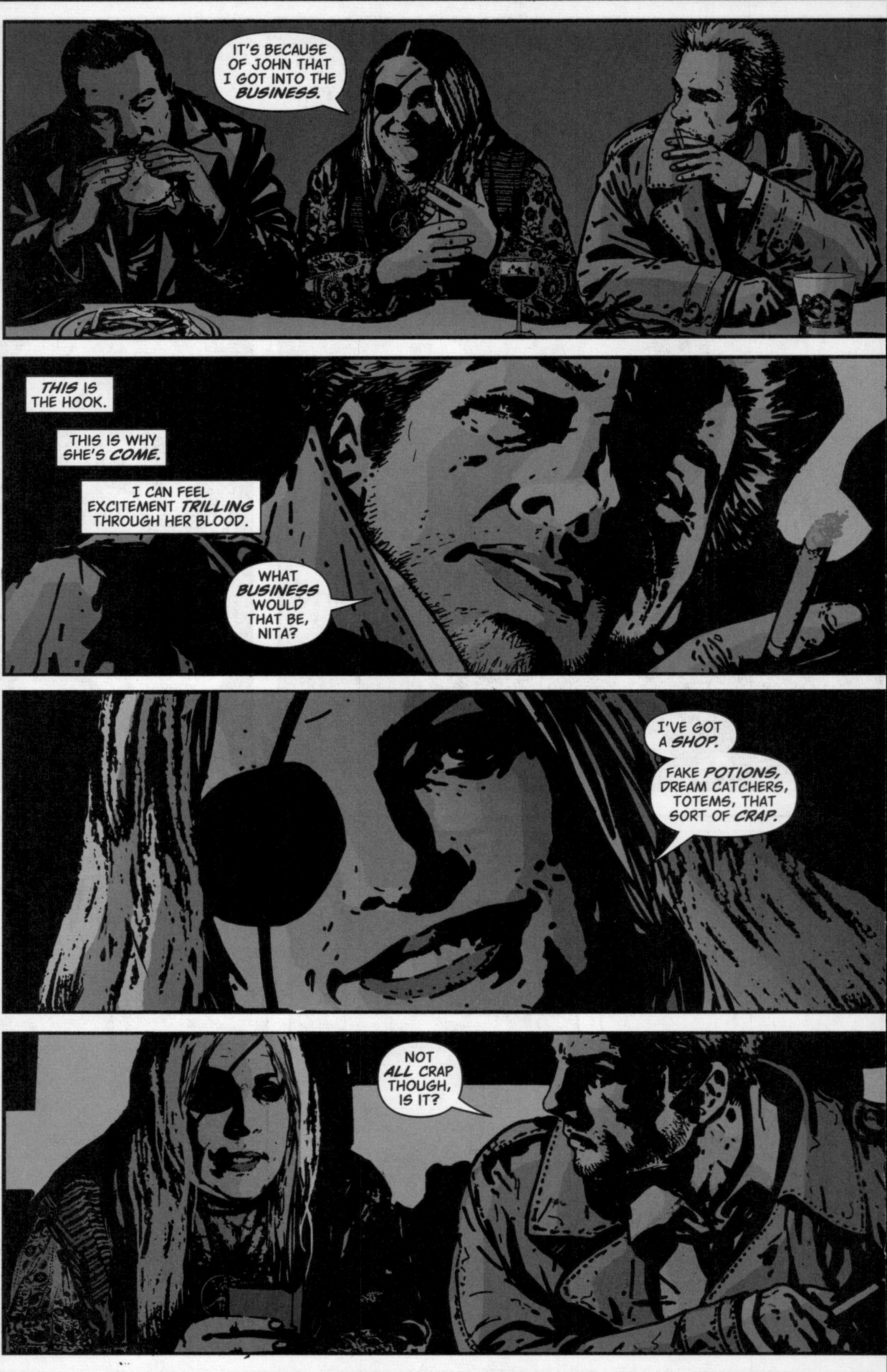
IT'S BECAUSE OF JOHN THAT I GOT INTO THE BUSINESS.
THIS IS THE HOOK.
THIS IS WHY SHE'S COME.
I CAN FEEL EXCITEMENT TRILLING THROUGH HER BLOOD.
WHAT BUSINESS WOULD THAT BE, NITA?
I'VE GOT A SHOP.
FAKE POTIONS, DREAM CATCHERS, TOTEMS, THAT SORT OF CRAP.
NOT ALL CRAP THOUGH, IS IT?

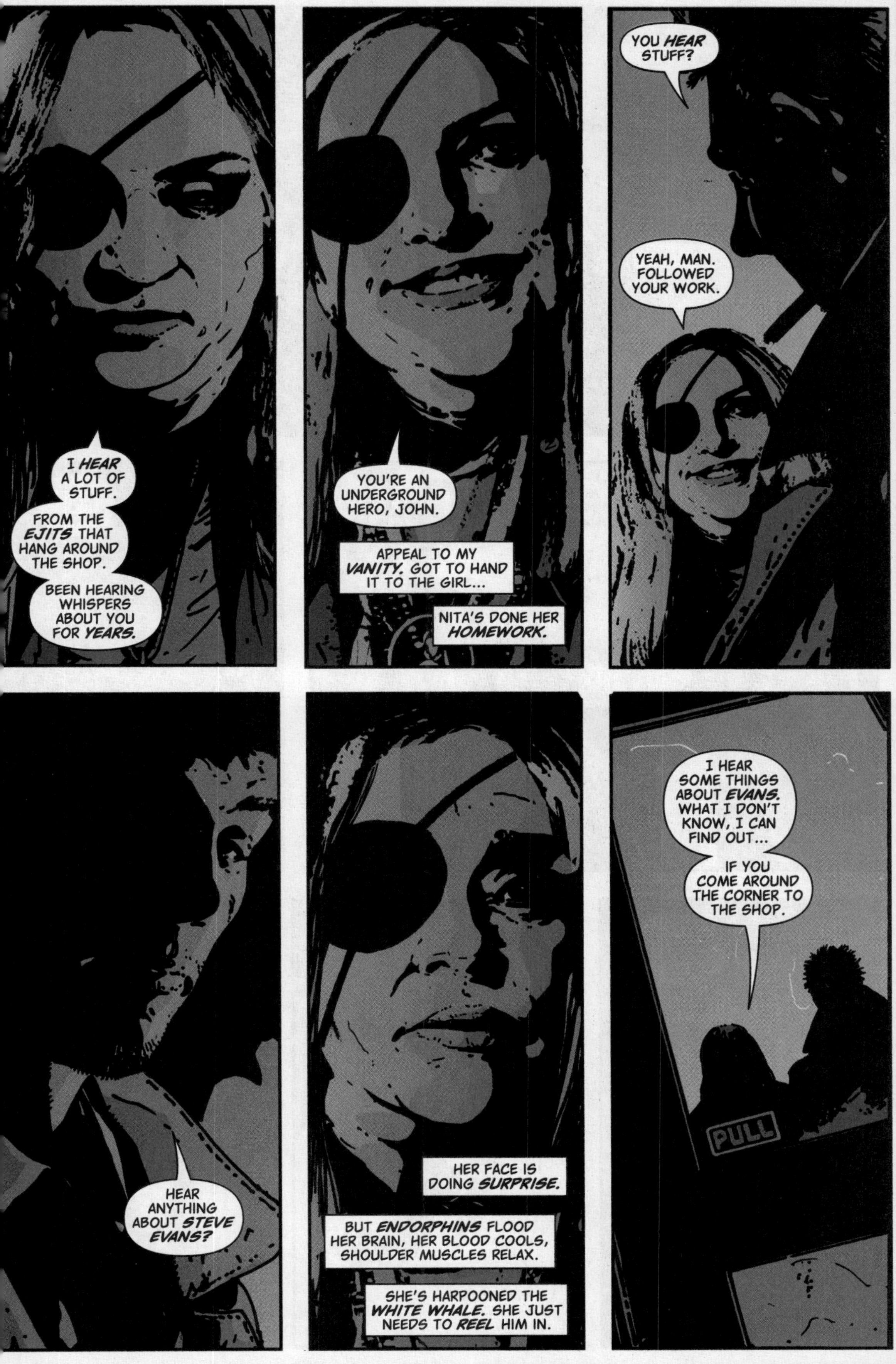
I HEAR A LOT OF STUFF.
FROM THE EJITS THAT HANG AROUND THE SHOP.
BEEN HEARING WHISPERS ABOUT YOU FOR YEARS.
YOU'RE AN UNDERGROUND HERO, JOHN.
APPEAL TO MY VANITY. GOT TO HAND IT TO THE GIRL...
NITA'S DONE HER HOMEWORK.
YOU HEAR STUFF?
YEAH, MAN. FOLLOWED YOUR WORK.
HEAR ANYTHING ABOUT STEVE EVANS?
HER FACE IS DOING SURPRISE.
BUT ENDORPHINS FLOOD HER BRAIN, HER BLOOD COOLS, SHOULDER MUSCLES RELAX.
SHE'S HARPOONED THE WHITE WHALE. SHE JUST NEEDS TO REEL HIM IN.
I HEAR SOME THINGS ABOUT EVANS. WHAT I DON'T KNOW, I CAN FIND OUT...
IF YOU COME AROUND THE CORNER TO THE SHOP.
PULL

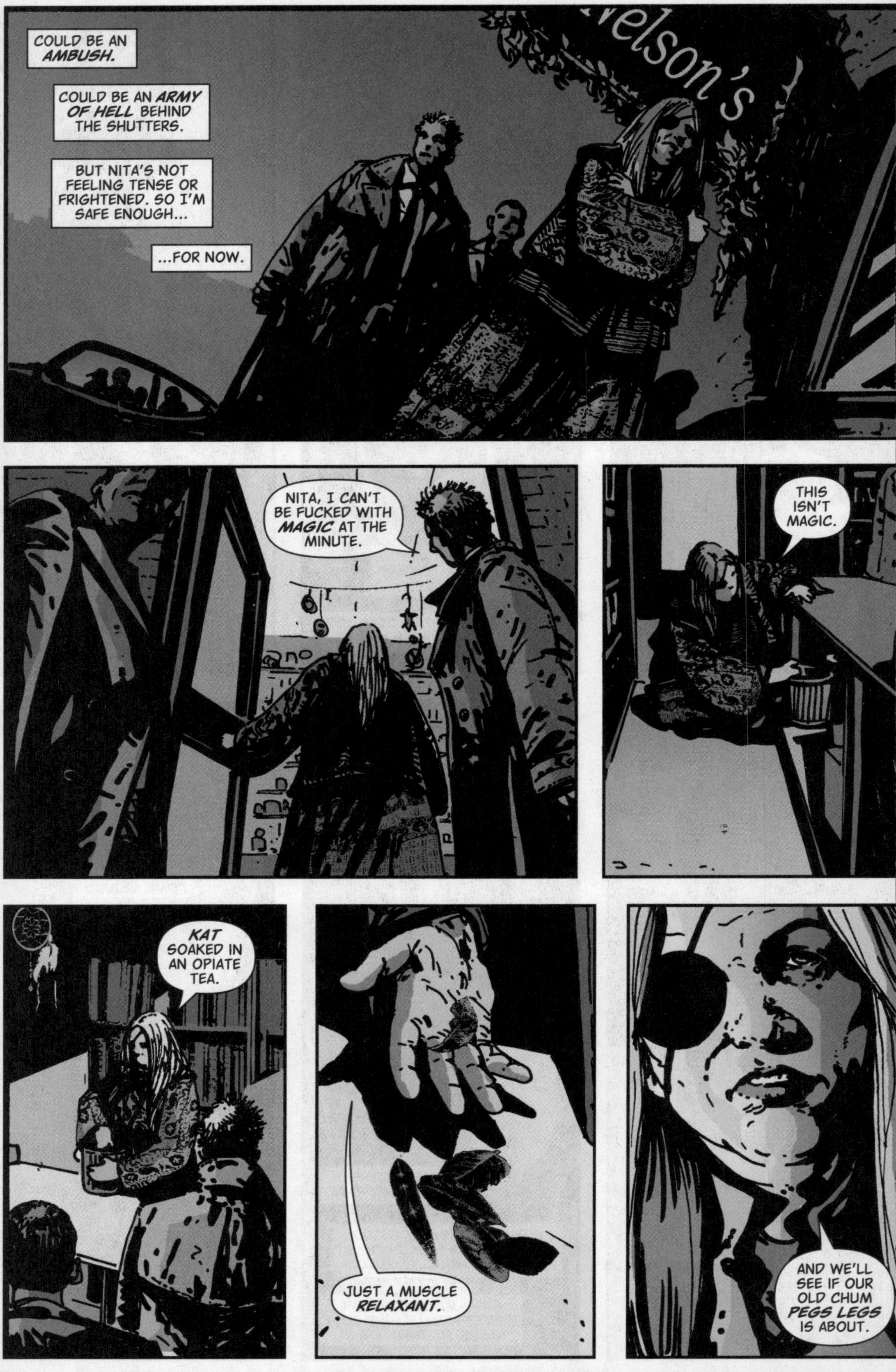

velson's
COULD BE AN AMBUSH.
COULD BE AN ARMY OF HELL BEHIND THE SHUTTERS.
BUT NITA'S NOT FEELING TENSE OR FRIGHTENED. SO I'M SAFE ENOUGH...
...FOR NOW.
NITA, I CAN'T BE FUCKED WITH MAGIC AT THE MINUTE.
THIS ISN'T MAGIC.
KAT SOAKED IN AN OPIATE TEA.
JUST A MUSCLE RELAXANT.
AND WE'LL SEE IF OUR OLD CHUM PEGS LEGS IS ABOUT.

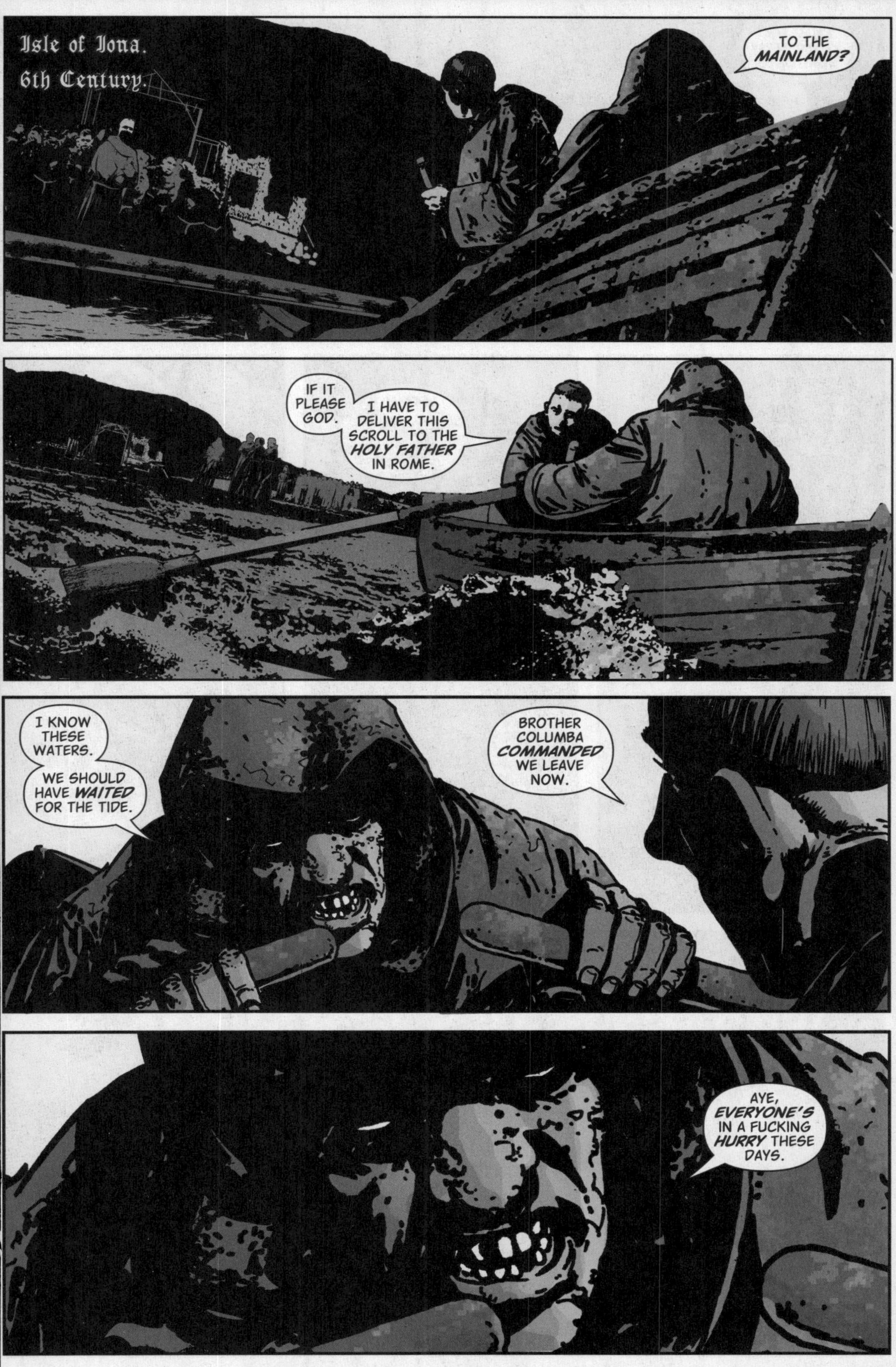
Isle of Iona.
6th Century.
TO THE MAINLAND?
IF IT PLEASE GOD.
I HAVE TO DELIVER THIS SCROLL TO THE HOLY FATHER IN ROME.
I KNOW THESE WATERS.
WE SHOULD HAVE WAITED FOR THE TIDE.
BROTHER COLUMBA COMMANDED WE LEAVE NOW.
AYE, EVERYONE'S IN A FUCKING HURRY THESE DAYS.

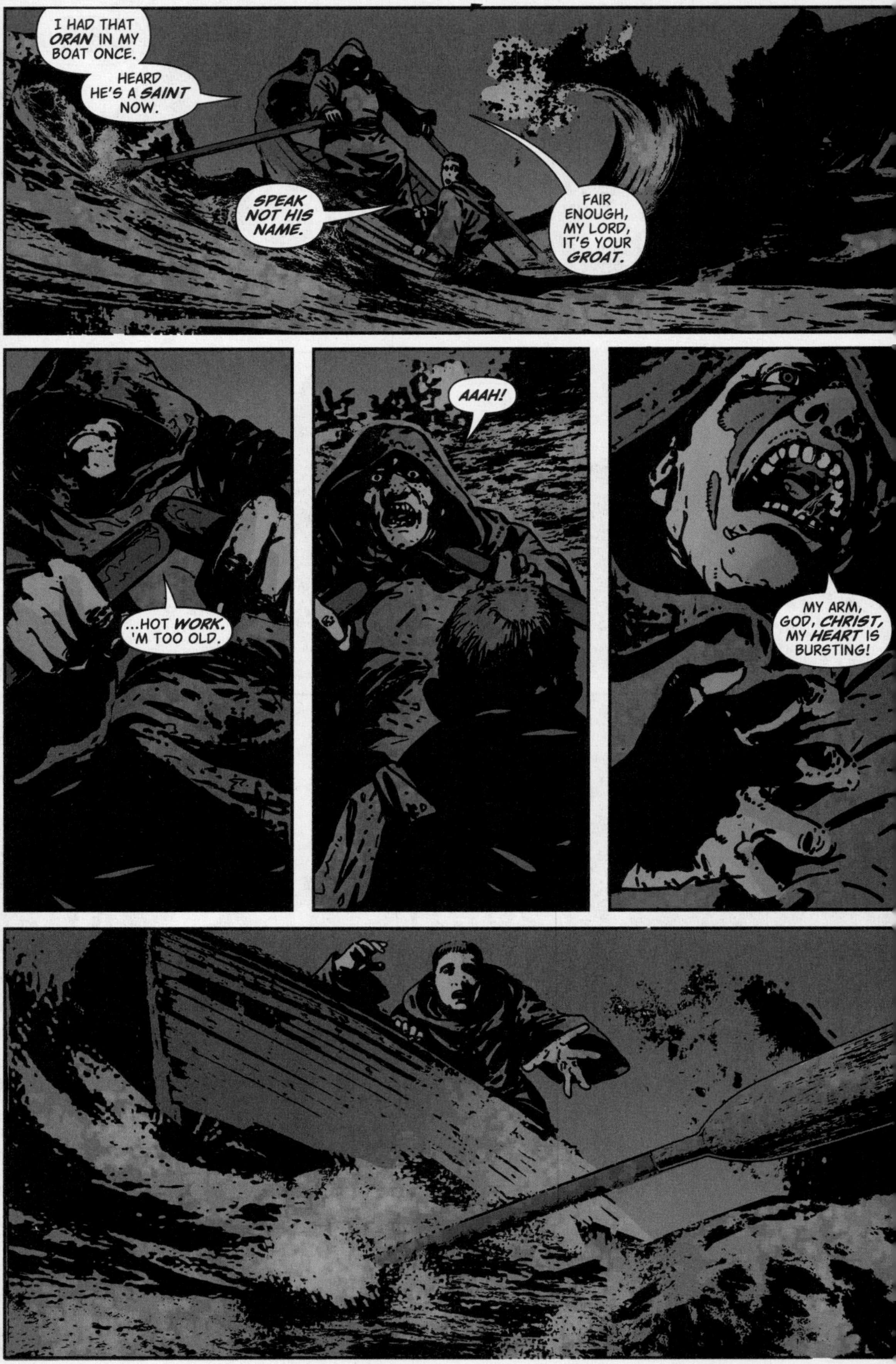
I HAD THAT ORAN IN MY BOAT ONCE.
HEARD HE'S A SAINT NOW.
SPEAK NOT HIS NAME.
FAIR ENOUGH, MY LORD, IT'S YOUR GROAT.
...HOT WORK. 'M TOO OLD.
AAAH!
MY ARM, GOD, CHRIST, MY HEART IS BURSTING!

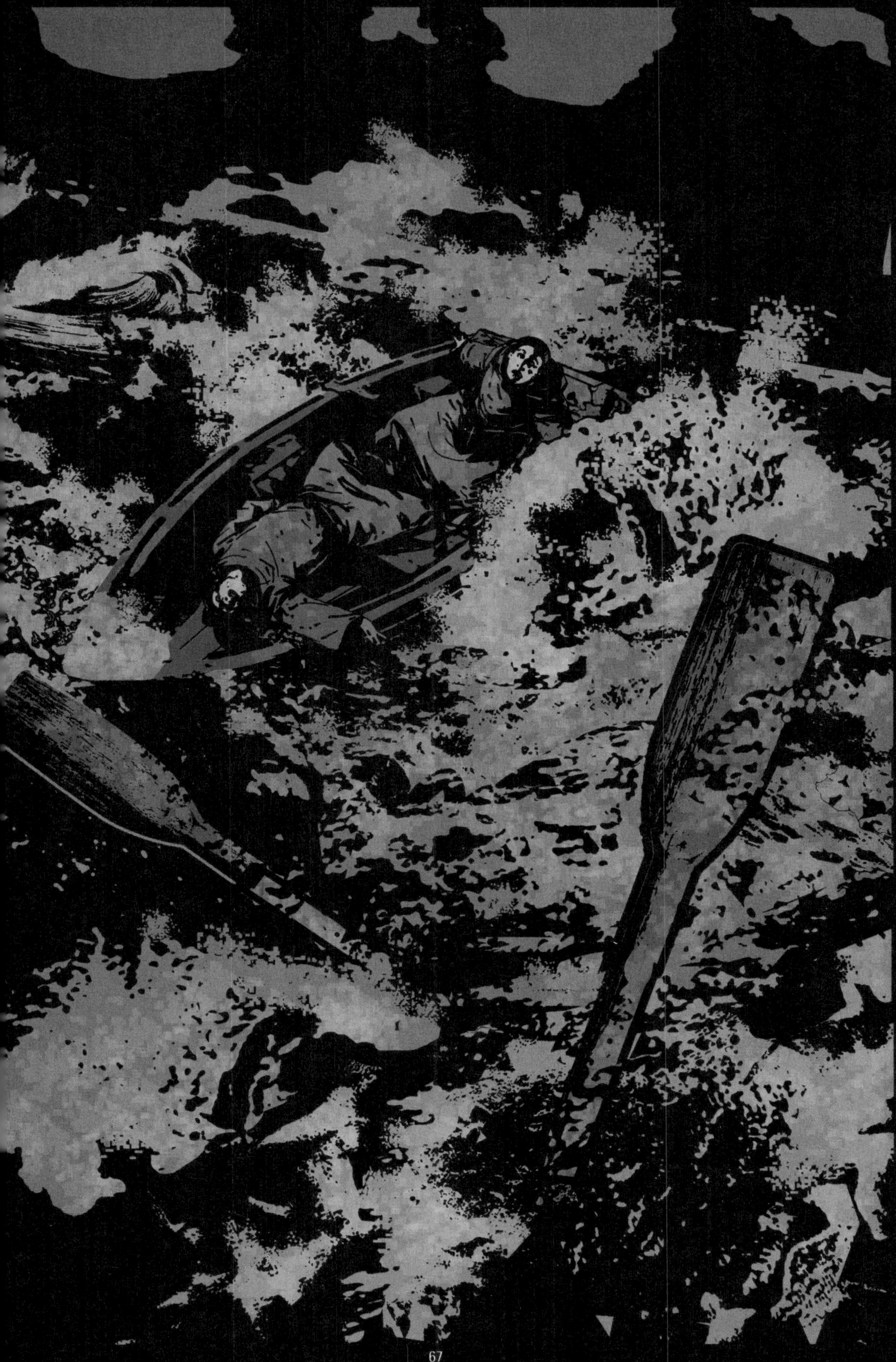

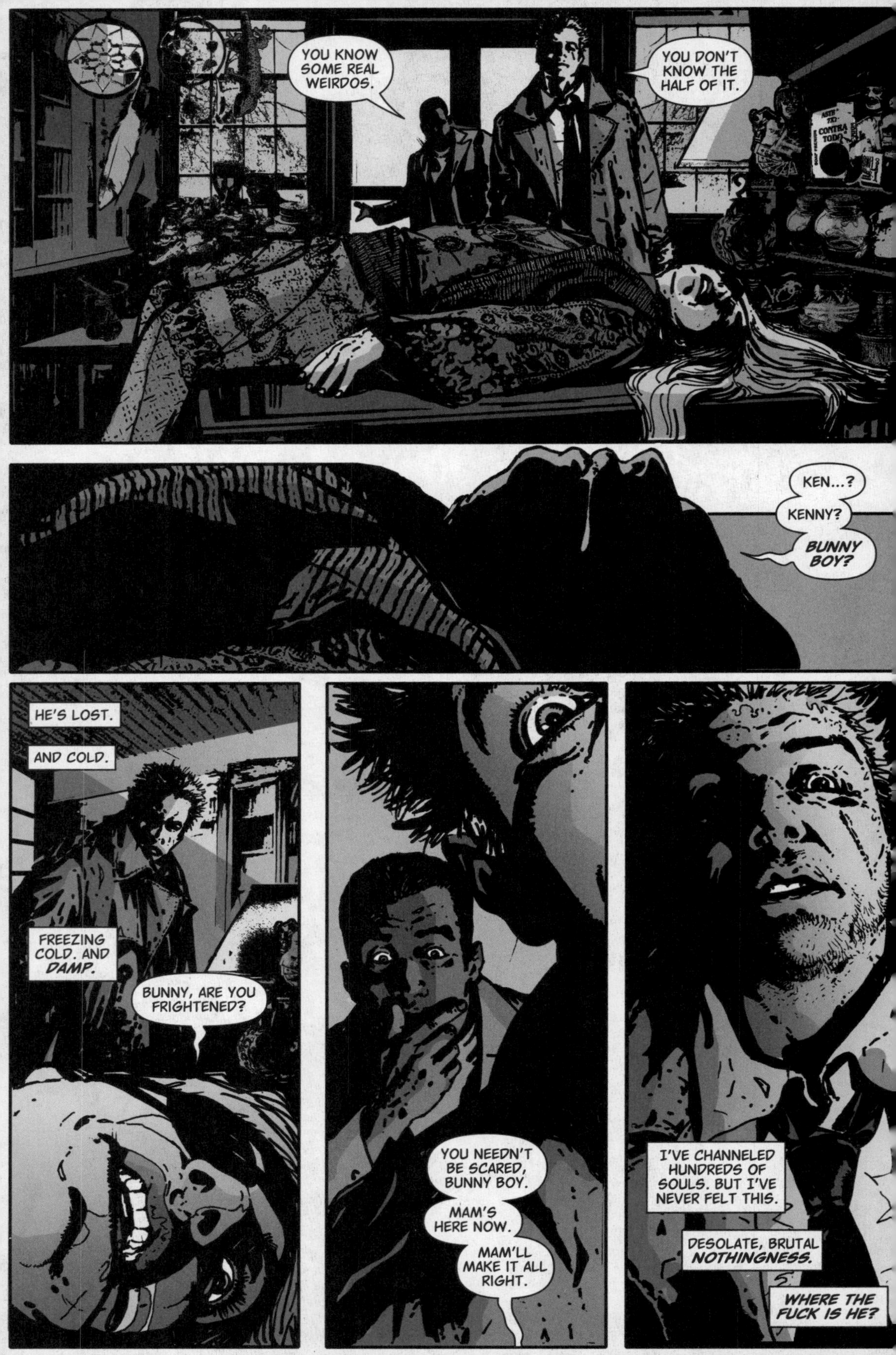
YOU KNOW SOME REAL WEIRDOS.
YOU DON'T KNOW THE HALF OF IT.
KEN...?
KENNY?
BUNNY BOY?
HE'S LOST.
AND COLD.
FREEZING COLD. AND DAMP.
BUNNY, ARE YOU FRIGHTENED?
YOU NEEDN'T BE SCARED, BUNNY BOY.
MAM'S HERE NOW.
MAM'LL MAKE IT ALL RIGHT.
I'VE CHANNELED HUNDREDS OF SOULS. BUT I'VE NEVER FELT THIS.
DESOLATE, BRUTAL NOTHINGNESS.
WHERE THE FUCK IS HE?

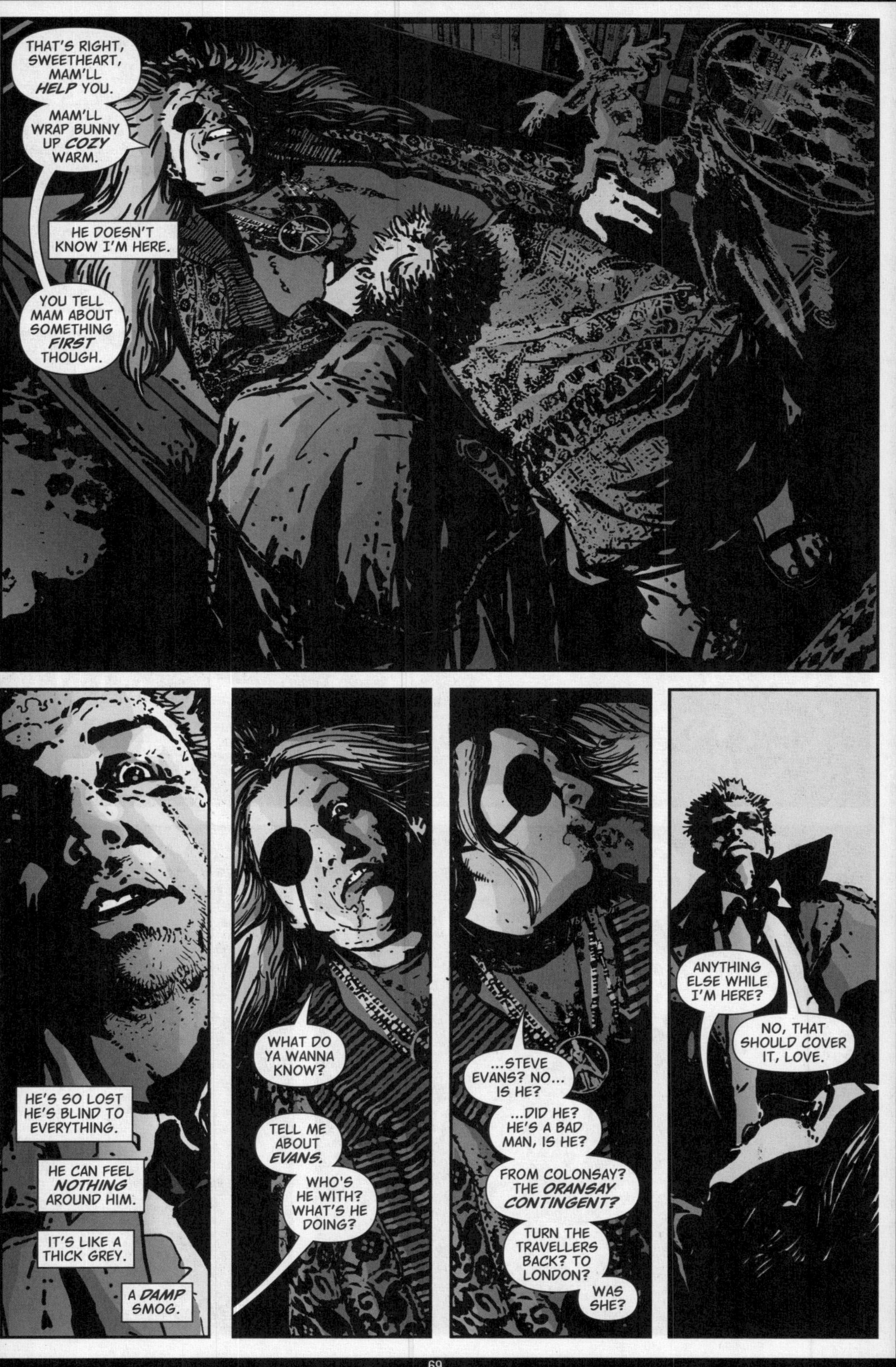
THAT'S RIGHT, SWEETHEART, MAM'LL HELP YOU.
MAM'LL WRAP BUNNY UP COZY WARM.
HE DOESN'T KNOW I'M HERE.
YOU TELL MAM ABOUT SOMETHING FIRST THOUGH.
HE'S SO LOST HE'S BLIND TO EVERYTHING.
HE CAN FEEL NOTHING AROUND HIM.
IT'S LIKE A THICK GREY.
A DAMP SMOG.
WHAT DO YA WANNA KNOW?
TELL ME ABOUT EVANS.
WHO'S HE WITH? WHAT'S HE DOING?
...STEVE EVANS? NO... IS HE?
...DID HE? HE'S A BAD MAN, IS HE?
FROM COLONSAY? THE ORANSAY CONTINGENT?
TURN THE TRAVELLERS BACK? TO LONDON?
WAS SHE?
ANYTHING ELSE WHILE I'M HERE?
NO, THAT SHOULD COVER IT, LOVE.

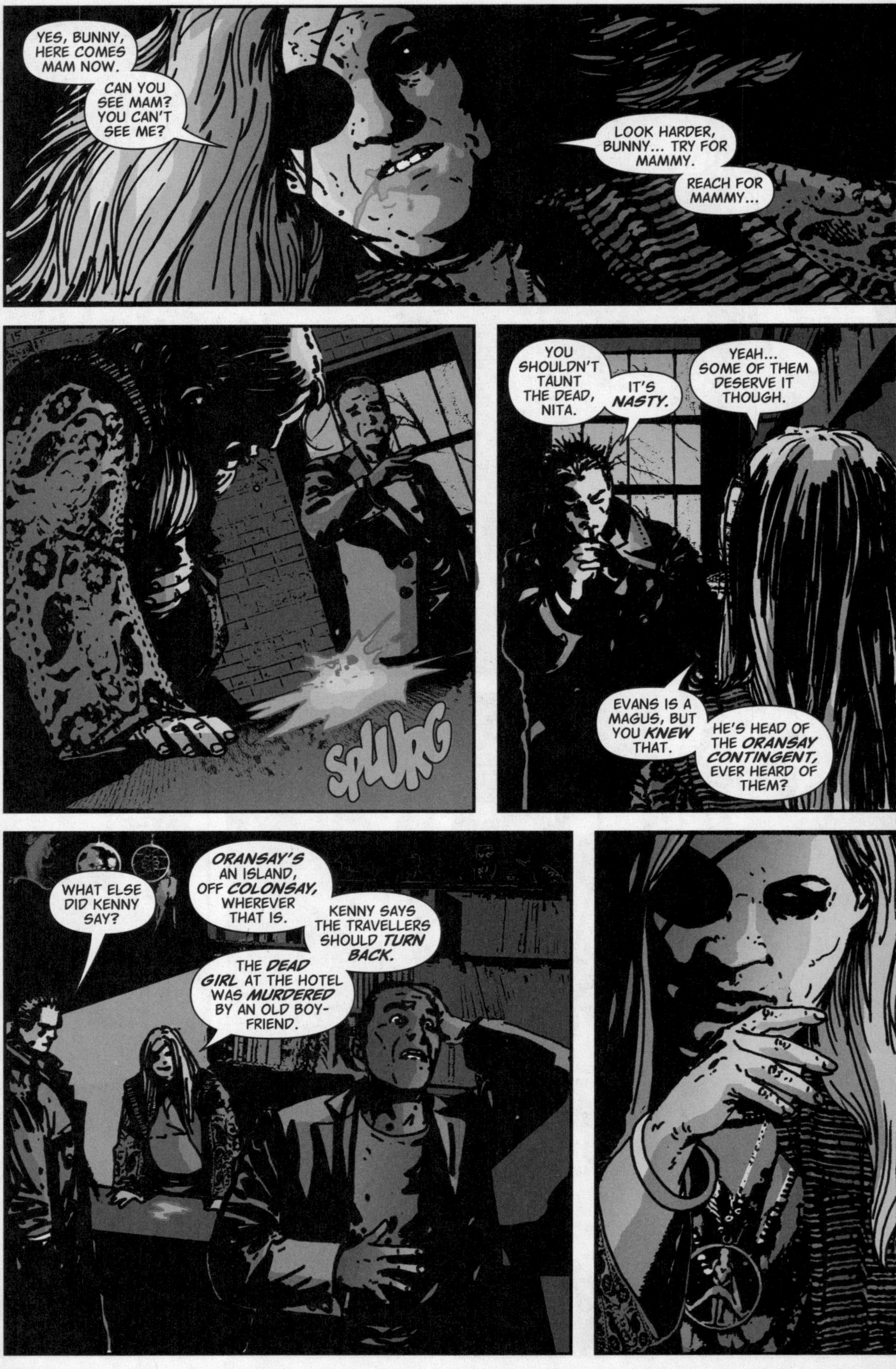
YES, BUNNY, HERE COMES MAM NOW.
CAN YOU SEE MAM? YOU CAN'T SEE ME?
LOOK HARDER, BUNNY... TRY FOR MAMMY.
REACH FOR MAMMY...
SPLURG
YOU SHOULDN'T TAUNT THE DEAD, NITA.
IT'S NASTY.
YEAH... SOME OF THEM DESERVE IT THOUGH.
EVANS IS A MAGUS, BUT YOU KNEW THAT.
HE'S HEAD OF THE ORANSAY CONTINGENT, EVER HEARD OF THEM?
WHAT ELSE DID KENNY SAY?
ORANSAY'S AN ISLAND, OFF COLONSAY, WHEREVER THAT IS.
KENNY SAYS THE TRAVELLERS SHOULD TURN BACK.
THE DEAD GIRL AT THE HOTEL WAS MURDERED BY AN OLD BOY-FRIEND.

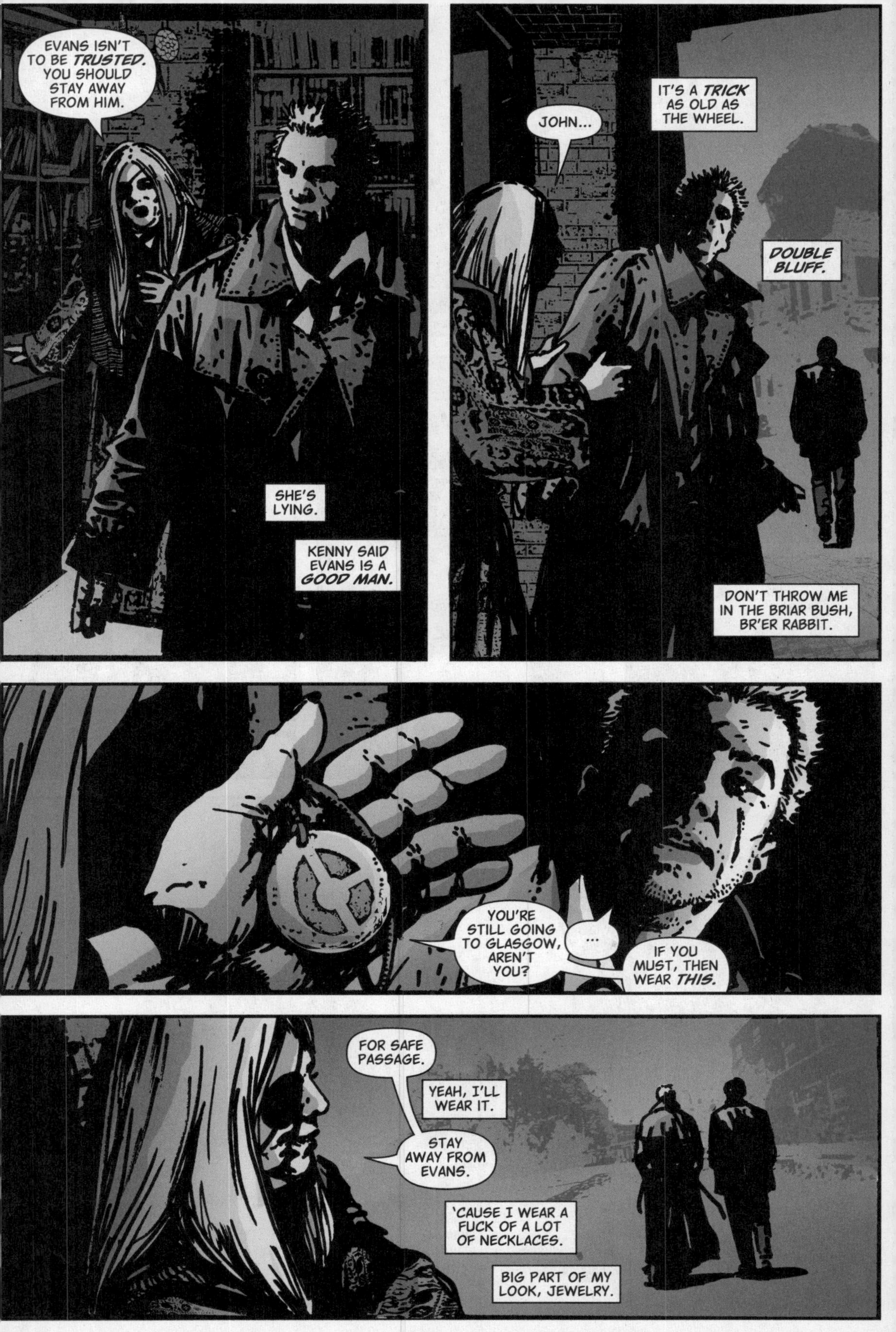

EVANS ISN'T TO BE TRUSTED. YOU SHOULD STAY AWAY FROM HIM.
SHE'S LYING.
KENNY SAID EVANS IS A GOOD MAN.
JOHN...
IT'S A TRICK AS OLD AS THE WHEEL.
DOUBLE BLUFF.
DON'T THROW ME IN THE BRIAR BUSH, BR'ER RABBIT.
YOU'RE STILL GOING TO GLASGOW, AREN'T YOU?
...
IF YOU MUST, THEN WEAR THIS.
FOR SAFE PASSAGE.
YEAH, I'LL WEAR IT.
STAY AWAY FROM EVANS.
'CAUSE I WEAR A FUCK OF A LOT OF NECKLACES.
BIG PART OF MY LOOK, JEWELRY.

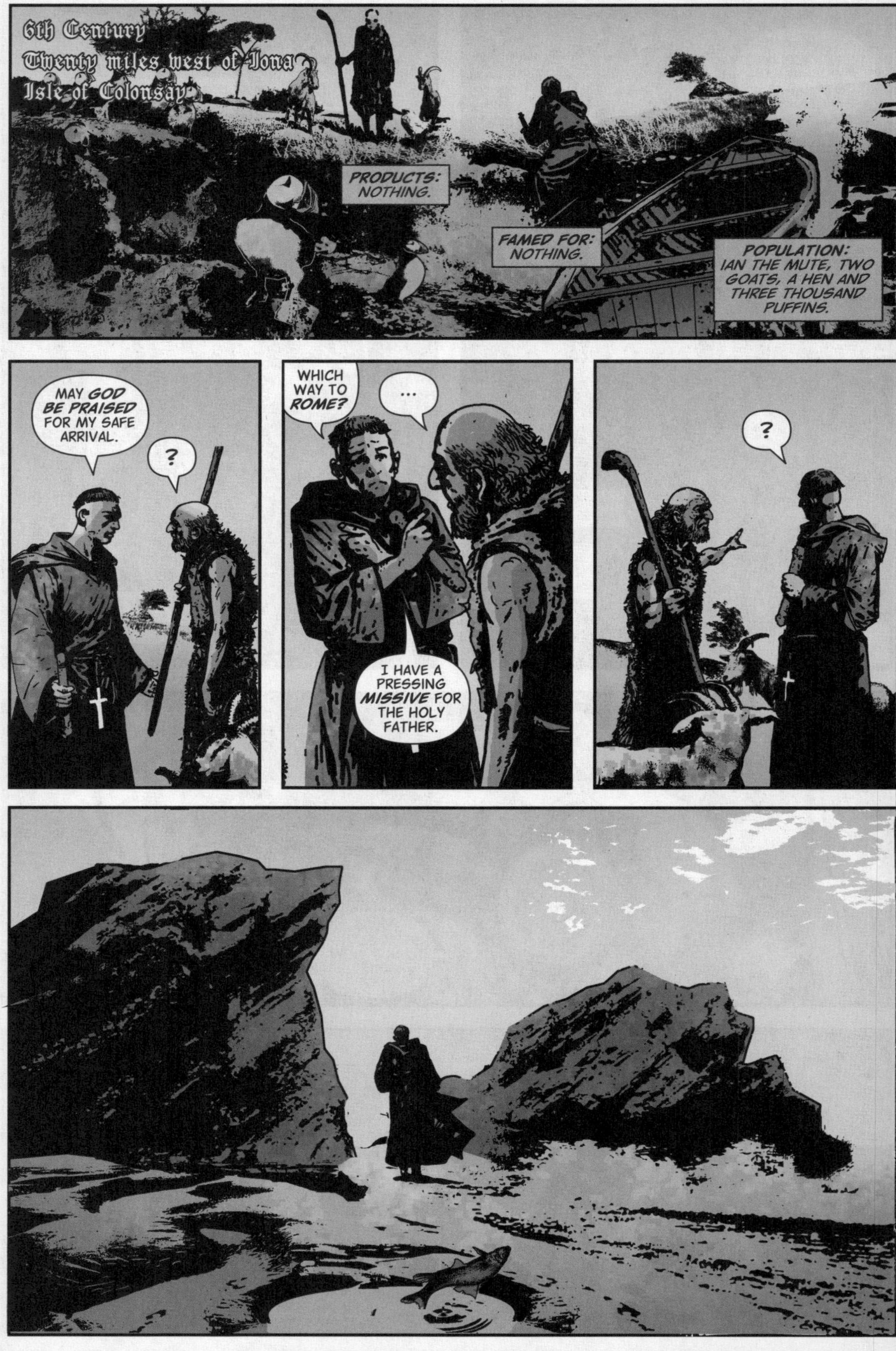
6th Century
Twenty miles west of Iona
Isle of Colonsay
PRODUCTS: NOTHING.
FAMED FOR: NOTHING.
POPULATION: IAN THE MUTE, TWO GOATS, A HEN AND THREE THOUSAND PUFFINS.
MAY GOD BE PRAISED FOR MY SAFE ARRIVAL.
?
WHICH WAY TO ROME?
...
I HAVE A PRESSING MISSIVE FOR THE HOLY FATHER.
?

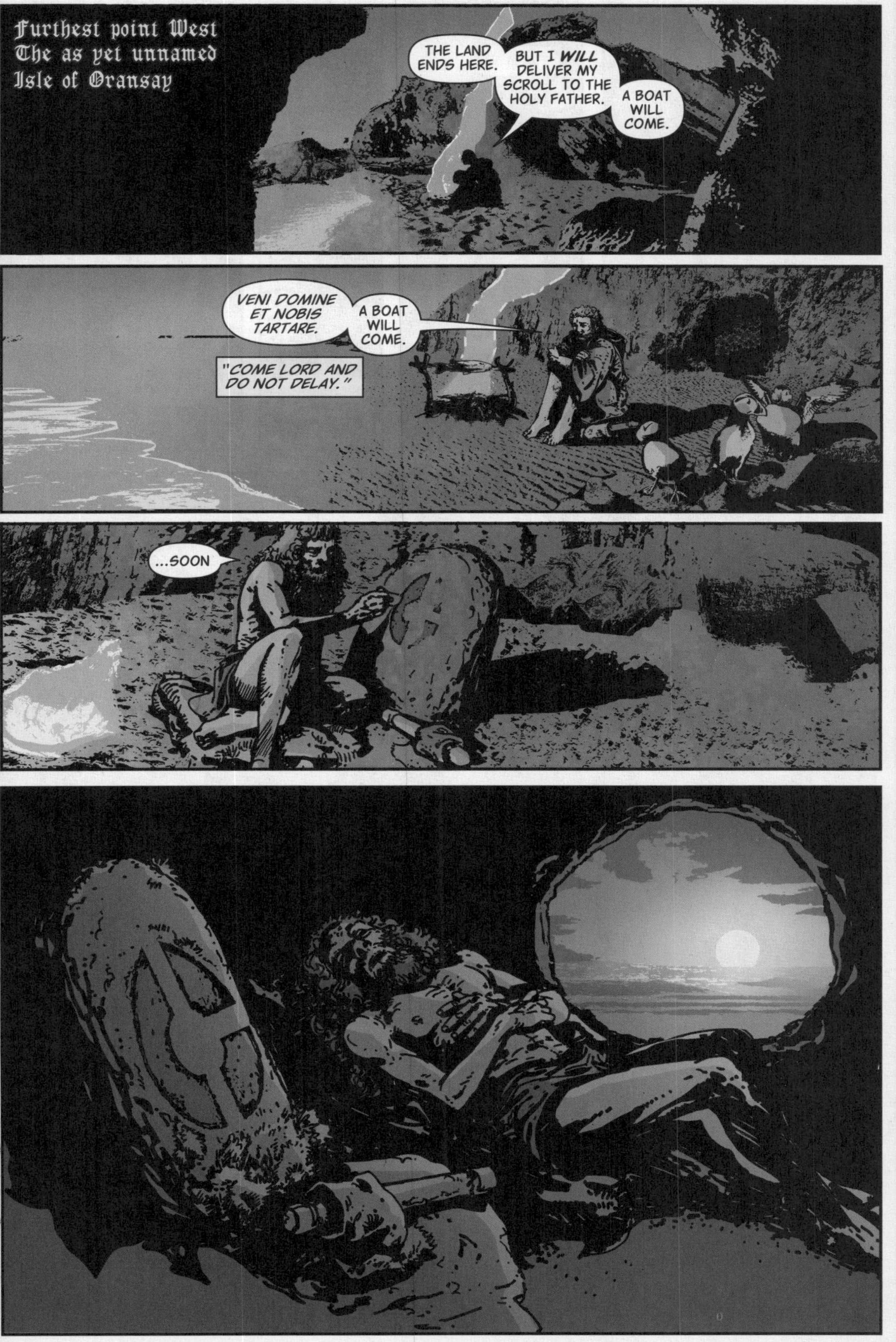
Furthest point West
The as yet unnamed
Isle of Oransay
THE LAND ENDS HERE.
BUT I WILL DELIVER MY SCROLL TO THE HOLY FATHER.
A BOAT WILL COME.
VENI DOMINE ET NOBIS TARTARE.
A BOAT WILL COME.
"COME LORD AND DO NOT DELAY."
...SOON

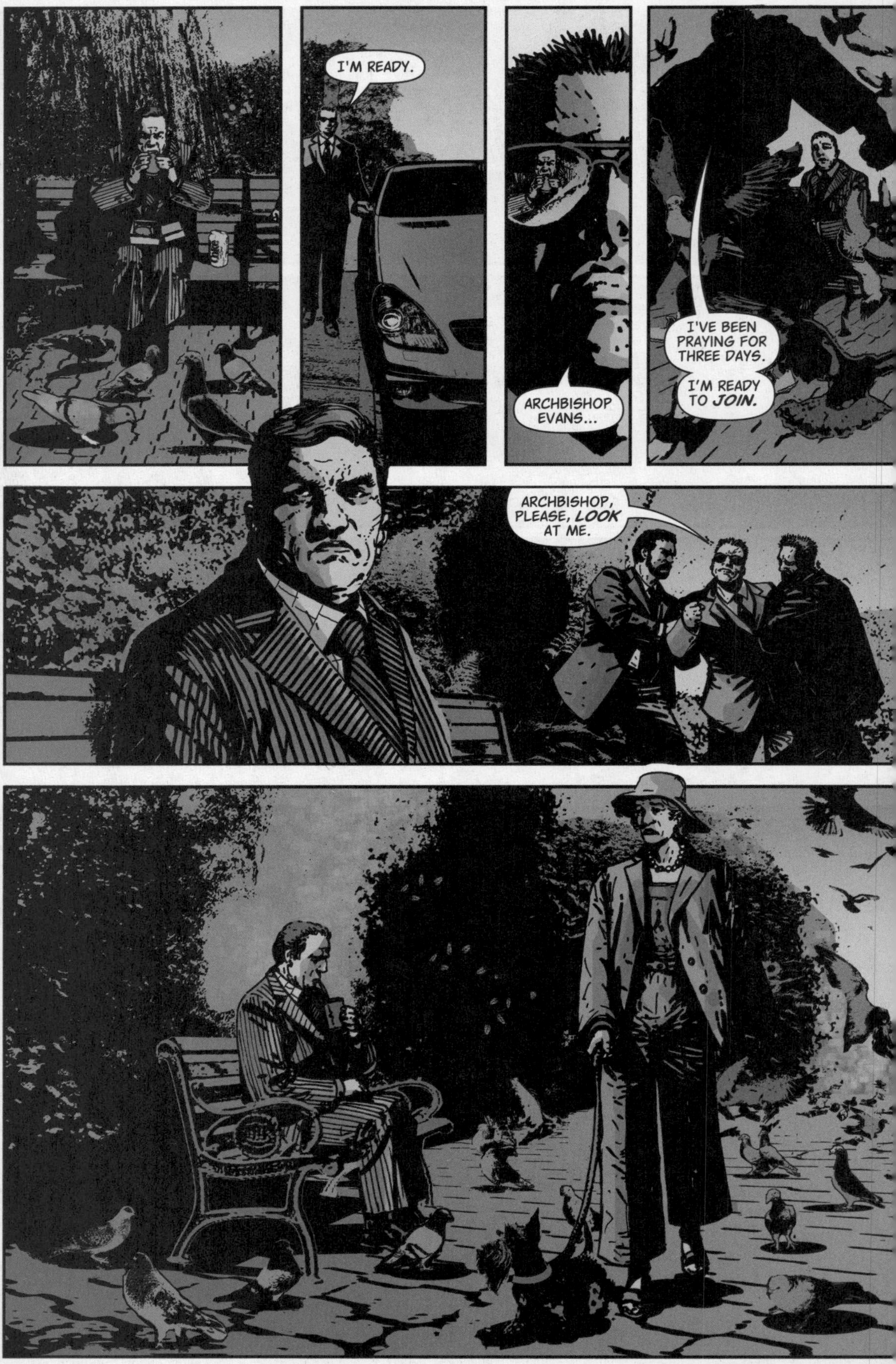
I'M READY.
ARCHBISHOP EVANS...
I'VE BEEN PRAYING FOR THREE DAYS.
I'M READY TO *JOIN.*
ARCHBISHOP, PLEASE, *LOOK* AT ME.

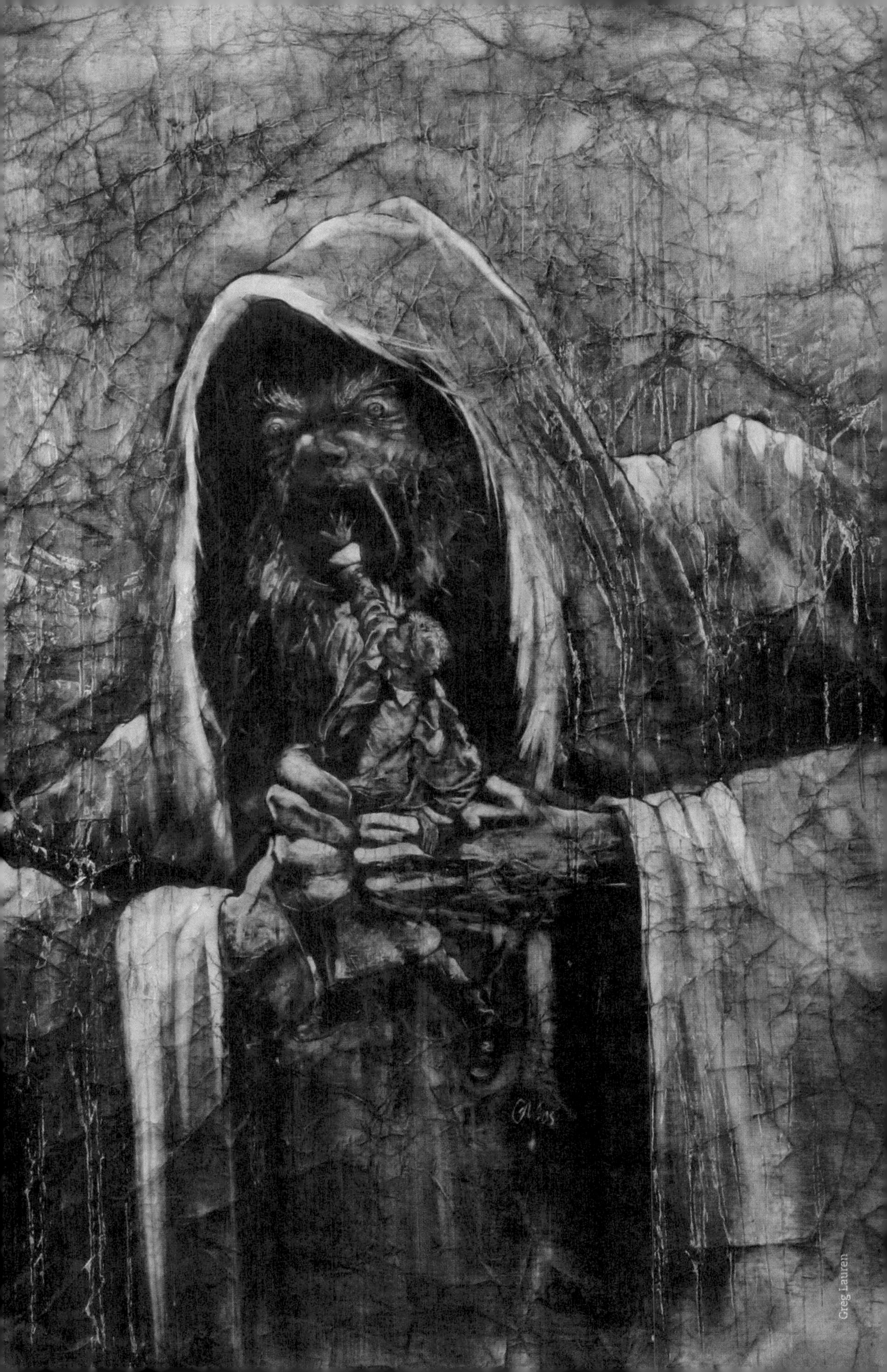

Greg Lauren

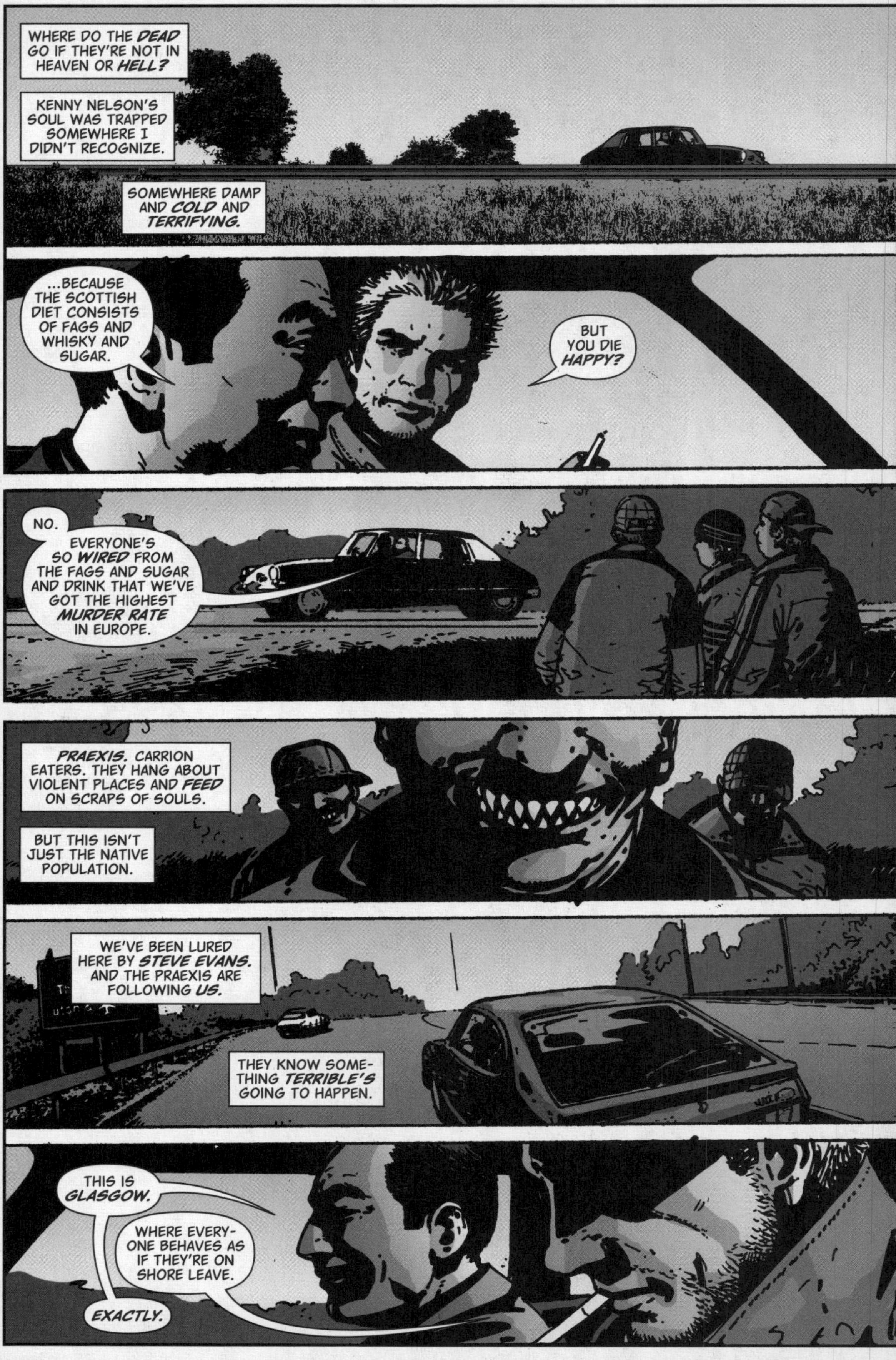
WHERE DO THE *DEAD* GO IF THEY'RE NOT IN HEAVEN OR *HELL?*
KENNY NELSON'S SOUL WAS TRAPPED SOMEWHERE I DIDN'T RECOGNIZE.
SOMEWHERE DAMP AND *COLD* AND *TERRIFYING.*
...BECAUSE THE SCOTTISH DIET CONSISTS OF FAGS AND WHISKY AND SUGAR.
BUT YOU DIE *HAPPY?*
NO.
EVERYONE'S SO *WIRED* FROM THE FAGS AND SUGAR AND DRINK THAT WE'VE GOT THE HIGHEST *MURDER RATE* IN EUROPE.
PRAEXIS. CARRION EATERS. THEY HANG ABOUT VIOLENT PLACES AND *FEED* ON SCRAPS OF SOULS.
BUT THIS ISN'T JUST THE NATIVE POPULATION.
WE'VE BEEN LURED HERE BY *STEVE EVANS.* AND THE PRAEXIS ARE FOLLOWING *US.*
THEY KNOW SOME-THING *TERRIBLE'S* GOING TO HAPPEN.
THIS IS *GLASGOW.*
WHERE EVERY-ONE BEHAVES AS IF THEY'RE ON SHORE LEAVE.
EXACTLY.

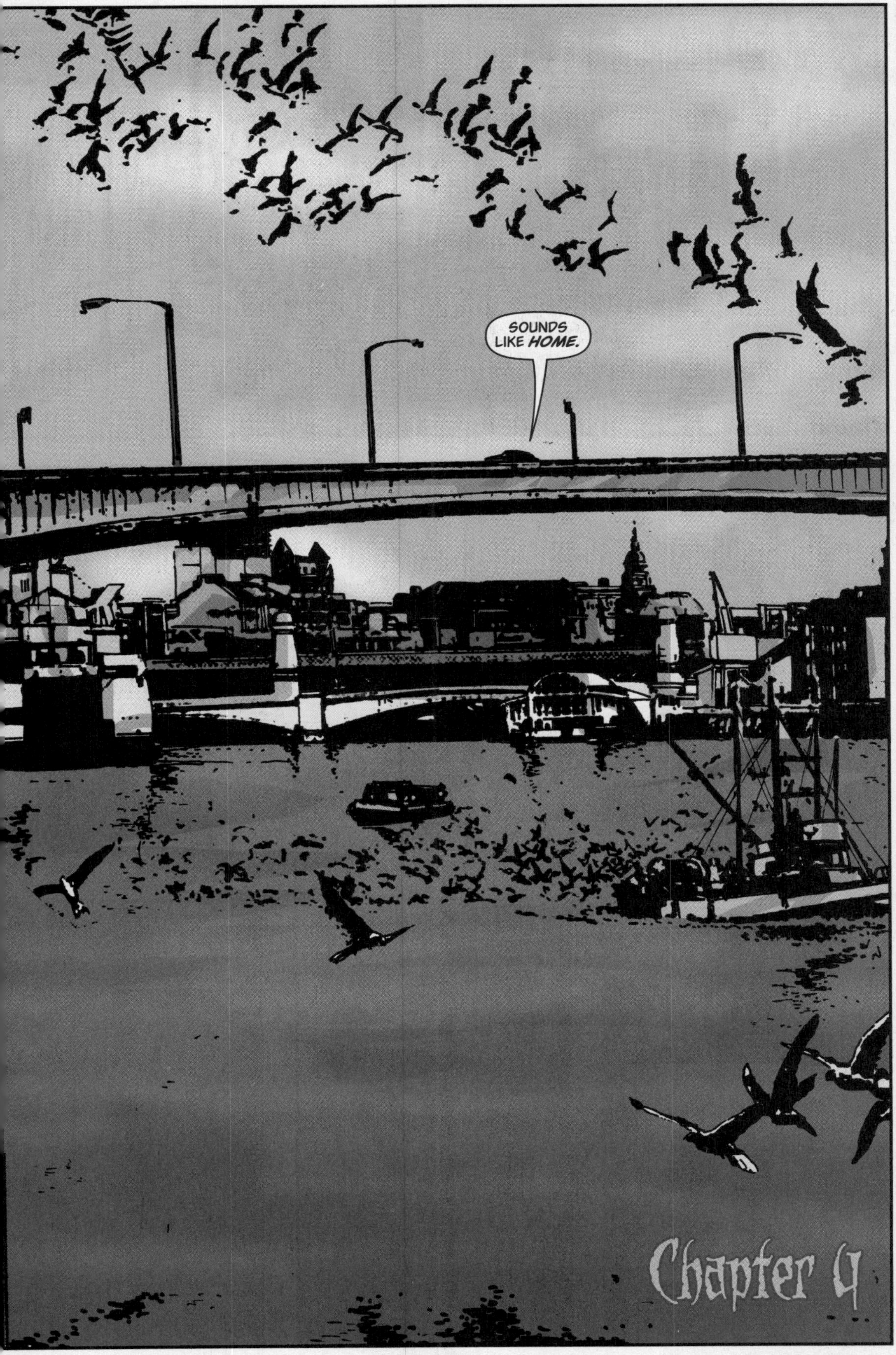
SOUNDS LIKE *HOME.*
Chapter 4

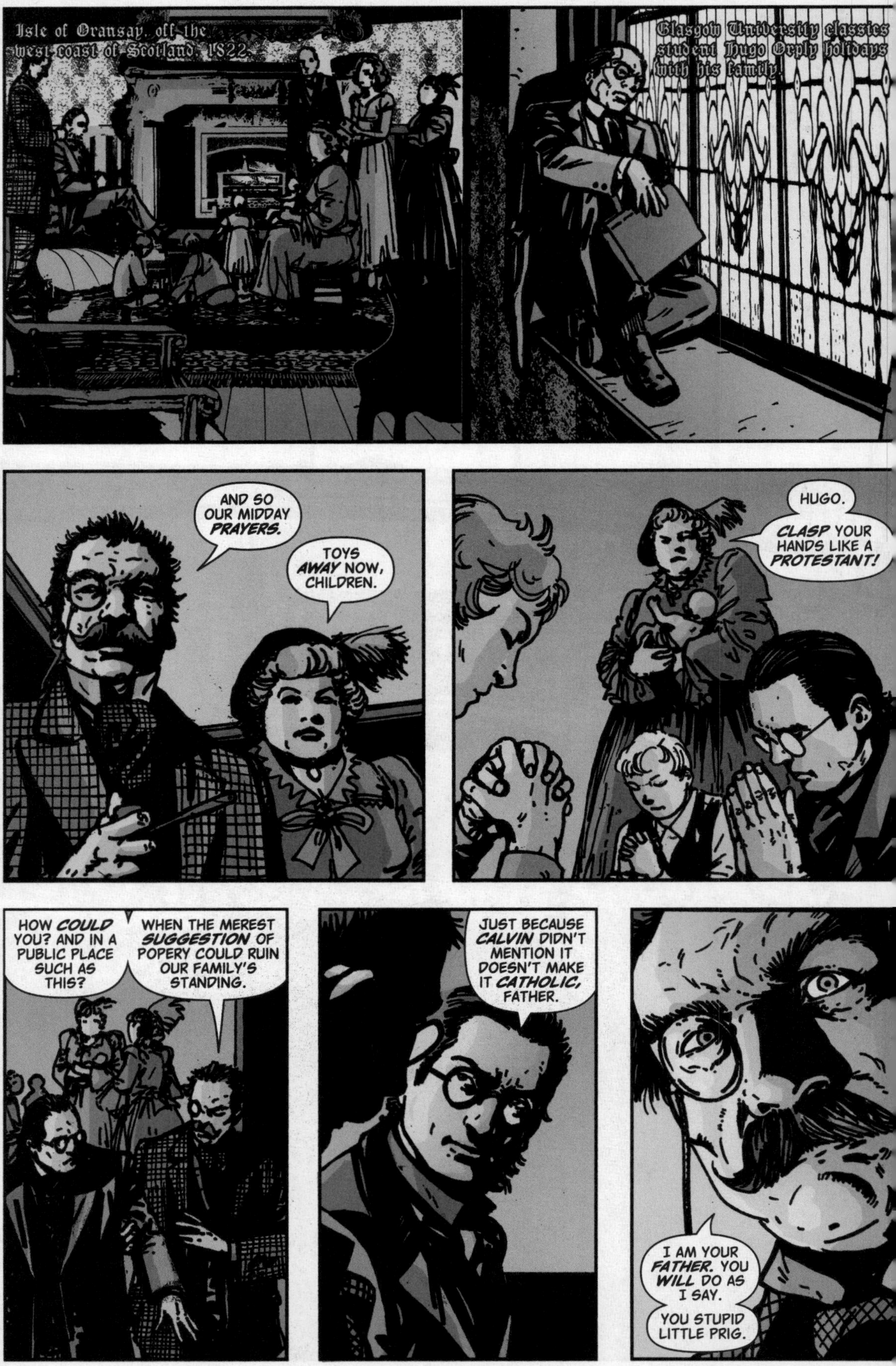

Isle of Oransay, off the west coast of Scotland, 1822.
Glasgow University classics student Hugo Orply holidays with his family.
AND SO OUR MIDDAY PRAYERS.
TOYS AWAY NOW, CHILDREN.
HUGO.
CLASP YOUR HANDS LIKE A PROTESTANT!
HOW COULD YOU? AND IN A PUBLIC PLACE SUCH AS THIS?
WHEN THE MEREST SUGGESTION OF POPERY COULD RUIN OUR FAMILY'S STANDING.
JUST BECAUSE CALVIN DIDN'T MENTION IT DOESN'T MAKE IT CATHOLIC, FATHER.
I AM YOUR FATHER. YOU WILL DO AS I SAY.
YOU STUPID LITTLE PRIG.

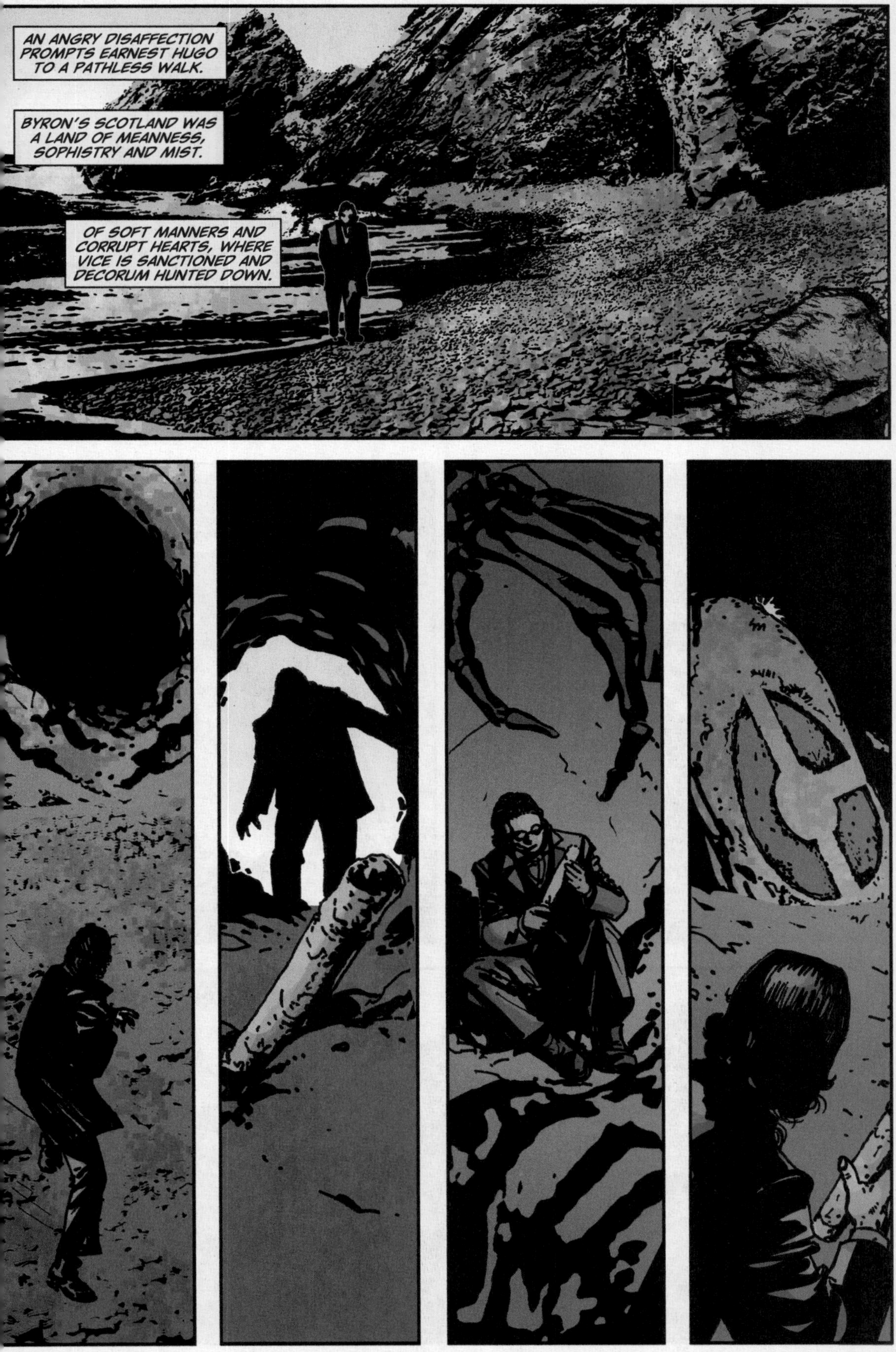
AN ANGRY DISAFFECTION PROMPTS EARNEST HUGO TO A PATHLESS WALK.
BYRON'S SCOTLAND WAS A LAND OF MEANNESS, SOPHISTRY AND MIST.
OF SOFT MANNERS AND CORRUPT HEARTS, WHERE VICE IS SANCTIONED AND DECORUM HUNTED DOWN.

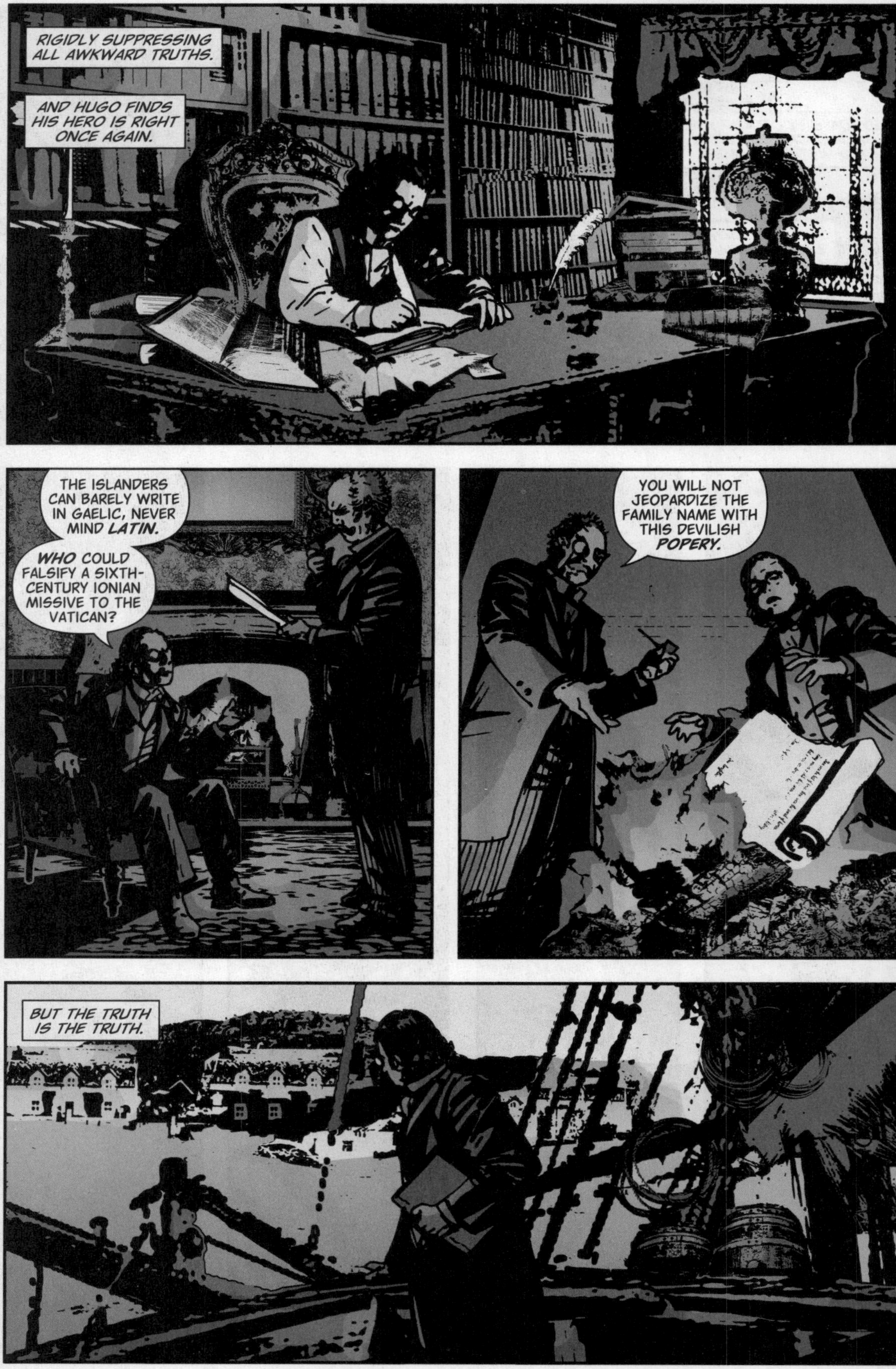
RIGIDLY SUPPRESSING ALL AWKWARD TRUTHS.
AND HUGO FINDS HIS HERO IS RIGHT ONCE AGAIN.
THE ISLANDERS CAN BARELY WRITE IN GAELIC, NEVER MIND LATIN.
WHO COULD FALSIFY A SIXTH-CENTURY IONIAN MISSIVE TO THE VATICAN?
YOU WILL NOT JEOPARDIZE THE FAMILY NAME WITH THIS DEVILISH POPERY.
BUT THE TRUTH IS THE TRUTH.

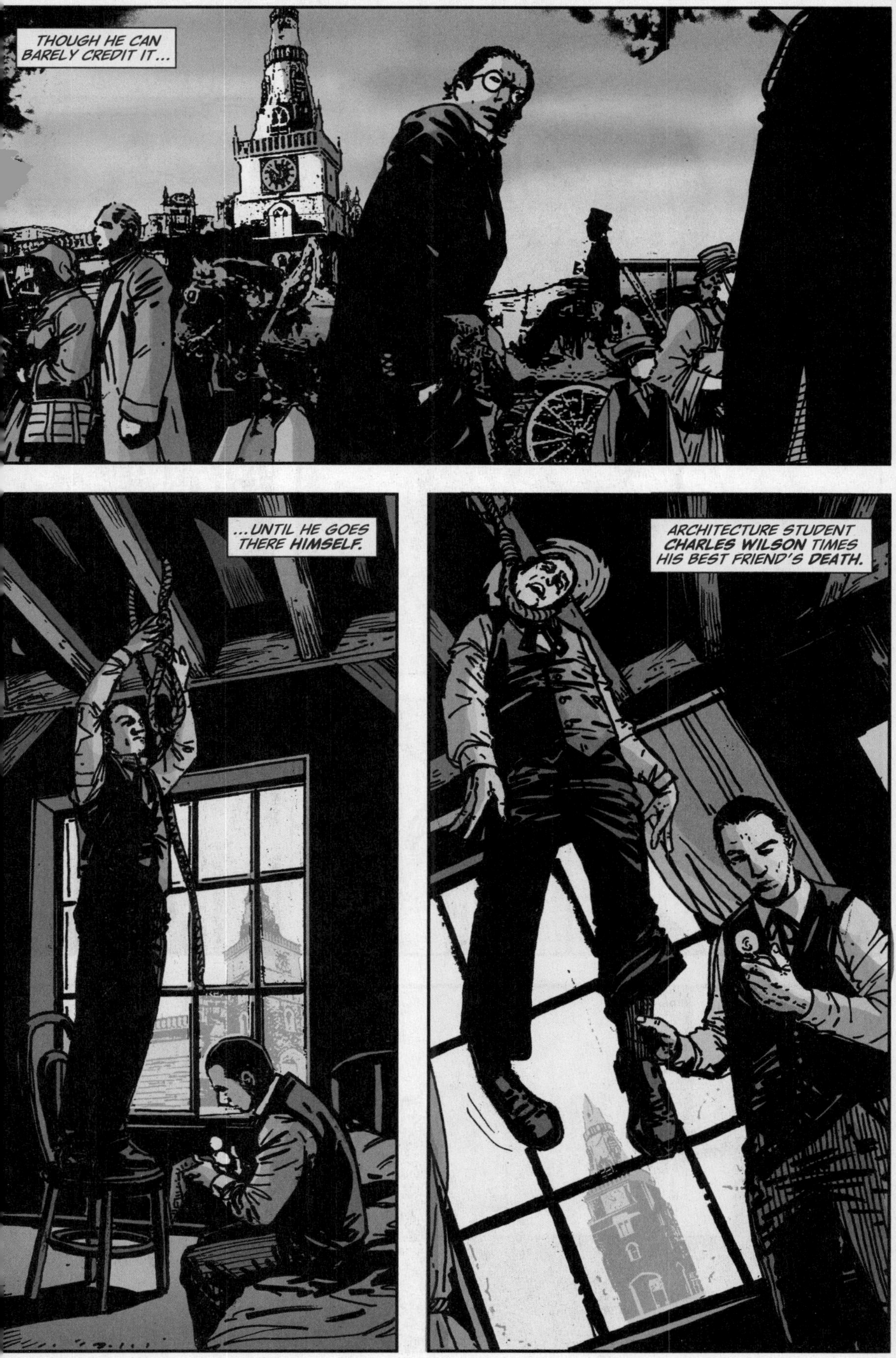

THOUGH HE CAN BARELY CREDIT IT...
...UNTIL HE GOES THERE HIMSELF.
ARCHITECTURE STUDENT CHARLES WILSON TIMES HIS BEST FRIEND'S DEATH.

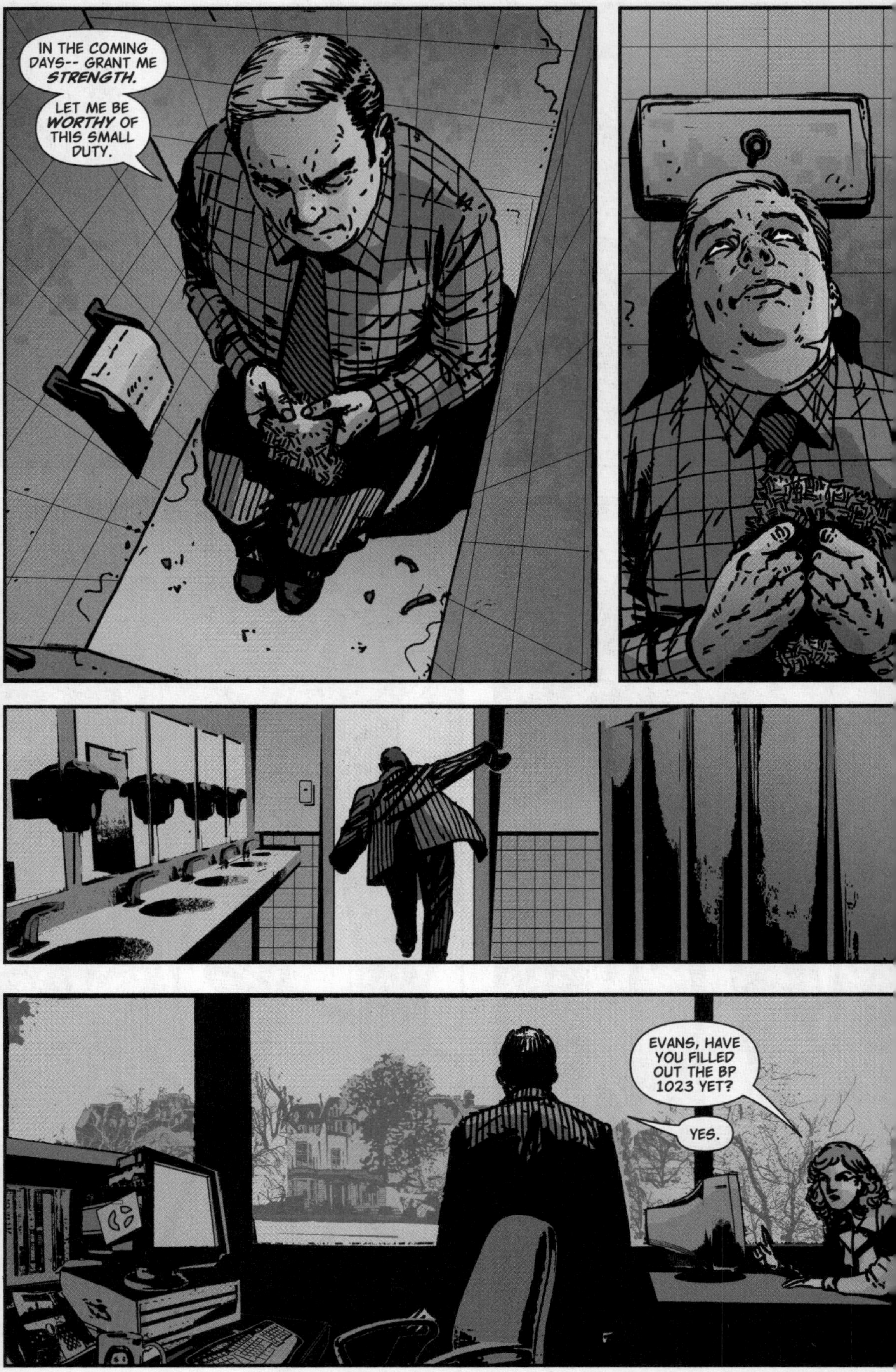
IN THE COMING DAYS-- GRANT ME *STRENGTH.*
LET ME BE *WORTHY* OF THIS SMALL DUTY.
EVANS, HAVE YOU FILLED OUT THE BP 1023 YET?
YES.

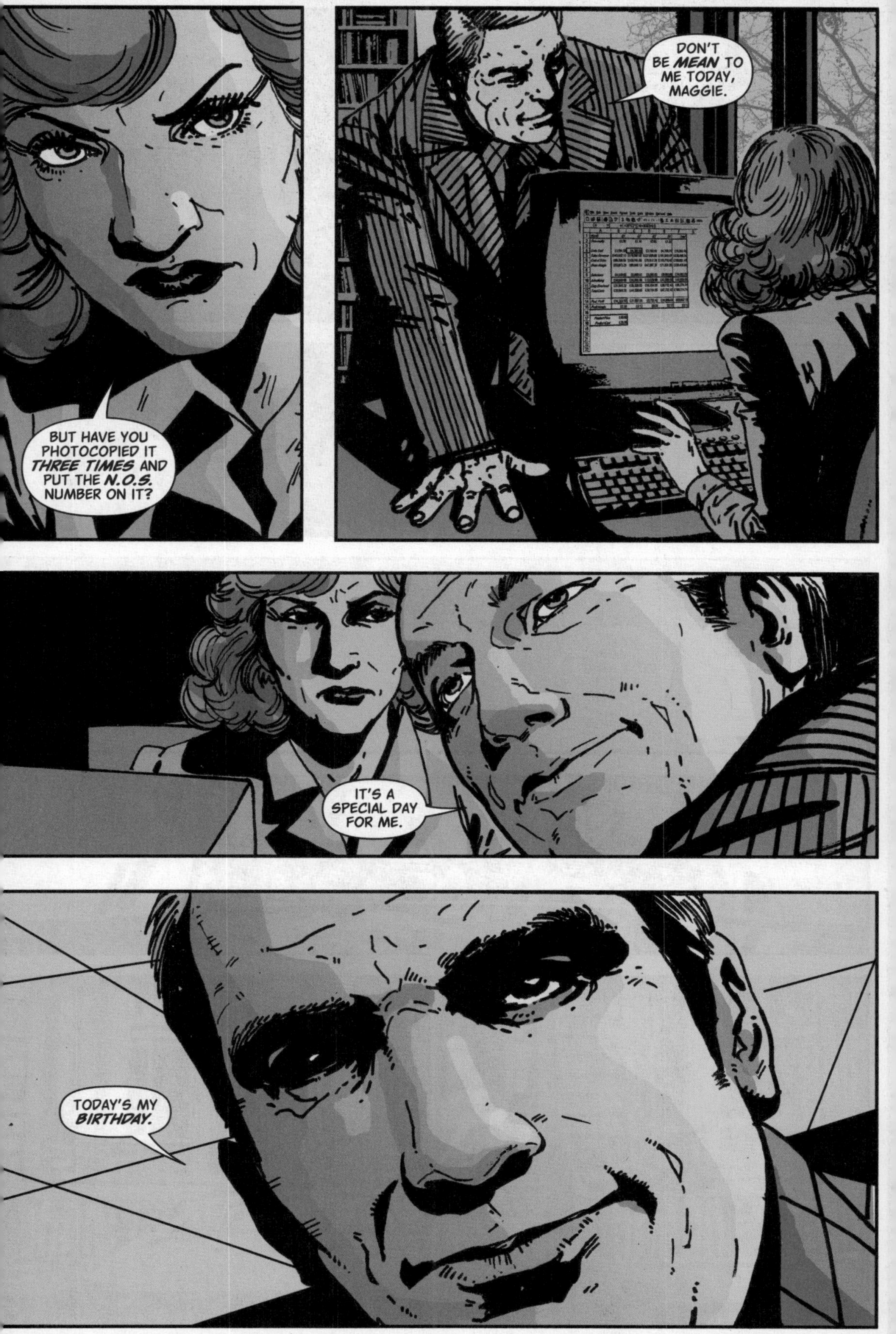
BUT HAVE YOU PHOTOCOPIED IT *THREE TIMES* AND PUT THE *N.O.S.* NUMBER ON IT?
DON'T BE *MEAN* TO ME TODAY, MAGGIE.
IT'S A SPECIAL DAY FOR ME.
TODAY'S MY *BIRTHDAY.*

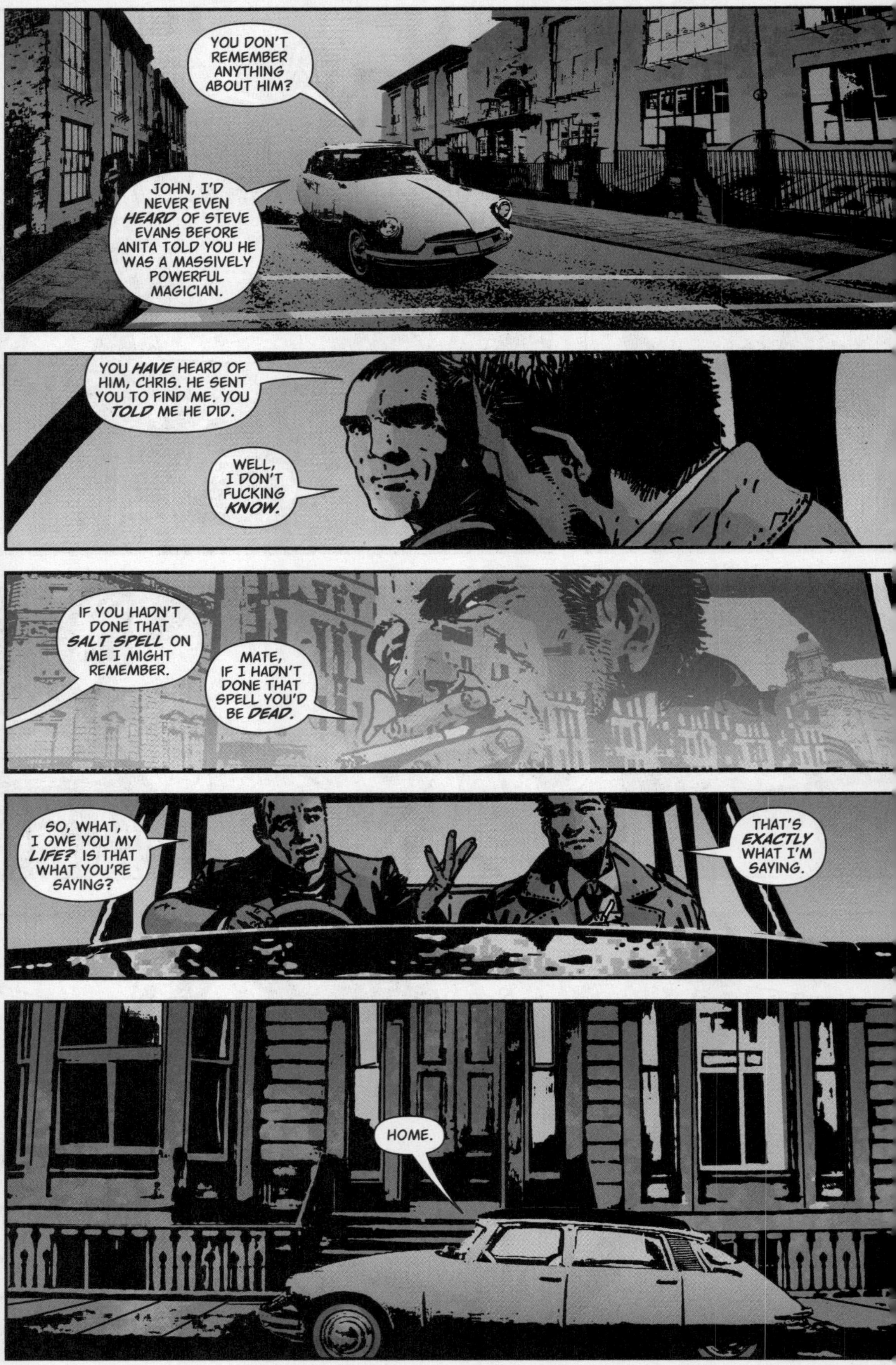
YOU DON'T REMEMBER ANYTHING ABOUT HIM?
JOHN, I'D NEVER EVEN HEARD OF STEVE EVANS BEFORE ANITA TOLD YOU HE WAS A MASSIVELY POWERFUL MAGICIAN.
YOU HAVE HEARD OF HIM, CHRIS. HE SENT YOU TO FIND ME. YOU TOLD ME HE DID.
WELL, I DON'T FUCKING KNOW.
IF YOU HADN'T DONE THAT SALT SPELL ON ME I MIGHT REMEMBER.
MATE, IF I HADN'T DONE THAT SPELL YOU'D BE DEAD.
SO, WHAT, I OWE YOU MY LIFE? IS THAT WHAT YOU'RE SAYING?
THAT'S EXACTLY WHAT I'M SAYING.
HOME.

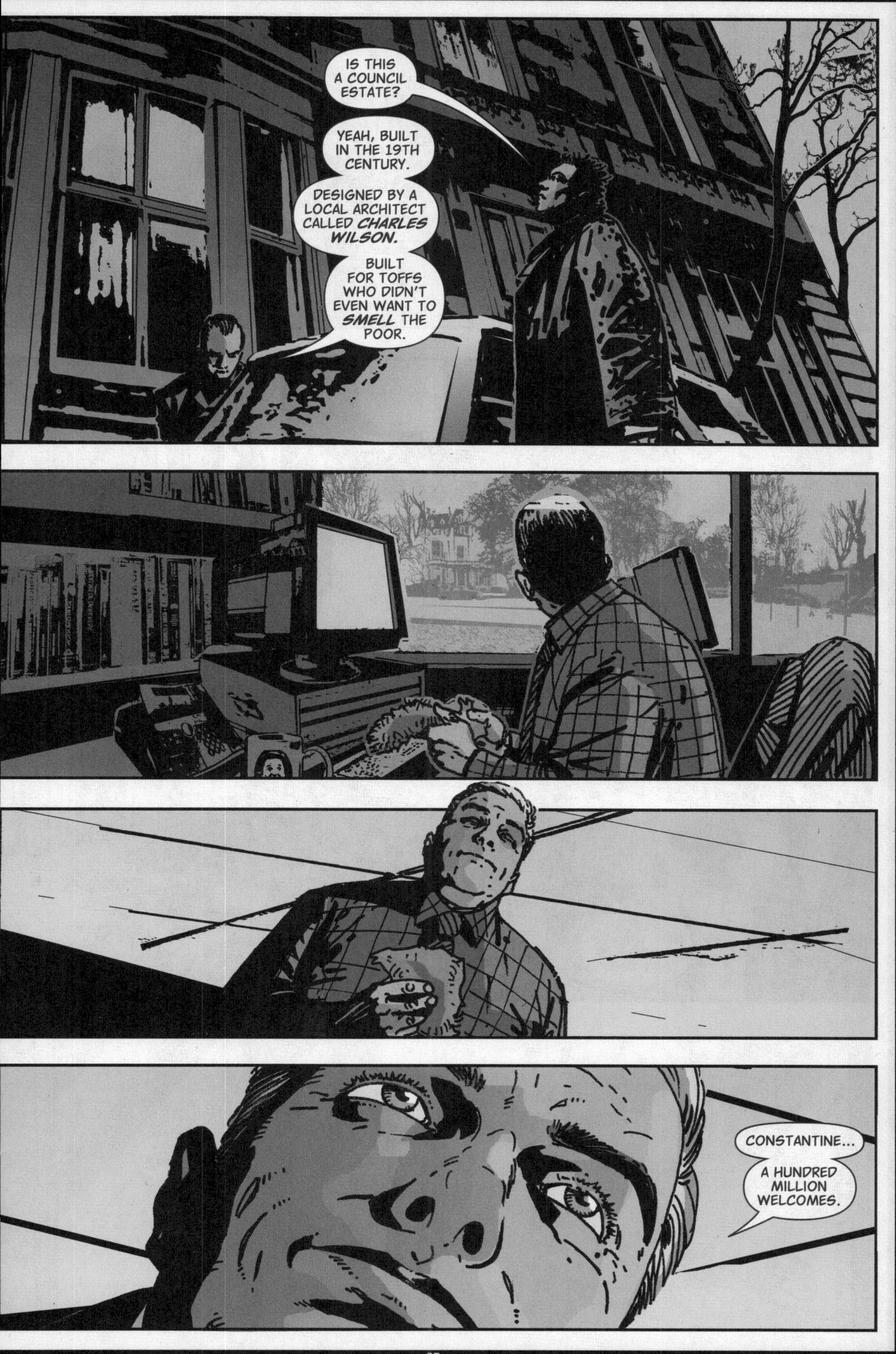
IS THIS A COUNCIL ESTATE?
YEAH, BUILT IN THE 19TH CENTURY.
DESIGNED BY A LOCAL ARCHITECT CALLED *CHARLES WILSON.*
BUILT FOR TOFFS WHO DIDN'T EVEN WANT TO *SMELL* THE POOR.
CONSTANTINE...
A HUNDRED MILLION WELCOMES.

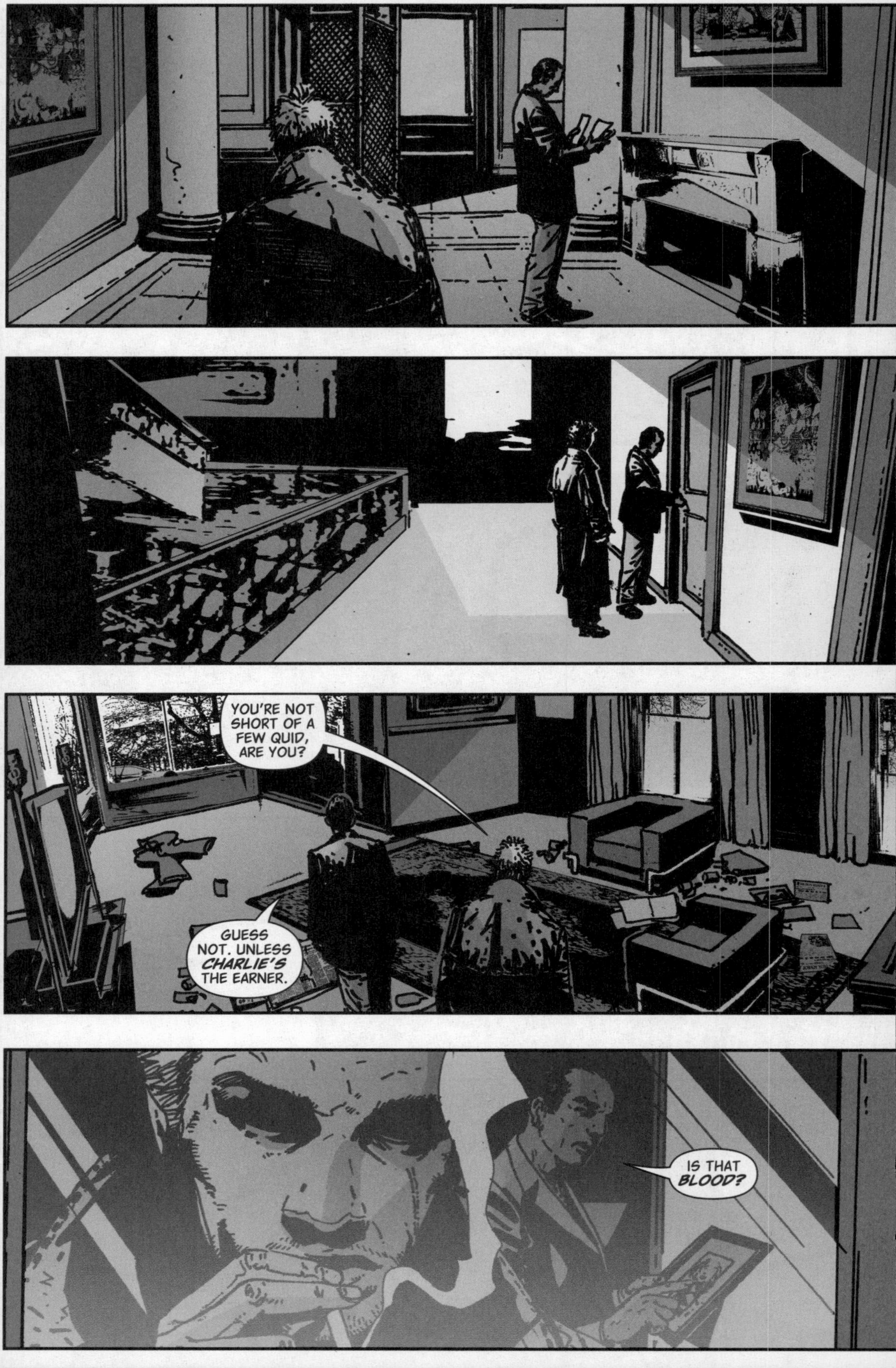
YOU'RE NOT SHORT OF A FEW QUID, ARE YOU?
GUESS NOT. UNLESS CHARLIE'S THE EARNER.
IS THAT BLOOD?

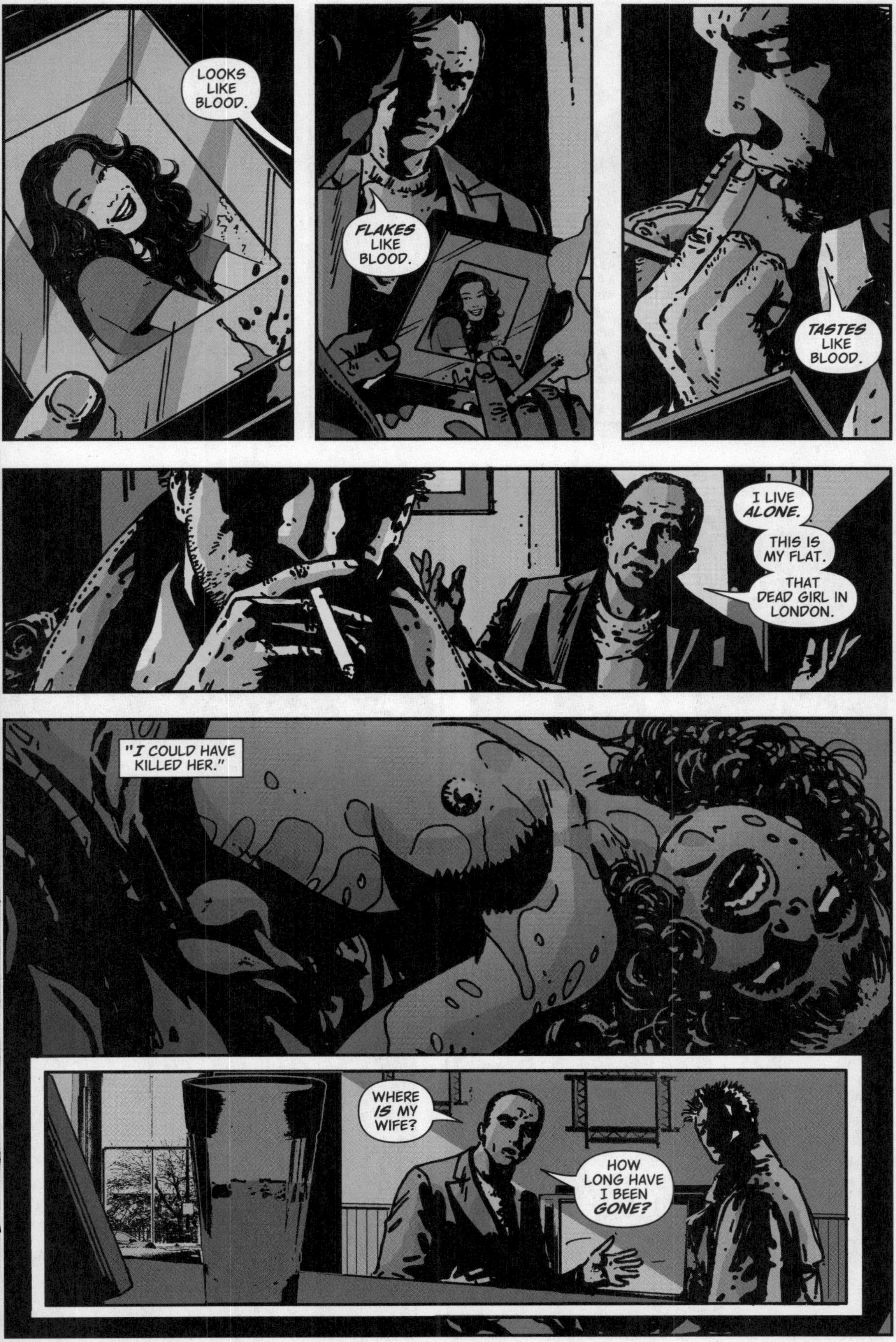
LOOKS LIKE BLOOD.
FLAKES LIKE BLOOD.
TASTES LIKE BLOOD.
I LIVE ALONE.
THIS IS MY FLAT.
THAT DEAD GIRL IN LONDON.
"I COULD HAVE KILLED HER."
WHERE IS MY WIFE?
HOW LONG HAVE I BEEN GONE?

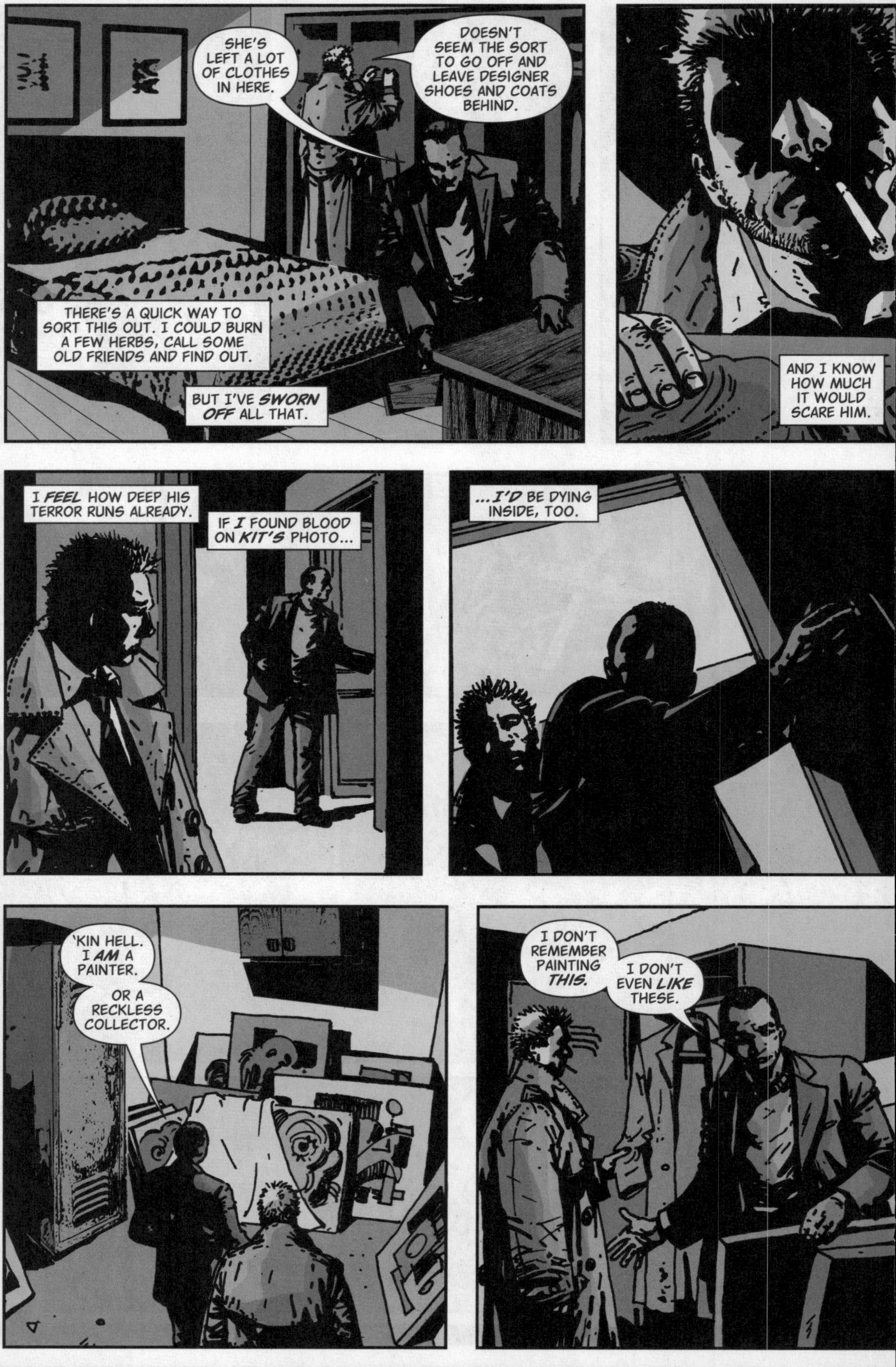
SHE'S LEFT A LOT OF CLOTHES IN HERE.
DOESN'T SEEM THE SORT TO GO OFF AND LEAVE DESIGNER SHOES AND COATS BEHIND.
THERE'S A QUICK WAY TO SORT THIS OUT. I COULD BURN A FEW HERBS, CALL SOME OLD FRIENDS AND FIND OUT.
BUT I'VE SWORN OFF ALL THAT.
AND I KNOW HOW MUCH IT WOULD SCARE HIM.
I FEEL HOW DEEP HIS TERROR RUNS ALREADY.
IF I FOUND BLOOD ON KIT'S PHOTO...
...I'D BE DYING INSIDE, TOO.
'KIN HELL. I AM A PAINTER.
OR A RECKLESS COLLECTOR.
I DON'T REMEMBER PAINTING THIS.
I DON'T EVEN LIKE THESE.

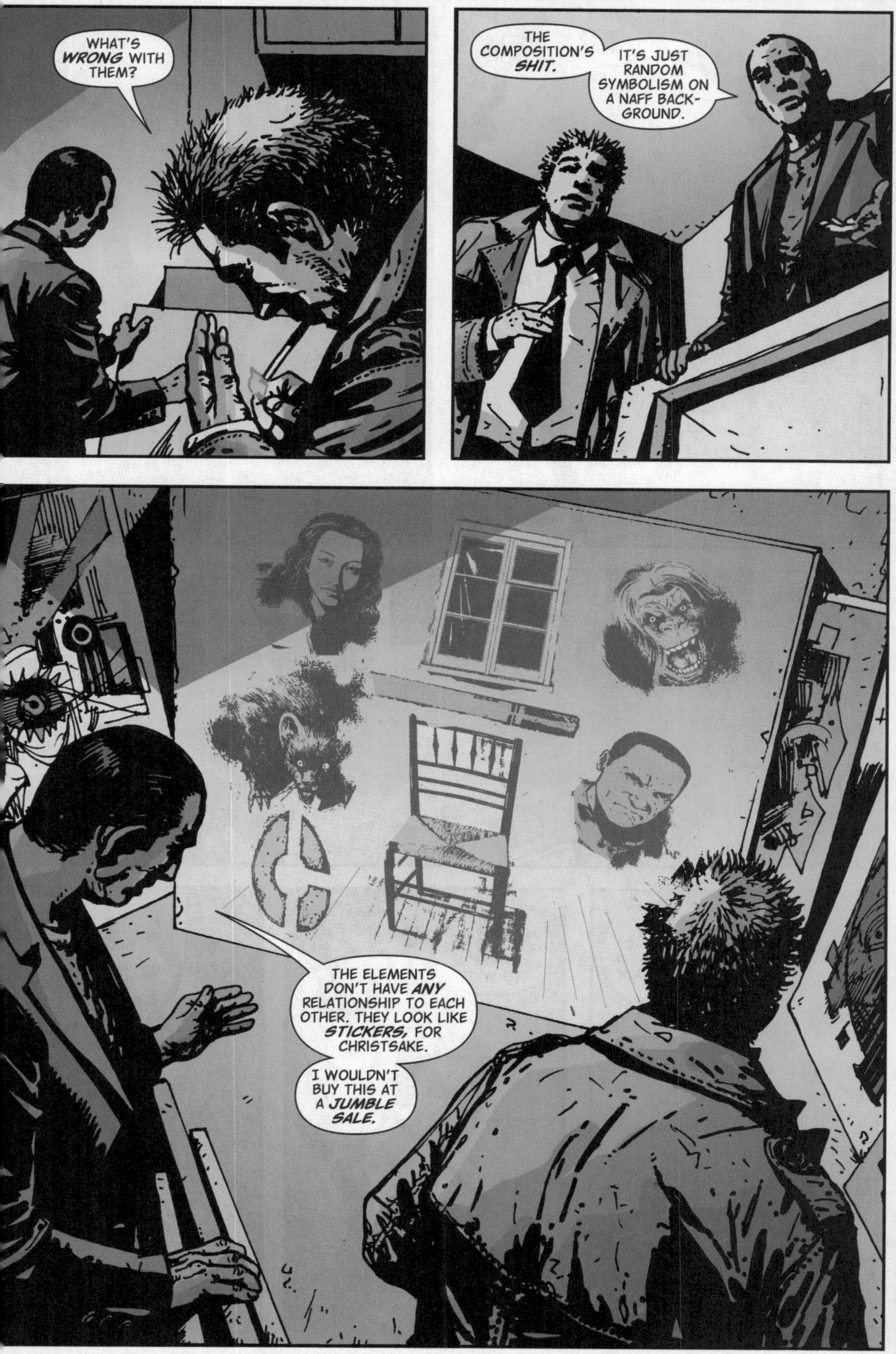
WHAT'S *WRONG* WITH THEM?
THE COMPOSITION'S *SHIT.*
IT'S JUST RANDOM SYMBOLISM ON A NAFF BACK-GROUND.
THE ELEMENTS DON'T HAVE *ANY* RELATIONSHIP TO EACH OTHER. THEY LOOK LIKE *STICKERS,* FOR CHRISTSAKE.
I WOULDN'T BUY THIS AT A *JUMBLE SALE.*

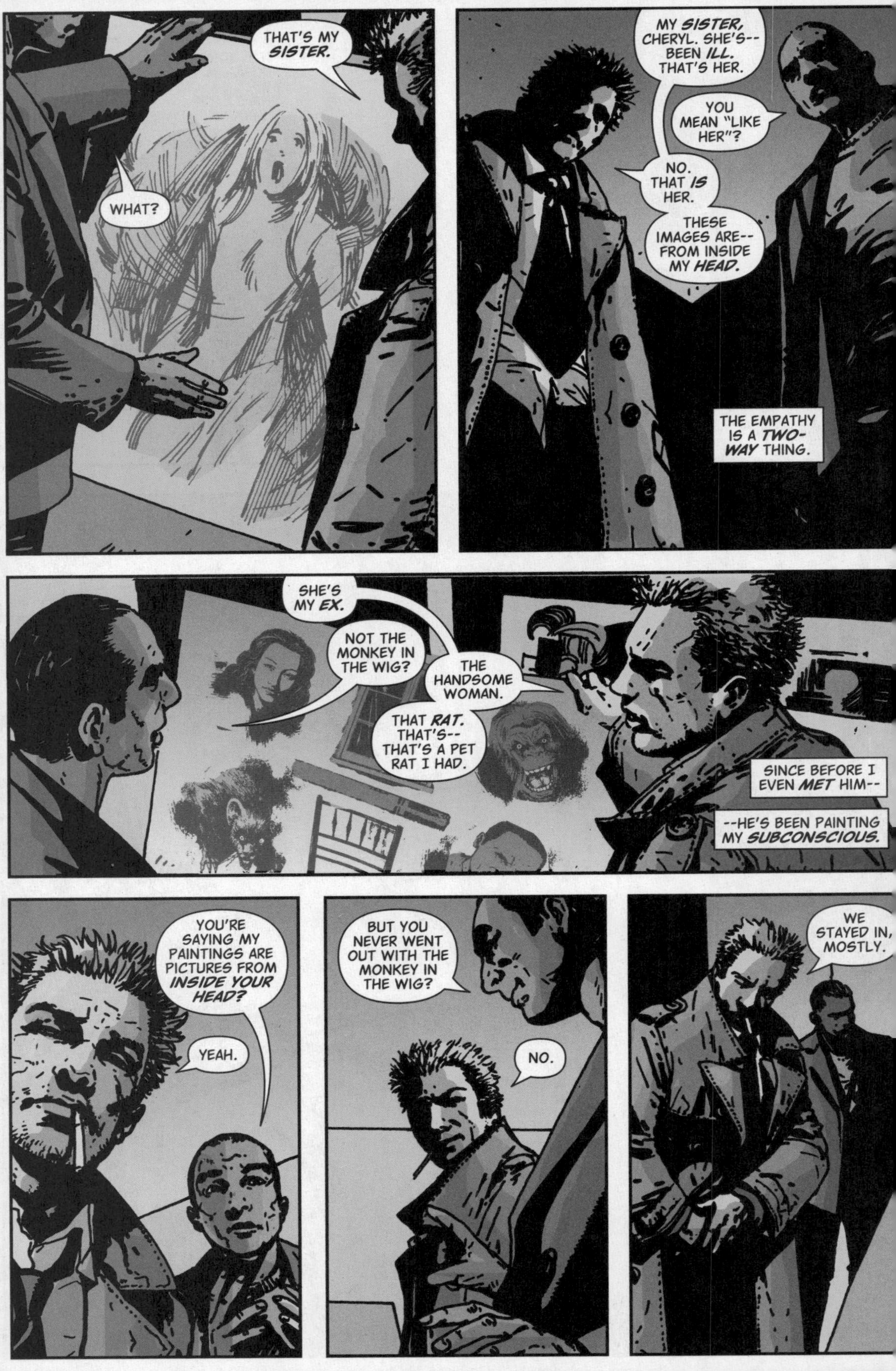

THAT'S MY SISTER.
WHAT?
MY SISTER, CHERYL. SHE'S-- BEEN ILL. THAT'S HER.
YOU MEAN "LIKE HER"?
NO. THAT IS HER.
THESE IMAGES ARE-- FROM INSIDE MY HEAD.
THE EMPATHY IS A TWO-WAY THING.
SHE'S MY EX.
NOT THE MONKEY IN THE WIG?
THE HANDSOME WOMAN.
THAT RAT. THAT'S-- THAT'S A PET RAT I HAD.
SINCE BEFORE I EVEN MET HIM--
--HE'S BEEN PAINTING MY SUBCONSCIOUS.
YOU'RE SAYING MY PAINTINGS ARE PICTURES FROM INSIDE YOUR HEAD?
YEAH.
BUT YOU NEVER WENT OUT WITH THE MONKEY IN THE WIG?
NO.
WE STAYED IN, MOSTLY.

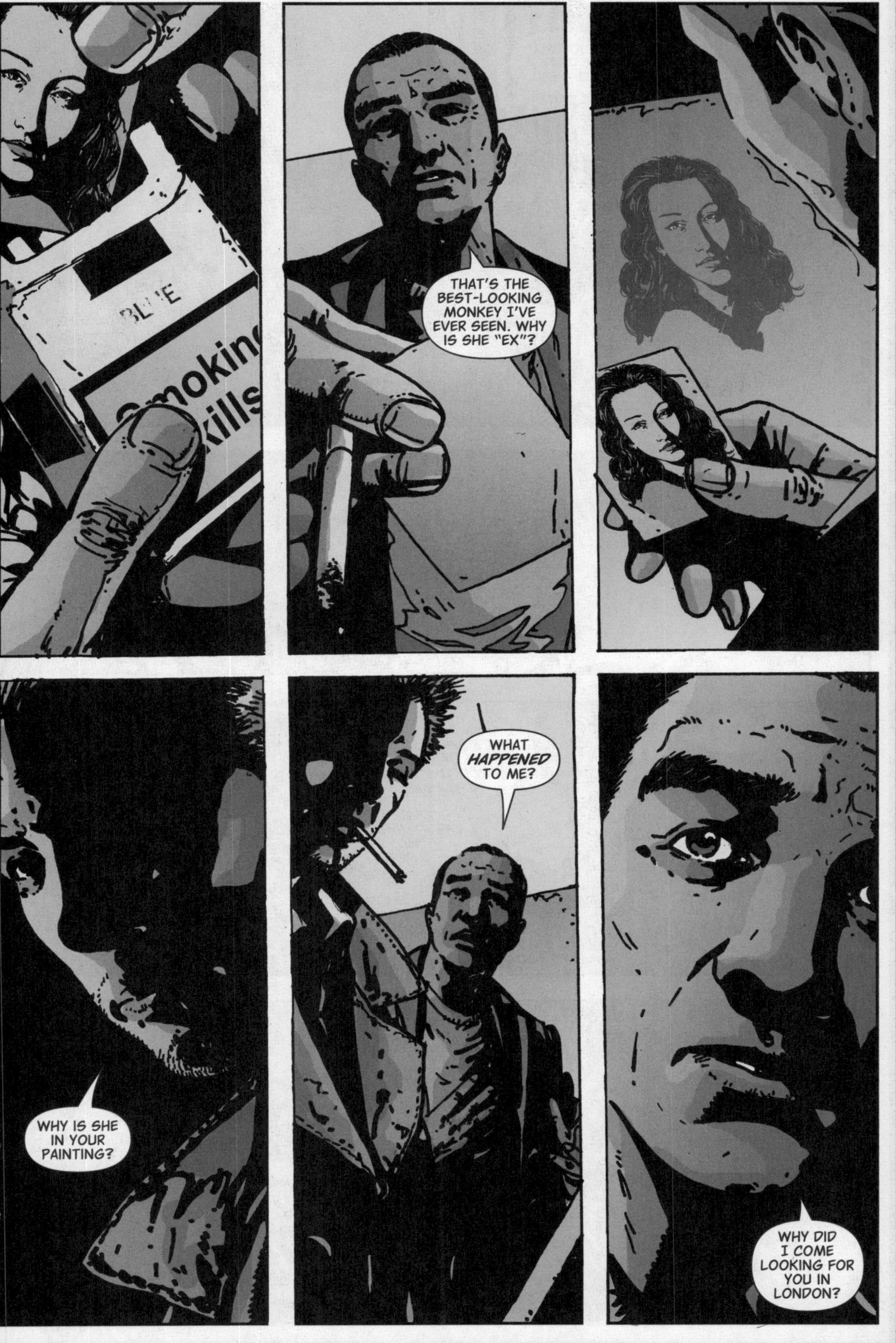
THAT'S THE BEST-LOOKING MONKEY I'VE EVER SEEN. WHY IS SHE "EX"?
WHY IS SHE IN YOUR PAINTING?
WHAT *HAPPENED* TO ME?
WHY DID I COME LOOKING FOR YOU IN LONDON?

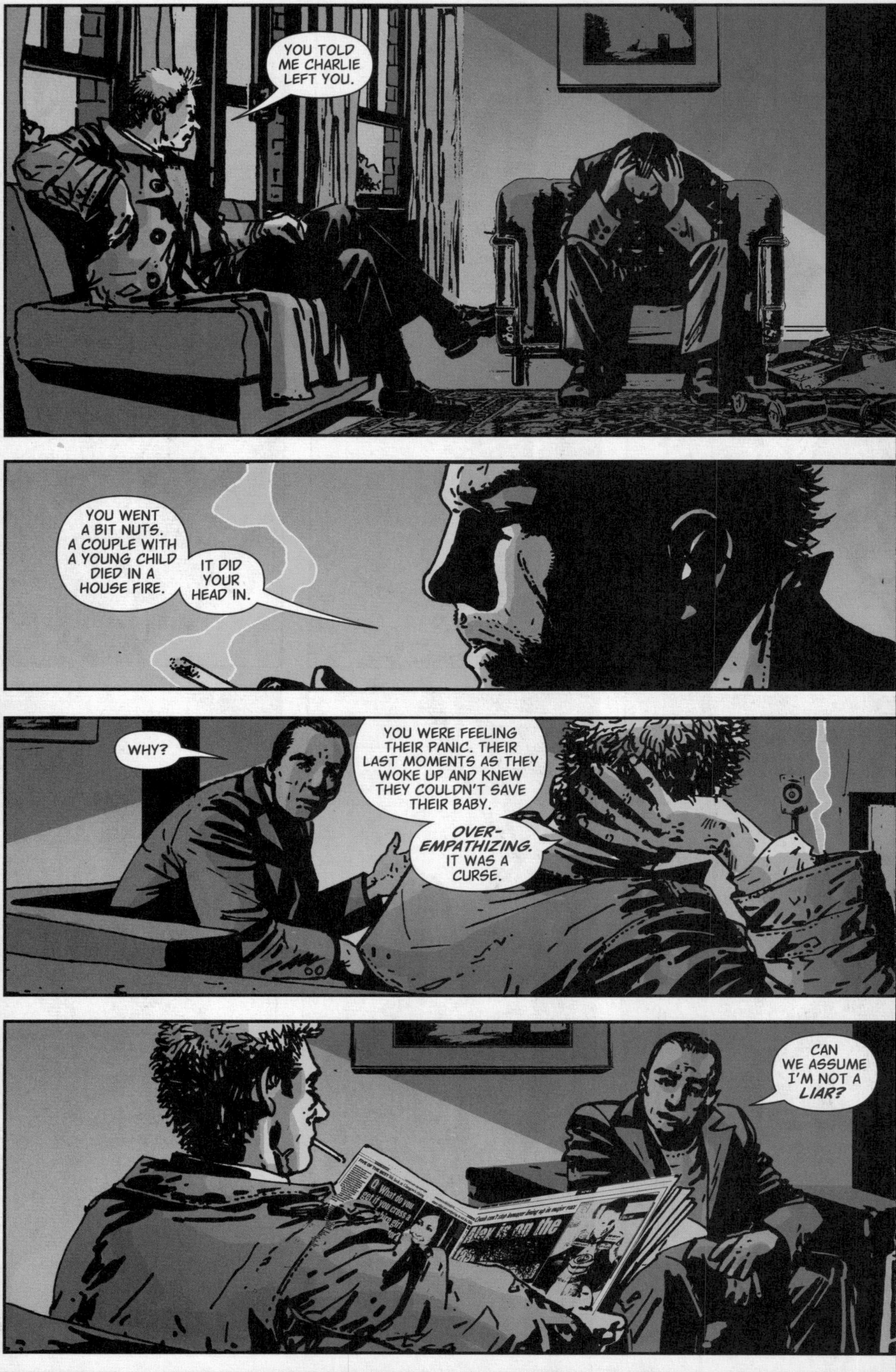
YOU TOLD ME CHARLIE LEFT YOU.
YOU WENT A BIT NUTS. A COUPLE WITH A YOUNG CHILD DIED IN A HOUSE FIRE.
IT DID YOUR HEAD IN.
WHY?
YOU WERE FEELING THEIR PANIC. THEIR LAST MOMENTS AS THEY WOKE UP AND KNEW THEY COULDN'T SAVE THEIR BABY.
OVER-EMPATHIZING. IT WAS A CURSE.
Alex is on the
CAN WE ASSUME I'M NOT A *LIAR?*

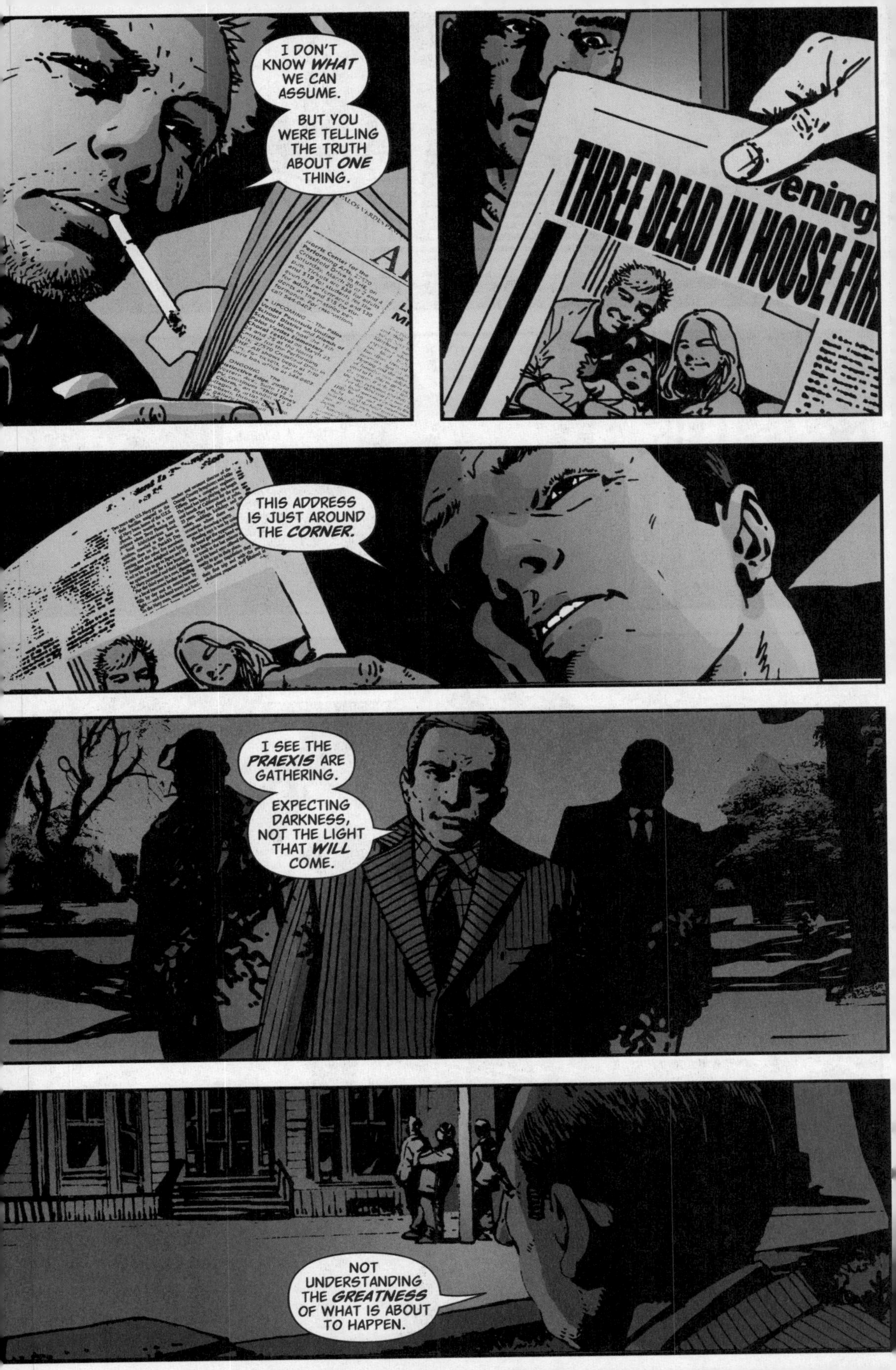

I DON'T KNOW WHAT WE CAN ASSUME.
BUT YOU WERE TELLING THE TRUTH ABOUT ONE THING.
THREE DEAD IN HOUSE FIR
THIS ADDRESS IS JUST AROUND THE CORNER.
I SEE THE PRAEXIS ARE GATHERING.
EXPECTING DARKNESS, NOT THE LIGHT THAT WILL COME.
NOT UNDERSTANDING THE GREATNESS OF WHAT IS ABOUT TO HAPPEN.

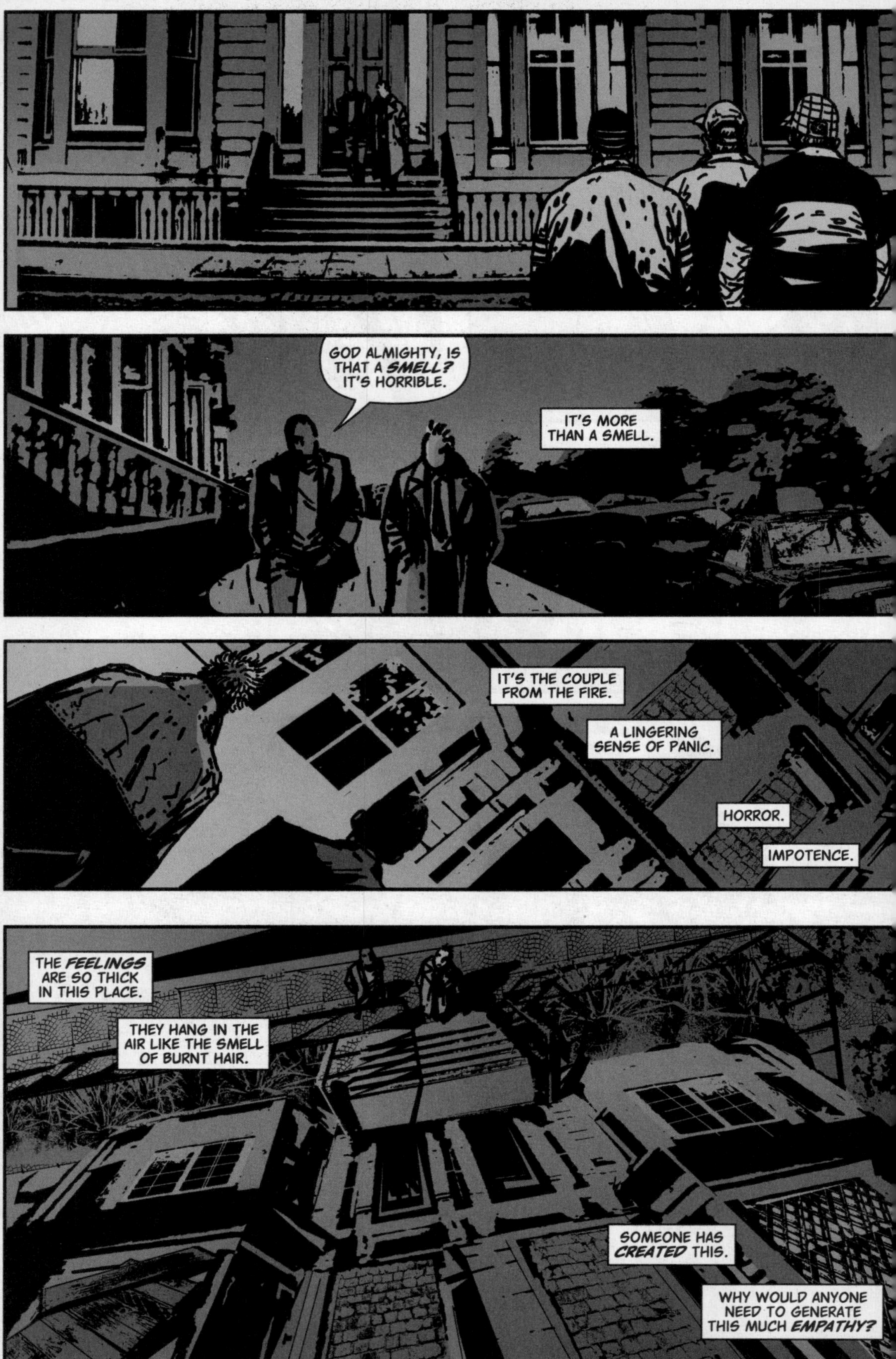
GOD ALMIGHTY, IS THAT A SMELL? IT'S HORRIBLE.
IT'S MORE THAN A SMELL.
IT'S THE COUPLE FROM THE FIRE.
A LINGERING SENSE OF PANIC.
HORROR.
IMPOTENCE.
THE FEELINGS ARE SO THICK IN THIS PLACE.
THEY HANG IN THE AIR LIKE THE SMELL OF BURNT HAIR.
SOMEONE HAS CREATED THIS.
WHY WOULD ANYONE NEED TO GENERATE THIS MUCH EMPATHY?

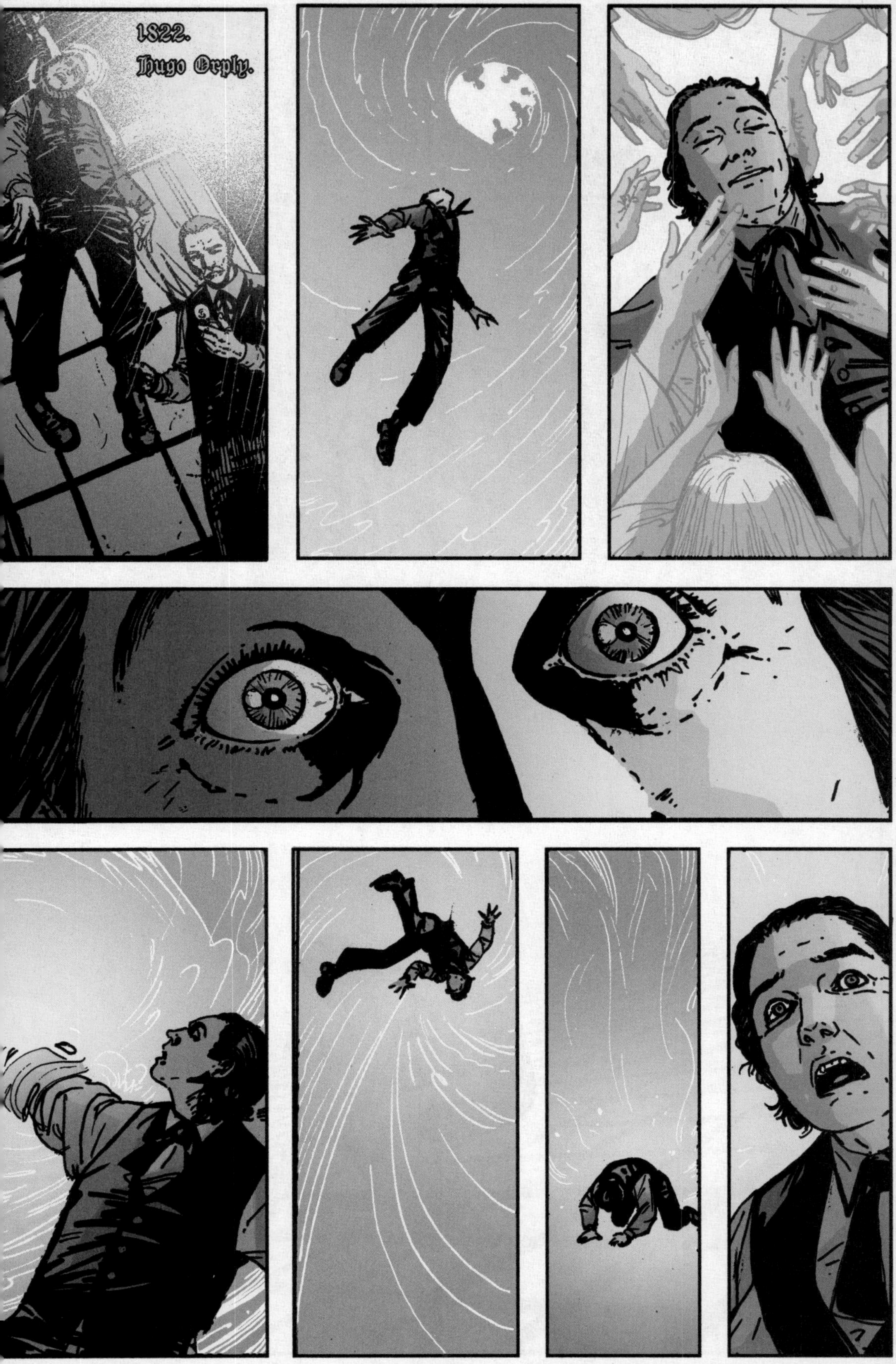
1822.
Hugo Orply.

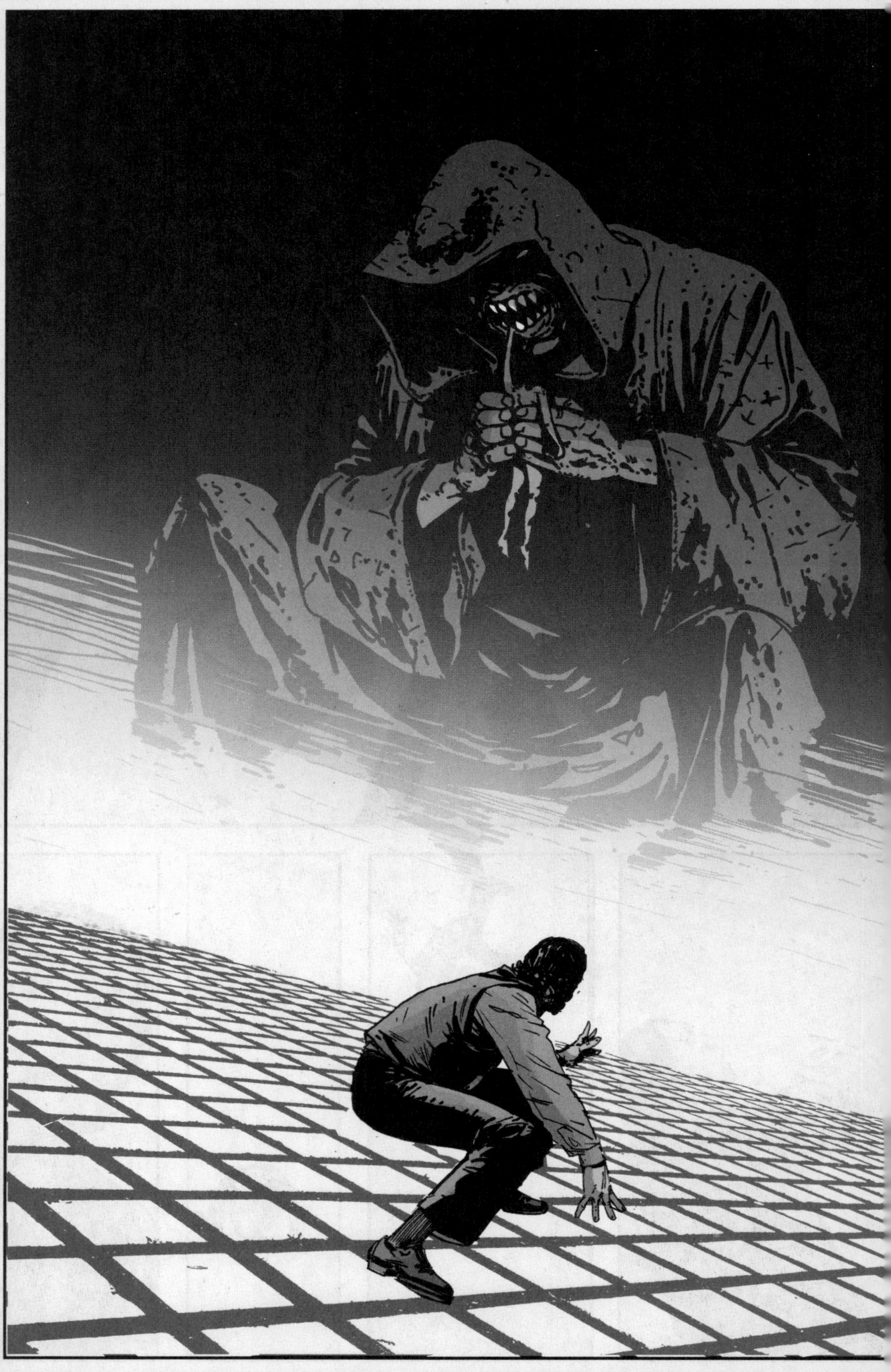

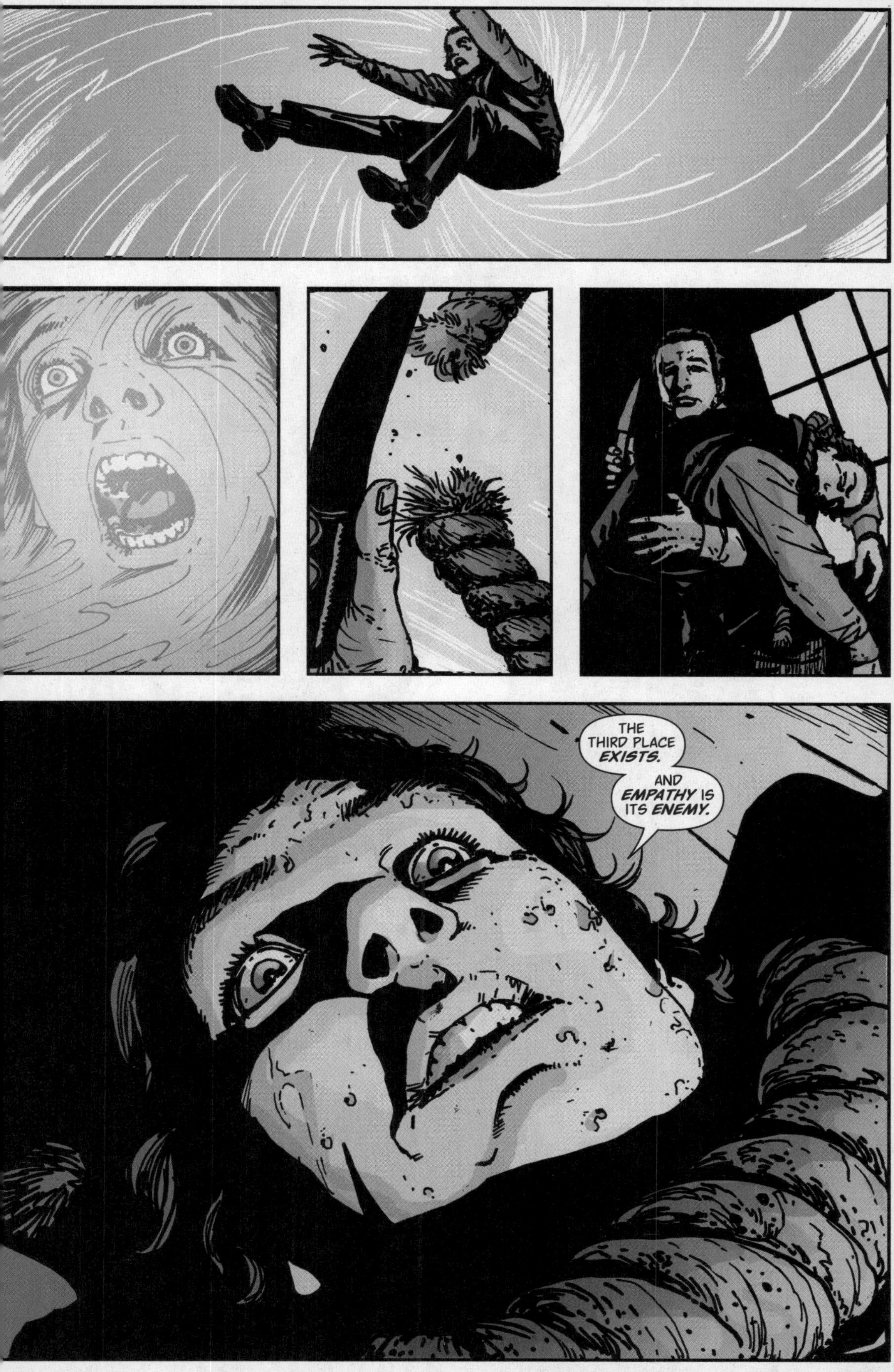
THE THIRD PLACE EXISTS.
AND EMPATHY IS ITS ENEMY.

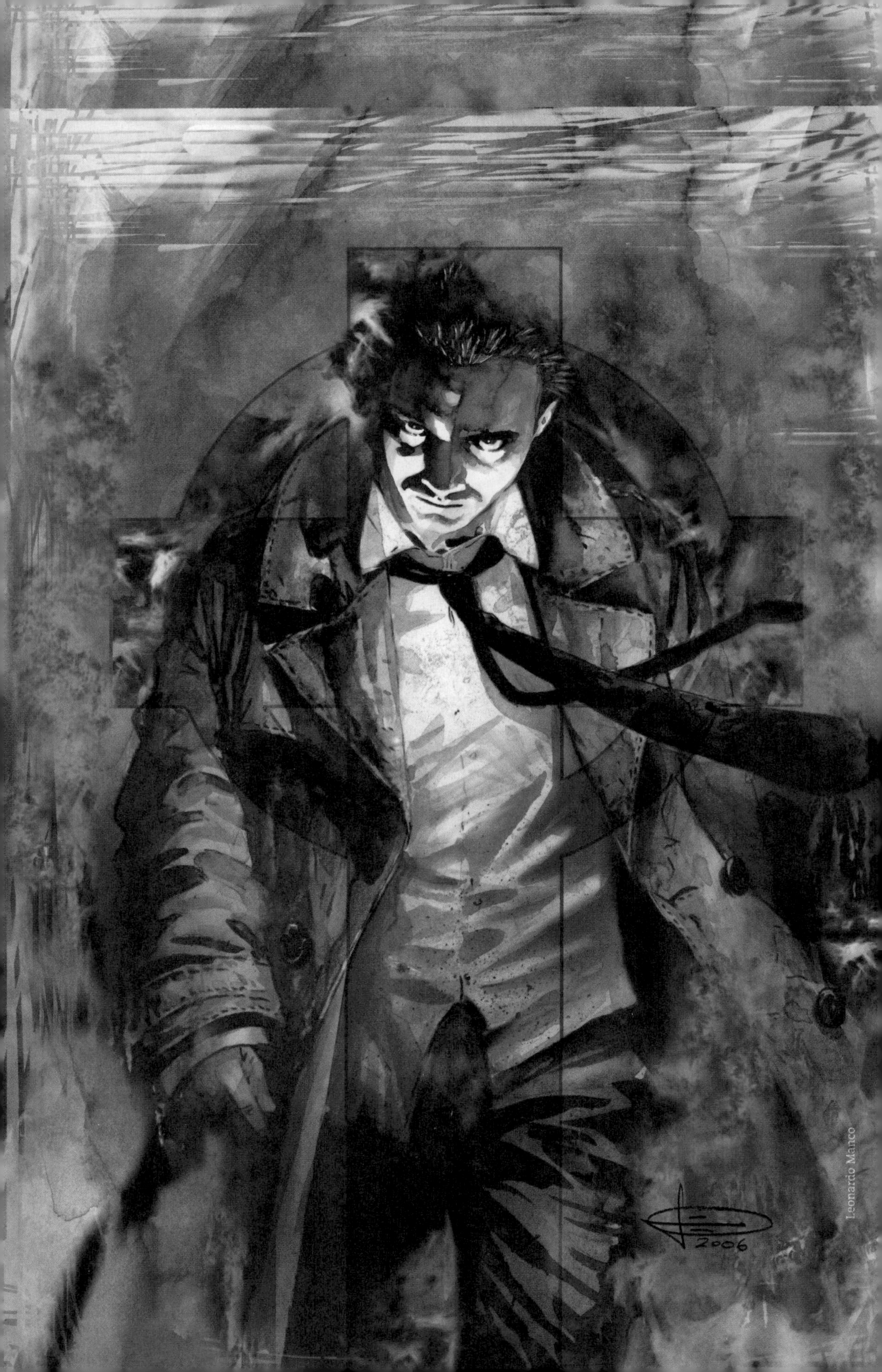
2006
Leonardo Manco

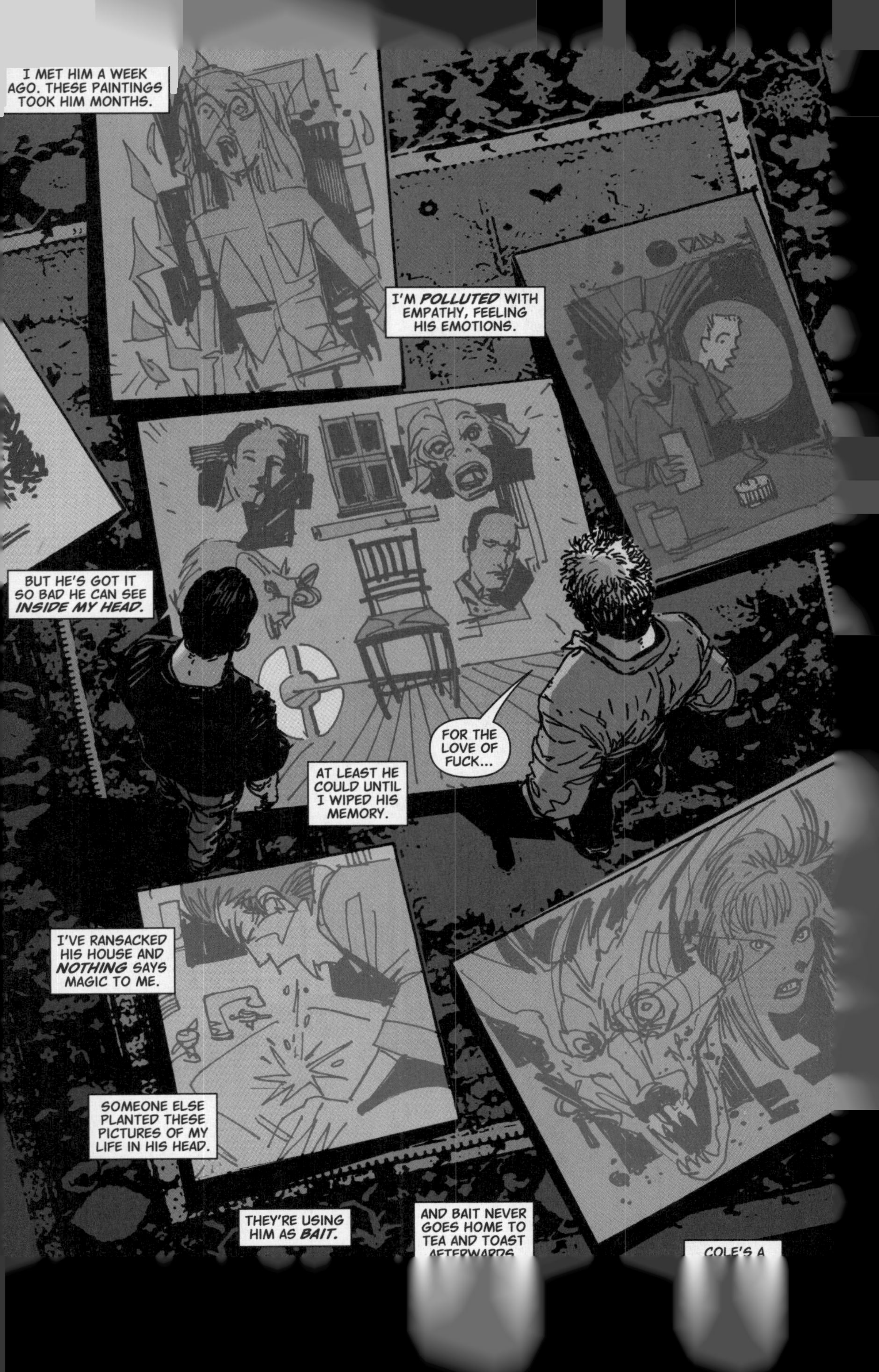
I MET HIM A WEEK AGO. THESE PAINTINGS TOOK HIM MONTHS.
I'M POLLUTED WITH EMPATHY, FEELING HIS EMOTIONS.
BUT HE'S GOT IT SO BAD HE CAN SEE INSIDE MY HEAD.
FOR THE LOVE OF FUCK...
AT LEAST HE COULD UNTIL I WIPED HIS MEMORY.
I'VE RANSACKED HIS HOUSE AND NOTHING SAYS MAGIC TO ME.
SOMEONE ELSE PLANTED THESE PICTURES OF MY LIFE IN HIS HEAD.
THEY'RE USING HIM AS BAIT.
AND BAIT NEVER GOES HOME TO TEA AND TOAST
COLE'S A

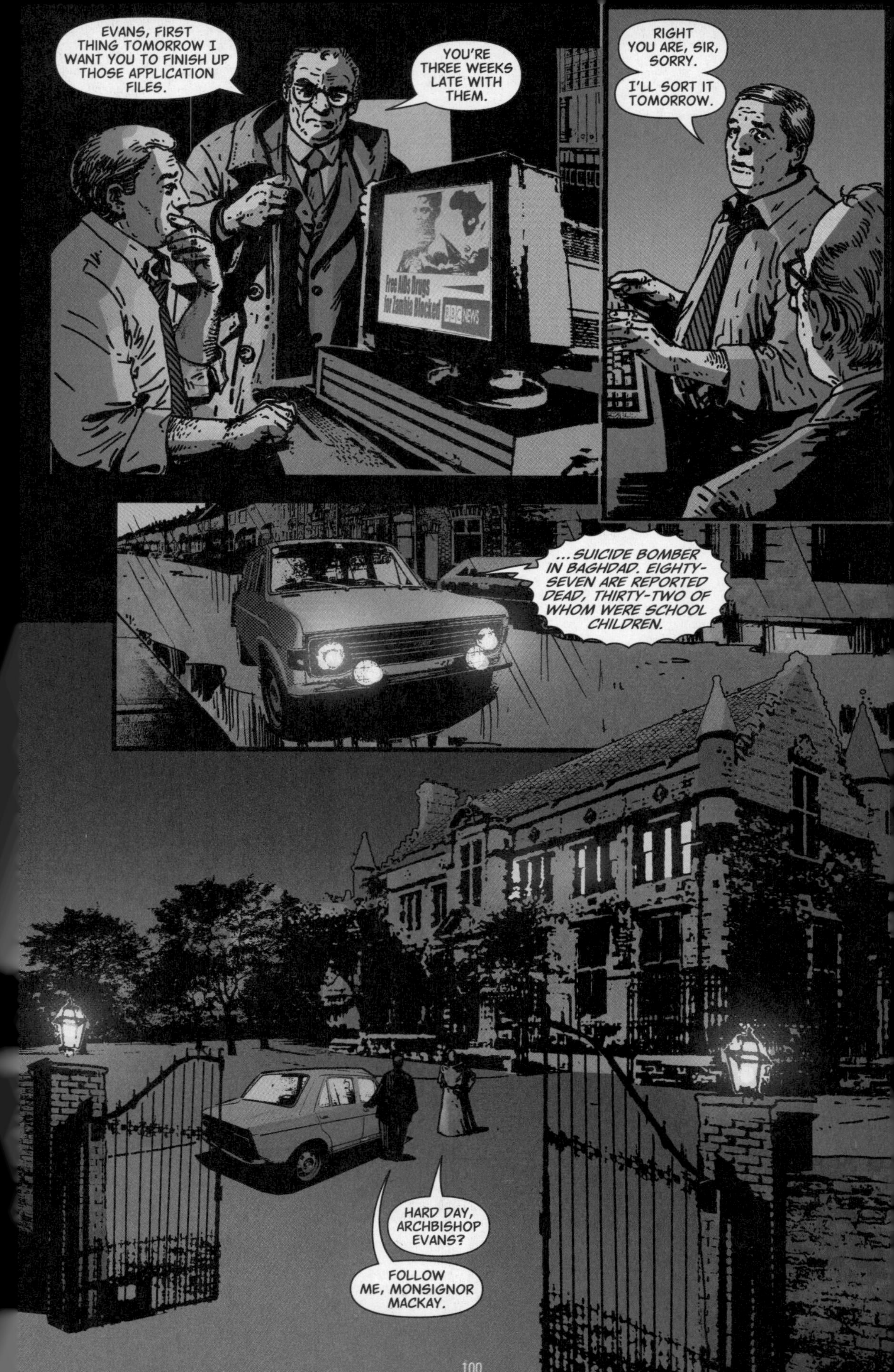
EVANS, FIRST THING TOMORROW I WANT YOU TO FINISH UP THOSE APPLICATION FILES.
YOU'RE THREE WEEKS LATE WITH THEM.
Free AIDs Drugs for Zambia Blocked
BBC NEWS
RIGHT YOU ARE, SIR, SORRY.
I'LL SORT IT TOMORROW.
...SUICIDE BOMBER IN BAGHDAD. EIGHTY-SEVEN ARE REPORTED DEAD, THIRTY-TWO OF WHOM WERE SCHOOL CHILDREN.
HARD DAY, ARCHBISHOP EVANS?
FOLLOW ME, MONSIGNOR MACKAY.

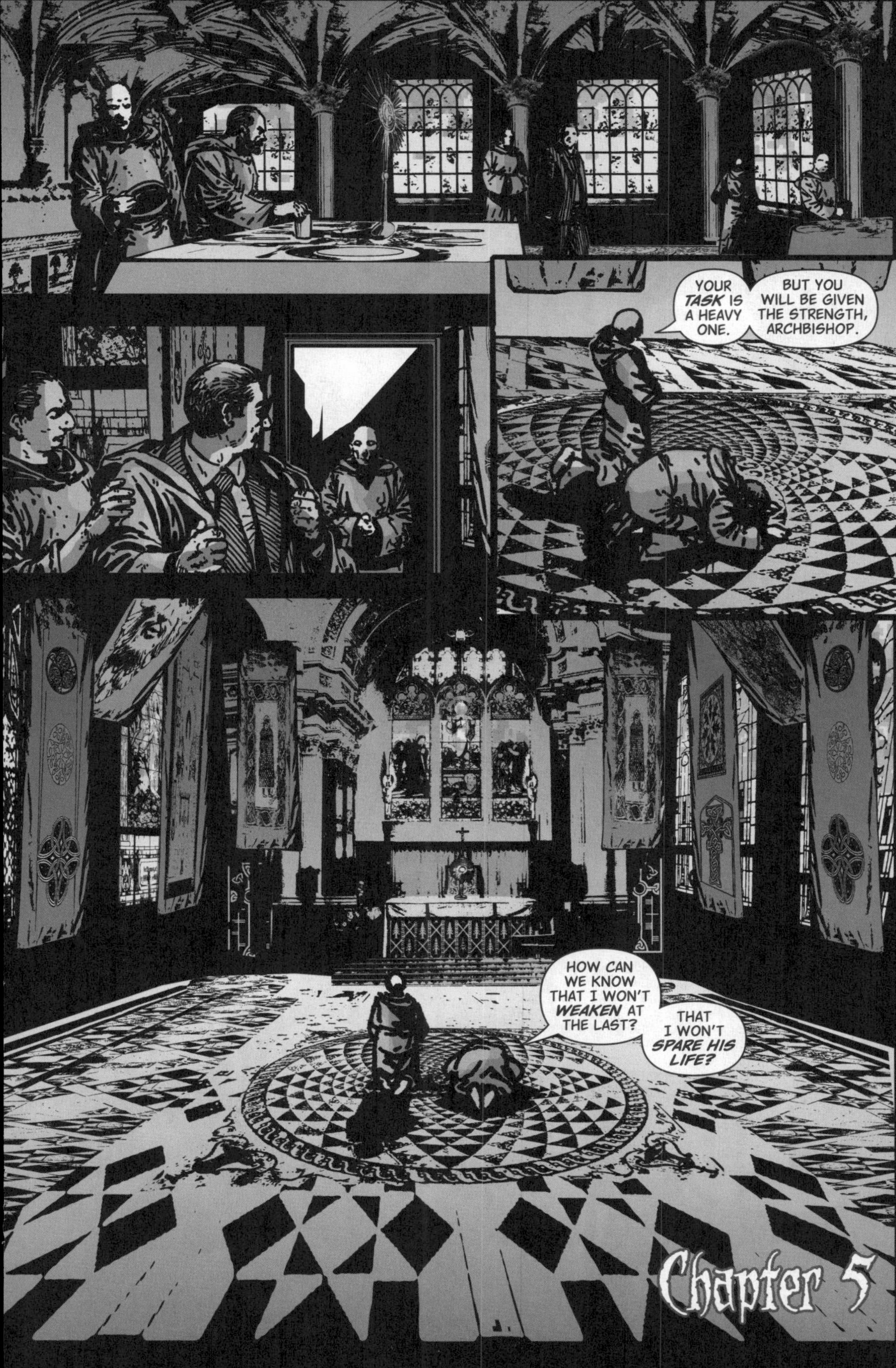
YOUR TASK IS A HEAVY ONE.
BUT YOU WILL BE GIVEN THE STRENGTH, ARCHBISHOP.
HOW CAN WE KNOW THAT I WON'T WEAKEN AT THE LAST?
THAT I WON'T SPARE HIS LIFE?
Chapter 5

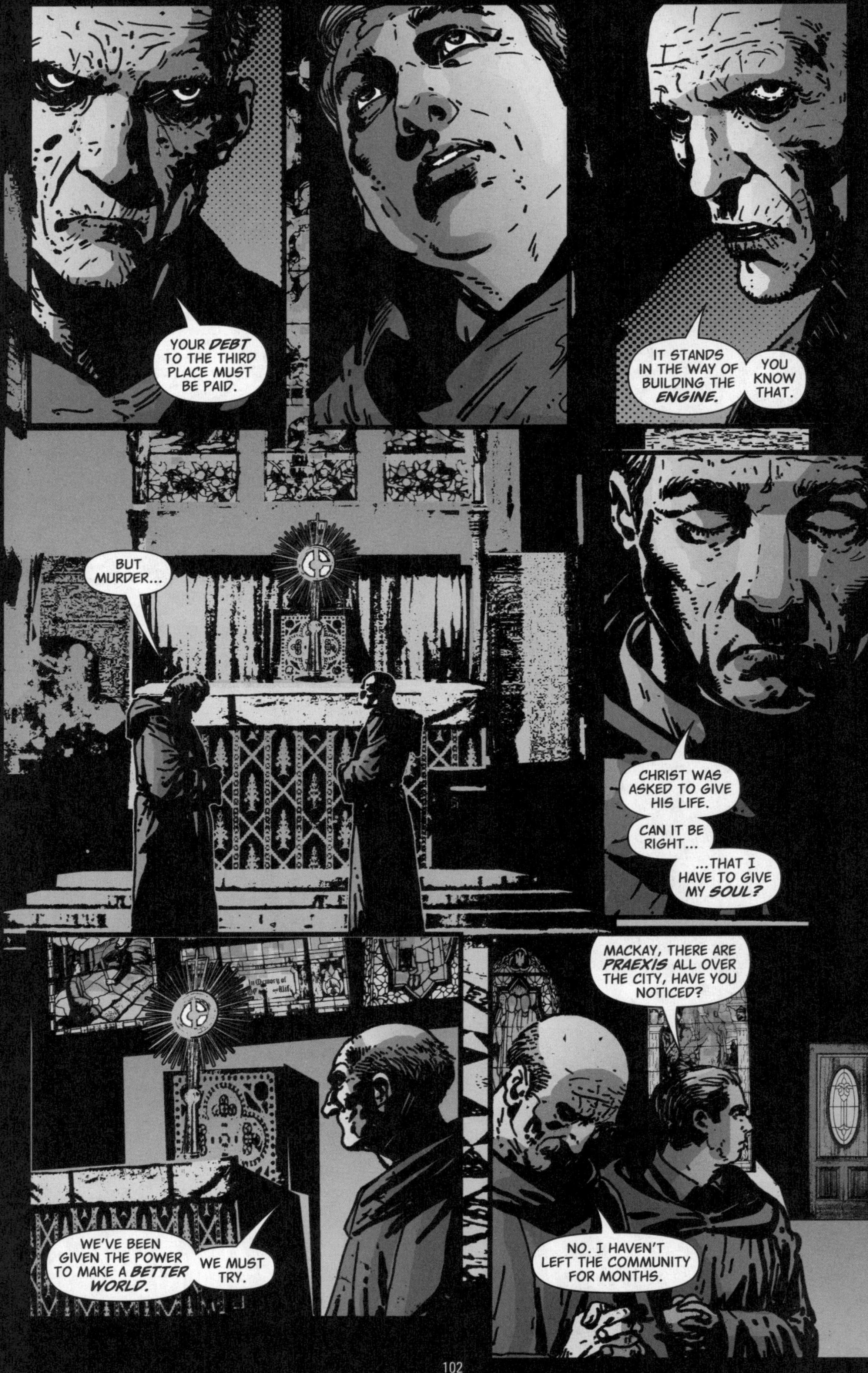
YOUR DEBT TO THE THIRD PLACE MUST BE PAID.
IT STANDS IN THE WAY OF BUILDING THE ENGINE.
YOU KNOW THAT.
BUT MURDER...
CHRIST WAS ASKED TO GIVE HIS LIFE.
CAN IT BE RIGHT...
...THAT I HAVE TO GIVE MY SOUL?
In Memory of
WE'VE BEEN GIVEN THE POWER TO MAKE A BETTER WORLD.
WE MUST TRY.
MACKAY, THERE ARE PRAEXIS ALL OVER THE CITY, HAVE YOU NOTICED?
NO. I HAVEN'T LEFT THE COMMUNITY FOR MONTHS.

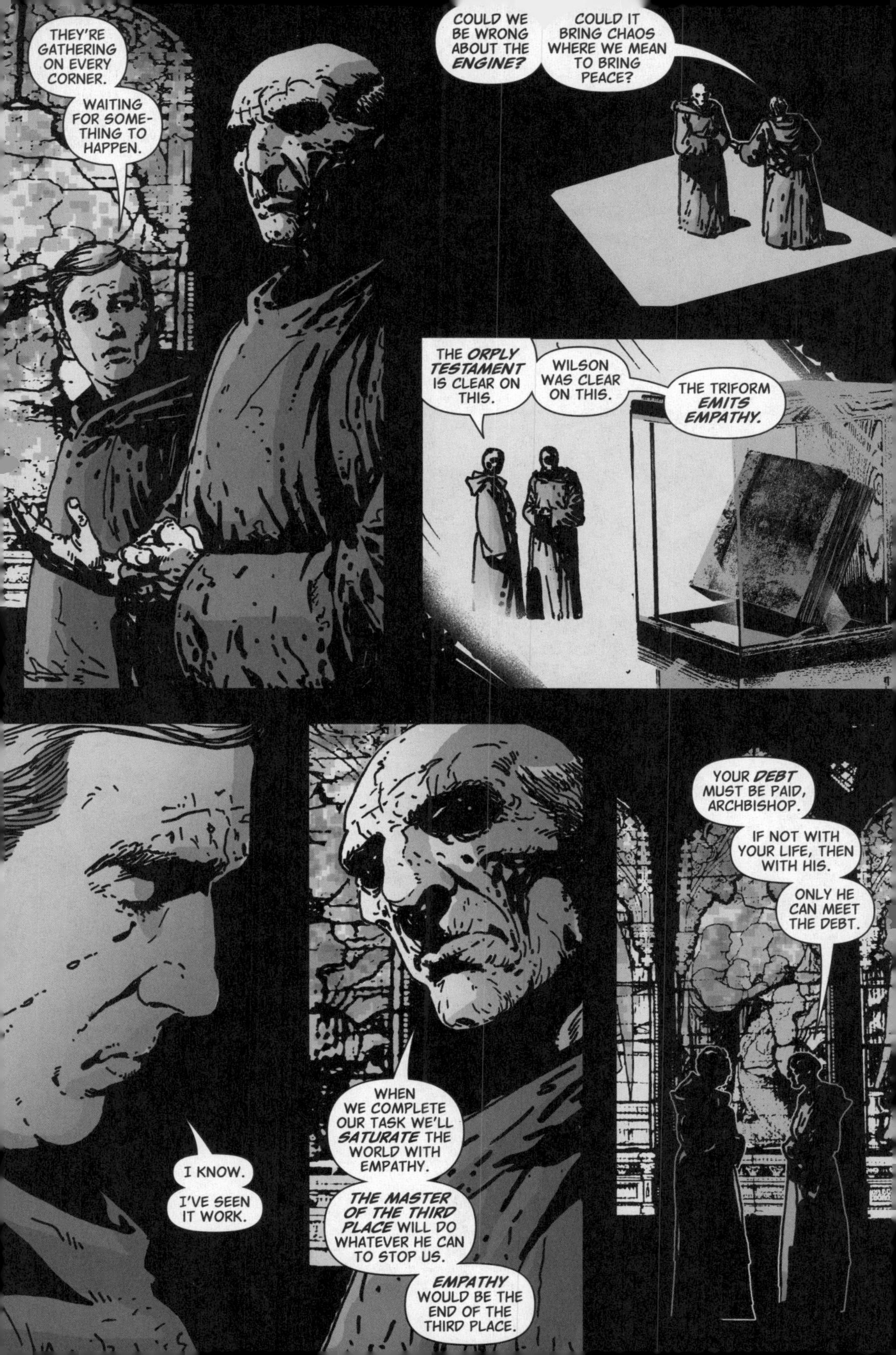

THEY'RE GATHERING ON EVERY CORNER.
WAITING FOR SOMETHING TO HAPPEN.
COULD WE BE WRONG ABOUT THE ENGINE?
COULD IT BRING CHAOS WHERE WE MEAN TO BRING PEACE?
THE ORPLY TESTAMENT IS CLEAR ON THIS.
WILSON WAS CLEAR ON THIS.
THE TRIFORM EMITS EMPATHY.
I KNOW.
I'VE SEEN IT WORK.
WHEN WE COMPLETE OUR TASK WE'LL SATURATE THE WORLD WITH EMPATHY.
THE MASTER OF THE THIRD PLACE WILL DO WHATEVER HE CAN TO STOP US.
EMPATHY WOULD BE THE END OF THE THIRD PLACE.
YOUR DEBT MUST BE PAID, ARCHBISHOP.
IF NOT WITH YOUR LIFE, THEN WITH HIS.
ONLY HE CAN MEET THE DEBT.

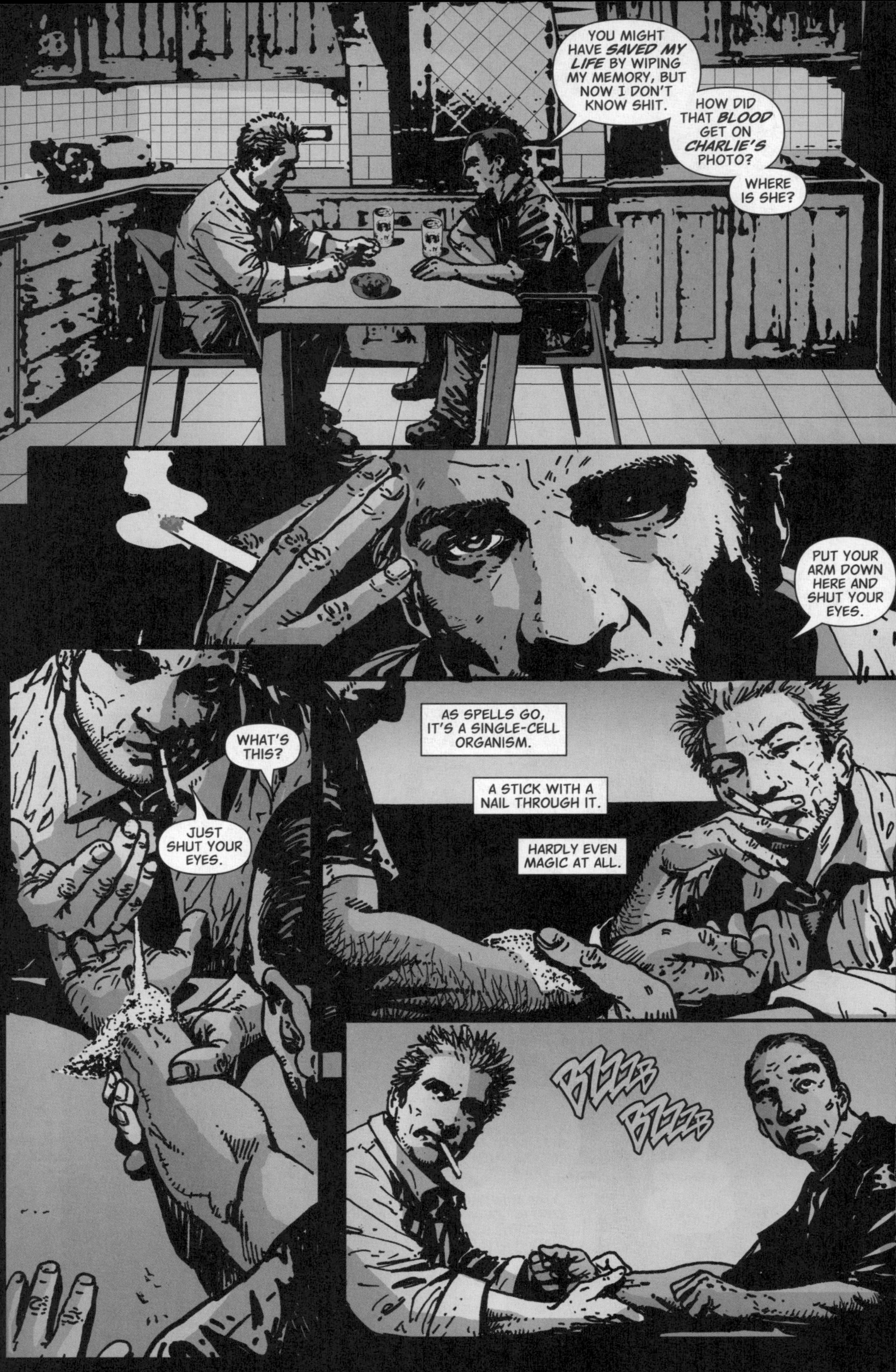
YOU MIGHT HAVE SAVED MY LIFE BY WIPING MY MEMORY, BUT NOW I DON'T KNOW SHIT.
HOW DID THAT BLOOD GET ON CHARLIE'S PHOTO?
WHERE IS SHE?
PUT YOUR ARM DOWN HERE AND SHUT YOUR EYES.
WHAT'S THIS?
JUST SHUT YOUR EYES.
AS SPELLS GO, IT'S A SINGLE-CELL ORGANISM.
A STICK WITH A NAIL THROUGH IT.
HARDLY EVEN MAGIC AT ALL.
BZZZB
BZZZB

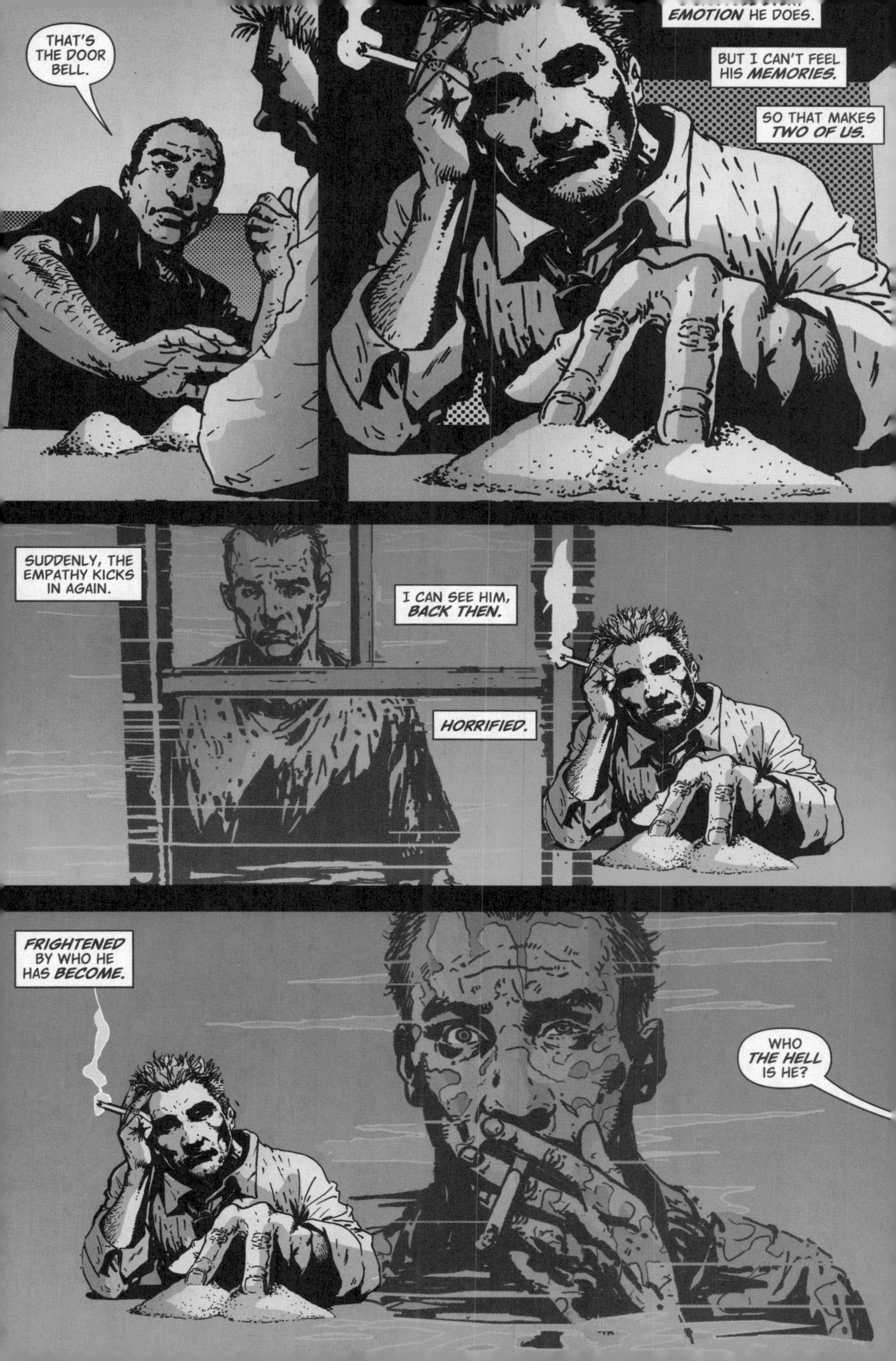

THAT'S THE DOOR BELL.
EMOTION HE DOES.
BUT I CAN'T FEEL HIS MEMORIES.
SO THAT MAKES TWO OF US.
SUDDENLY, THE EMPATHY KICKS IN AGAIN.
I CAN SEE HIM, BACK THEN.
HORRIFIED.
FRIGHTENED BY WHO HE HAS BECOME.
WHO THE HELL IS HE?

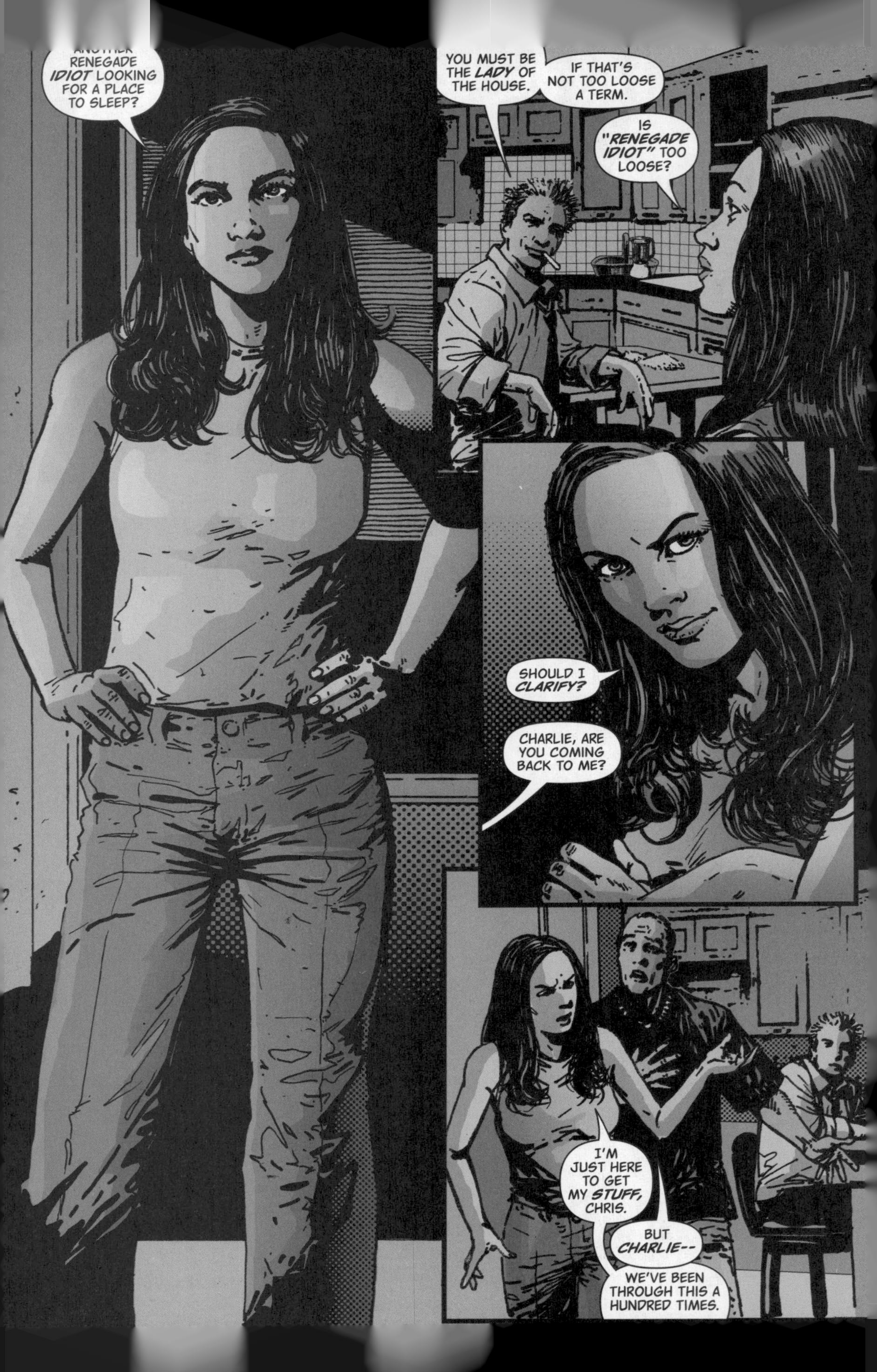

ANOTHER RENEGADE IDIOT LOOKING FOR A PLACE TO SLEEP?
YOU MUST BE THE LADY OF THE HOUSE.
IF THAT'S NOT TOO LOOSE A TERM.
IS "RENEGADE IDIOT" TOO LOOSE?
SHOULD I CLARIFY?
CHARLIE, ARE YOU COMING BACK TO ME?
I'M JUST HERE TO GET MY STUFF, CHRIS.
BUT CHARLIE--
WE'VE BEEN THROUGH THIS A HUNDRED TIMES.

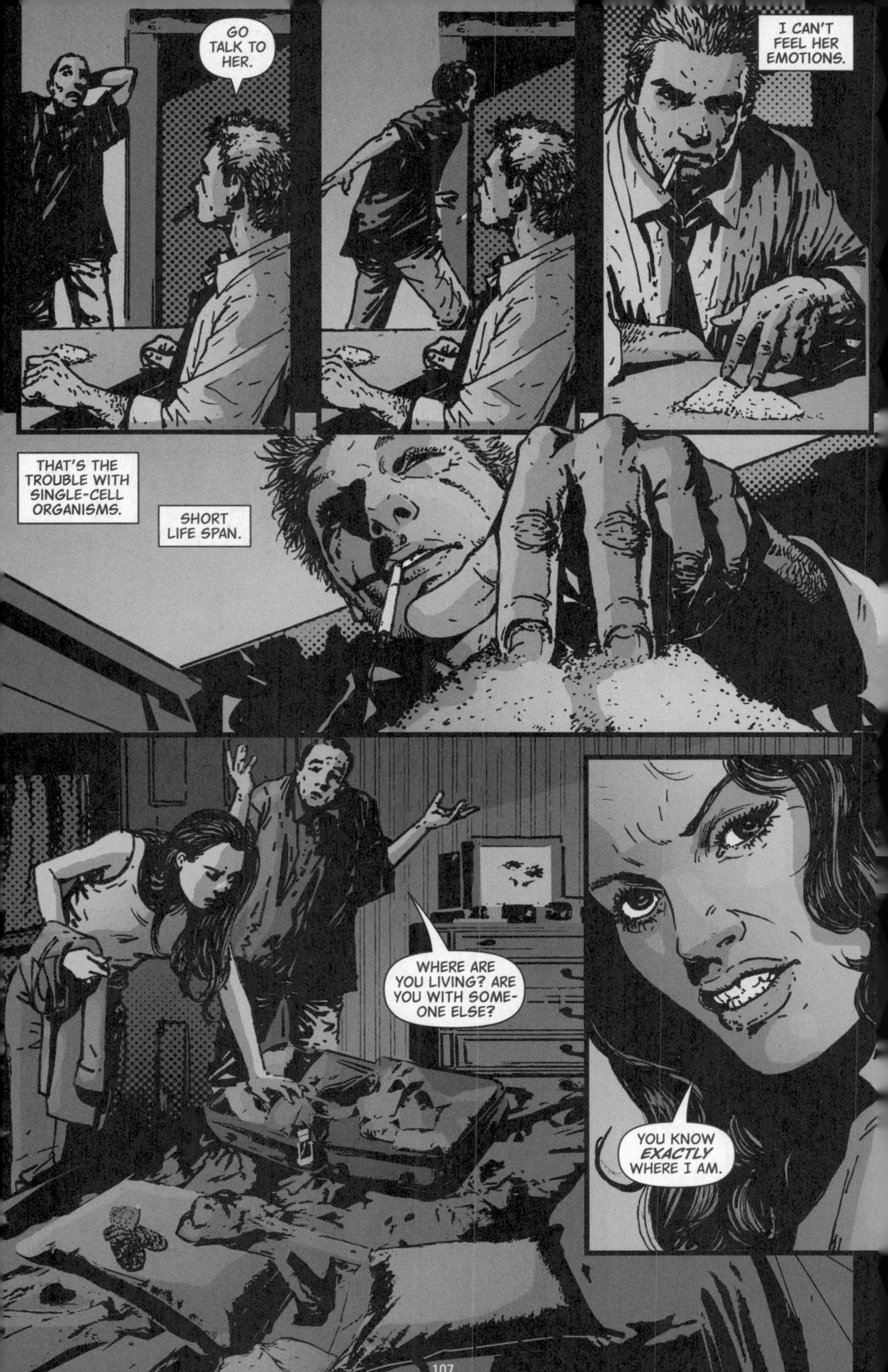
GO TALK TO HER.
I CAN'T FEEL HER EMOTIONS.
THAT'S THE TROUBLE WITH SINGLE-CELL ORGANISMS.
SHORT LIFE SPAN.
WHERE ARE YOU LIVING? ARE YOU WITH SOME-ONE ELSE?
YOU KNOW EXACTLY WHERE I AM.

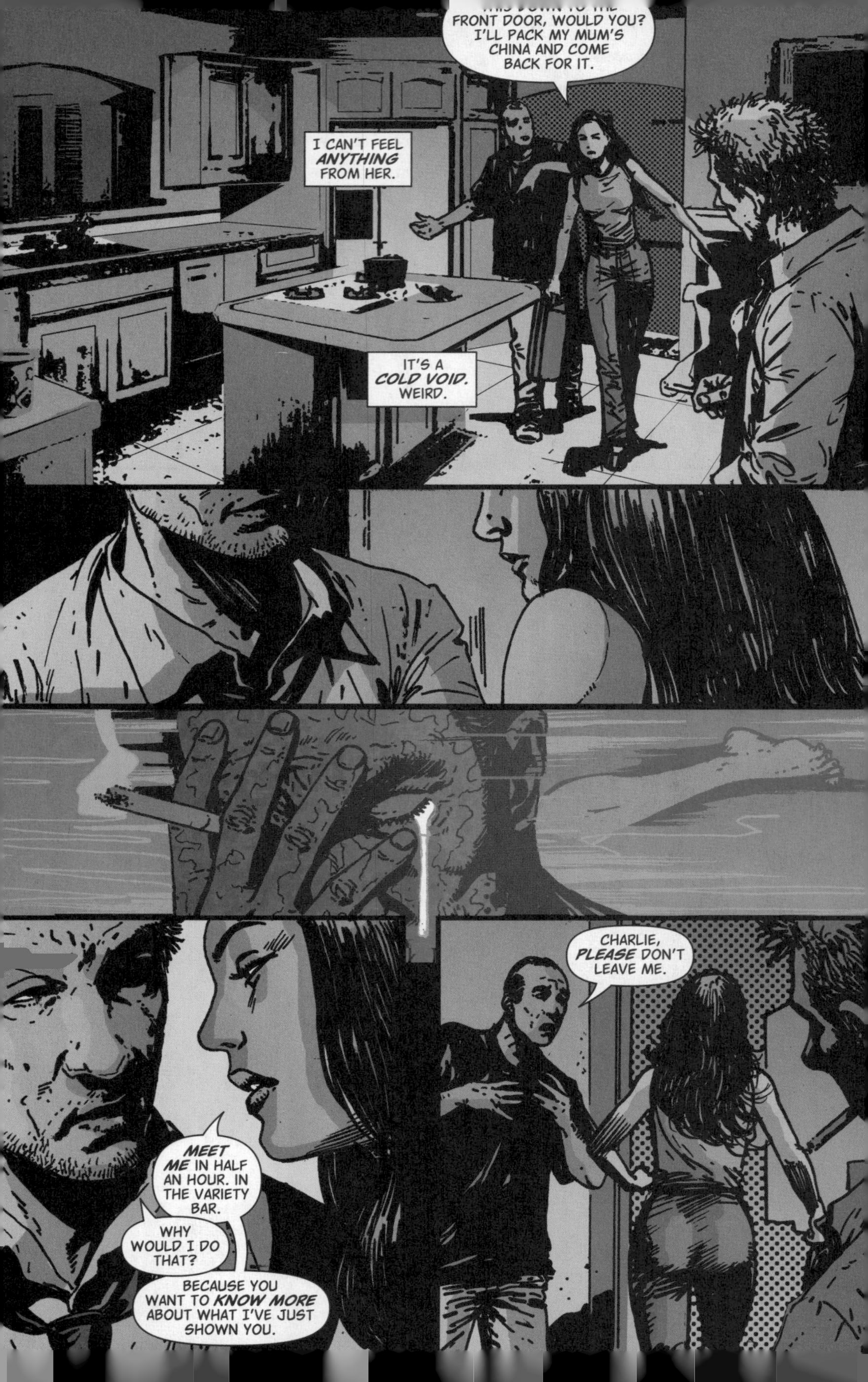
FRONT DOOR, WOULD YOU? I'LL PACK MY MUM'S CHINA AND COME BACK FOR IT.
I CAN'T FEEL ANYTHING FROM HER.
IT'S A COLD VOID. WEIRD.
CHARLIE, PLEASE DON'T LEAVE ME.
MEET ME IN HALF AN HOUR. IN THE VARIETY BAR.
WHY WOULD I DO THAT?
BECAUSE YOU WANT TO KNOW MORE ABOUT WHAT I'VE JUST SHOWN YOU.

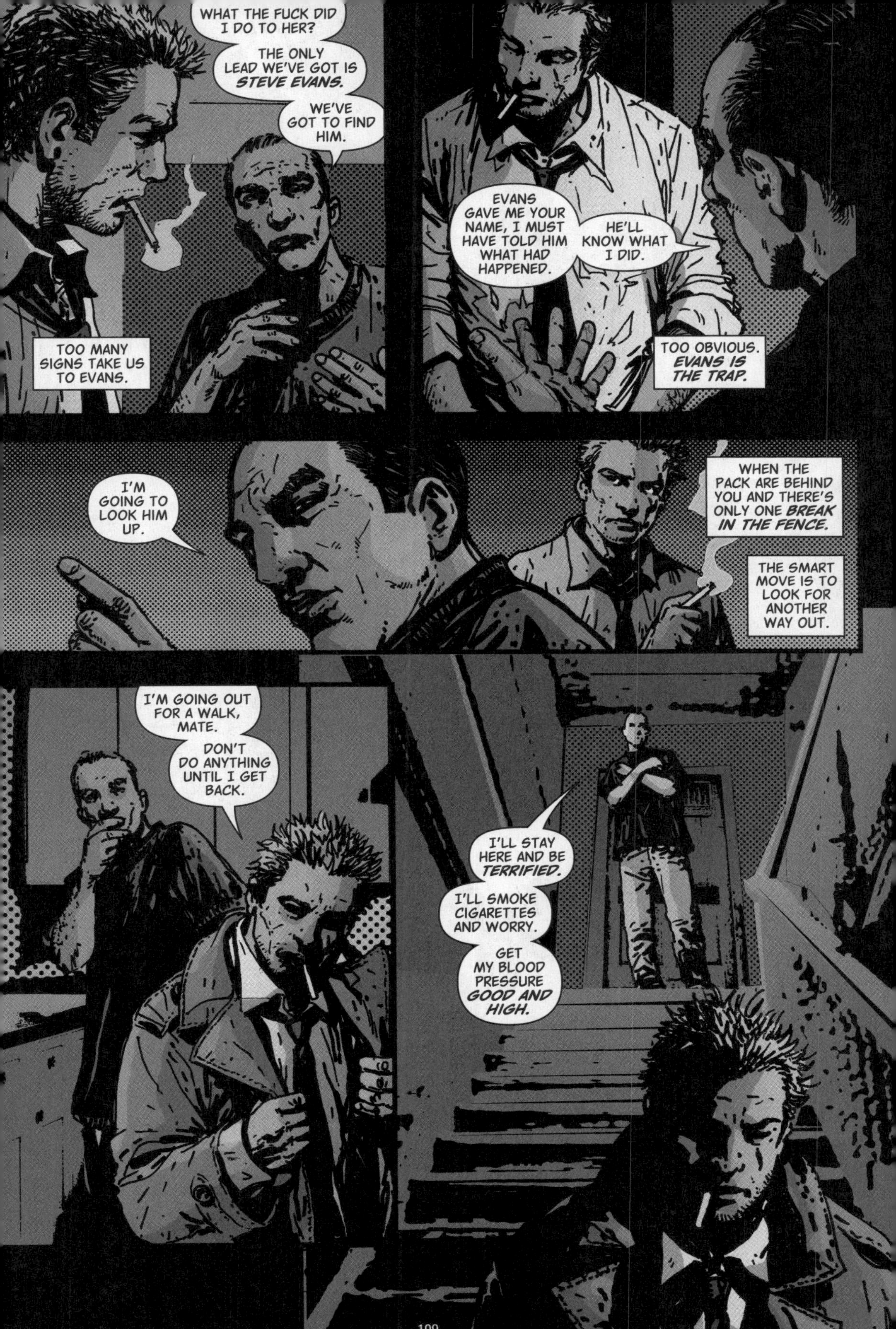
WHAT THE FUCK DID I DO TO HER?
THE ONLY LEAD WE'VE GOT IS *STEVE EVANS.*
WE'VE GOT TO FIND HIM.
TOO MANY SIGNS TAKE US TO EVANS.
EVANS GAVE ME YOUR NAME, I MUST HAVE TOLD HIM WHAT HAD HAPPENED.
HE'LL KNOW WHAT I DID.
TOO OBVIOUS. *EVANS IS THE TRAP.*
I'M GOING TO LOOK HIM UP.
WHEN THE PACK ARE BEHIND YOU AND THERE'S ONLY ONE *BREAK IN THE FENCE.*
THE SMART MOVE IS TO LOOK FOR ANOTHER WAY OUT.
I'M GOING OUT FOR A WALK, MATE.
DON'T DO ANYTHING UNTIL I GET BACK.
I'LL STAY HERE AND BE *TERRIFIED.*
I'LL SMOKE CIGARETTES AND WORRY.
GET MY BLOOD PRESSURE *GOOD AND HIGH.*

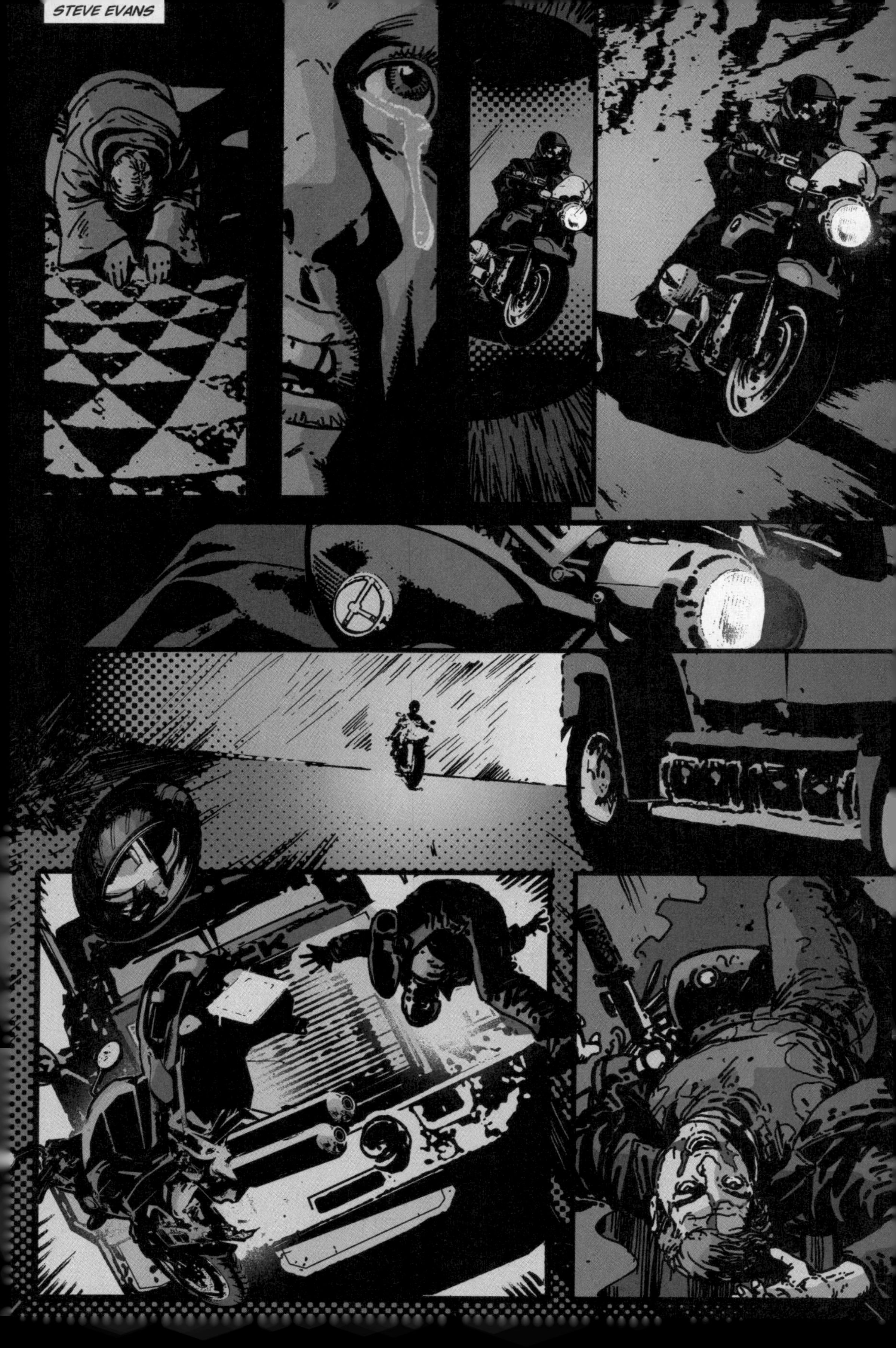
STEVE EVANS

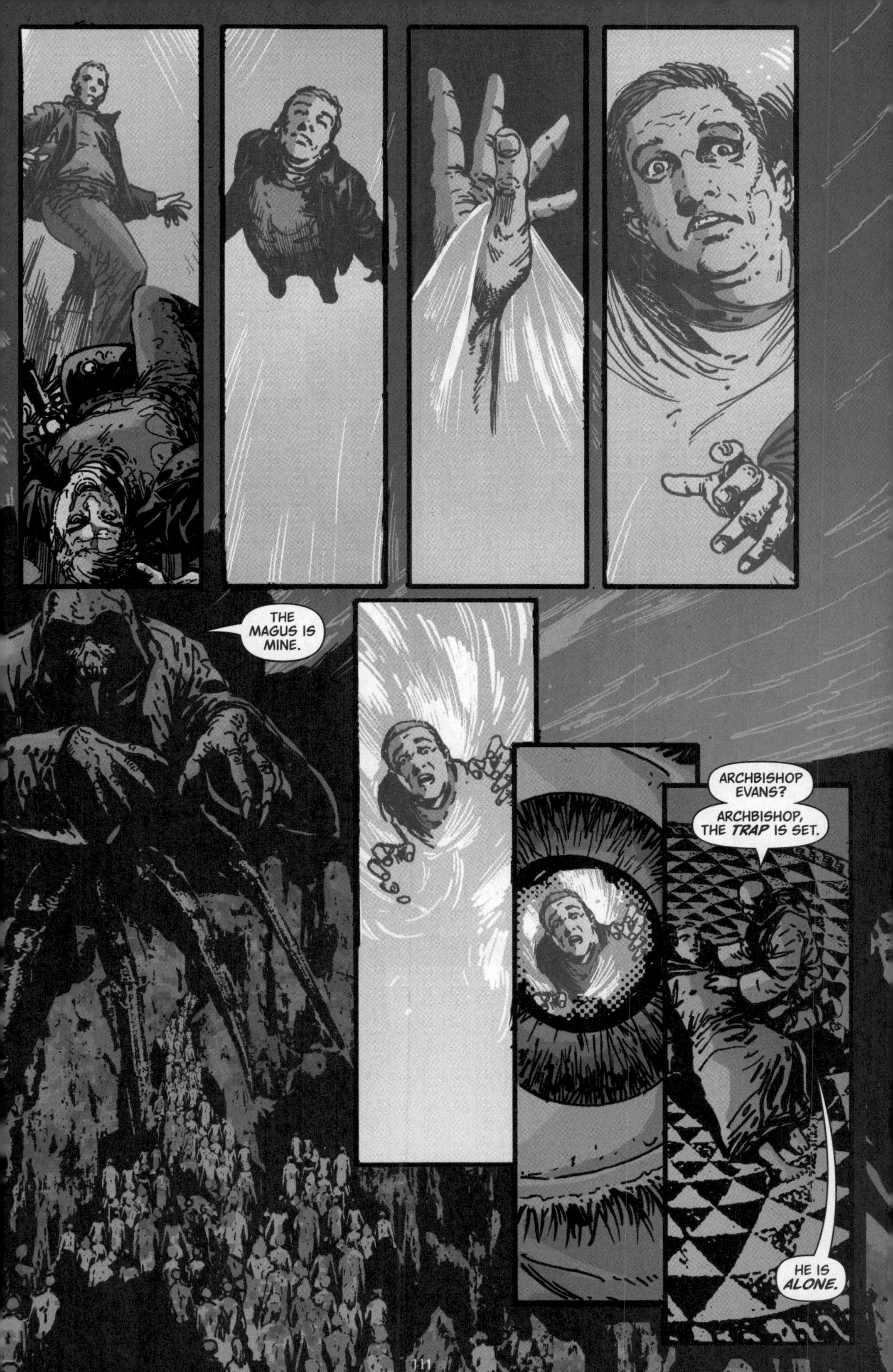
THE MAGUS IS MINE.
ARCHBISHOP EVANS?
ARCHBISHOP, THE *TRAP* IS SET.
HE IS *ALONE.*

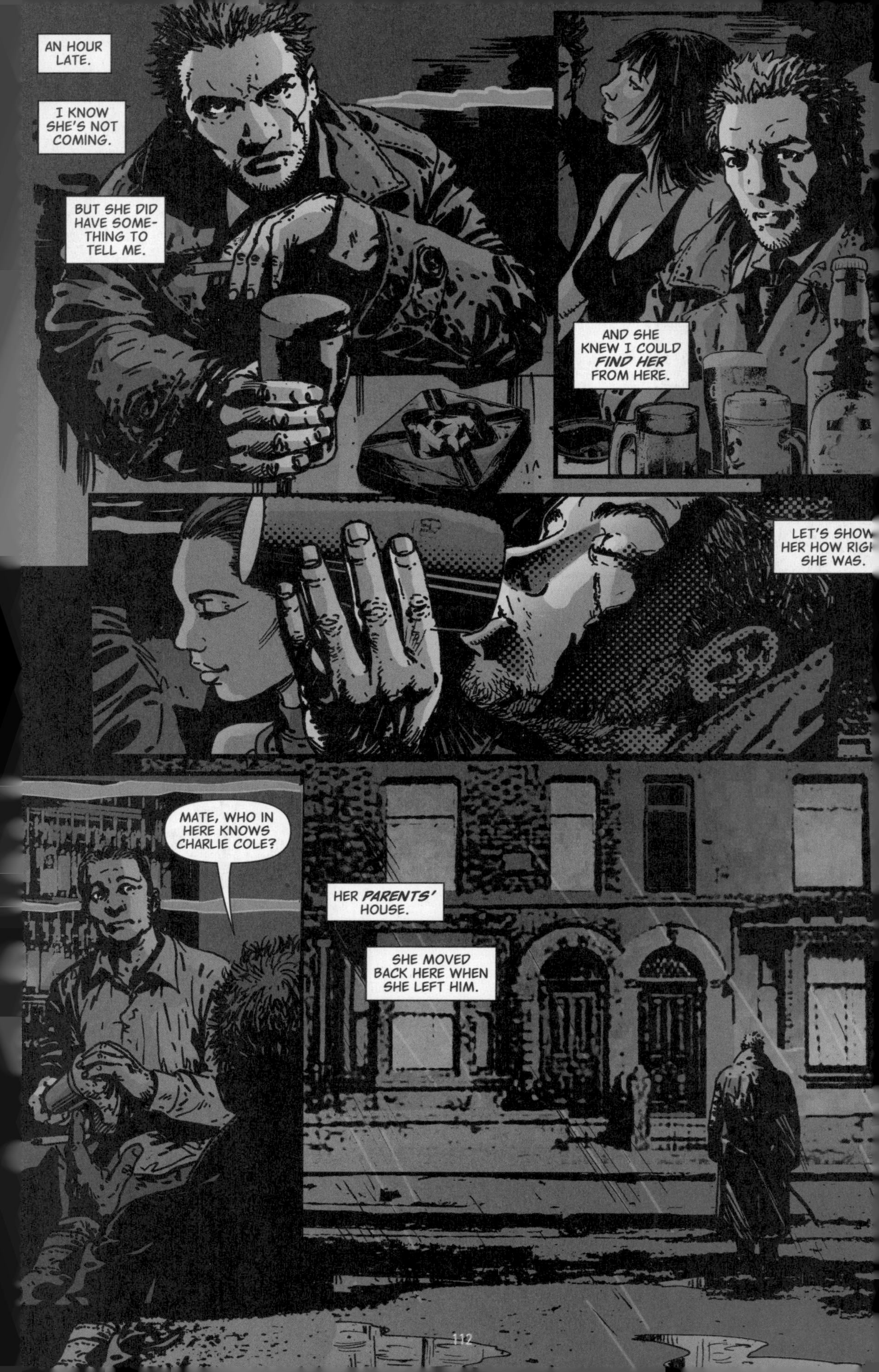
AN HOUR LATE.
I KNOW SHE'S NOT COMING.
BUT SHE DID HAVE SOME-THING TO TELL ME.
AND SHE KNEW I COULD *FIND HER* FROM HERE.
MATE, WHO IN HERE KNOWS CHARLIE COLE?
HER *PARENTS'* HOUSE.
SHE MOVED BACK HERE WHEN SHE LEFT HIM.

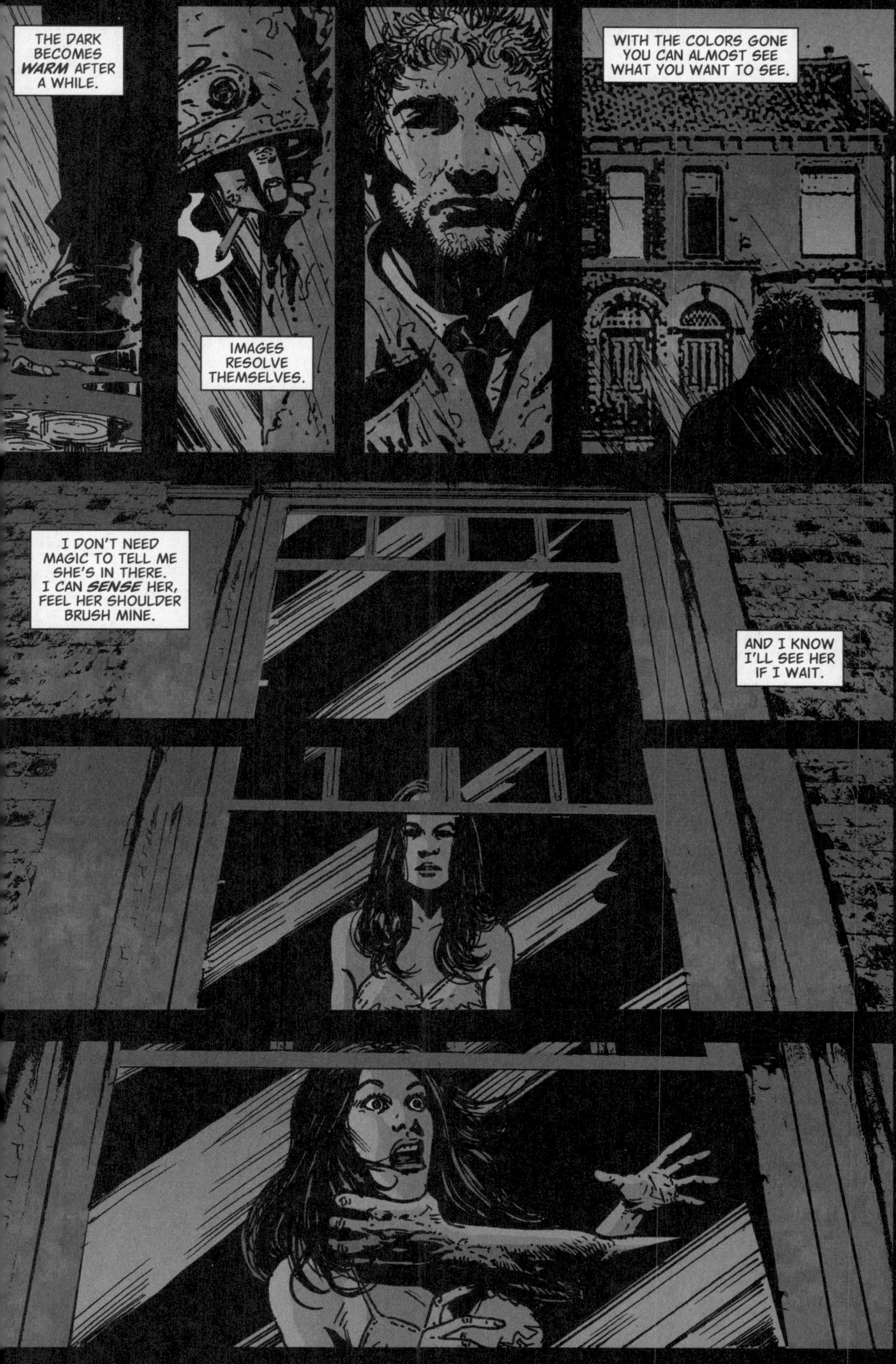
THE DARK BECOMES *WARM* AFTER A WHILE.
IMAGES RESOLVE THEMSELVES.
WITH THE COLORS GONE YOU CAN ALMOST SEE WHAT YOU WANT TO SEE.
I DON'T NEED MAGIC TO TELL ME SHE'S IN THERE. I CAN *SENSE* HER, FEEL HER SHOULDER BRUSH MINE.
AND I KNOW I'LL SEE HER IF I WAIT.

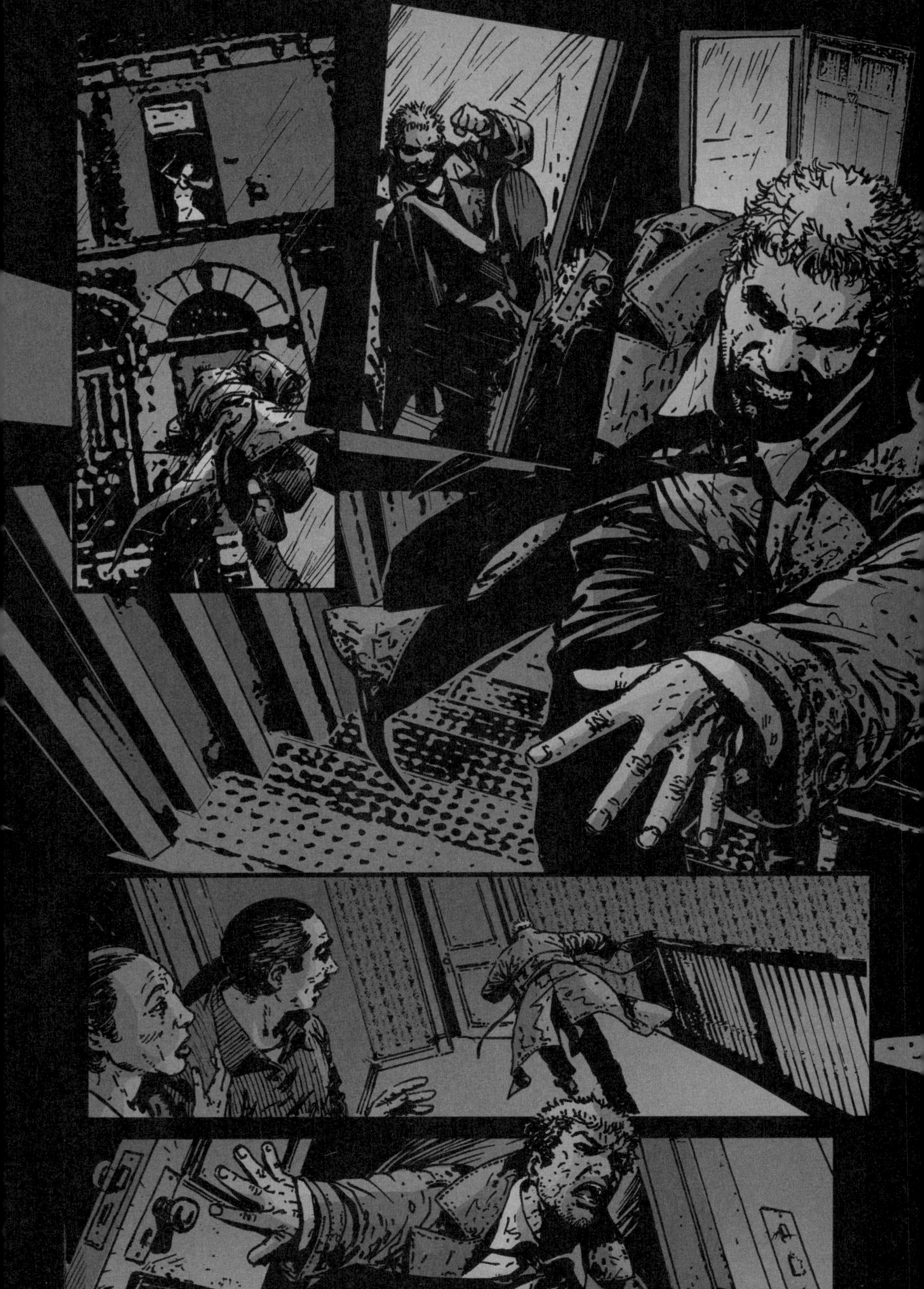

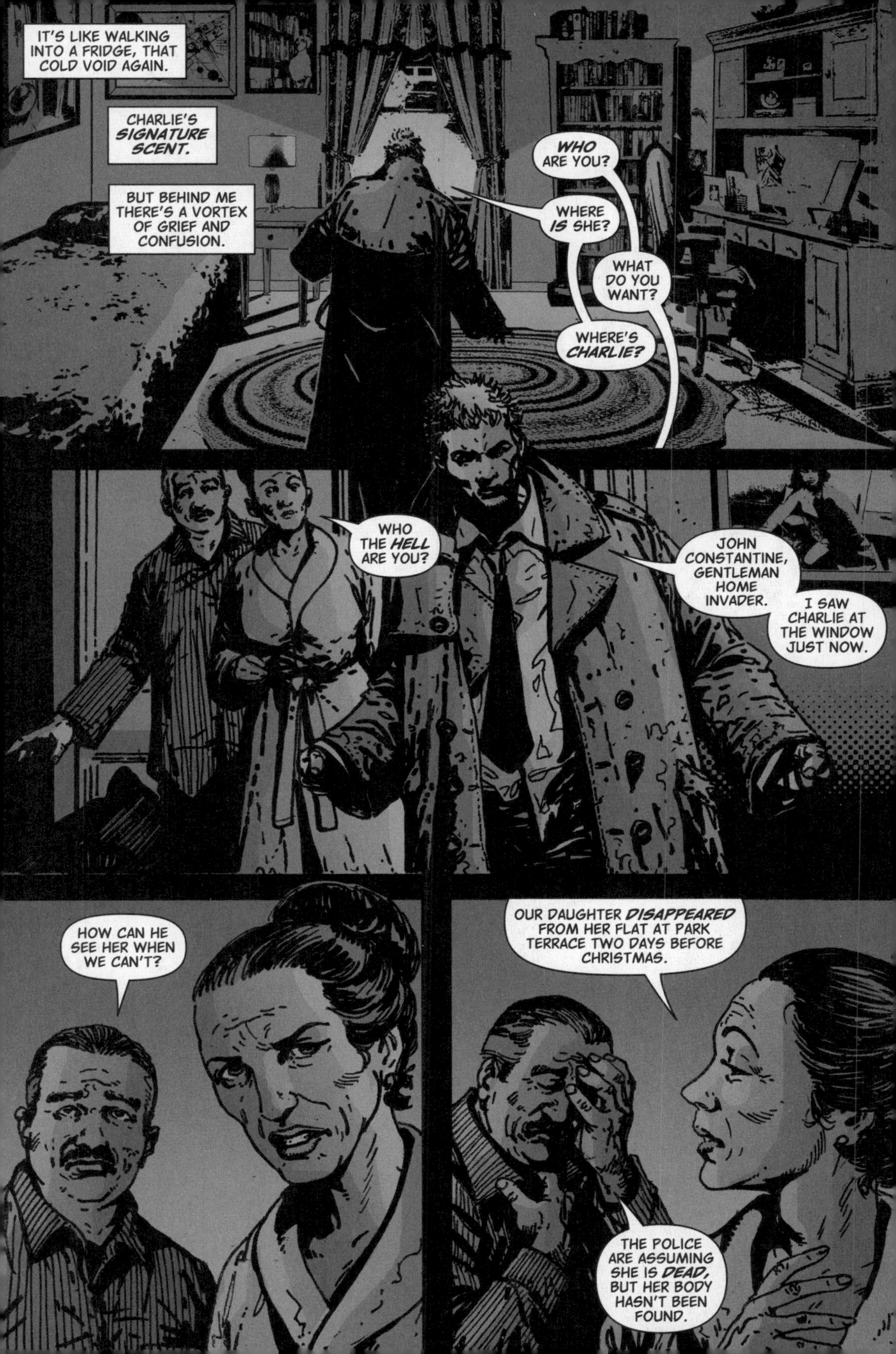
IT'S LIKE WALKING INTO A FRIDGE, THAT COLD VOID AGAIN.
CHARLIE'S *SIGNATURE SCENT.*
BUT BEHIND ME THERE'S A VORTEX OF GRIEF AND CONFUSION.
WHO ARE YOU?
WHERE *IS* SHE?
WHAT DO YOU WANT?
WHERE'S *CHARLIE?*
WHO THE *HELL* ARE YOU?
JOHN CONSTANTINE, GENTLEMAN HOME INVADER.
I SAW CHARLIE AT THE WINDOW JUST NOW.
HOW CAN HE SEE HER WHEN WE CAN'T?
OUR DAUGHTER *DISAPPEARED* FROM HER FLAT AT PARK TERRACE TWO DAYS BEFORE CHRISTMAS.
THE POLICE ARE ASSUMING SHE IS *DEAD,* BUT HER BODY HASN'T BEEN FOUND.

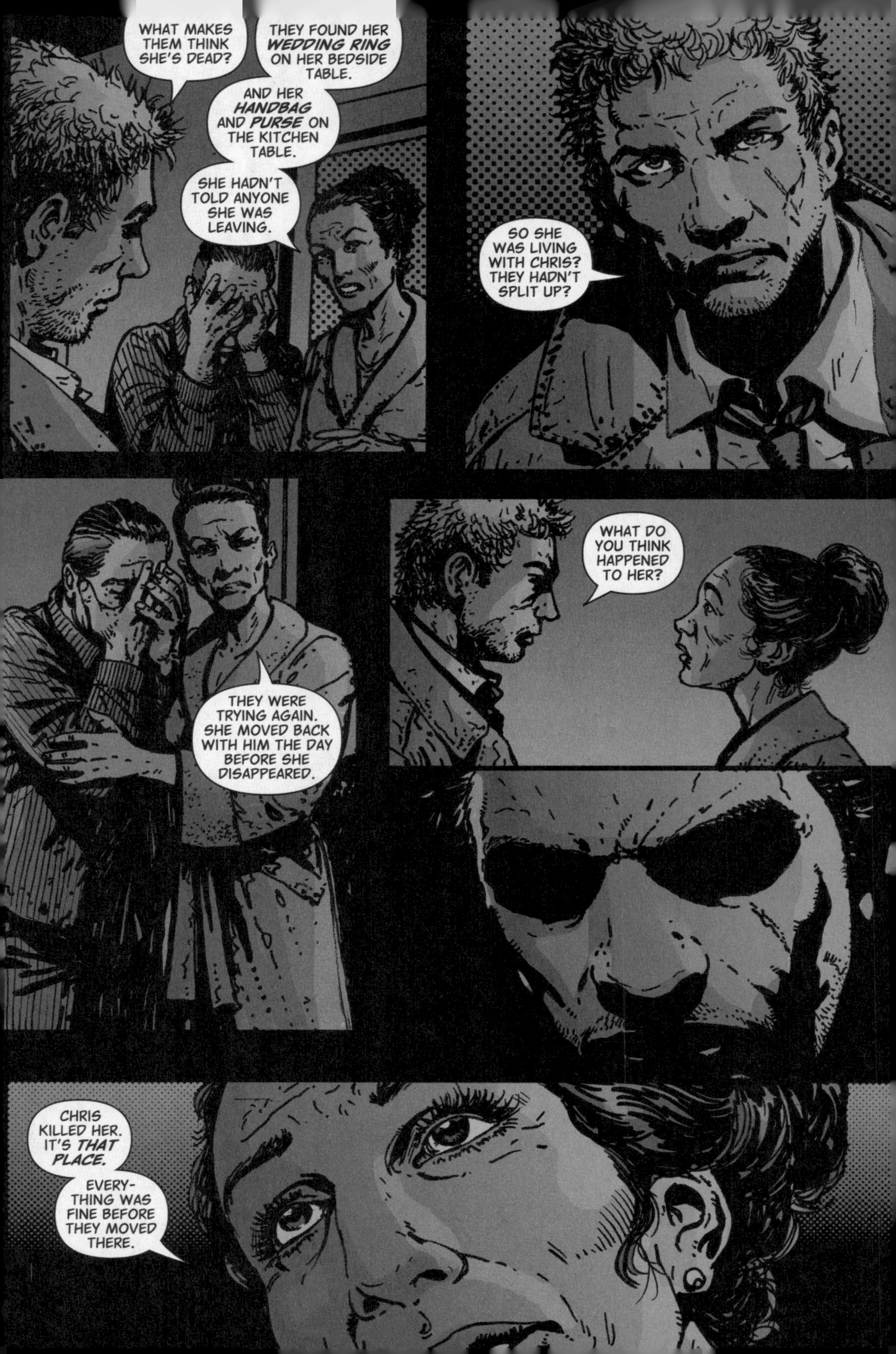
WHAT MAKES THEM THINK SHE'S DEAD?
THEY FOUND HER *WEDDING RING* ON HER BEDSIDE TABLE.
AND HER *HANDBAG* AND *PURSE* ON THE KITCHEN TABLE.
SHE HADN'T TOLD ANYONE SHE WAS LEAVING.
SO SHE WAS LIVING WITH CHRIS? THEY HADN'T SPLIT UP?
THEY WERE TRYING AGAIN. SHE MOVED BACK WITH HIM THE DAY BEFORE SHE DISAPPEARED.
WHAT DO YOU THINK HAPPENED TO HER?
CHRIS KILLED HER. IT'S *THAT PLACE.*
EVERY-THING WAS FINE BEFORE THEY MOVED THERE.

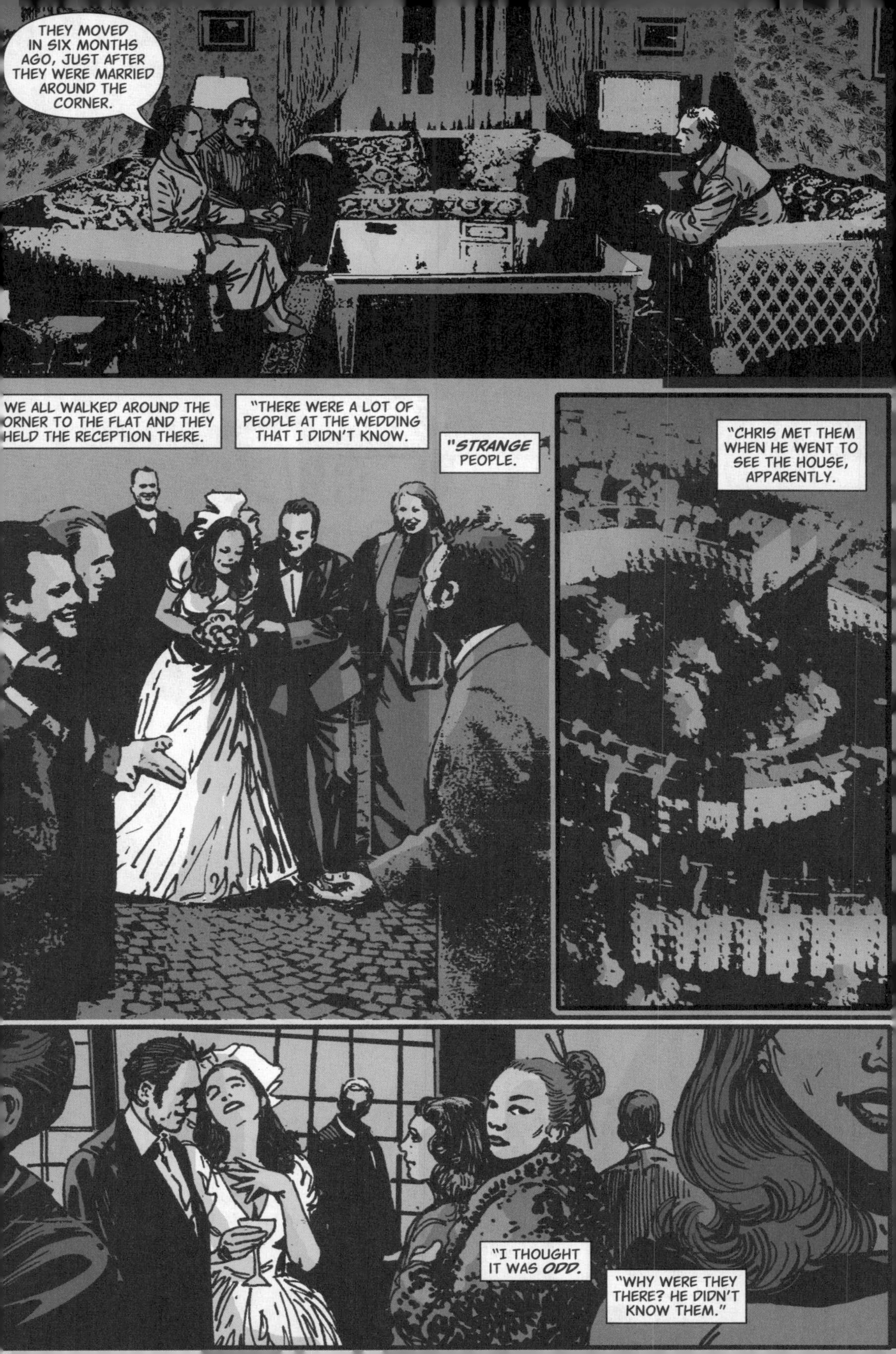
THEY MOVED IN SIX MONTHS AGO, JUST AFTER THEY WERE MARRIED AROUND THE CORNER.
WE ALL WALKED AROUND THE ORNER TO THE FLAT AND THEY HELD THE RECEPTION THERE.
"THERE WERE A LOT OF PEOPLE AT THE WEDDING THAT I DIDN'T KNOW.
"STRANGE PEOPLE.
"CHRIS MET THEM WHEN HE WENT TO SEE THE HOUSE, APPARENTLY.
"I THOUGHT IT WAS ODD.
"WHY WERE THEY THERE? HE DIDN'T KNOW THEM."

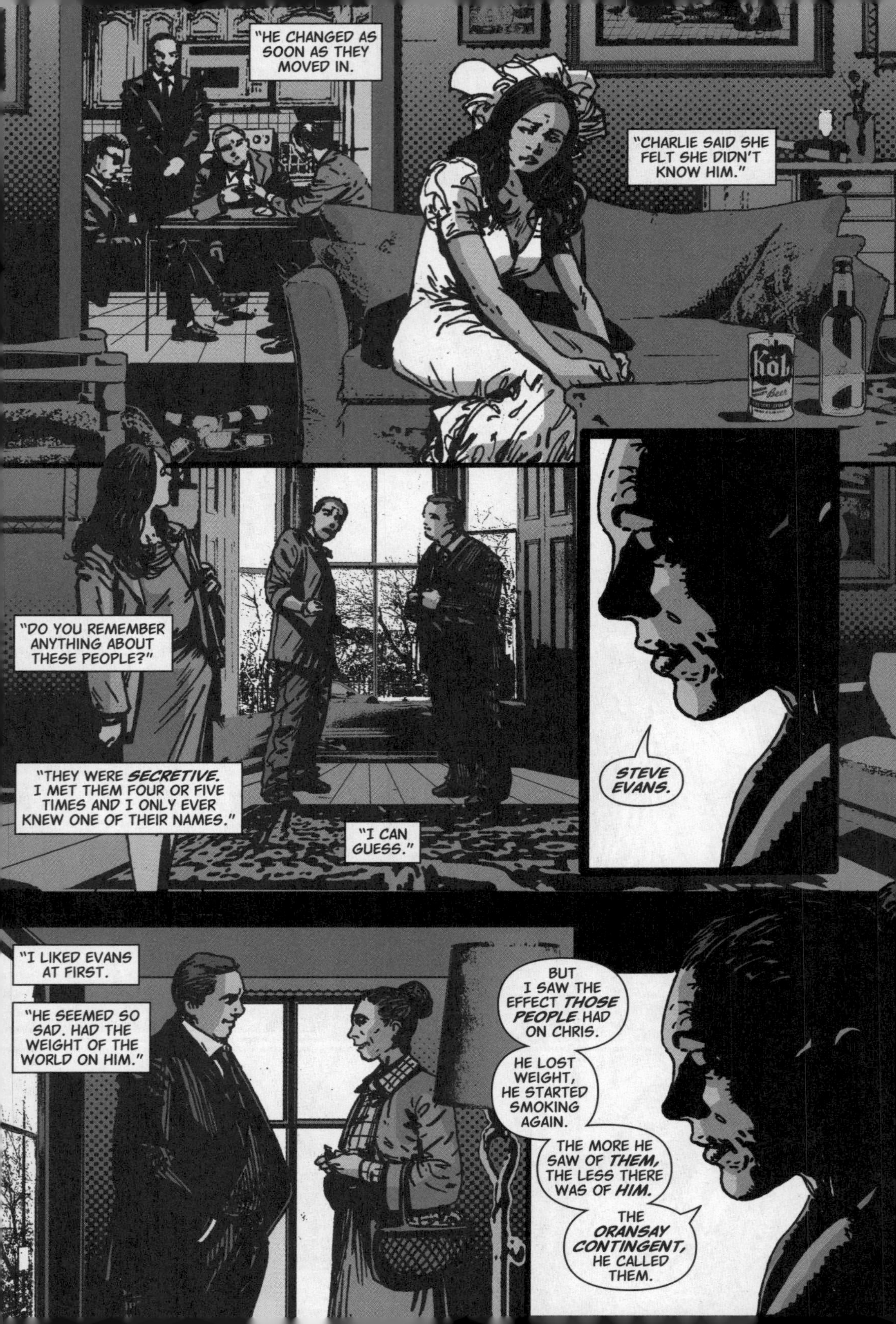
"HE CHANGED AS SOON AS THEY MOVED IN.
"CHARLIE SAID SHE FELT SHE DIDN'T KNOW HIM."
Kol Beer
"DO YOU REMEMBER ANYTHING ABOUT THESE PEOPLE?"
"THEY WERE SECRETIVE. I MET THEM FOUR OR FIVE TIMES AND I ONLY EVER KNEW ONE OF THEIR NAMES."
"I CAN GUESS."
STEVE EVANS.
"I LIKED EVANS AT FIRST.
"HE SEEMED SO SAD. HAD THE WEIGHT OF THE WORLD ON HIM."
BUT I SAW THE EFFECT THOSE PEOPLE HAD ON CHRIS.
HE LOST WEIGHT, HE STARTED SMOKING AGAIN.
THE MORE HE SAW OF THEM, THE LESS THERE WAS OF HIM.
THE ORANSAY CONTINGENT, HE CALLED THEM.

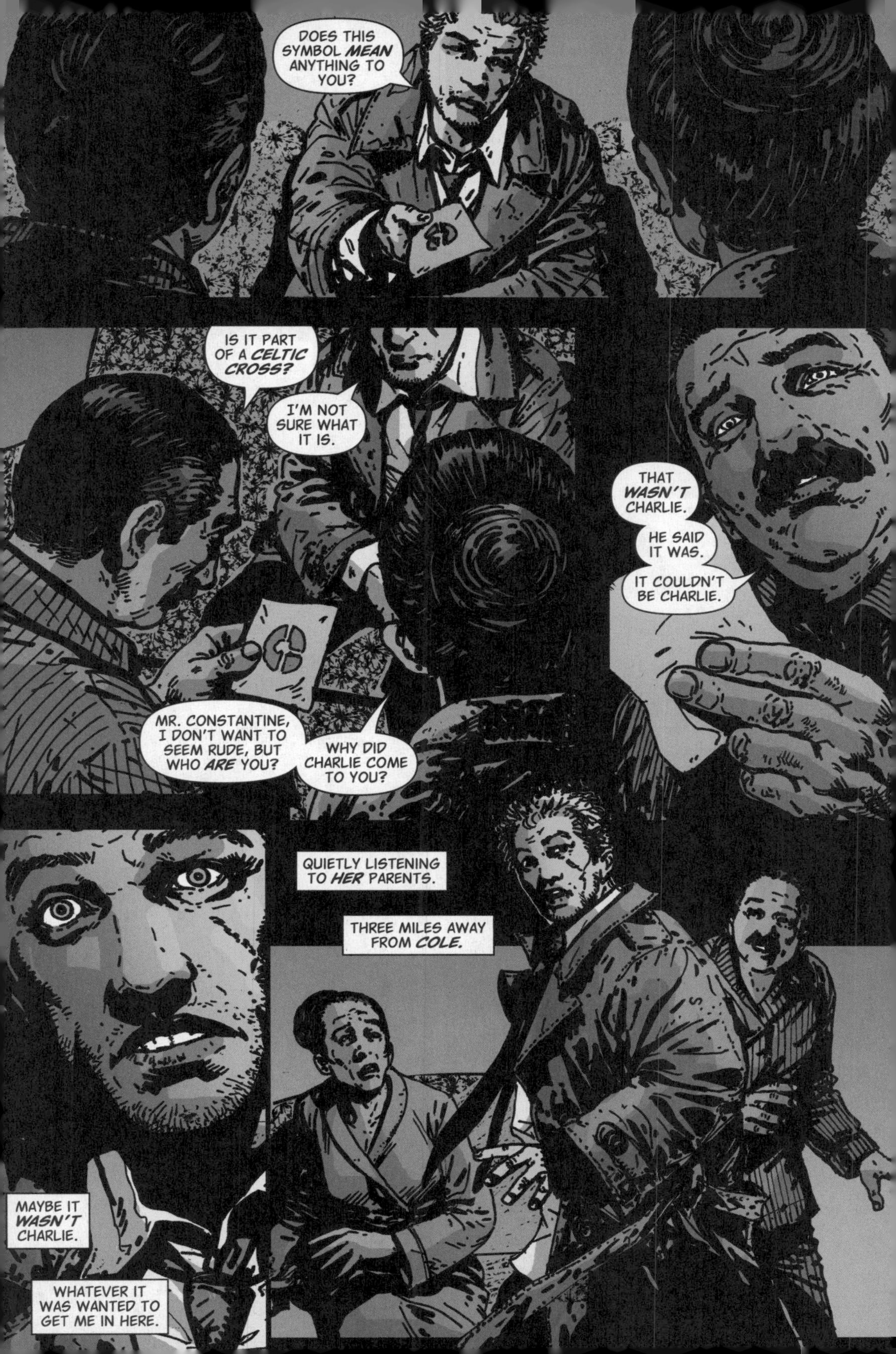
DOES THIS SYMBOL MEAN ANYTHING TO YOU?
IS IT PART OF A CELTIC CROSS?
I'M NOT SURE WHAT IT IS.
MR. CONSTANTINE, I DON'T WANT TO SEEM RUDE, BUT WHO ARE YOU?
WHY DID CHARLIE COME TO YOU?
THAT WASN'T CHARLIE.
HE SAID IT WAS.
IT COULDN'T BE CHARLIE.
MAYBE IT WASN'T CHARLIE.
WHATEVER IT WAS WANTED TO GET ME IN HERE.
QUIETLY LISTENING TO HER PARENTS.
THREE MILES AWAY FROM COLE.

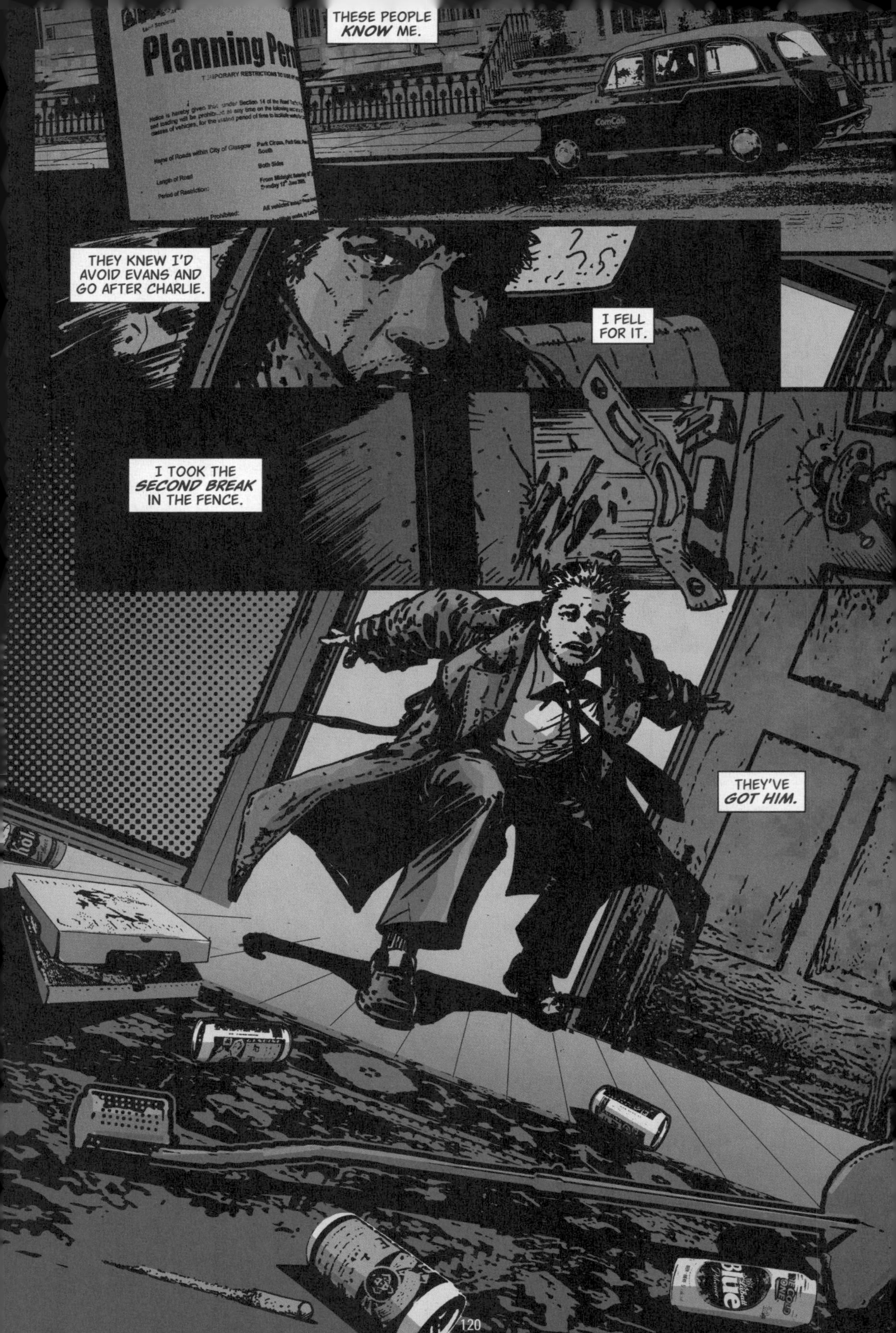
THESE PEOPLE KNOW ME.
THEY KNEW I'D AVOID EVANS AND GO AFTER CHARLIE.
I FELL FOR IT.
I TOOK THE SECOND BREAK IN THE FENCE.
THEY'VE GOT HIM.

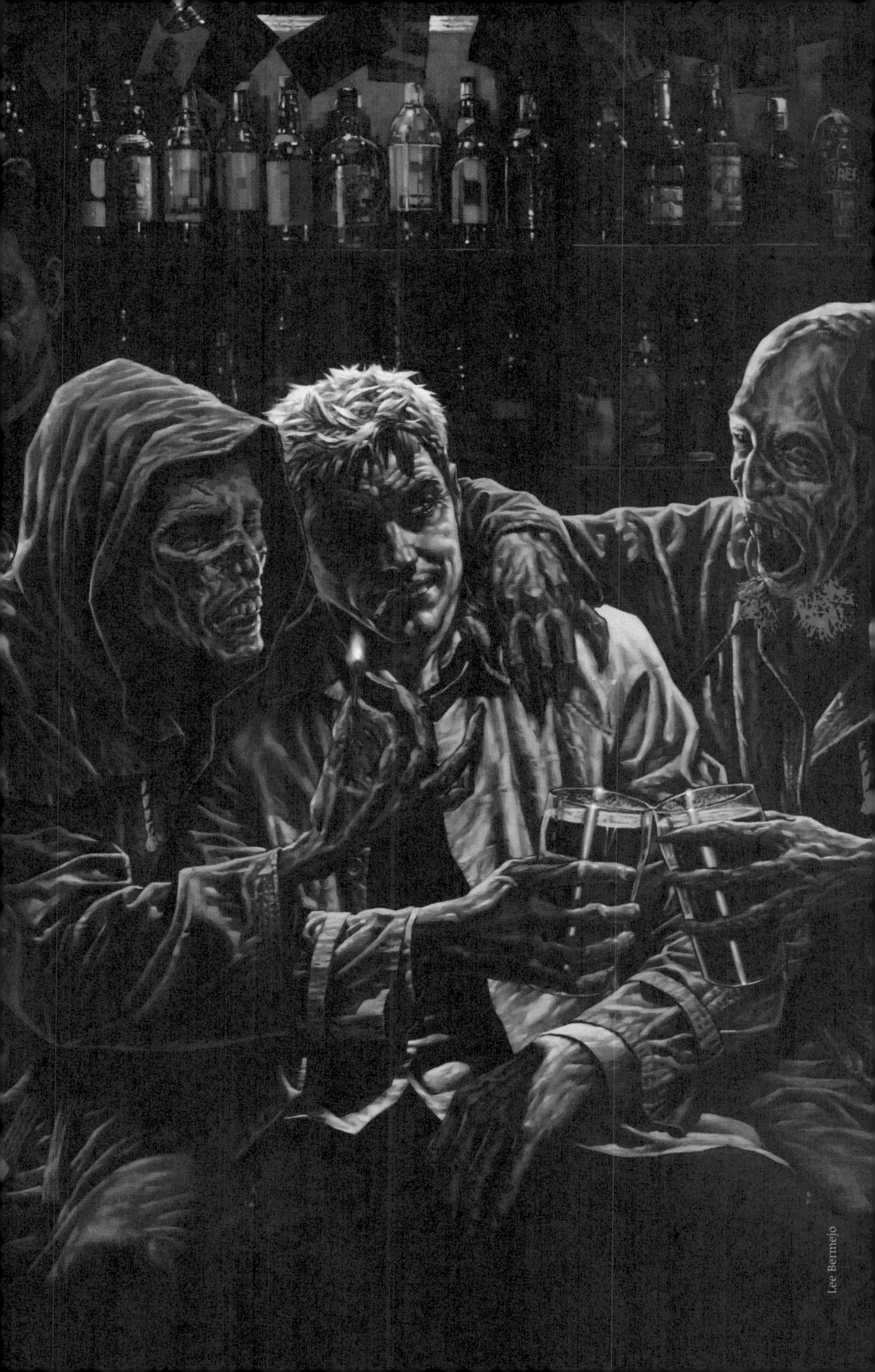
Lee Bermejo

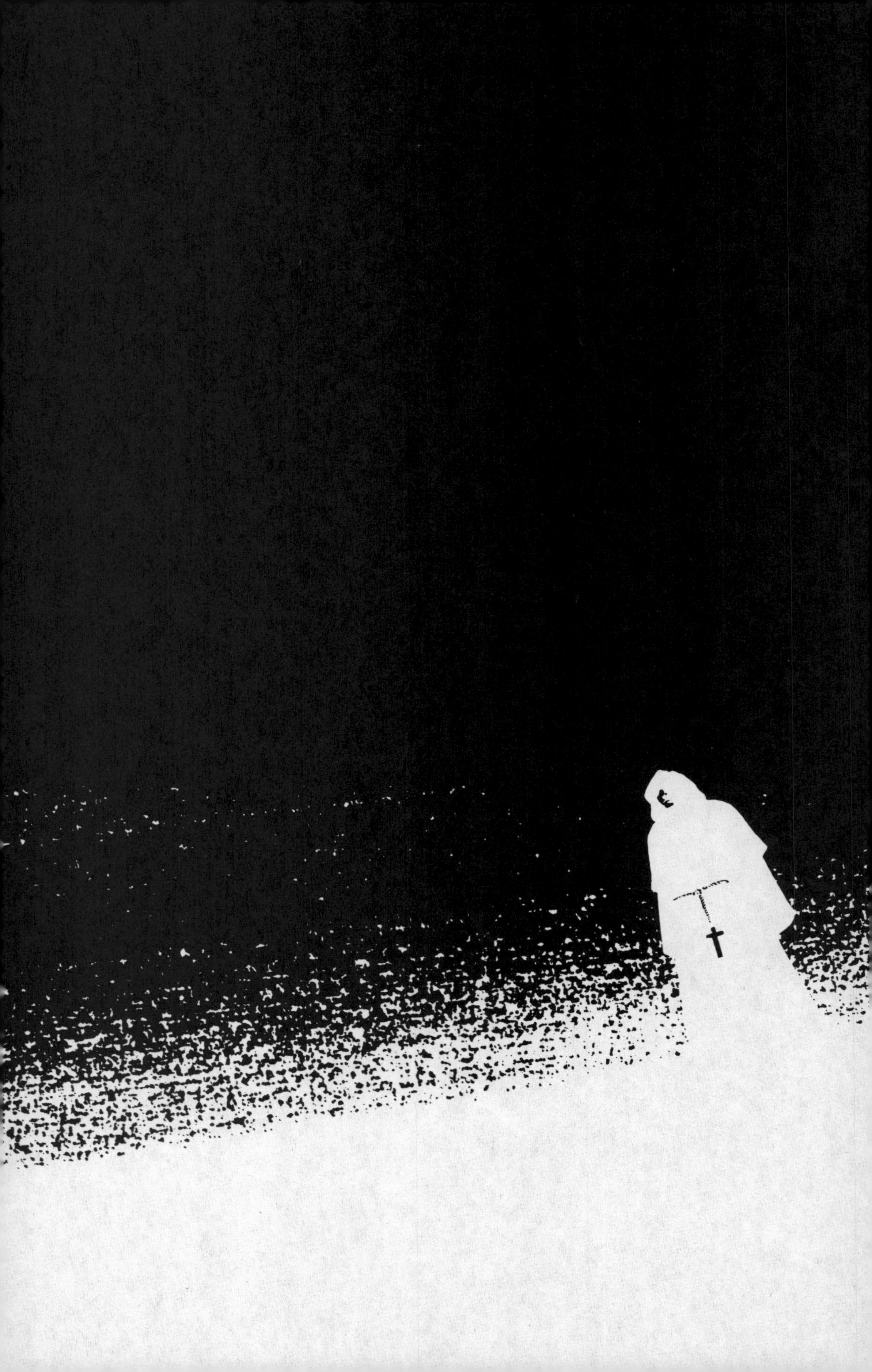

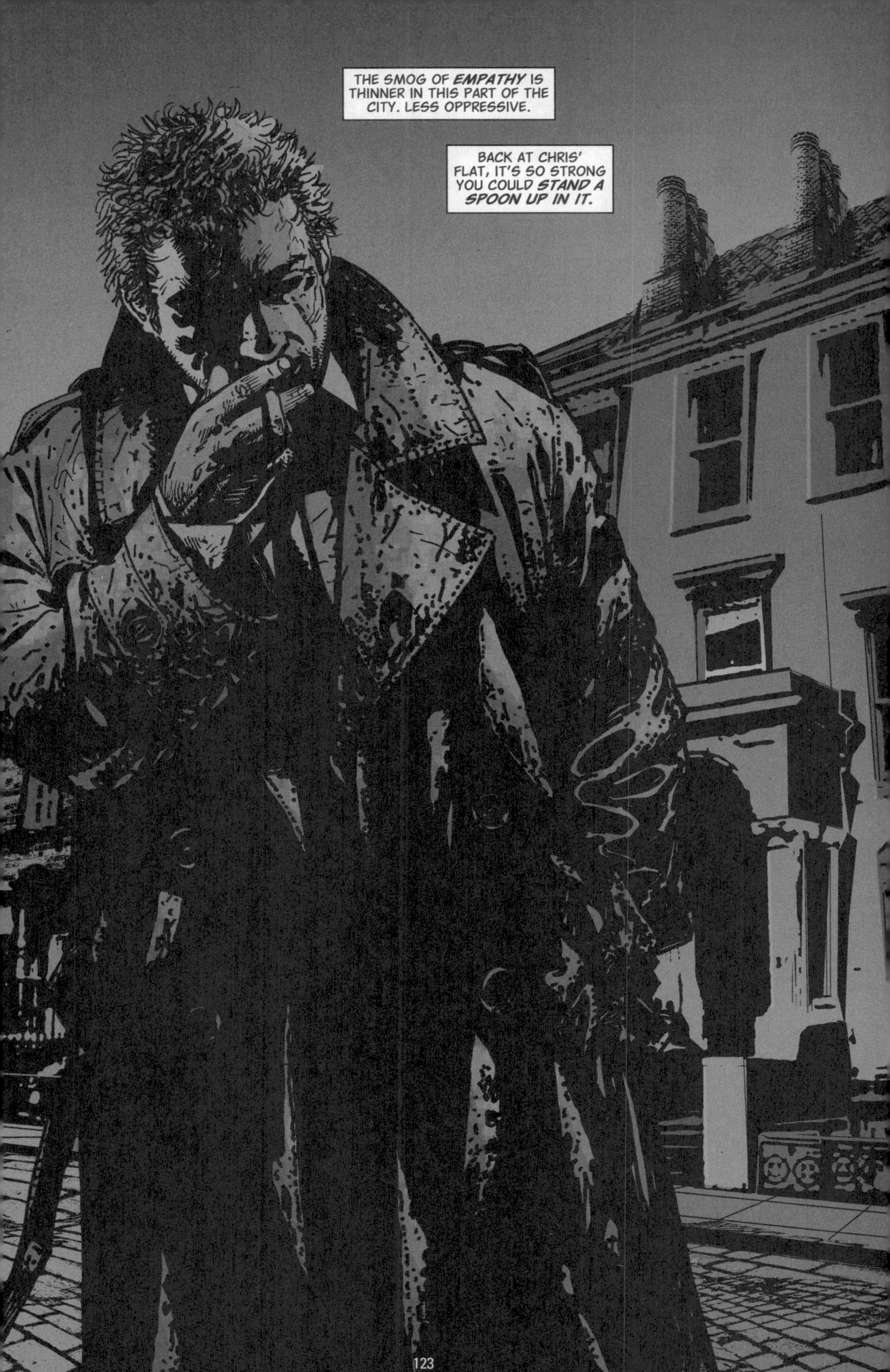
THE SMOG OF EMPATHY IS THINNER IN THIS PART OF THE CITY. LESS OPPRESSIVE.
BACK AT CHRIS' FLAT, IT'S SO STRONG YOU COULD STAND A SPOON UP IN IT.

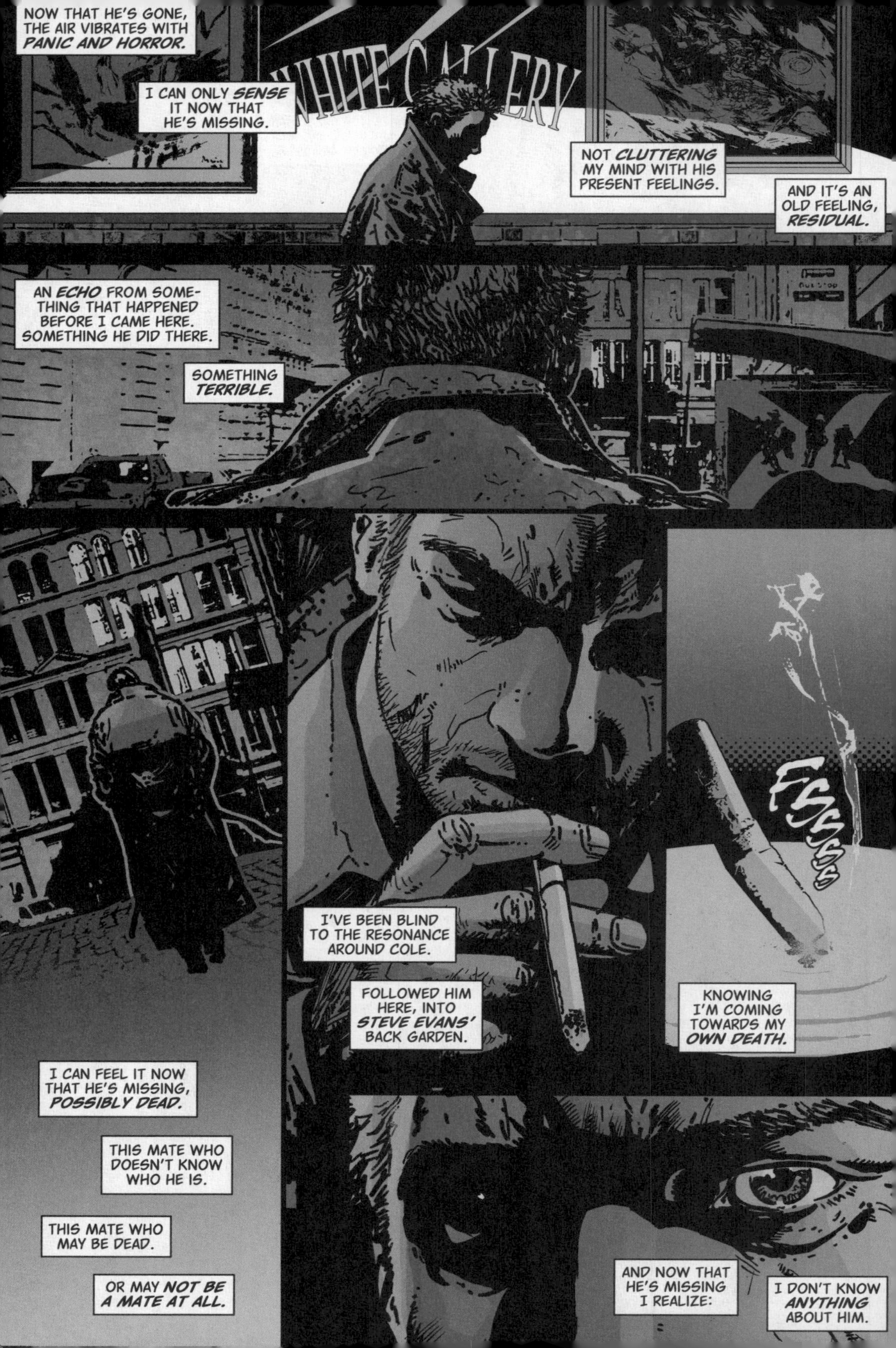

WHITE GALLERY
NOW THAT HE'S GONE, THE AIR VIBRATES WITH PANIC AND HORROR.
I CAN ONLY SENSE IT NOW THAT HE'S MISSING.
NOT CLUTTERING MY MIND WITH HIS PRESENT FEELINGS.
AND IT'S AN OLD FEELING, RESIDUAL.
AN ECHO FROM SOMETHING THAT HAPPENED BEFORE I CAME HERE. SOMETHING HE DID THERE.
SOMETHING TERRIBLE.
I CAN FEEL IT NOW THAT HE'S MISSING, POSSIBLY DEAD.
THIS MATE WHO DOESN'T KNOW WHO HE IS.
THIS MATE WHO MAY BE DEAD.
OR MAY NOT BE A MATE AT ALL.
I'VE BEEN BLIND TO THE RESONANCE AROUND COLE.
FOLLOWED HIM HERE, INTO STEVE EVANS' BACK GARDEN.
FSSSSS
KNOWING I'M COMING TOWARDS MY OWN DEATH.
AND NOW THAT HE'S MISSING I REALIZE:
I DON'T KNOW ANYTHING ABOUT HIM.

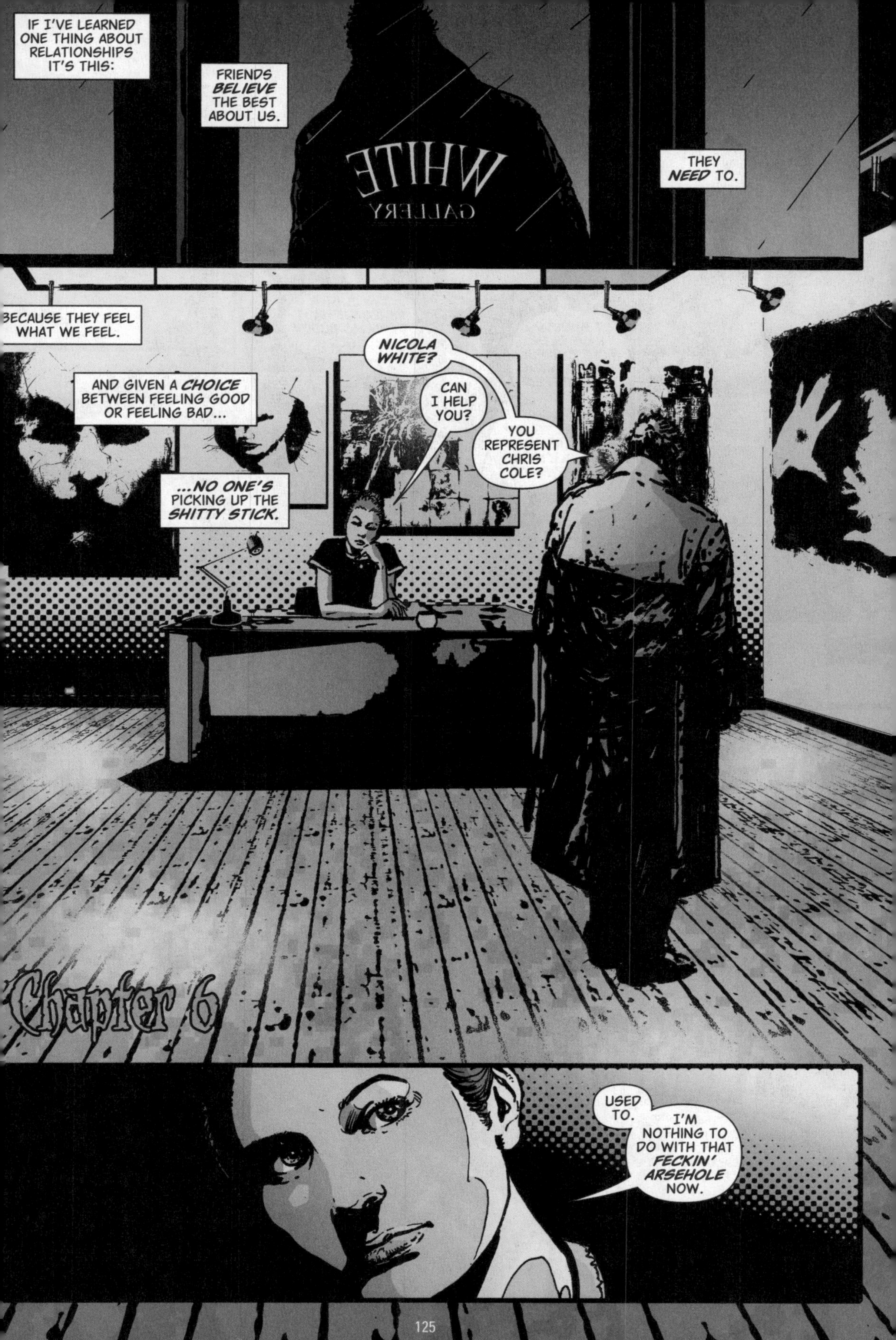
IF I'VE LEARNED ONE THING ABOUT RELATIONSHIPS IT'S THIS:
FRIENDS BELIEVE THE BEST ABOUT US.
THEY NEED TO.
WHITE GALLERY
BECAUSE THEY FEEL WHAT WE FEEL.
AND GIVEN A CHOICE BETWEEN FEELING GOOD OR FEELING BAD...
...NO ONE'S PICKING UP THE SHITTY STICK.
CAN I HELP YOU?
NICOLA WHITE?
YOU REPRESENT CHRIS COLE?
Chapter 6
USED TO.
I'M NOTHING TO DO WITH THAT FECKIN' ARSEHOLE NOW.

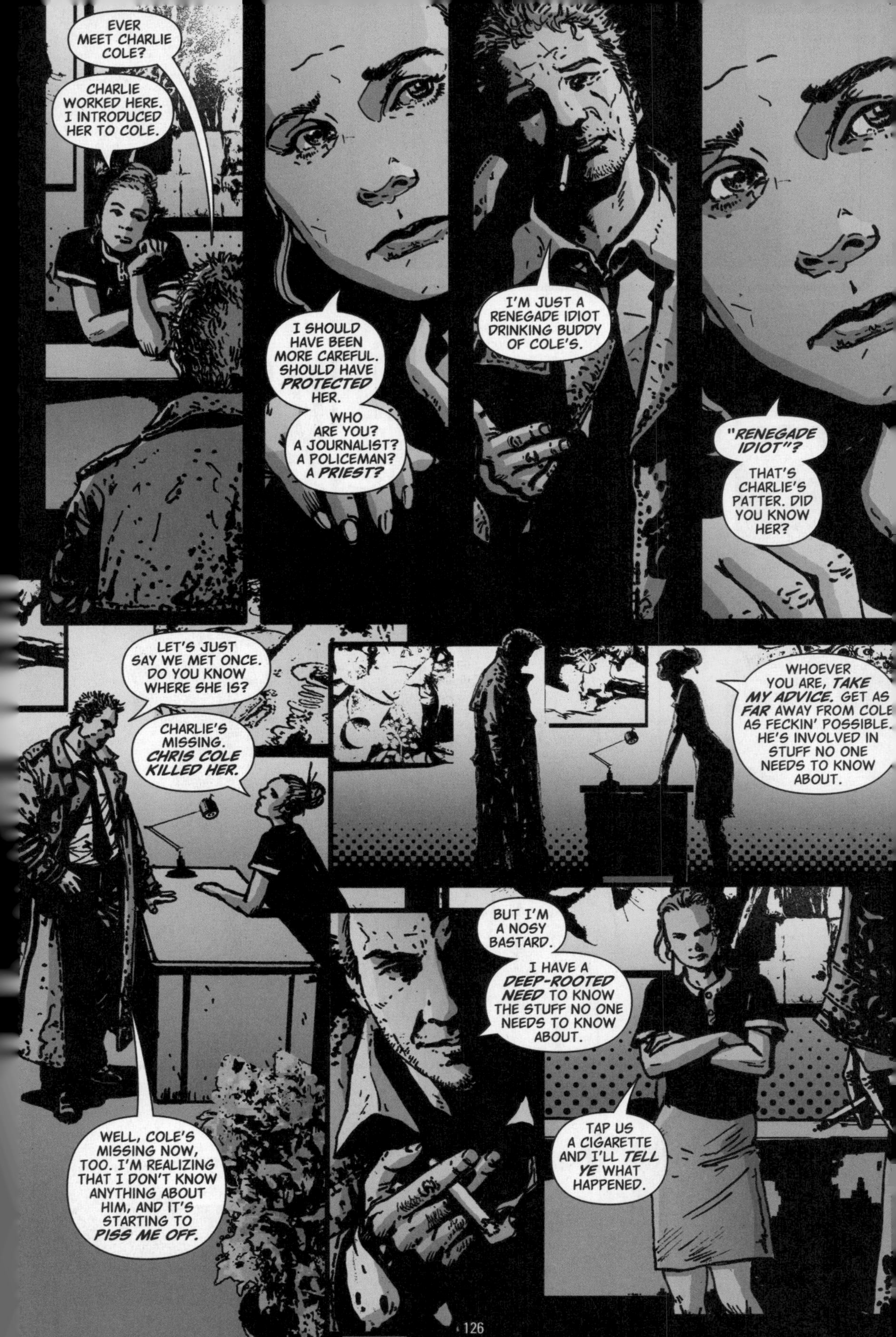
EVER MEET CHARLIE COLE?
CHARLIE WORKED HERE. I INTRODUCED HER TO COLE.
I SHOULD HAVE BEEN MORE CAREFUL. SHOULD HAVE PROTECTED HER.
WHO ARE YOU? A JOURNALIST? A POLICEMAN? A PRIEST?
I'M JUST A RENEGADE IDIOT DRINKING BUDDY OF COLE'S.
"RENEGADE IDIOT"?
THAT'S CHARLIE'S PATTER. DID YOU KNOW HER?
LET'S JUST SAY WE MET ONCE. DO YOU KNOW WHERE SHE IS?
CHARLIE'S MISSING. CHRIS COLE KILLED HER.
WELL, COLE'S MISSING NOW, TOO. I'M REALIZING THAT I DON'T KNOW ANYTHING ABOUT HIM, AND IT'S STARTING TO PISS ME OFF.
WHOEVER YOU ARE, TAKE MY ADVICE. GET AS FAR AWAY FROM COLE AS FECKIN' POSSIBLE. HE'S INVOLVED IN STUFF NO ONE NEEDS TO KNOW ABOUT.
BUT I'M A NOSY BASTARD.
I HAVE A DEEP-ROOTED NEED TO KNOW THE STUFF NO ONE NEEDS TO KNOW ABOUT.
TAP US A CIGARETTE AND I'LL TELL YE WHAT HAPPENED.

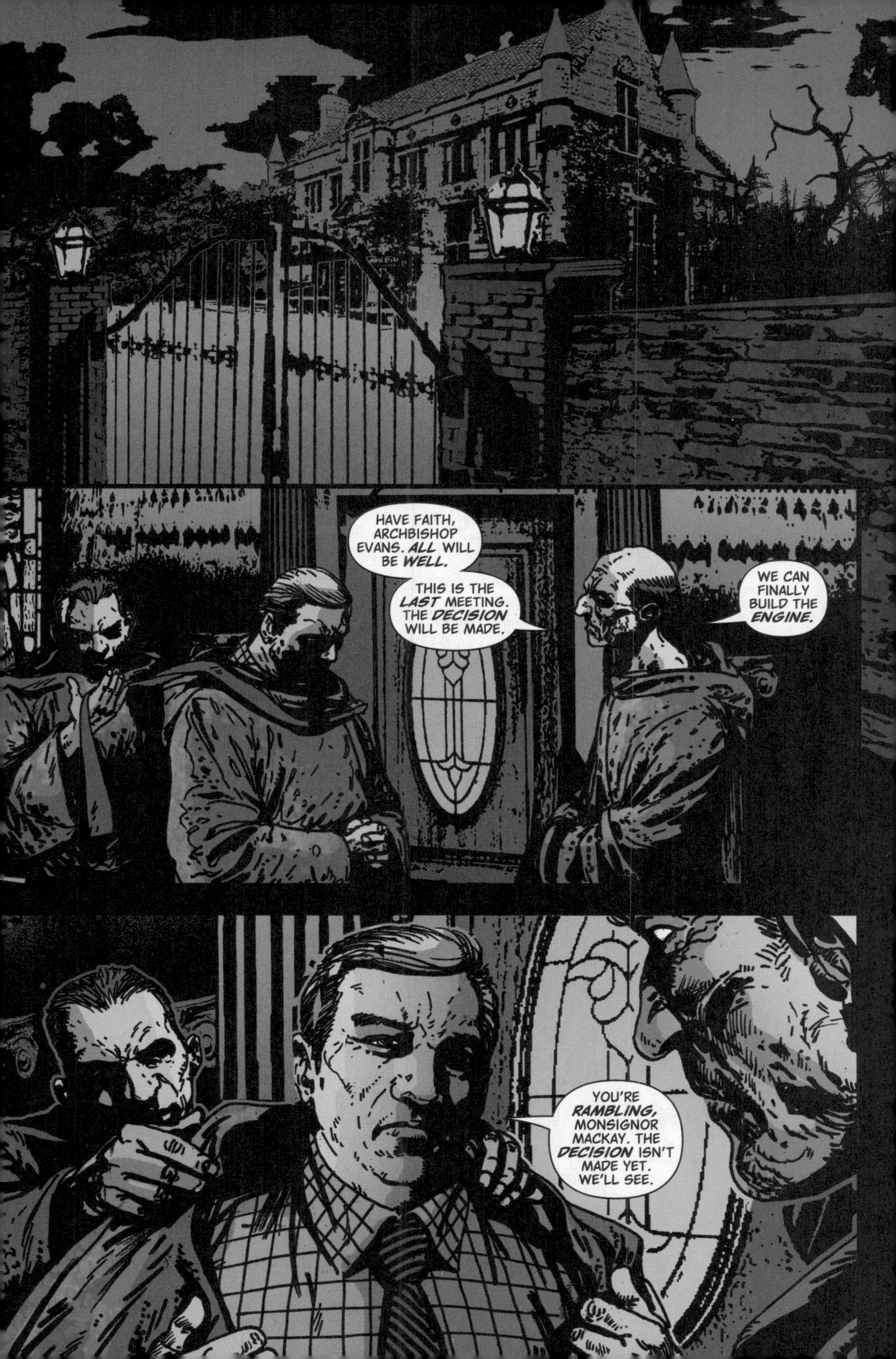
HAVE FAITH, ARCHBISHOP EVANS. ALL WILL BE WELL.
THIS IS THE LAST MEETING. THE DECISION WILL BE MADE.
WE CAN FINALLY BUILD THE ENGINE.
YOU'RE RAMBLING, MONSIGNOR MACKAY. THE DECISION ISN'T MADE YET. WE'LL SEE.

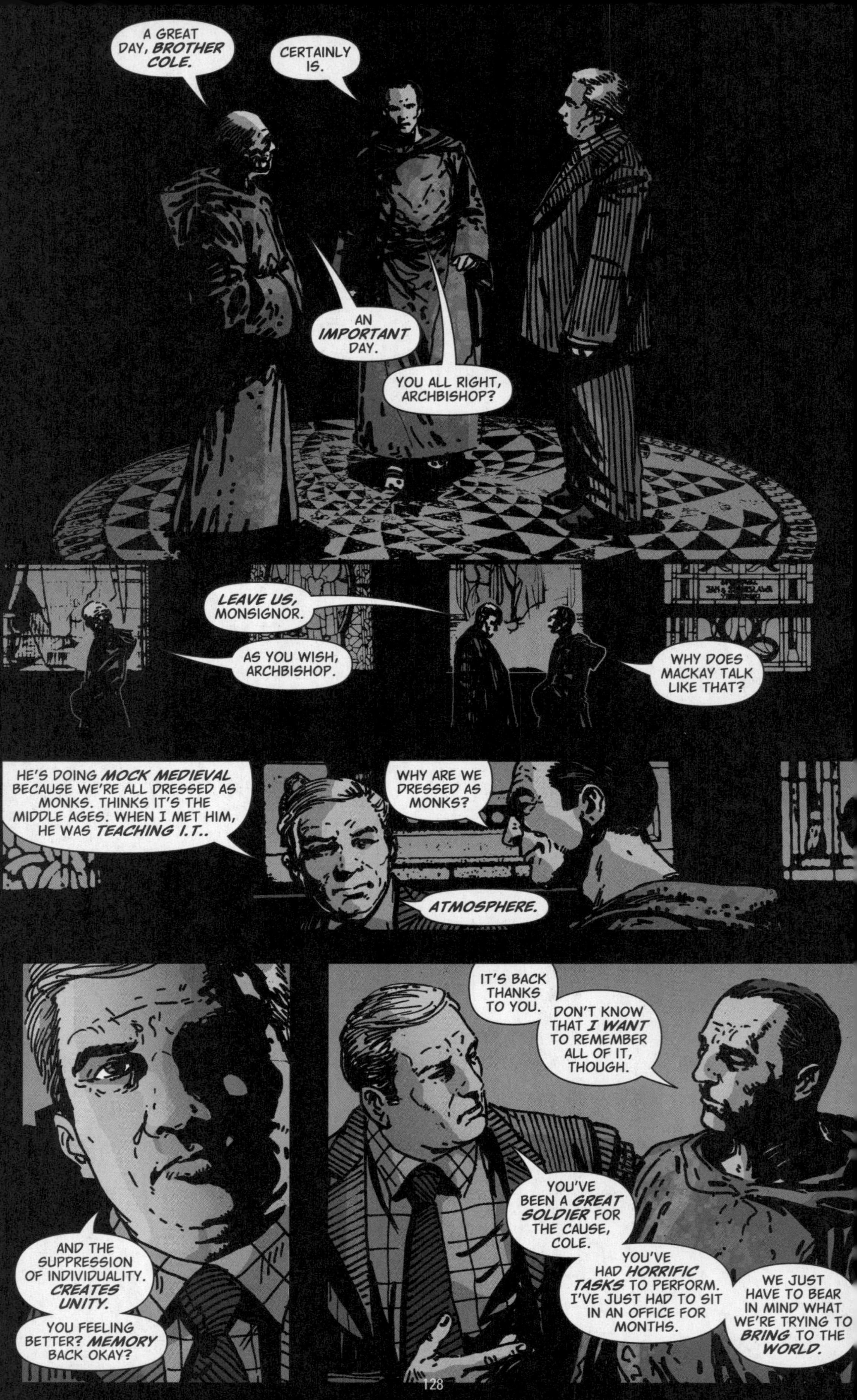

A GREAT DAY, BROTHER COLE.
CERTAINLY IS.
AN IMPORTANT DAY.
YOU ALL RIGHT, ARCHBISHOP?
LEAVE US, MONSIGNOR.
AS YOU WISH, ARCHBISHOP.
WHY DOES MACKAY TALK LIKE THAT?
HE'S DOING MOCK MEDIEVAL BECAUSE WE'RE ALL DRESSED AS MONKS. THINKS IT'S THE MIDDLE AGES. WHEN I MET HIM, HE WAS TEACHING I.T..
WHY ARE WE DRESSED AS MONKS?
ATMOSPHERE.
AND THE SUPPRESSION OF INDIVIDUALITY. CREATES UNITY.
YOU FEELING BETTER? MEMORY BACK OKAY?
IT'S BACK THANKS TO YOU.
DON'T KNOW THAT I WANT TO REMEMBER ALL OF IT, THOUGH.
YOU'VE BEEN A GREAT SOLDIER FOR THE CAUSE, COLE.
YOU'VE HAD HORRIFIC TASKS TO PERFORM. I'VE JUST HAD TO SIT IN AN OFFICE FOR MONTHS.
WE JUST HAVE TO BEAR IN MIND WHAT WE'RE TRYING TO BRING TO THE WORLD.

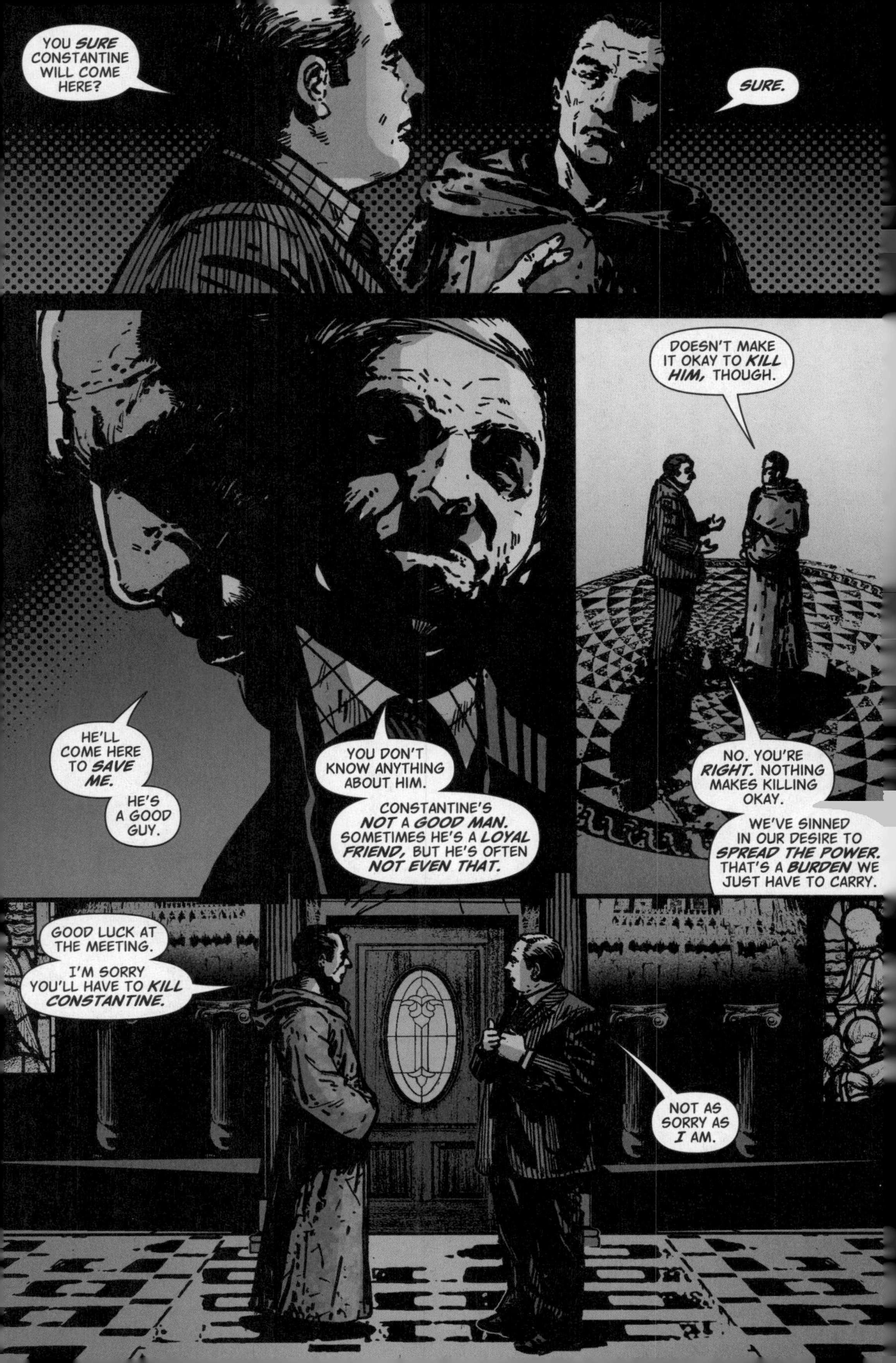
YOU SURE CONSTANTINE WILL COME HERE?
SURE.
HE'LL COME HERE TO SAVE ME.
HE'S A GOOD GUY.
YOU DON'T KNOW ANYTHING ABOUT HIM.
CONSTANTINE'S NOT A GOOD MAN. SOMETIMES HE'S A LOYAL FRIEND, BUT HE'S OFTEN NOT EVEN THAT.
DOESN'T MAKE IT OKAY TO KILL HIM, THOUGH.
NO. YOU'RE RIGHT. NOTHING MAKES KILLING OKAY.
WE'VE SINNED IN OUR DESIRE TO SPREAD THE POWER. THAT'S A BURDEN WE JUST HAVE TO CARRY.
GOOD LUCK AT THE MEETING.
I'M SORRY YOU'LL HAVE TO KILL CONSTANTINE.
NOT AS SORRY AS I AM.

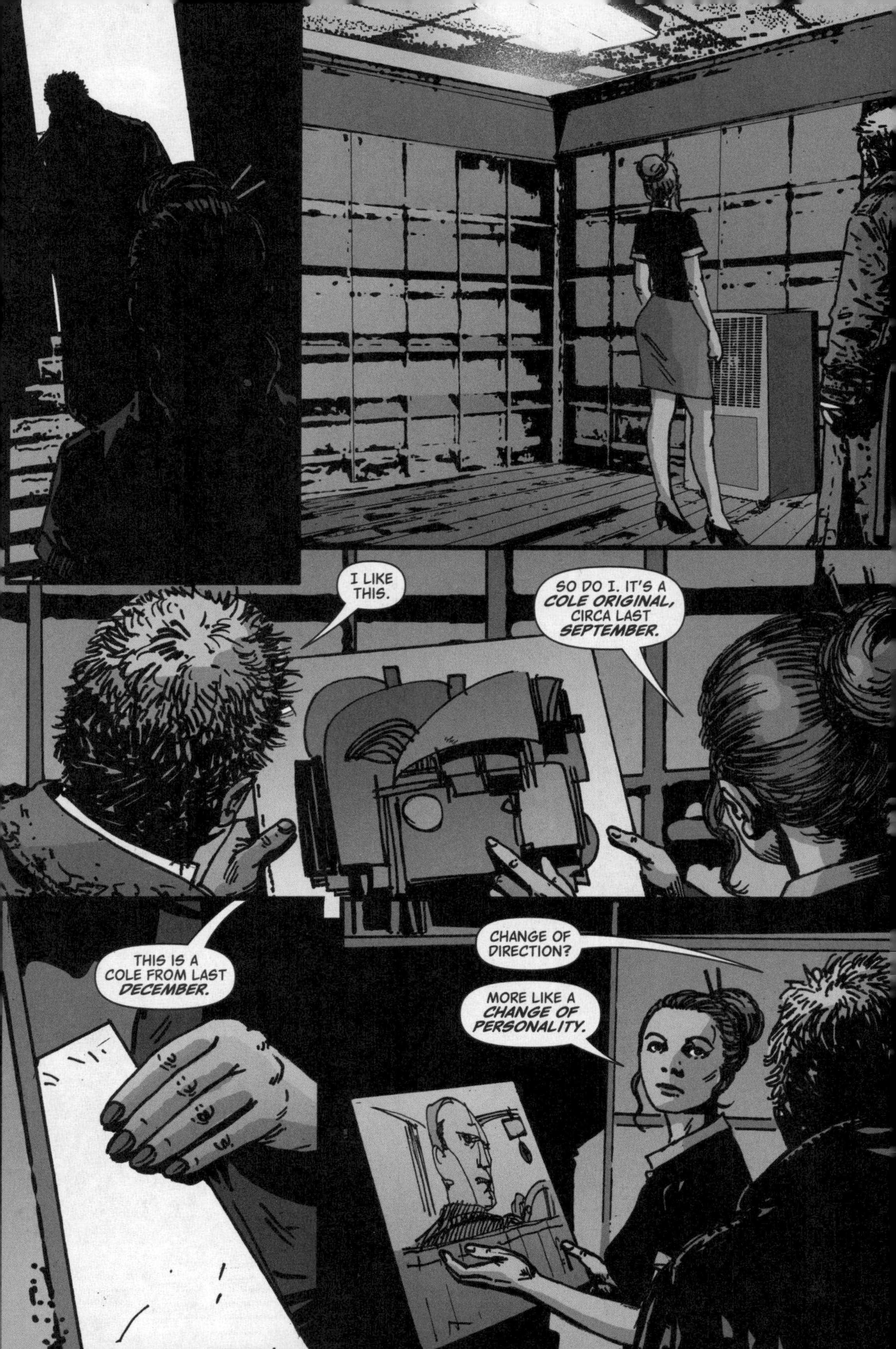
I LIKE THIS.
SO DO I. IT'S A *COLE ORIGINAL,* CIRCA LAST *SEPTEMBER.*
THIS IS A COLE FROM LAST *DECEMBER.*
CHANGE OF DIRECTION?
MORE LIKE A *CHANGE OF PERSONALITY.*

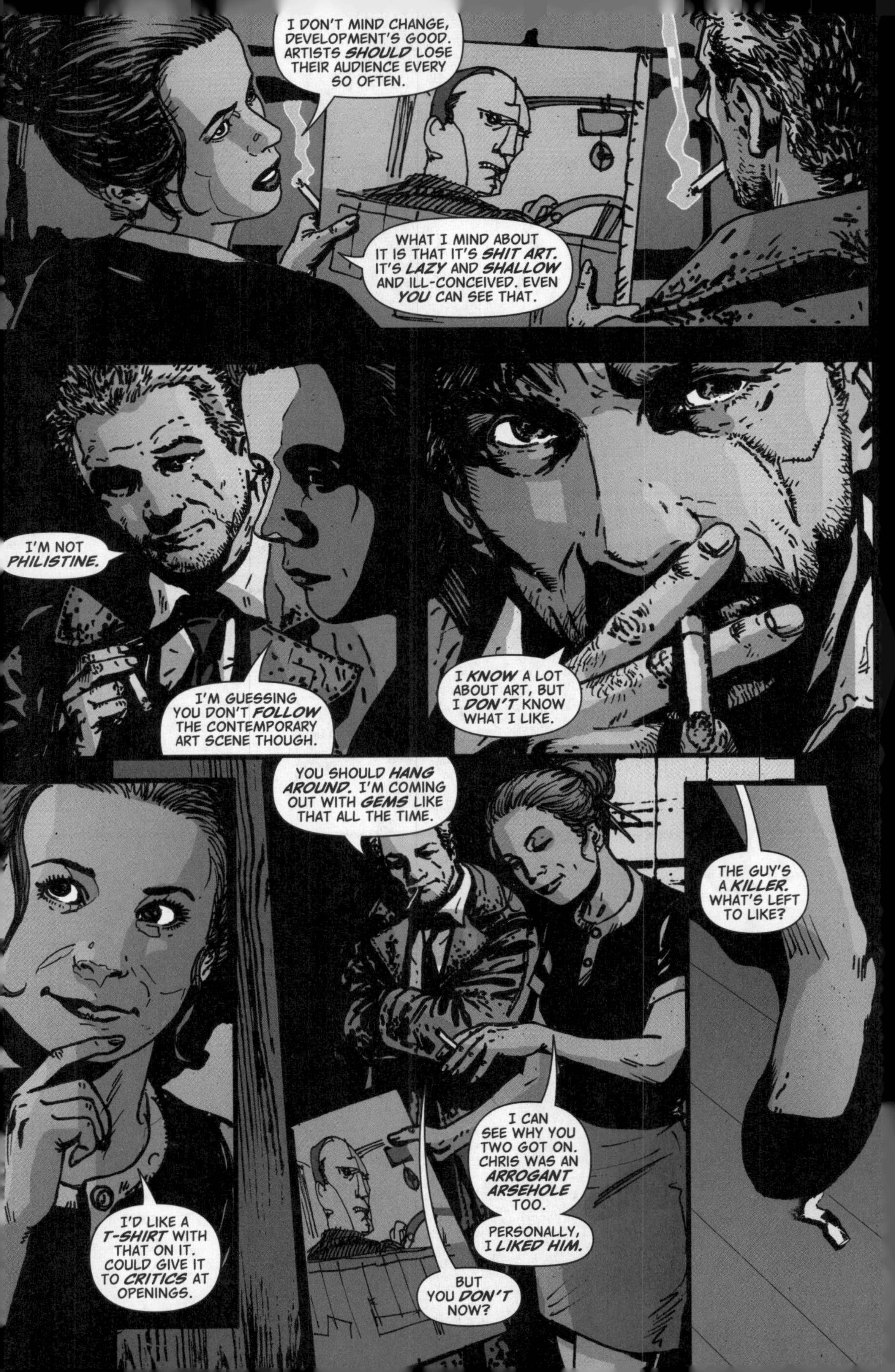
I DON'T MIND CHANGE, DEVELOPMENT'S GOOD. ARTISTS SHOULD LOSE THEIR AUDIENCE EVERY SO OFTEN.
WHAT I MIND ABOUT IT IS THAT IT'S SHIT ART. IT'S LAZY AND SHALLOW AND ILL-CONCEIVED. EVEN YOU CAN SEE THAT.
I'M NOT PHILISTINE.
I'M GUESSING YOU DON'T FOLLOW THE CONTEMPORARY ART SCENE THOUGH.
I KNOW A LOT ABOUT ART, BUT I DON'T KNOW WHAT I LIKE.
I'D LIKE A T-SHIRT WITH THAT ON IT. COULD GIVE IT TO CRITICS AT OPENINGS.
YOU SHOULD HANG AROUND. I'M COMING OUT WITH GEMS LIKE THAT ALL THE TIME.
I CAN SEE WHY YOU TWO GOT ON. CHRIS WAS AN ARROGANT ARSEHOLE TOO.
PERSONALLY, I LIKED HIM.
BUT YOU DON'T NOW?
THE GUY'S A KILLER. WHAT'S LEFT TO LIKE?

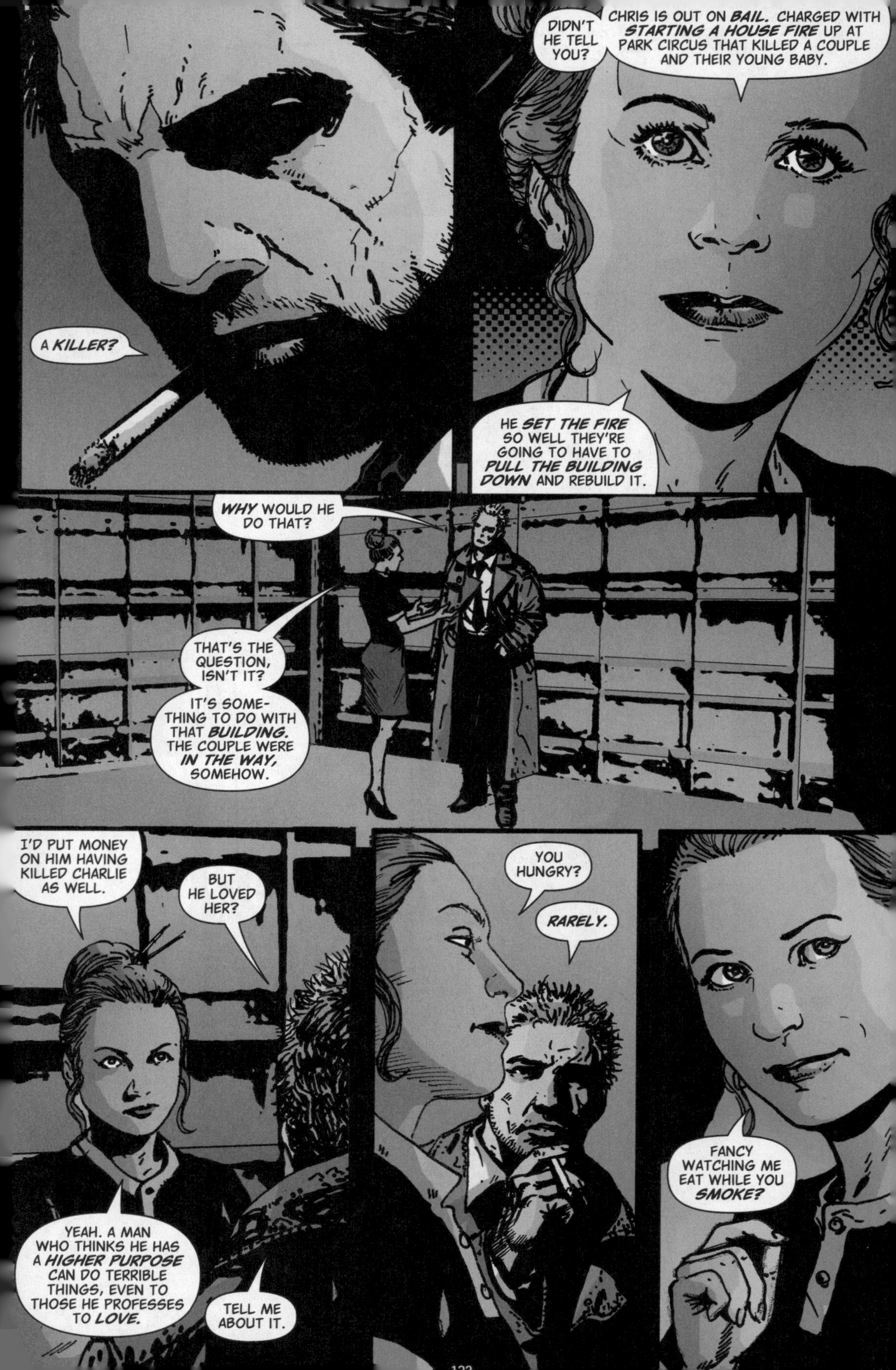

DIDN'T HE TELL YOU?
CHRIS IS OUT ON BAIL. CHARGED WITH STARTING A HOUSE FIRE UP AT PARK CIRCUS THAT KILLED A COUPLE AND THEIR YOUNG BABY.
A KILLER?
HE SET THE FIRE SO WELL THEY'RE GOING TO HAVE TO PULL THE BUILDING DOWN AND REBUILD IT.
WHY WOULD HE DO THAT?
THAT'S THE QUESTION, ISN'T IT?
IT'S SOME-THING TO DO WITH THAT BUILDING. THE COUPLE WERE IN THE WAY, SOMEHOW.
I'D PUT MONEY ON HIM HAVING KILLED CHARLIE AS WELL.
BUT HE LOVED HER?
YEAH. A MAN WHO THINKS HE HAS A HIGHER PURPOSE CAN DO TERRIBLE THINGS, EVEN TO THOSE HE PROFESSES TO LOVE.
TELL ME ABOUT IT.
YOU HUNGRY?
RARELY.
FANCY WATCHING ME EAT WHILE YOU SMOKE?

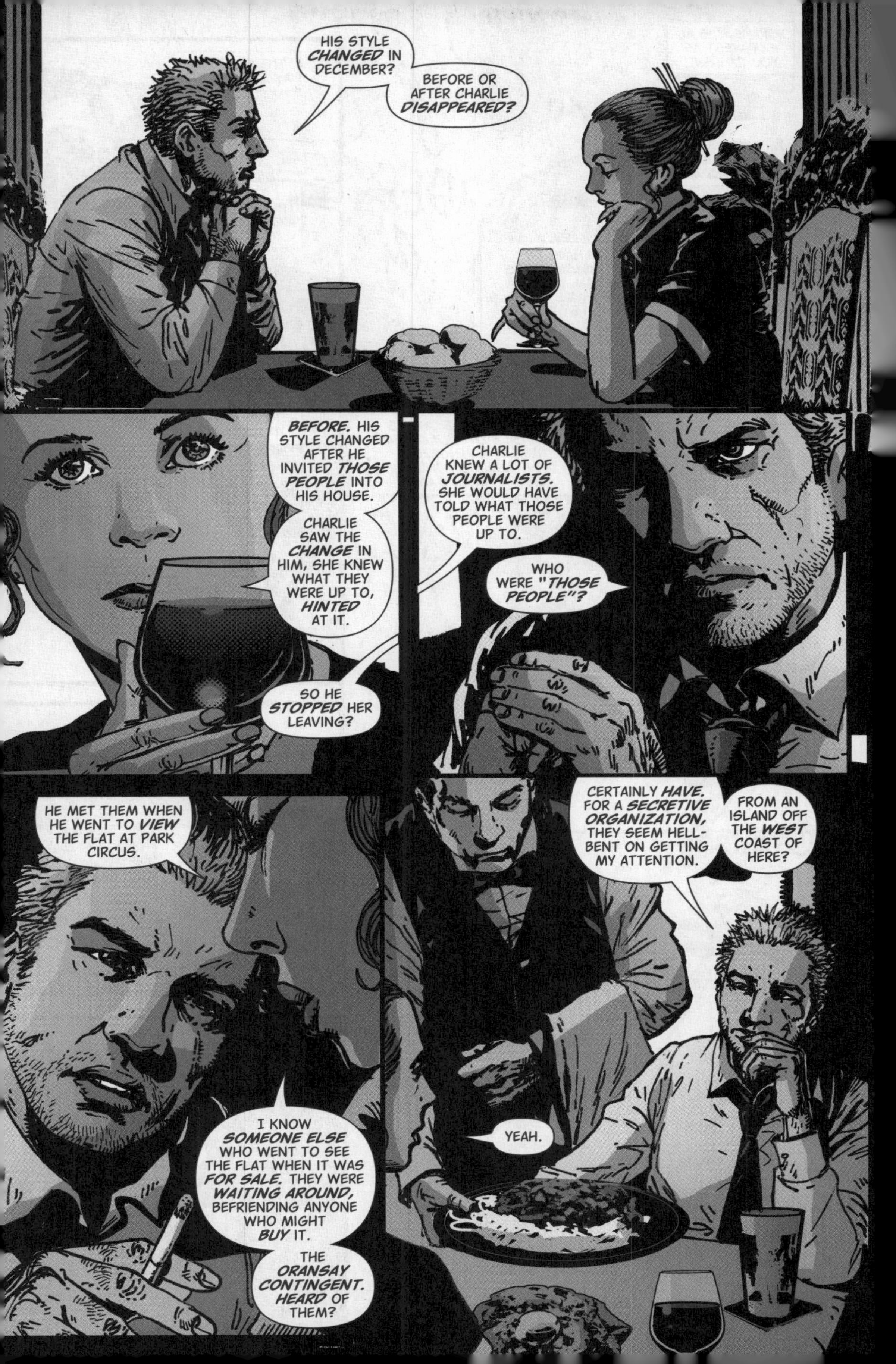
HIS STYLE CHANGED IN DECEMBER?
BEFORE OR AFTER CHARLIE DISAPPEARED?
BEFORE. HIS STYLE CHANGED AFTER HE INVITED THOSE PEOPLE INTO HIS HOUSE.
CHARLIE SAW THE CHANGE IN HIM, SHE KNEW WHAT THEY WERE UP TO, HINTED AT IT.
SO HE STOPPED HER LEAVING?
CHARLIE KNEW A LOT OF JOURNALISTS. SHE WOULD HAVE TOLD WHAT THOSE PEOPLE WERE UP TO.
WHO WERE "THOSE PEOPLE"?
HE MET THEM WHEN HE WENT TO VIEW THE FLAT AT PARK CIRCUS.
I KNOW SOMEONE ELSE WHO WENT TO SEE THE FLAT WHEN IT WAS FOR SALE. THEY WERE WAITING AROUND, BEFRIENDING ANYONE WHO MIGHT BUY IT.
THE ORANSAY CONTINGENT. HEARD OF THEM?
YEAH.
CERTAINLY HAVE. FOR A SECRETIVE ORGANIZATION, THEY SEEM HELL-BENT ON GETTING MY ATTENTION.
FROM AN ISLAND OFF THE WEST COAST OF HERE?

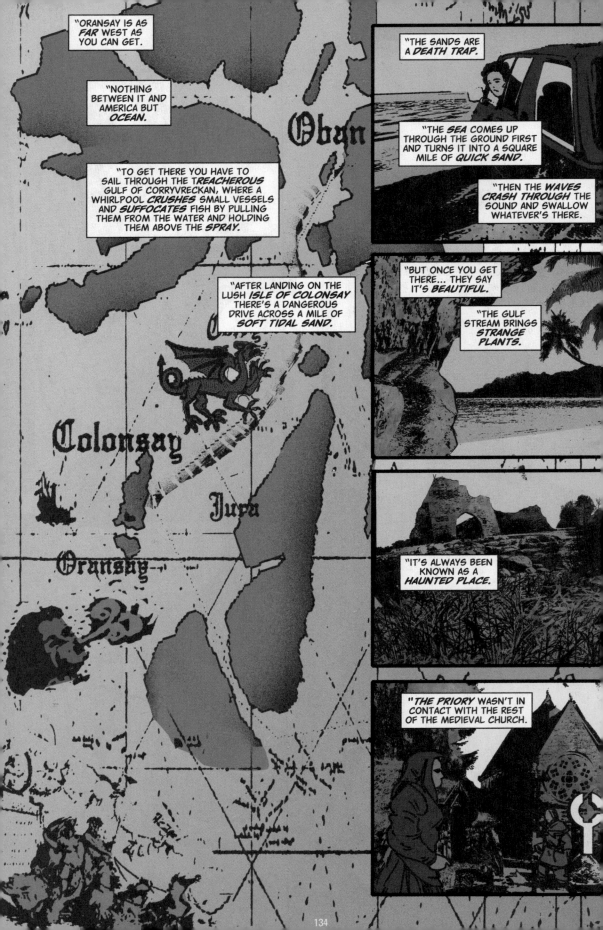

"ORANSAY IS AS *FAR* WEST AS YOU CAN GET.

"NOTHING BETWEEN IT AND AMERICA BUT *OCEAN*.

"TO GET THERE YOU HAVE TO SAIL THROUGH THE *TREACHEROUS* GULF OF CORRYVRECKAN, WHERE A WHIRLPOOL *CRUSHES* SMALL VESSELS AND *SUFFOCATES* FISH BY PULLING THEM FROM THE WATER AND HOLDING THEM ABOVE THE *SPRAY*.

"AFTER LANDING ON THE LUSH *ISLE OF COLONSAY* THERE'S A DANGEROUS DRIVE ACROSS A MILE OF *SOFT TIDAL SAND*.

"THE SANDS ARE A *DEATH TRAP*.

"THE *SEA* COMES UP THROUGH THE GROUND FIRST AND TURNS IT INTO A SQUARE MILE OF *QUICK SAND*.

"THEN THE *WAVES CRASH THROUGH* THE SOUND AND SWALLOW WHATEVER'S THERE.

"BUT ONCE YOU GET THERE... THEY SAY IT'S *BEAUTIFUL*.

"THE *GULF STREAM* BRINGS *STRANGE PLANTS*.

"IT'S ALWAYS BEEN KNOWN AS A *HAUNTED PLACE*.

"*THE PRIORY* WASN'T IN CONTACT WITH THE REST OF THE MEDIEVAL CHURCH.

Oban

Colonsay

Jura

Oransay

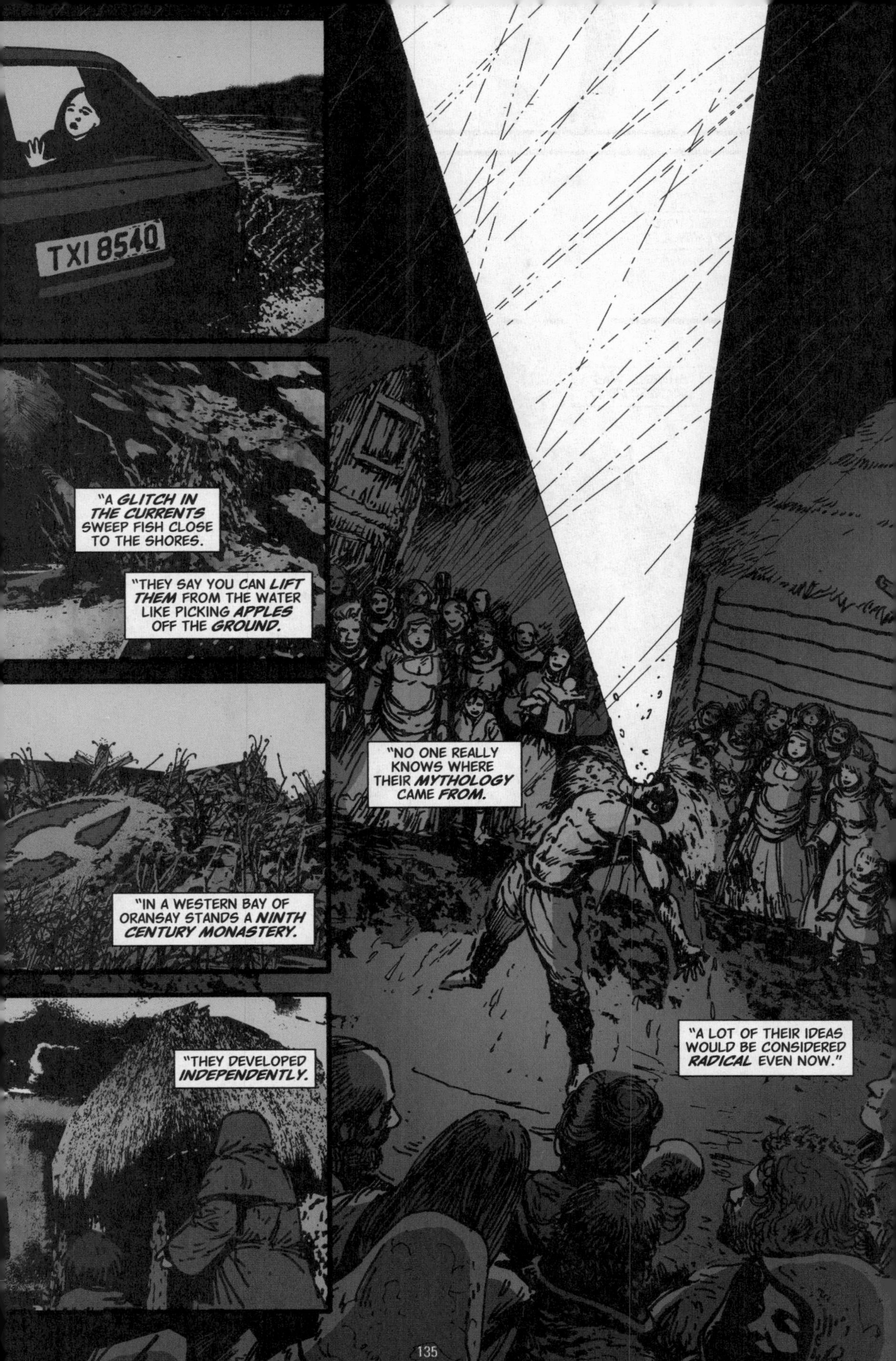
TXI 854Q
"A GLITCH IN THE CURRENTS SWEEP FISH CLOSE TO THE SHORES.
"THEY SAY YOU CAN LIFT THEM FROM THE WATER LIKE PICKING APPLES OFF THE GROUND.
"IN A WESTERN BAY OF ORANSAY STANDS A NINTH CENTURY MONASTERY.
"THEY DEVELOPED INDEPENDENTLY.
"NO ONE REALLY KNOWS WHERE THEIR MYTHOLOGY CAME FROM.
"A LOT OF THEIR IDEAS WOULD BE CONSIDERED RADICAL EVEN NOW."

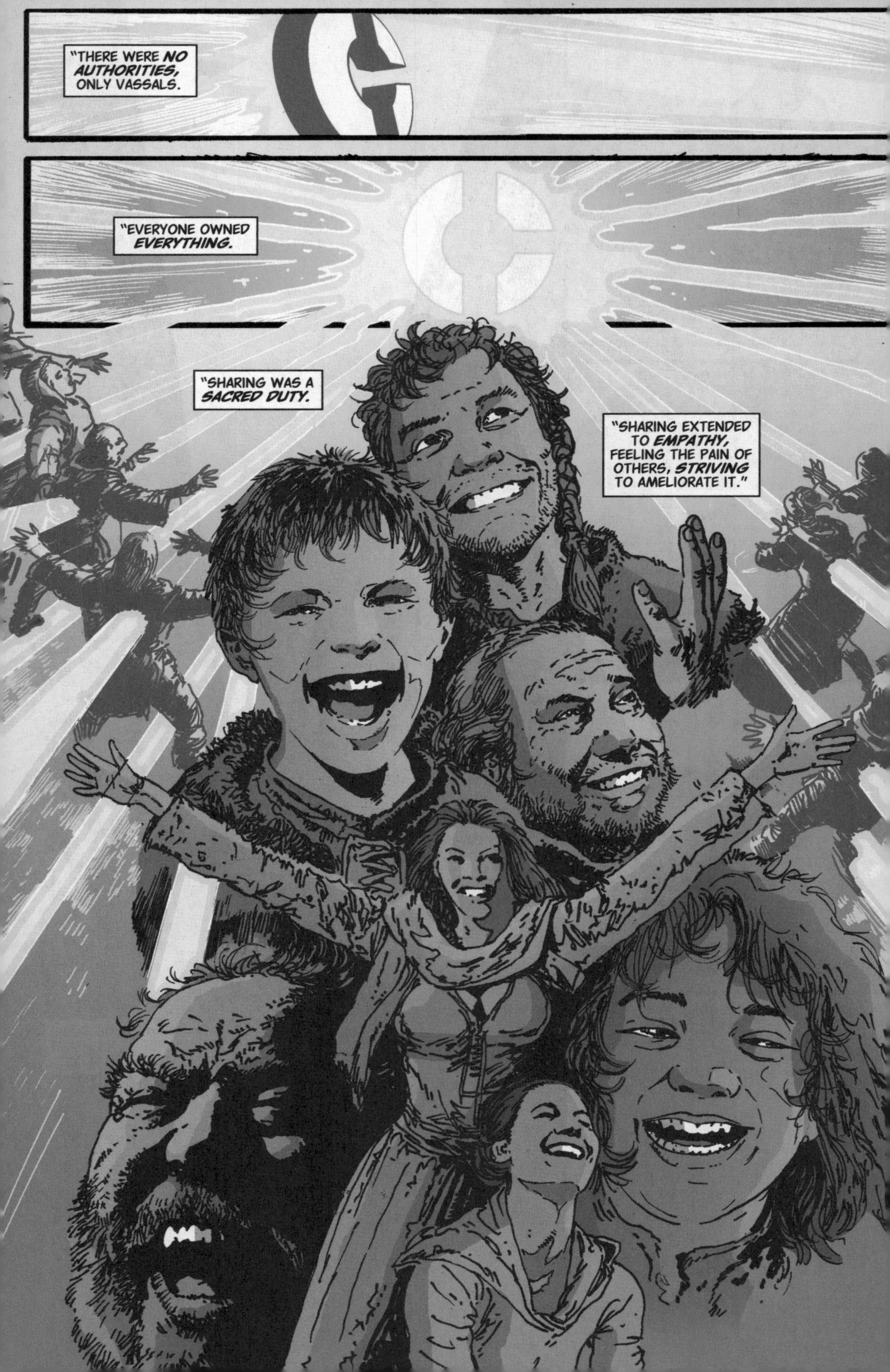
"THERE WERE NO AUTHORITIES, ONLY VASSALS.
"EVERYONE OWNED EVERYTHING.
"SHARING WAS A SACRED DUTY.
"SHARING EXTENDED TO EMPATHY, FEELING THE PAIN OF OTHERS, STRIVING TO AMELIORATE IT."

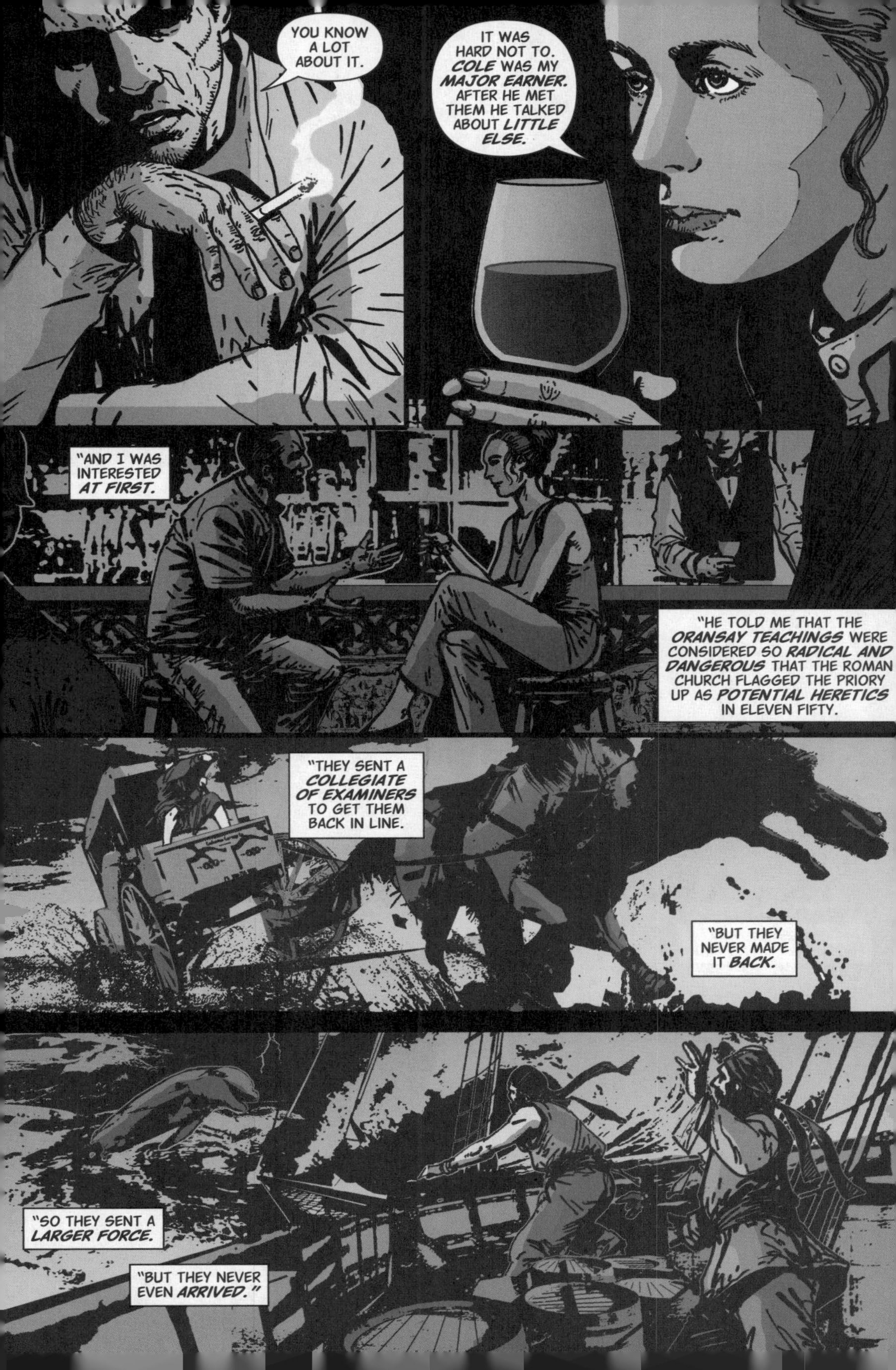
YOU KNOW A LOT ABOUT IT.
IT WAS HARD NOT TO. COLE WAS MY MAJOR EARNER. AFTER HE MET THEM HE TALKED ABOUT LITTLE ELSE.
"AND I WAS INTERESTED AT FIRST.
"HE TOLD ME THAT THE ORANSAY TEACHINGS WERE CONSIDERED SO RADICAL AND DANGEROUS THAT THE ROMAN CHURCH FLAGGED THE PRIORY UP AS POTENTIAL HERETICS IN ELEVEN FIFTY.
"THEY SENT A COLLEGIATE OF EXAMINERS TO GET THEM BACK IN LINE.
"BUT THEY NEVER MADE IT BACK.
"SO THEY SENT A LARGER FORCE.
"BUT THEY NEVER EVEN ARRIVED."

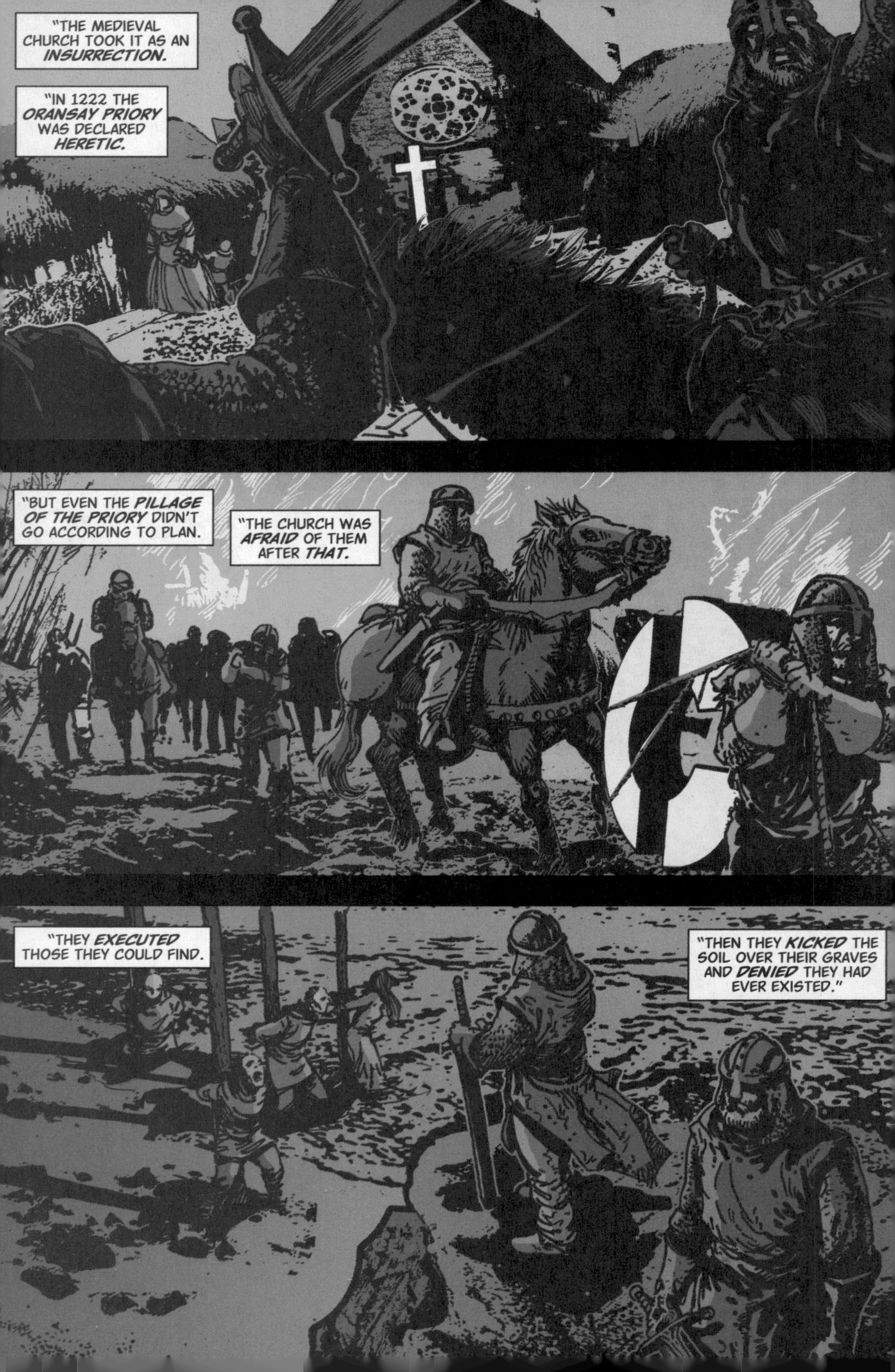
"THE MEDIEVAL CHURCH TOOK IT AS AN *INSURRECTION.*
"IN 1222 THE *ORANSAY PRIORY* WAS DECLARED *HERETIC.*
"BUT EVEN THE *PILLAGE OF THE PRIORY* DIDN'T GO ACCORDING TO PLAN.
"THE CHURCH WAS *AFRAID* OF THEM AFTER *THAT.*
"THEY *EXECUTED* THOSE THEY COULD FIND.
"THEN THEY *KICKED* THE SOIL OVER THEIR GRAVES AND *DENIED* THEY HAD EVER EXISTED."

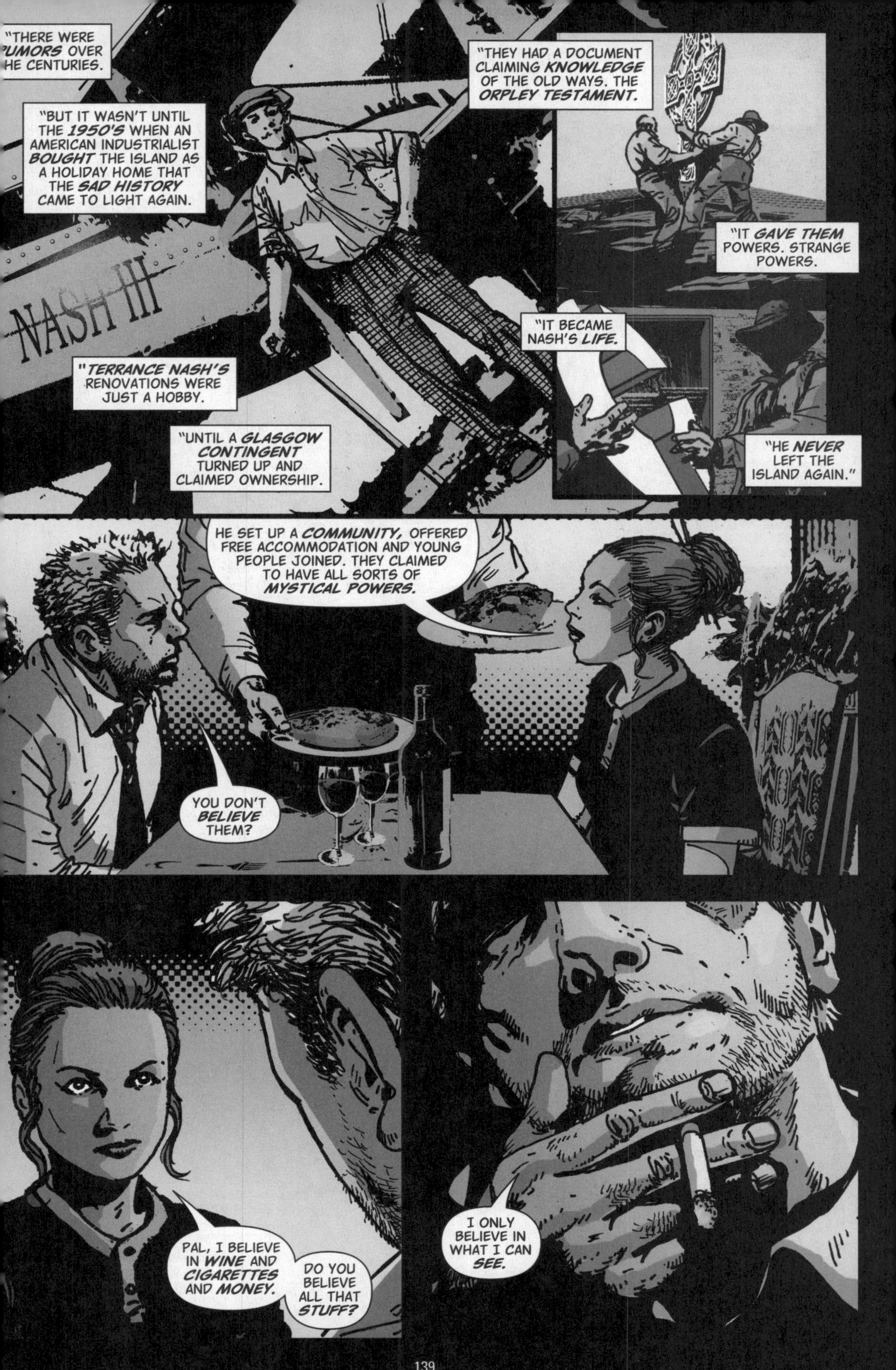
"THERE WERE RUMORS OVER THE CENTURIES.
"BUT IT WASN'T UNTIL THE 1950'S WHEN AN AMERICAN INDUSTRIALIST BOUGHT THE ISLAND AS A HOLIDAY HOME THAT THE SAD HISTORY CAME TO LIGHT AGAIN.
NASH III
"TERRANCE NASH'S RENOVATIONS WERE JUST A HOBBY.
"UNTIL A GLASGOW CONTINGENT TURNED UP AND CLAIMED OWNERSHIP.
"THEY HAD A DOCUMENT CLAIMING KNOWLEDGE OF THE OLD WAYS. THE ORPLEY TESTAMENT.
"IT GAVE THEM POWERS. STRANGE POWERS.
"IT BECAME NASH'S LIFE.
"HE NEVER LEFT THE ISLAND AGAIN."
HE SET UP A COMMUNITY, OFFERED FREE ACCOMMODATION AND YOUNG PEOPLE JOINED. THEY CLAIMED TO HAVE ALL SORTS OF MYSTICAL POWERS.
YOU DON'T BELIEVE THEM?
PAL, I BELIEVE IN WINE AND CIGARETTES AND MONEY.
DO YOU BELIEVE ALL THAT STUFF?
I ONLY BELIEVE IN WHAT I CAN SEE.

"IT WAS ALL KEPT ON THE ISLAND UNTIL A *NEW LEADER* EMERGED. HE TOOK OVER WHEN NASH DIED.

"HE WAS AS *NON-DESCRIPT* AS YOU COULD IMAGINE. EVEN HIS NAME WAS BLAND: *STEVE EVANS.*

"I NEVER UNDERSTOOD THE *ATTRACTION.*

"*EVANS* WAS THEIR FIRST *EVANGELIST.*

"DISTURBED BY THE *BRUTALITY* OF LIFE IN GLASGOW, HE WANTED TO TAKE THEIR MESSAGE TO THE WORLD.

"FIRST HE SENT ENVOYS. PRETTY GIRLS AND BOYS. SENT THEM TO PARTIES AND SO ON, TO SPREAD THE WORD, TRAVELLING THE WORLD, SEEDING THE MESSAGE.

"EVANS WAS *RECRUITING* THEM ALL HIMSELF.

"HE WAS DRIVING *BACK AND FORTH* TO THE ISLAND THREE TIMES A WEEK, UNTIL HE HAD A B..

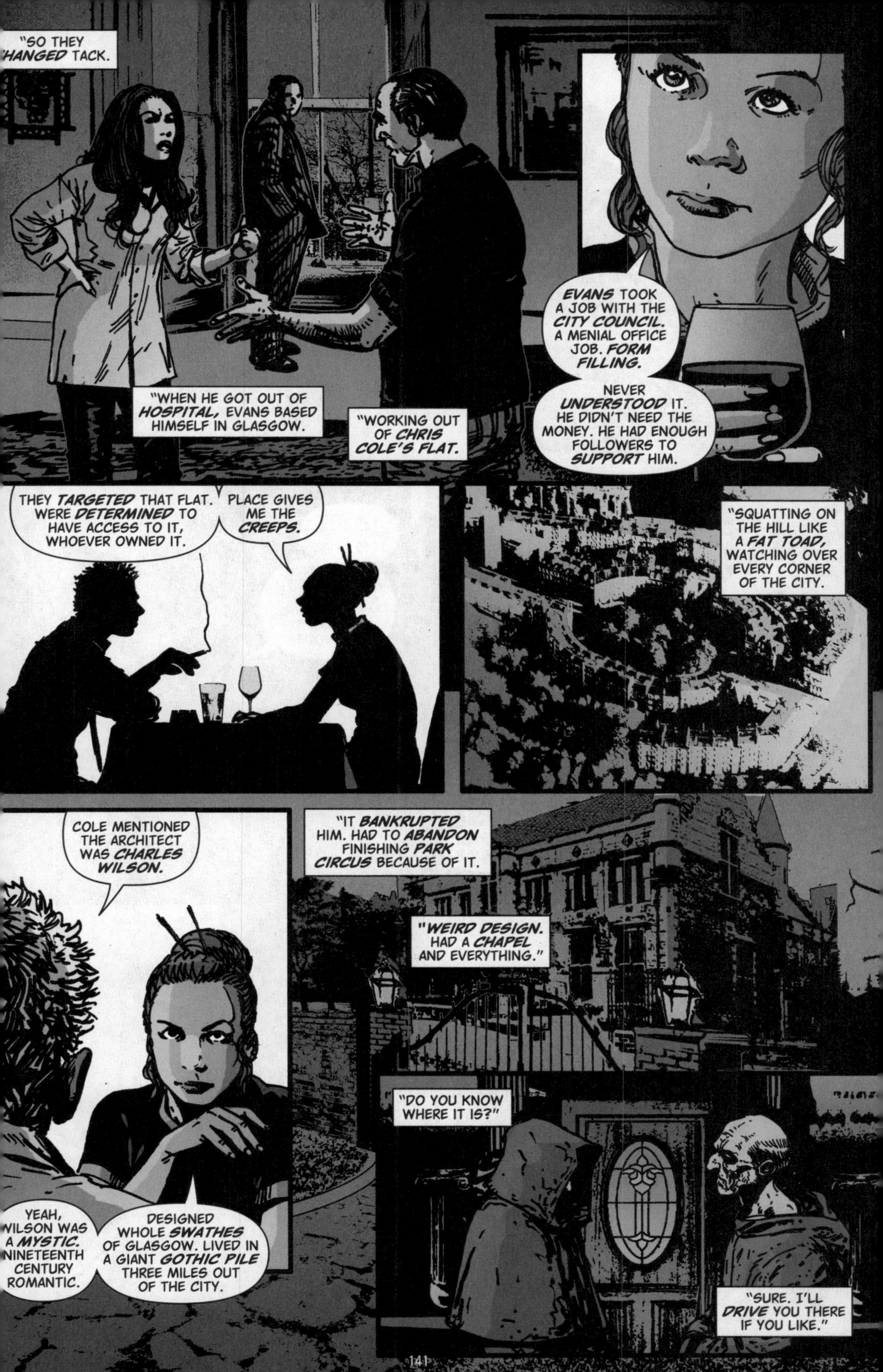
"SO THEY CHANGED TACK.
"WHEN HE GOT OUT OF HOSPITAL, EVANS BASED HIMSELF IN GLASGOW.
"WORKING OUT OF CHRIS COLE'S FLAT.
EVANS TOOK A JOB WITH THE CITY COUNCIL. A MENIAL OFFICE JOB. FORM FILLING.
NEVER UNDERSTOOD IT. HE DIDN'T NEED THE MONEY. HE HAD ENOUGH FOLLOWERS TO SUPPORT HIM.
THEY TARGETED THAT FLAT. WERE DETERMINED TO HAVE ACCESS TO IT, WHOEVER OWNED IT.
PLACE GIVES ME THE CREEPS.
"SQUATTING ON THE HILL LIKE A FAT TOAD, WATCHING OVER EVERY CORNER OF THE CITY.
COLE MENTIONED THE ARCHITECT WAS CHARLES WILSON.
YEAH, WILSON WAS A MYSTIC. NINETEENTH CENTURY ROMANTIC.
DESIGNED WHOLE SWATHES OF GLASGOW. LIVED IN A GIANT GOTHIC PILE THREE MILES OUT OF THE CITY.
"IT BANKRUPTED HIM. HAD TO ABANDON FINISHING PARK CIRCUS BECAUSE OF IT.
"WEIRD DESIGN. HAD A CHAPEL AND EVERYTHING."
"DO YOU KNOW WHERE IT IS?"
"SURE. I'LL DRIVE YOU THERE IF YOU LIKE."

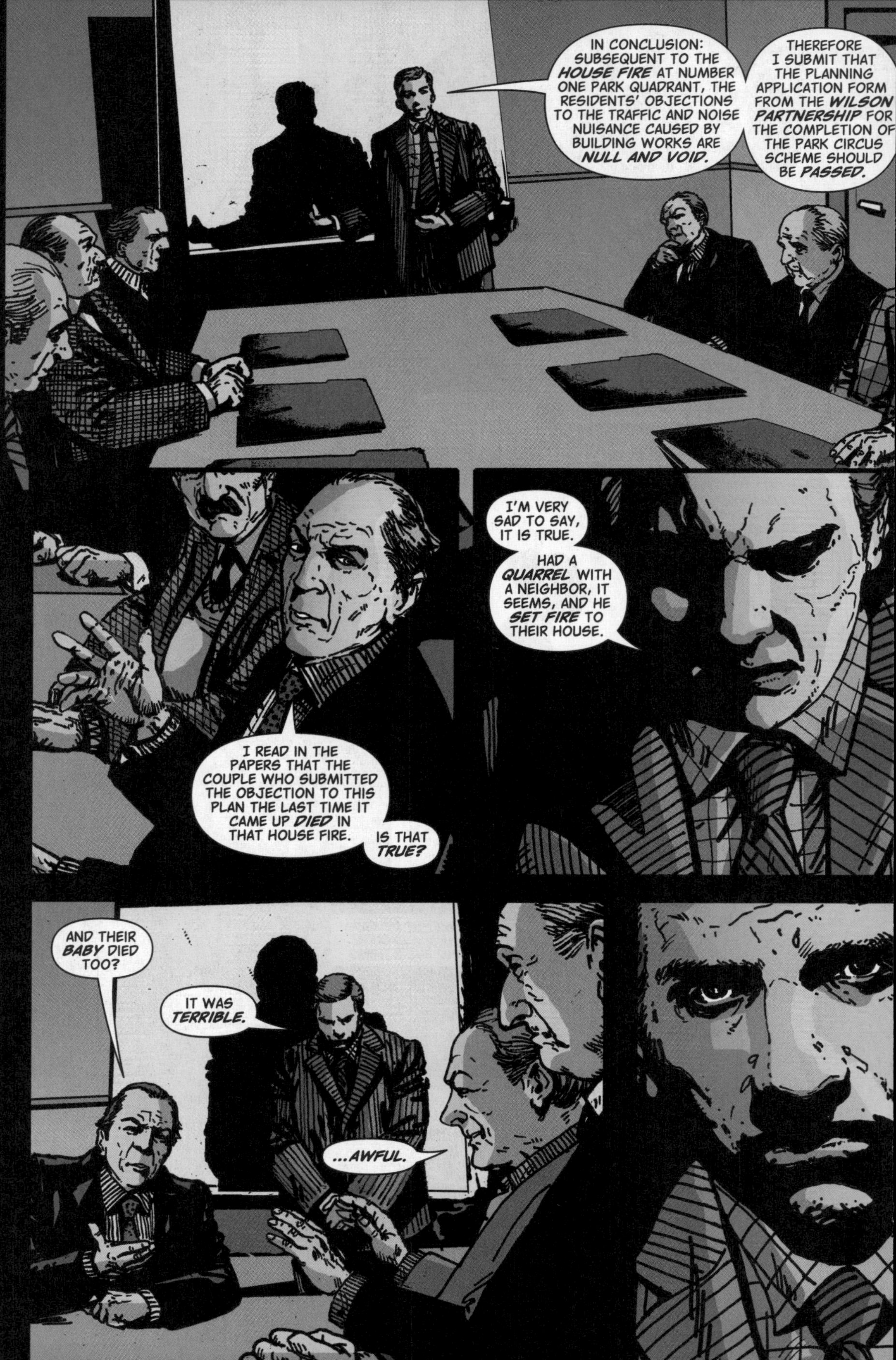
IN CONCLUSION: SUBSEQUENT TO THE HOUSE FIRE AT NUMBER ONE PARK QUADRANT, THE RESIDENTS' OBJECTIONS TO THE TRAFFIC AND NOISE NUISANCE CAUSED BY BUILDING WORKS ARE NULL AND VOID.
THEREFORE I SUBMIT THAT THE PLANNING APPLICATION FORM FROM THE WILSON PARTNERSHIP FOR THE COMPLETION OF THE PARK CIRCUS SCHEME SHOULD BE PASSED.
I READ IN THE PAPERS THAT THE COUPLE WHO SUBMITTED THE OBJECTION TO THIS PLAN THE LAST TIME IT CAME UP DIED IN THAT HOUSE FIRE.
IS THAT TRUE?
I'M VERY SAD TO SAY, IT IS TRUE.
HAD A QUARREL WITH A NEIGHBOR, IT SEEMS, AND HE SET FIRE TO THEIR HOUSE.
AND THEIR BABY DIED TOO?
IT WAS TERRIBLE.
...AWFUL.

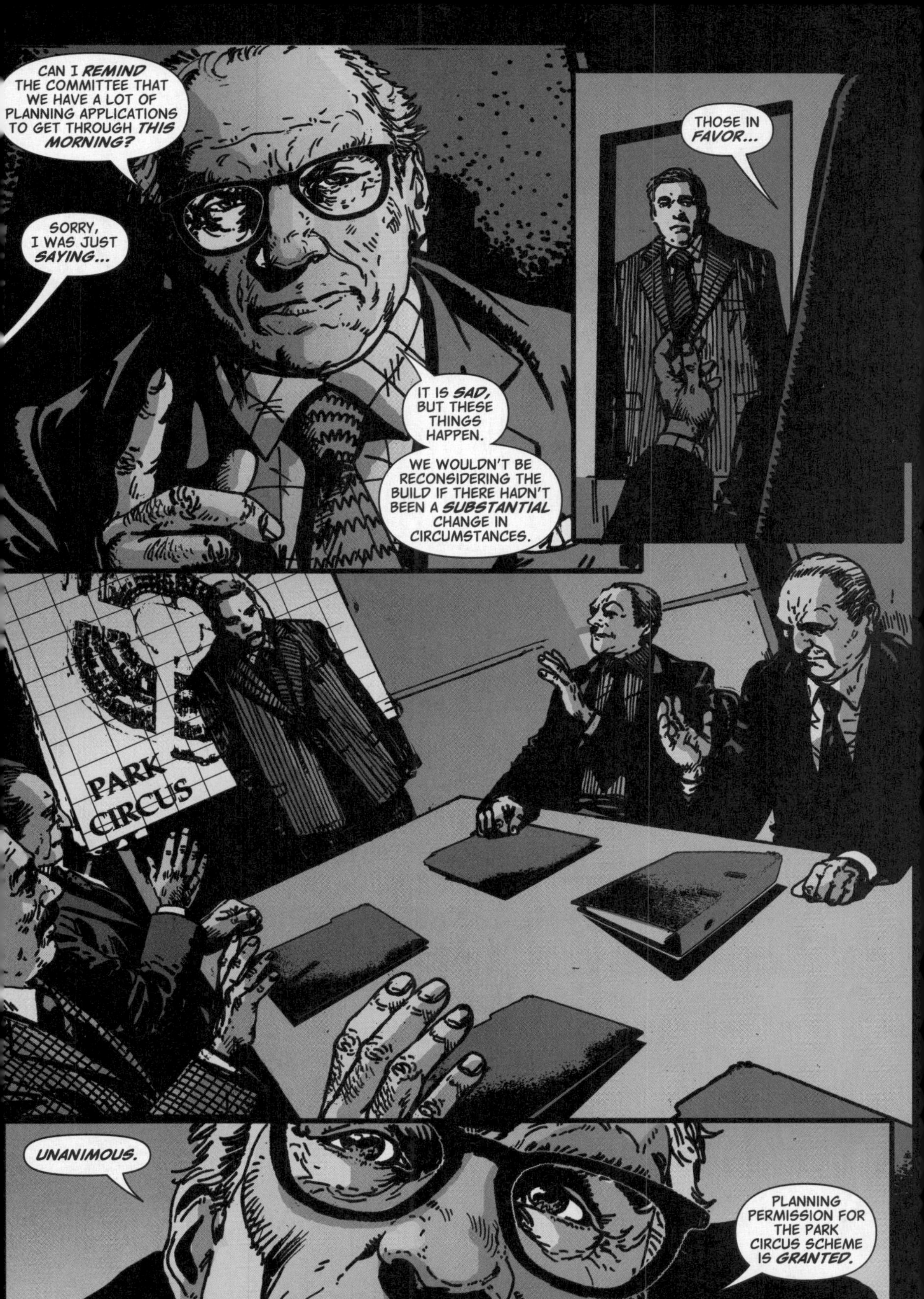
CAN I *REMIND* THE COMMITTEE THAT WE HAVE A LOT OF PLANNING APPLICATIONS TO GET THROUGH *THIS MORNING?*
SORRY, I WAS JUST *SAYING...*
IT IS *SAD,* BUT THESE THINGS HAPPEN.
WE WOULDN'T BE RECONSIDERING THE BUILD IF THERE HADN'T BEEN A *SUBSTANTIAL* CHANGE IN CIRCUMSTANCES.
THOSE IN *FAVOR...*
PARK CIRCUS
UNANIMOUS.
PLANNING PERMISSION FOR THE PARK CIRCUS SCHEME IS *GRANTED.*

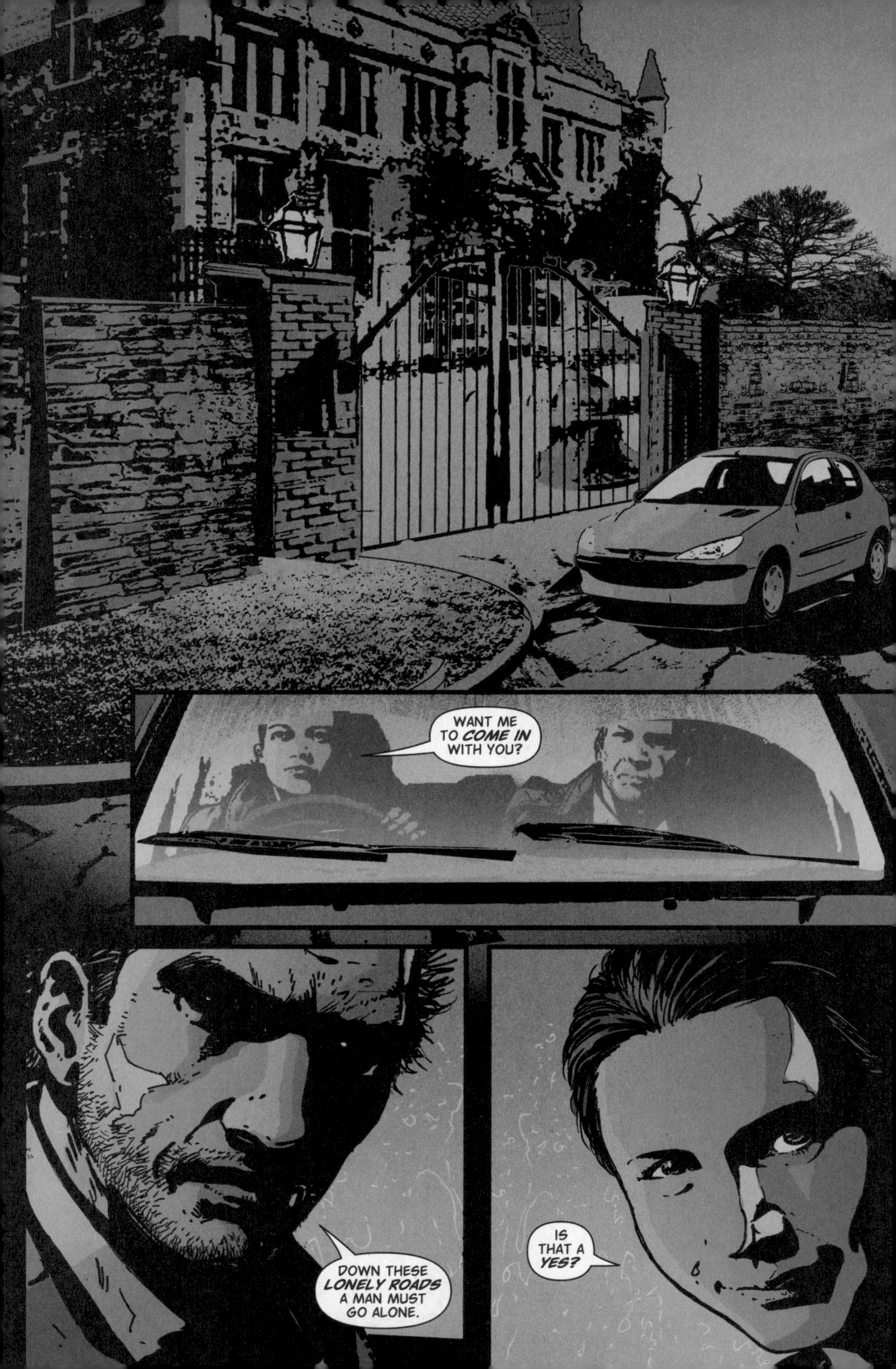
WANT ME TO *COME IN* WITH YOU?
DOWN THESE *LONELY ROADS* A MAN MUST GO ALONE.
IS THAT A *YES?*

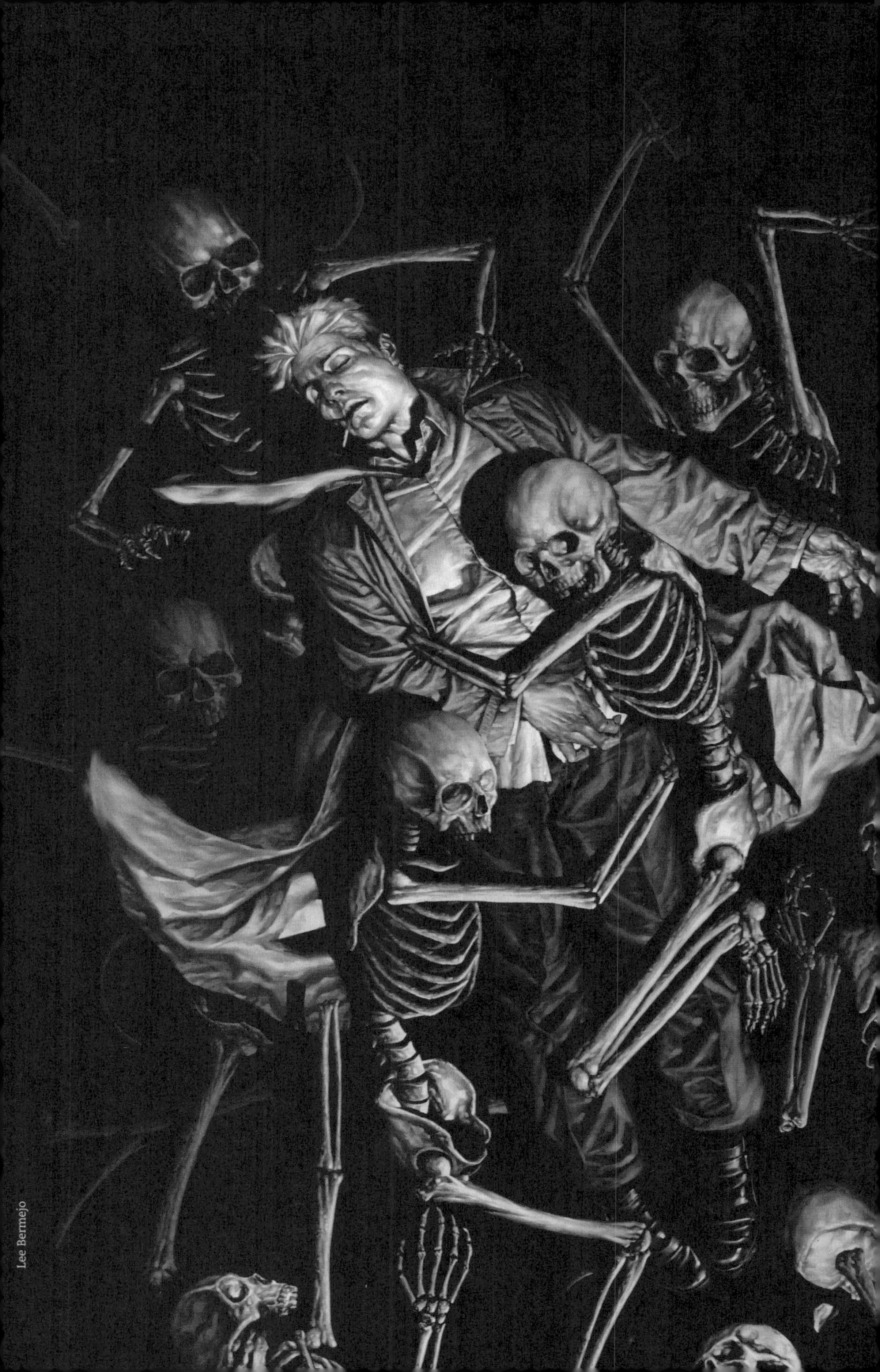

Lee Bermejo

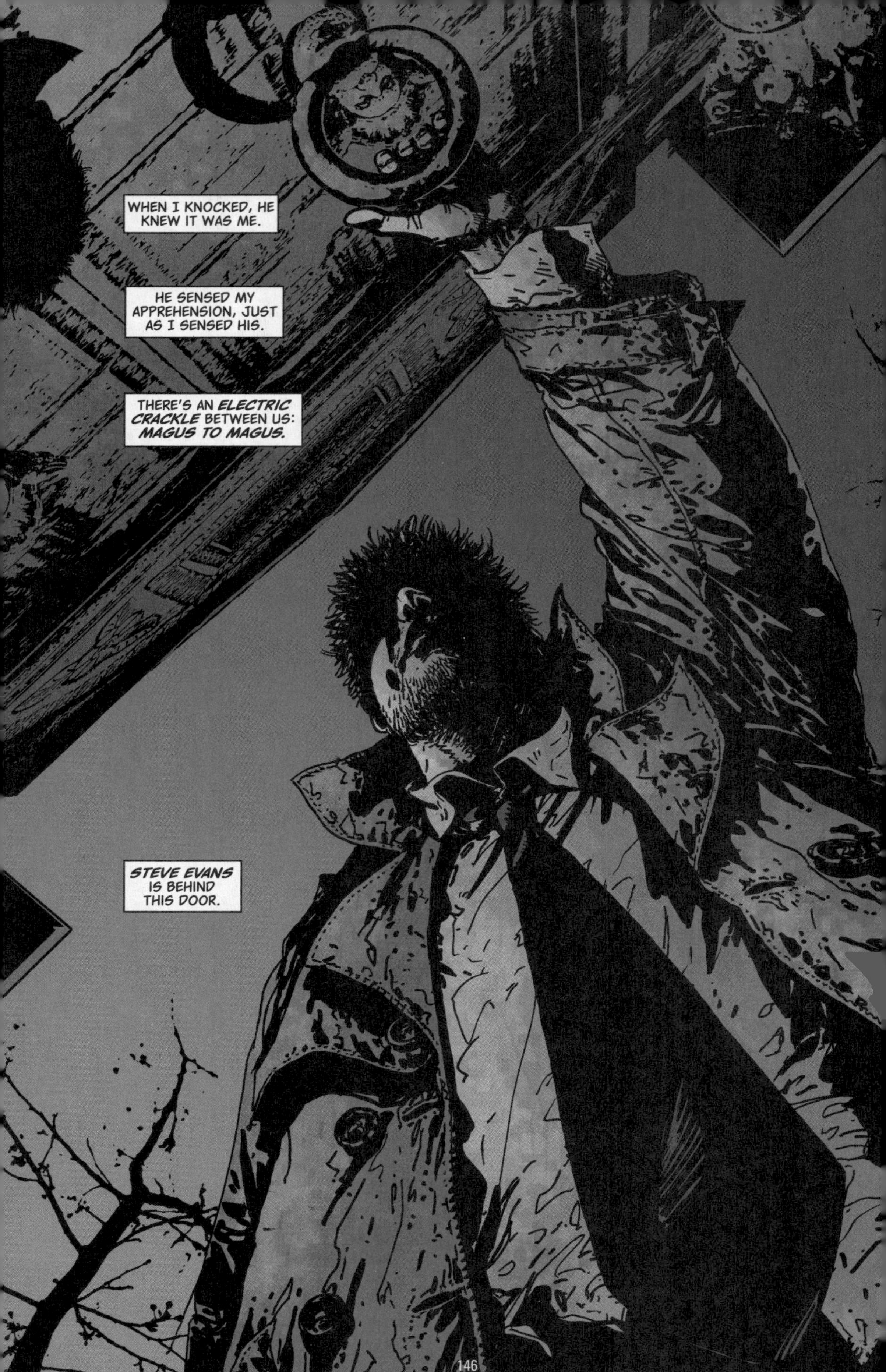
WHEN I KNOCKED, HE KNEW IT WAS ME.
HE SENSED MY APPREHENSION, JUST AS I SENSED HIS.
THERE'S AN *ELECTRIC CRACKLE* BETWEEN US: *MAGUS TO MAGUS.*
STEVE EVANS IS BEHIND THIS DOOR.

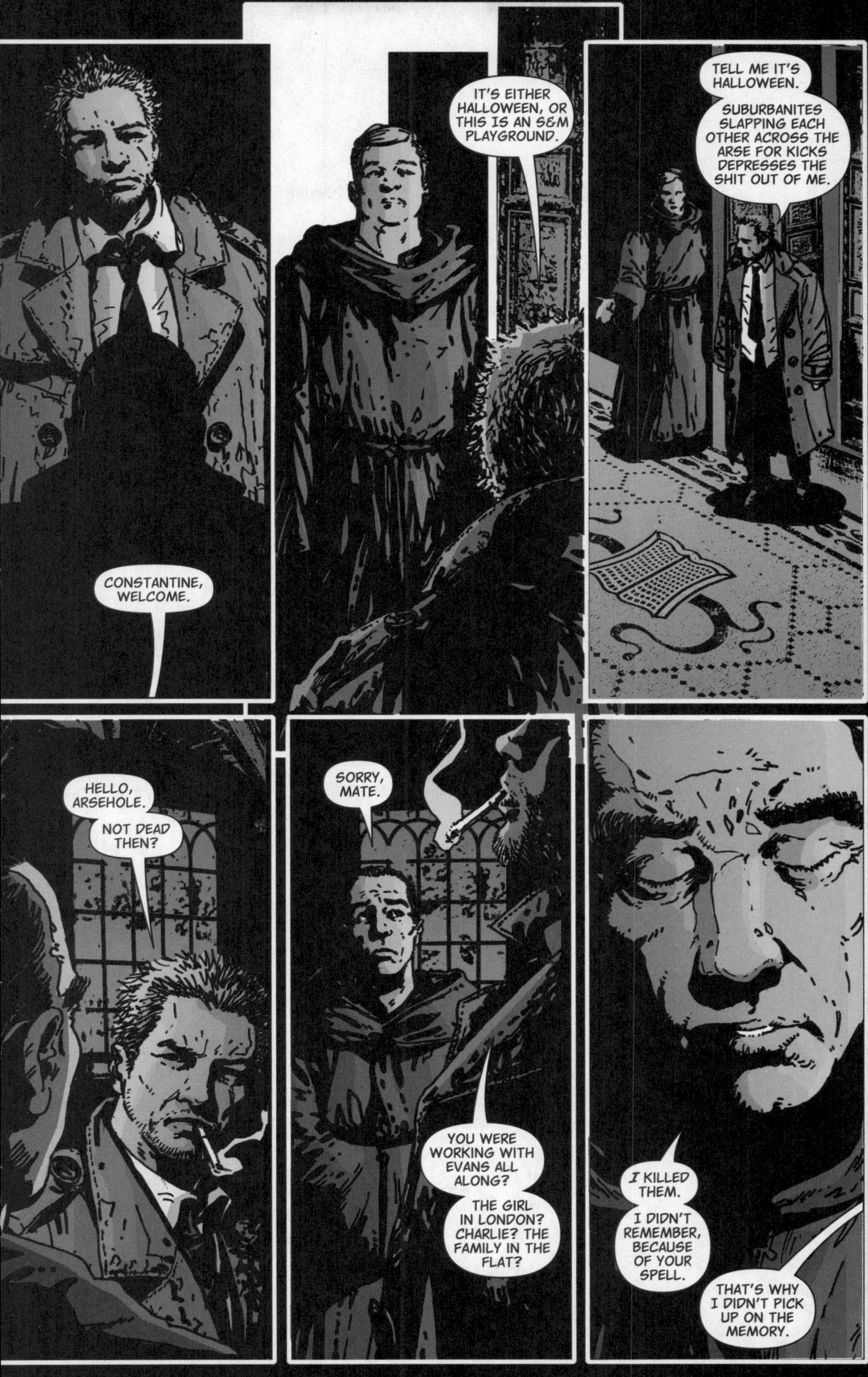
CONSTANTINE, WELCOME.
IT'S EITHER HALLOWEEN, OR THIS IS AN S&M PLAYGROUND.
TELL ME IT'S HALLOWEEN.
SUBURBANITES SLAPPING EACH OTHER ACROSS THE ARSE FOR KICKS DEPRESSES THE SHIT OUT OF ME.
HELLO, ARSEHOLE.
NOT DEAD THEN?
SORRY, MATE.
YOU WERE WORKING WITH EVANS ALL ALONG?
THE GIRL IN LONDON? CHARLIE? THE FAMILY IN THE FLAT?
I KILLED THEM.
I DIDN'T REMEMBER, BECAUSE OF YOUR SPELL.
THAT'S WHY I DIDN'T PICK UP ON THE MEMORY.

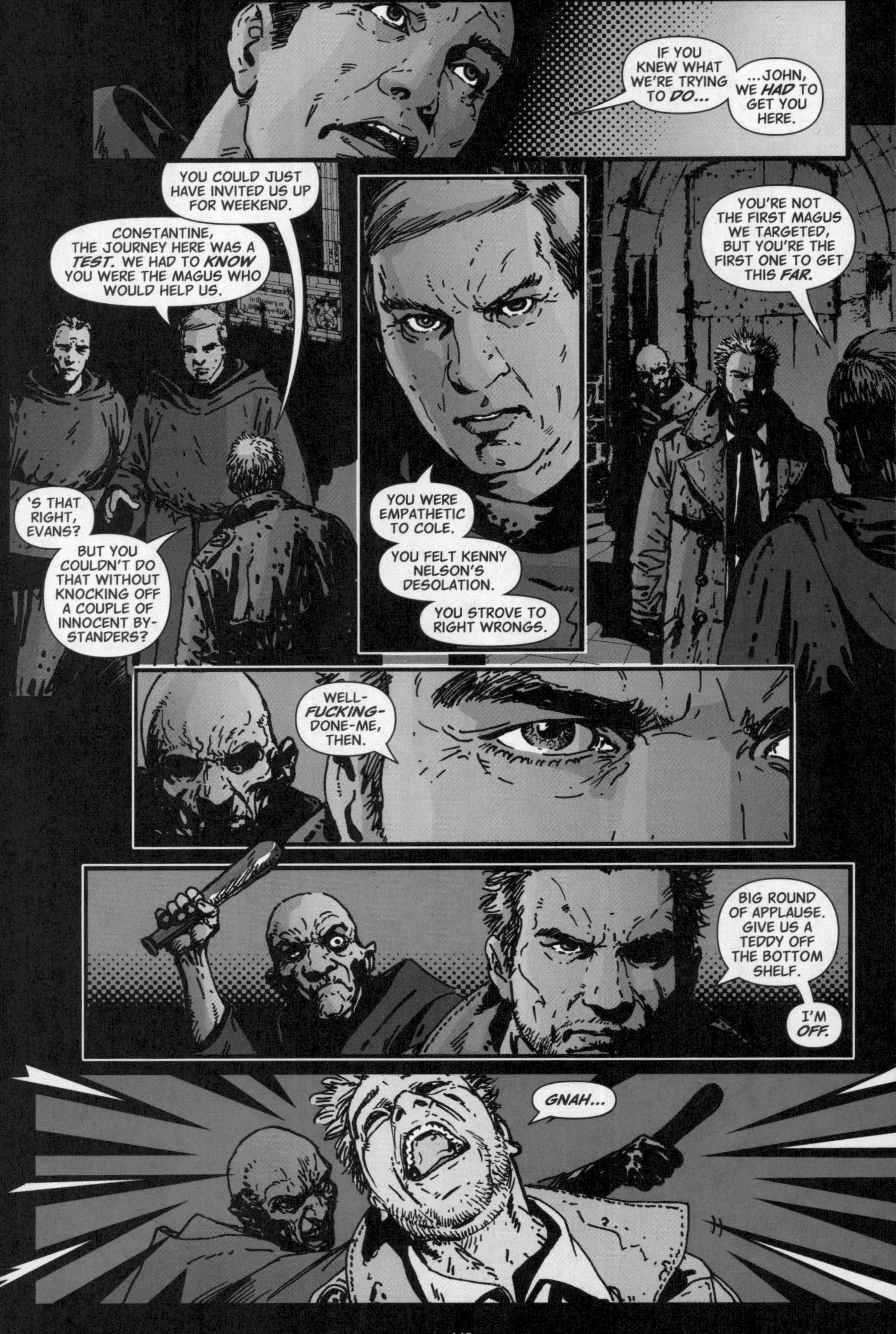
IF YOU KNEW WHAT WE'RE TRYING TO *DO*...
...JOHN, WE *HAD* TO GET YOU HERE.
YOU COULD JUST HAVE INVITED US UP FOR WEEKEND.
CONSTANTINE, THE JOURNEY HERE WAS A *TEST.* WE HAD TO *KNOW* YOU WERE THE MAGUS WHO WOULD HELP US.
'S THAT RIGHT, EVANS?
BUT YOU COULDN'T DO THAT WITHOUT KNOCKING OFF A COUPLE OF INNOCENT BY-STANDERS?
YOU WERE EMPATHETIC TO COLE.
YOU FELT KENNY NELSON'S DESOLATION.
YOU STROVE TO RIGHT WRONGS.
YOU'RE NOT THE FIRST MAGUS WE TARGETED, BUT YOU'RE THE FIRST ONE TO GET THIS *FAR.*
WELL-*FUCKING*-DONE-ME, THEN.
BIG ROUND OF APPLAUSE. GIVE US A TEDDY OFF THE BOTTOM SHELF.
I'M *OFF.*
GNAH...

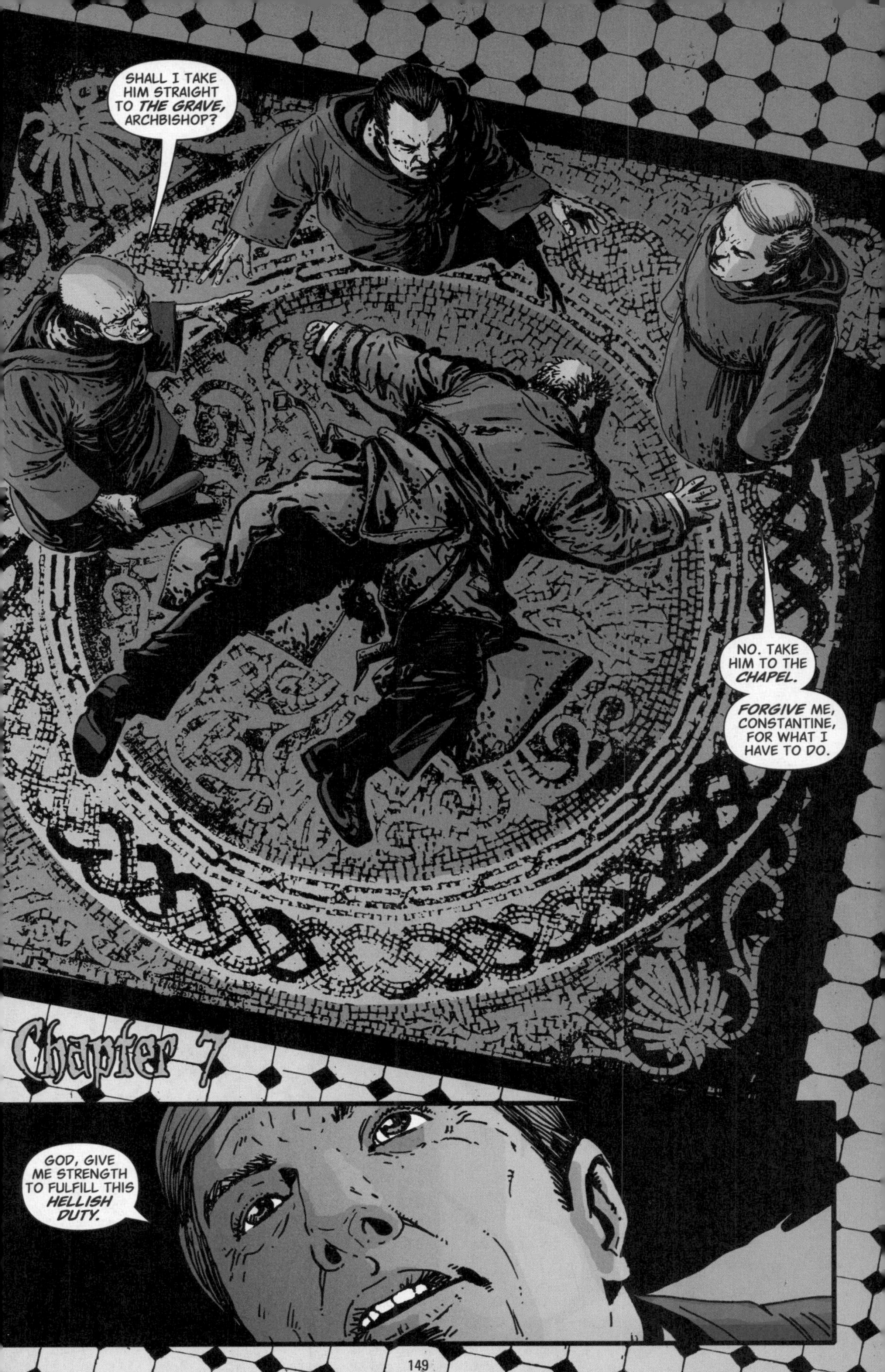
SHALL I TAKE HIM STRAIGHT TO THE GRAVE, ARCHBISHOP?
NO. TAKE HIM TO THE CHAPEL.
FORGIVE ME, CONSTANTINE, FOR WHAT I HAVE TO DO.
Chapter 7
GOD, GIVE ME STRENGTH TO FULFILL THIS HELLISH DUTY.

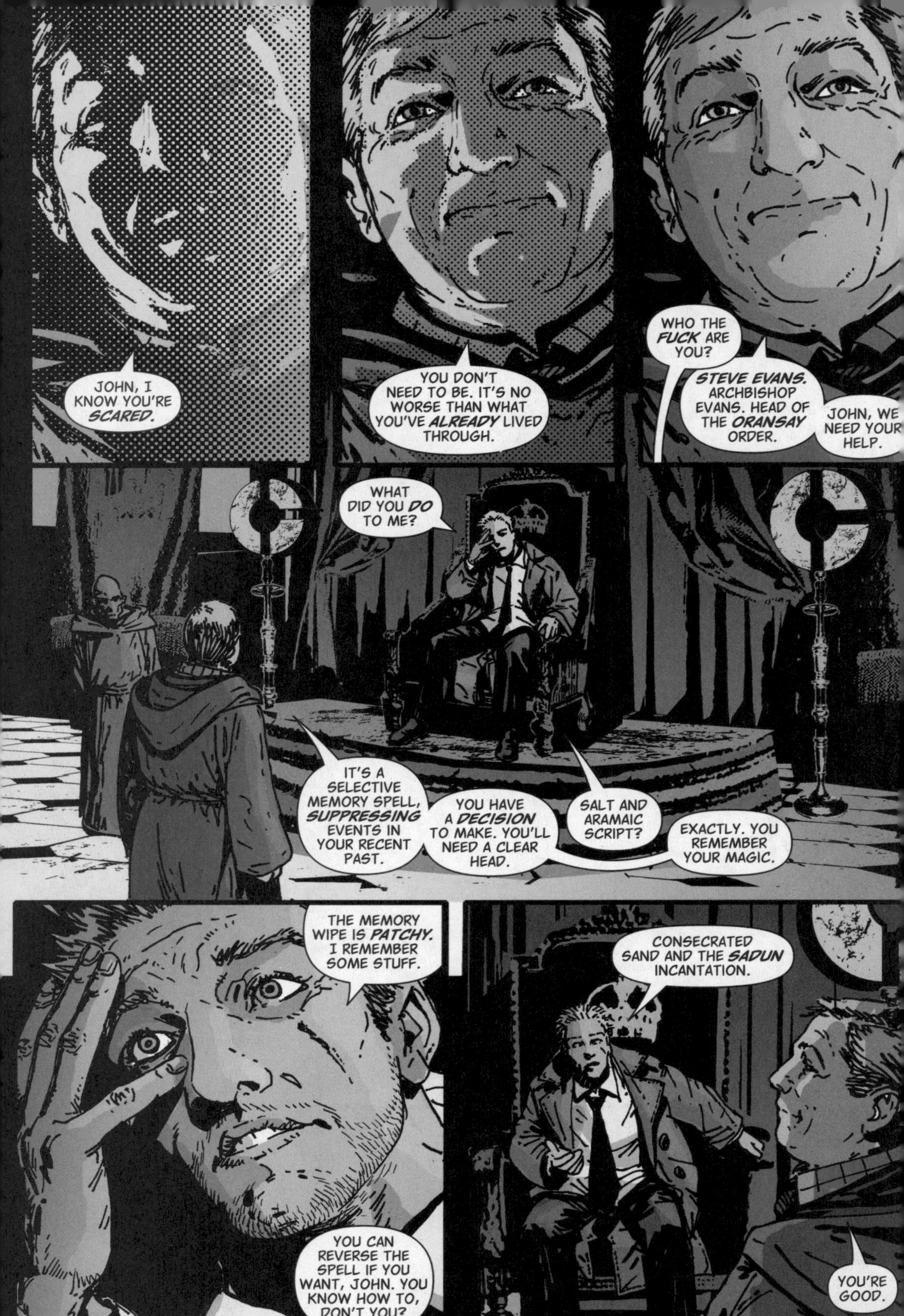
JOHN, I KNOW YOU'RE SCARED.
YOU DON'T NEED TO BE. IT'S NO WORSE THAN WHAT YOU'VE ALREADY LIVED THROUGH.
WHO THE FUCK ARE YOU?
STEVE EVANS. ARCHBISHOP EVANS. HEAD OF THE ORANSAY ORDER.
JOHN, WE NEED YOUR HELP.
WHAT DID YOU DO TO ME?
IT'S A SELECTIVE MEMORY SPELL, SUPPRESSING EVENTS IN YOUR RECENT PAST.
YOU HAVE A DECISION TO MAKE. YOU'LL NEED A CLEAR HEAD.
SALT AND ARAMAIC SCRIPT?
EXACTLY. YOU REMEMBER YOUR MAGIC.
THE MEMORY WIPE IS PATCHY. I REMEMBER SOME STUFF.
YOU CAN REVERSE THE SPELL IF YOU WANT, JOHN. YOU KNOW HOW TO, DON'T YOU?
CONSECRATED SAND AND THE SADUN INCANTATION.
YOU'RE GOOD.

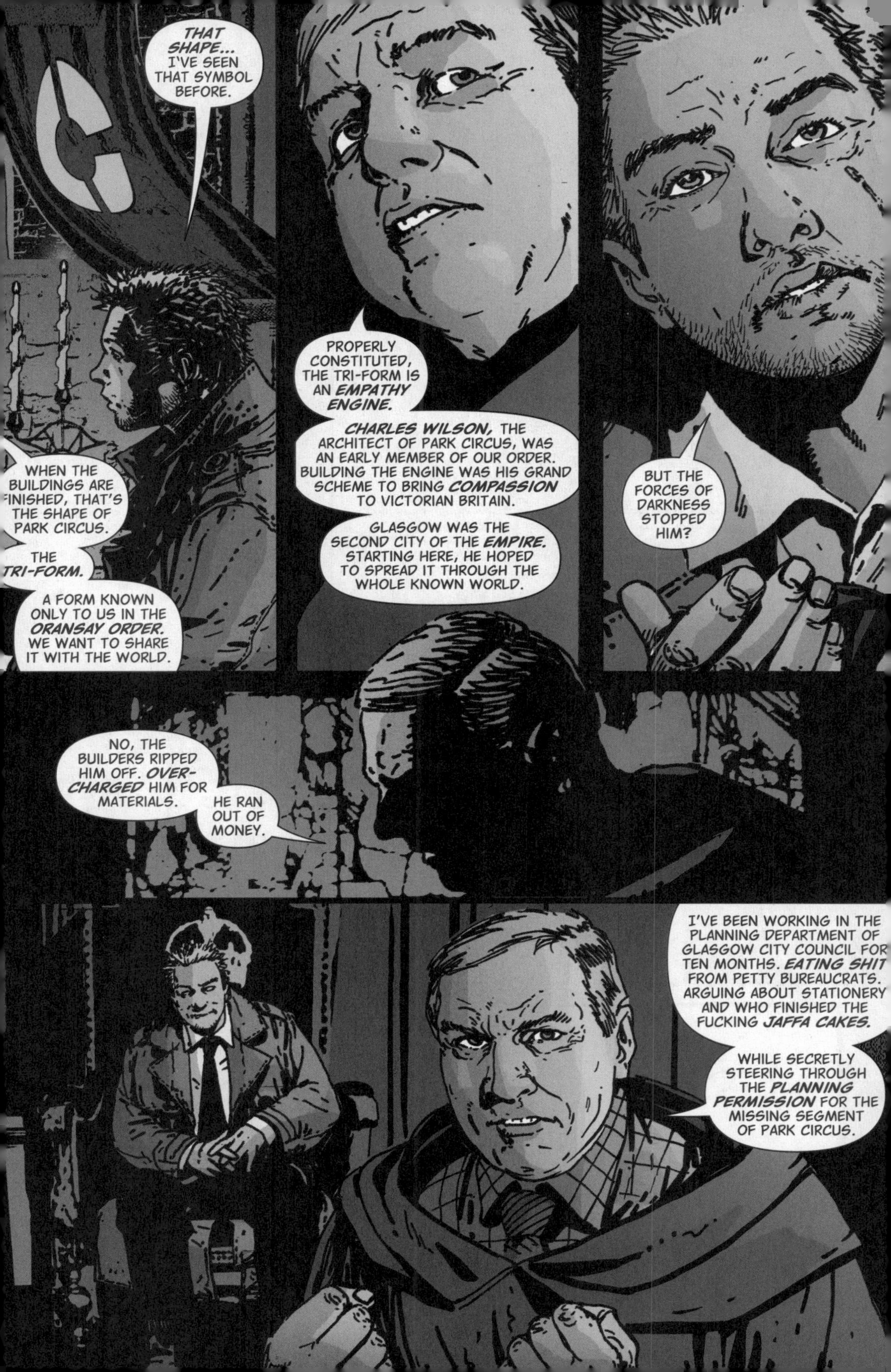
THAT SHAPE... I'VE SEEN THAT SYMBOL BEFORE.
PROPERLY CONSTITUTED, THE TRI-FORM IS AN EMPATHY ENGINE.
CHARLES WILSON, THE ARCHITECT OF PARK CIRCUS, WAS AN EARLY MEMBER OF OUR ORDER. BUILDING THE ENGINE WAS HIS GRAND SCHEME TO BRING COMPASSION TO VICTORIAN BRITAIN.
GLASGOW WAS THE SECOND CITY OF THE EMPIRE. STARTING HERE, HE HOPED TO SPREAD IT THROUGH THE WHOLE KNOWN WORLD.
WHEN THE BUILDINGS ARE FINISHED, THAT'S THE SHAPE OF PARK CIRCUS.
THE TRI-FORM.
A FORM KNOWN ONLY TO US IN THE ORANSAY ORDER. WE WANT TO SHARE IT WITH THE WORLD.
BUT THE FORCES OF DARKNESS STOPPED HIM?
NO, THE BUILDERS RIPPED HIM OFF. OVER-CHARGED HIM FOR MATERIALS.
HE RAN OUT OF MONEY.
I'VE BEEN WORKING IN THE PLANNING DEPARTMENT OF GLASGOW CITY COUNCIL FOR TEN MONTHS. EATING SHIT FROM PETTY BUREAUCRATS. ARGUING ABOUT STATIONERY AND WHO FINISHED THE FUCKING JAFFA CAKES.
WHILE SECRETLY STEERING THROUGH THE PLANNING PERMISSION FOR THE MISSING SEGMENT OF PARK CIRCUS.

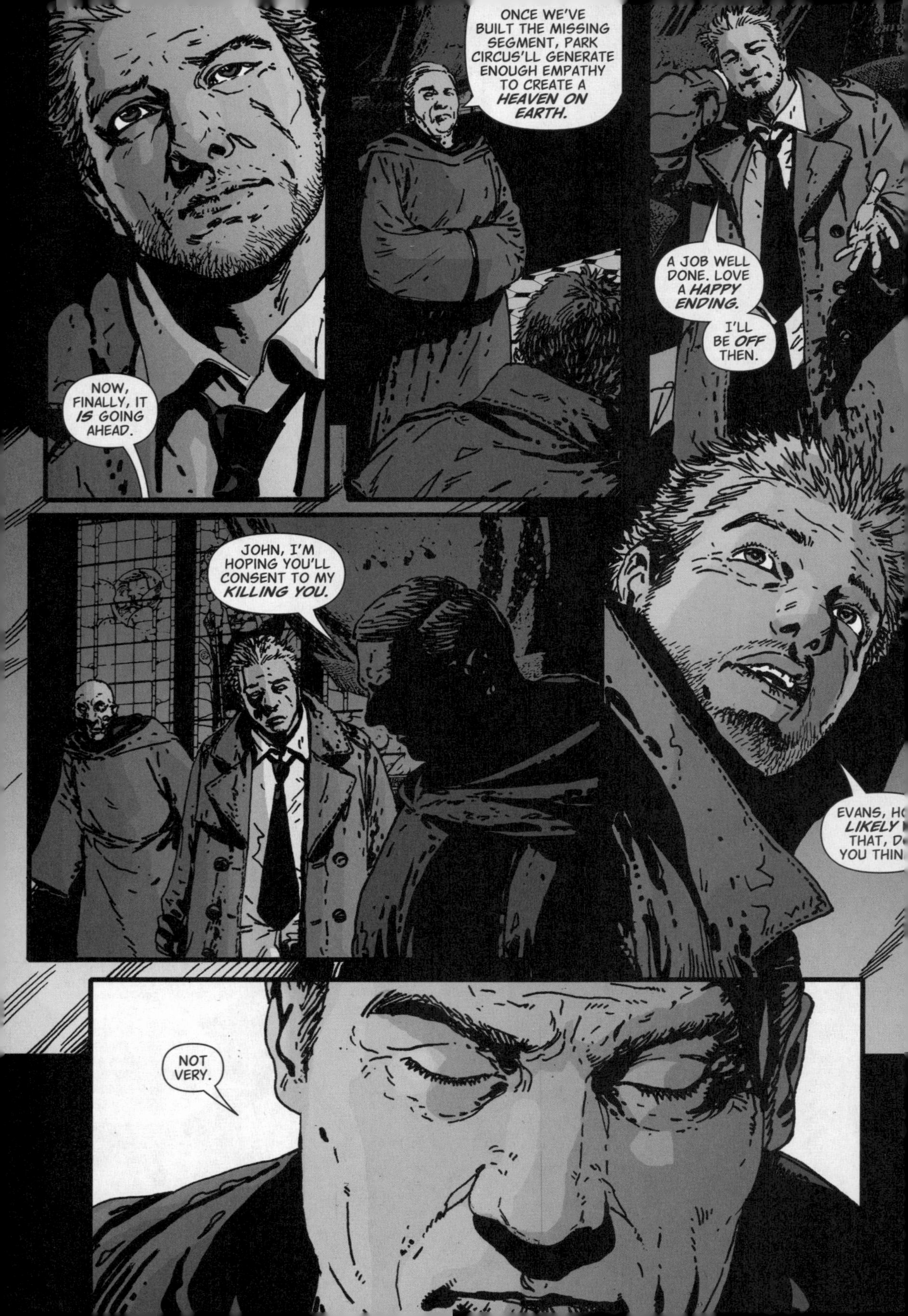
NOW, FINALLY, IT *IS* GOING AHEAD.
ONCE WE'VE BUILT THE MISSING SEGMENT, PARK CIRCUS'LL GENERATE ENOUGH EMPATHY TO CREATE A *HEAVEN ON EARTH.*
A JOB WELL DONE. LOVE A *HAPPY ENDING.*
I'LL BE *OFF* THEN.
JOHN, I'M HOPING YOU'LL CONSENT TO MY *KILLING YOU.*
EVANS, HO *LIKELY* THAT, D YOU THIN
NOT VERY.

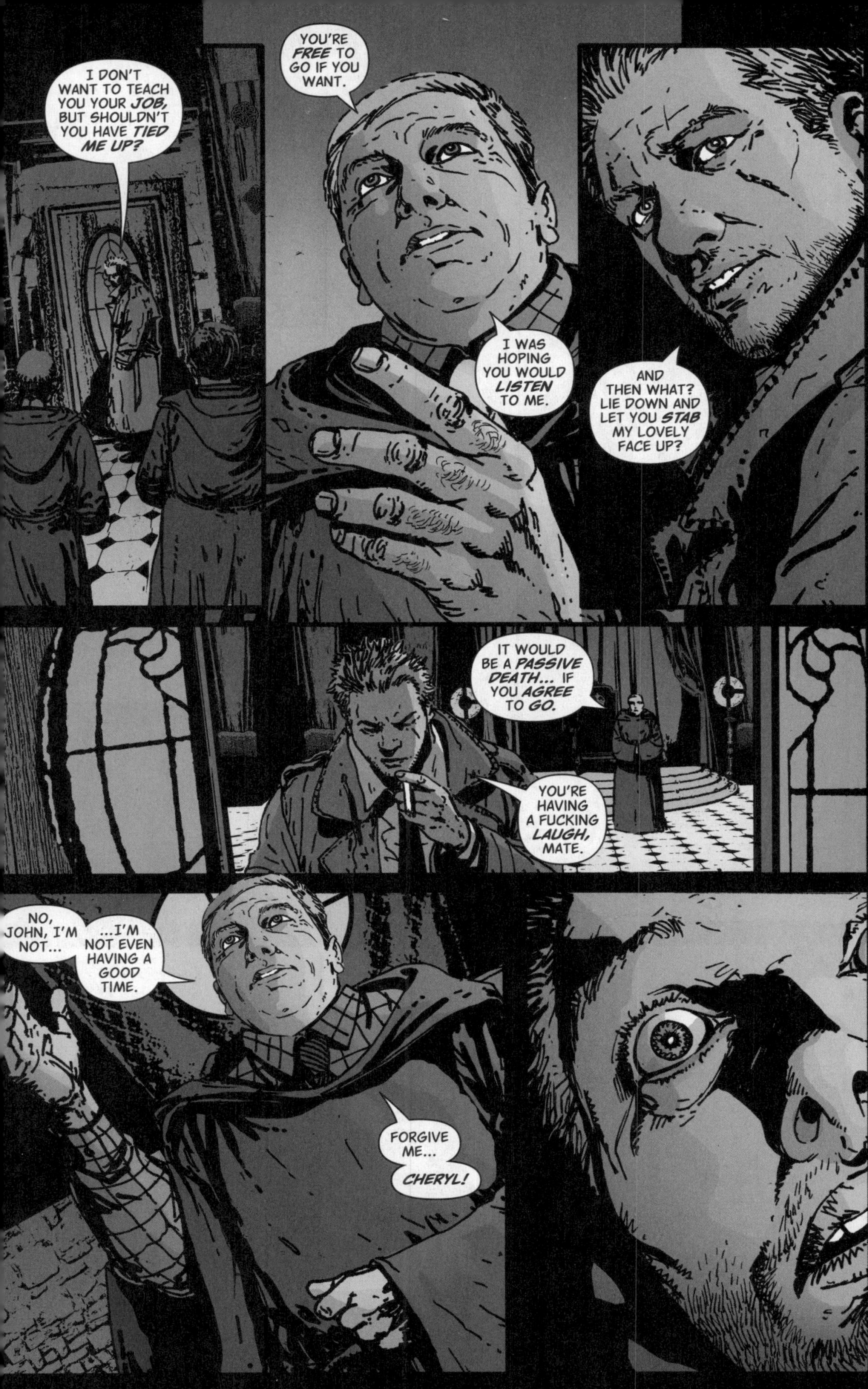
I DON'T WANT TO TEACH YOU YOUR JOB, BUT SHOULDN'T YOU HAVE TIED ME UP?
YOU'RE FREE TO GO IF YOU WANT.
I WAS HOPING YOU WOULD LISTEN TO ME.
AND THEN WHAT? LIE DOWN AND LET YOU STAB MY LOVELY FACE UP?
IT WOULD BE A PASSIVE DEATH... IF YOU AGREE TO GO.
YOU'RE HAVING A FUCKING LAUGH, MATE.
NO, JOHN, I'M NOT...
...I'M NOT EVEN HAVING A GOOD TIME.
FORGIVE ME...
CHERYL!

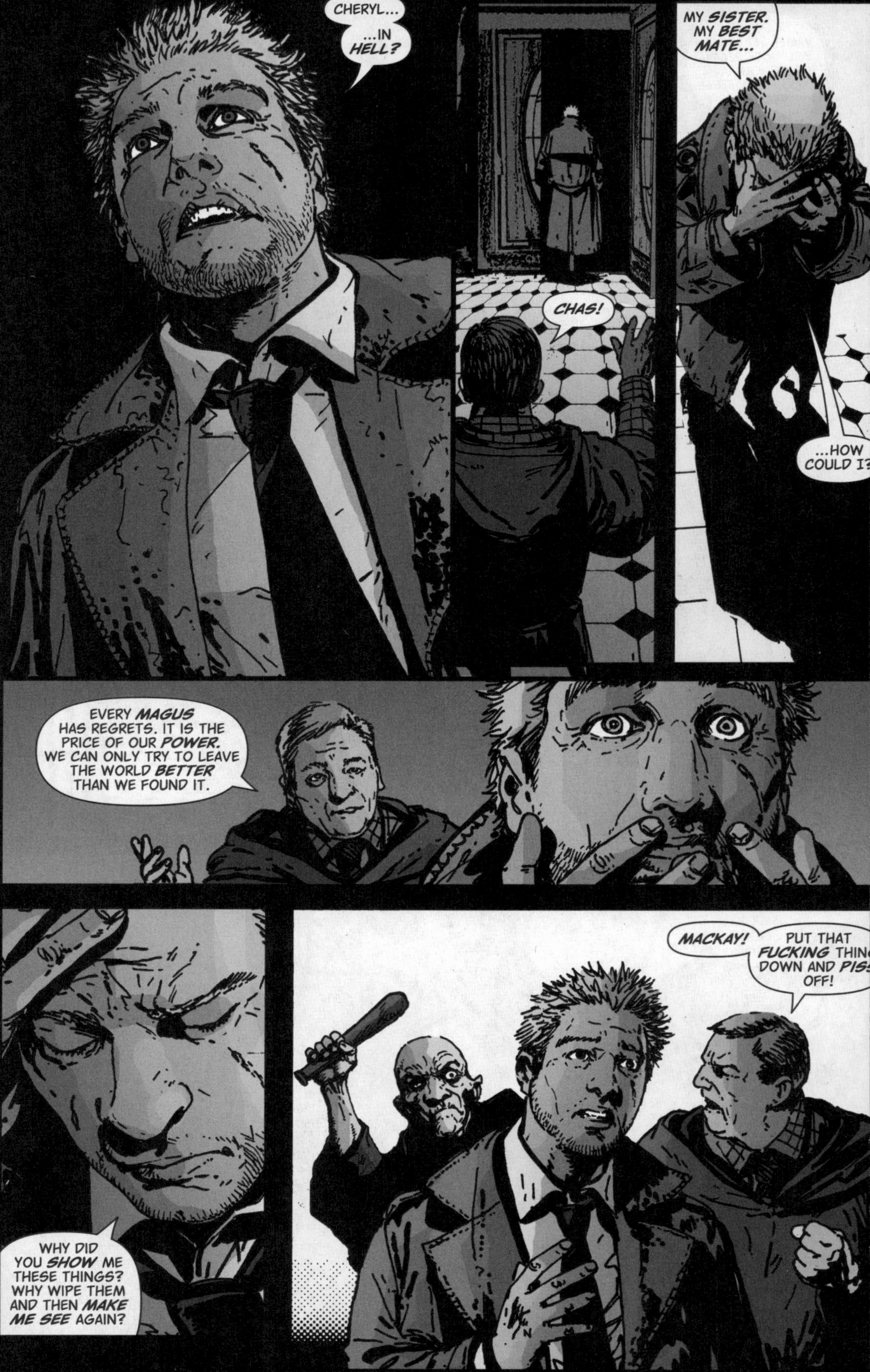
CHERYL...
...IN HELL?
CHAS!
MY SISTER. MY BEST MATE...
...HOW COULD I?
EVERY MAGUS HAS REGRETS. IT IS THE PRICE OF OUR POWER. WE CAN ONLY TRY TO LEAVE THE WORLD BETTER THAN WE FOUND IT.
WHY DID YOU SHOW ME THESE THINGS? WHY WIPE THEM AND THEN MAKE ME SEE AGAIN?
MACKAY!
PUT THAT FUCKING THING DOWN AND PISS OFF!

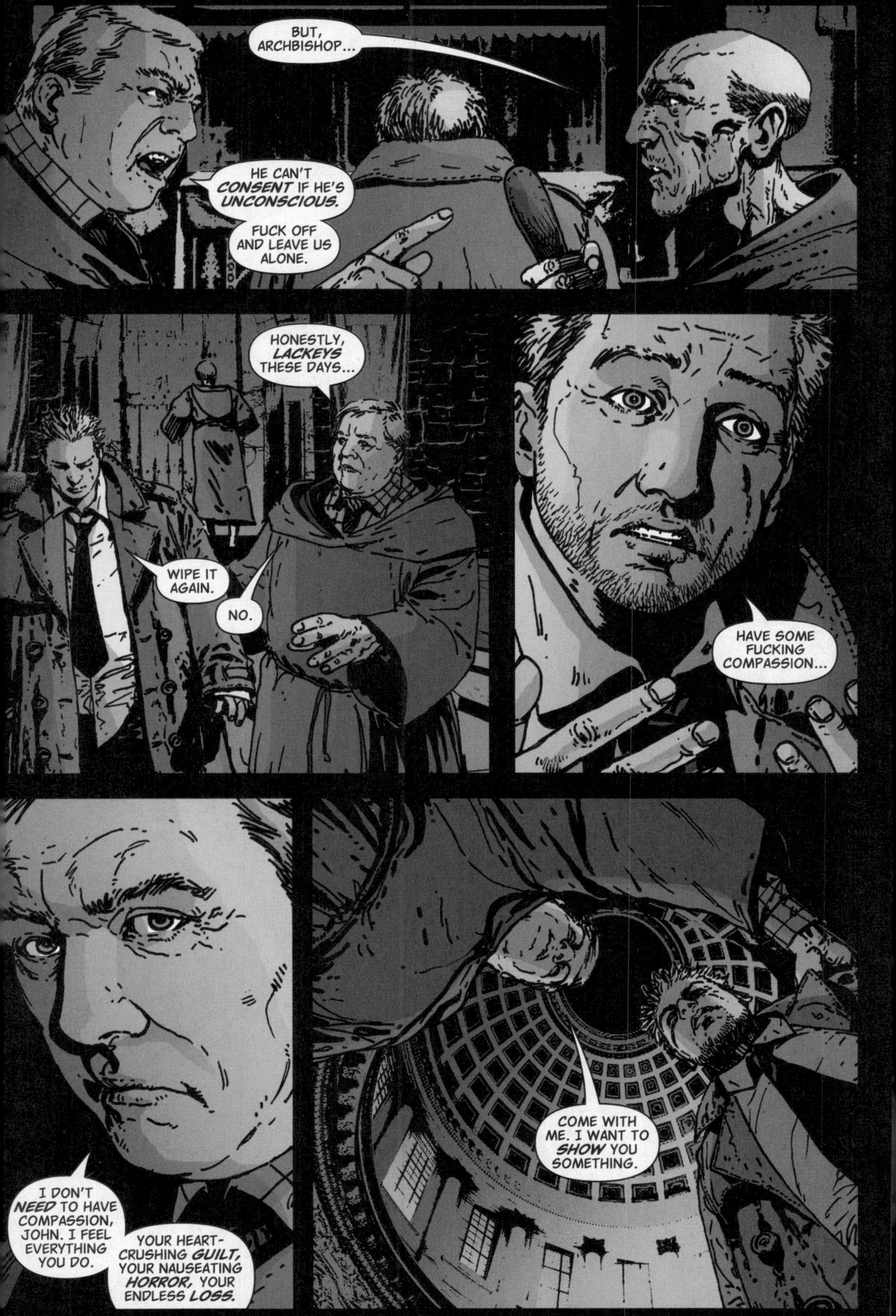
BUT, ARCHBISHOP...
HE CAN'T CONSENT IF HE'S UNCONSCIOUS.
FUCK OFF AND LEAVE US ALONE.
HONESTLY, LACKEYS THESE DAYS...
WIPE IT AGAIN.
NO.
HAVE SOME FUCKING COMPASSION...
I DON'T NEED TO HAVE COMPASSION, JOHN. I FEEL EVERYTHING YOU DO.
YOUR HEART-CRUSHING GUILT, YOUR NAUSEATING HORROR, YOUR ENDLESS LOSS.
COME WITH ME. I WANT TO SHOW YOU SOMETHING.

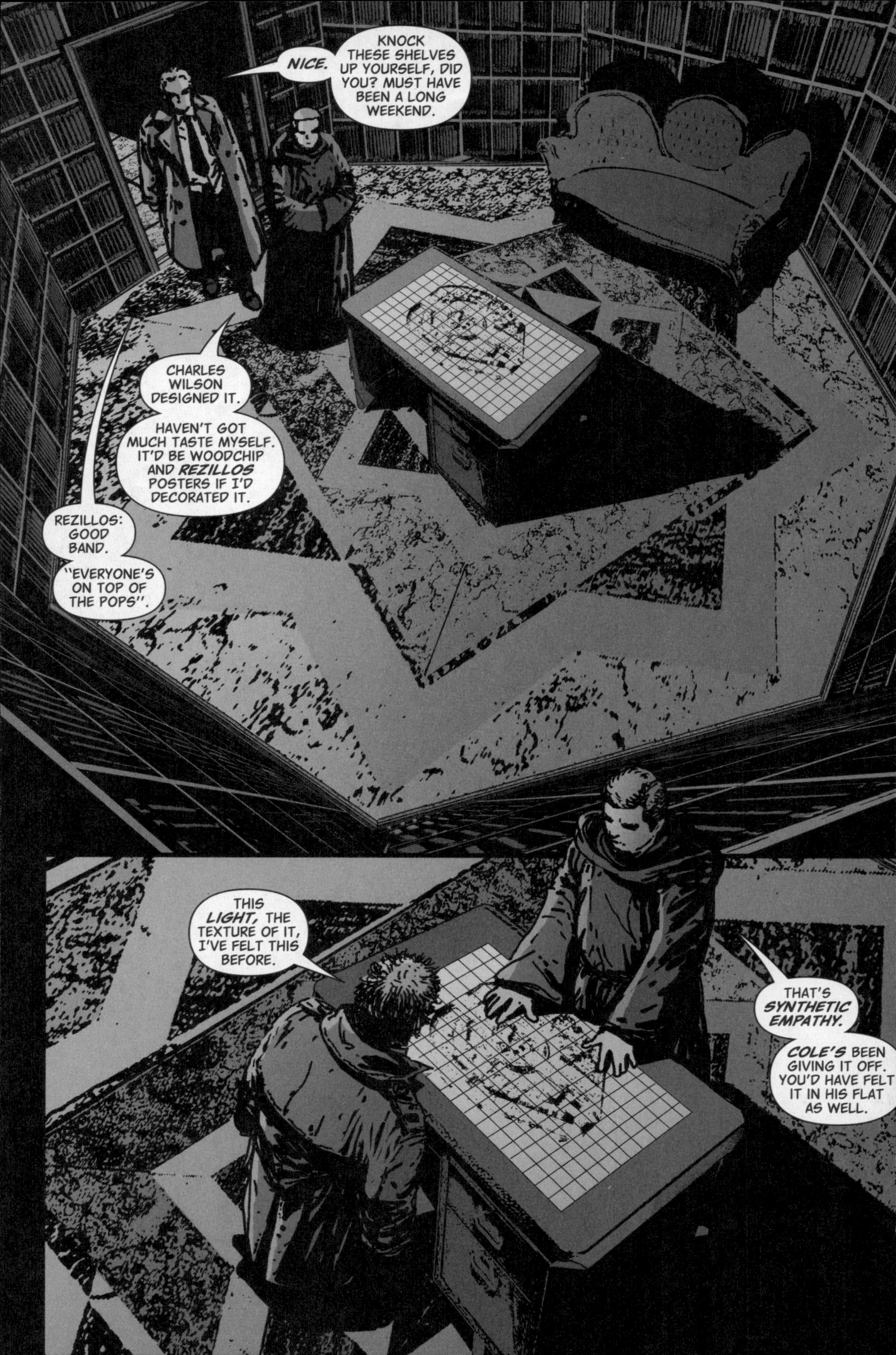

NICE.
KNOCK THESE SHELVES UP YOURSELF, DID YOU? MUST HAVE BEEN A LONG WEEKEND.
CHARLES WILSON DESIGNED IT.
HAVEN'T GOT MUCH TASTE MYSELF. IT'D BE WOODCHIP AND REZILLOS POSTERS IF I'D DECORATED IT.
REZILLOS: GOOD BAND.
"EVERYONE'S ON TOP OF THE POPS".
THIS LIGHT, THE TEXTURE OF IT, I'VE FELT THIS BEFORE.
THAT'S SYNTHETIC EMPATHY.
COLE'S BEEN GIVING IT OFF. YOU'D HAVE FELT IT IN HIS FLAT AS WELL.

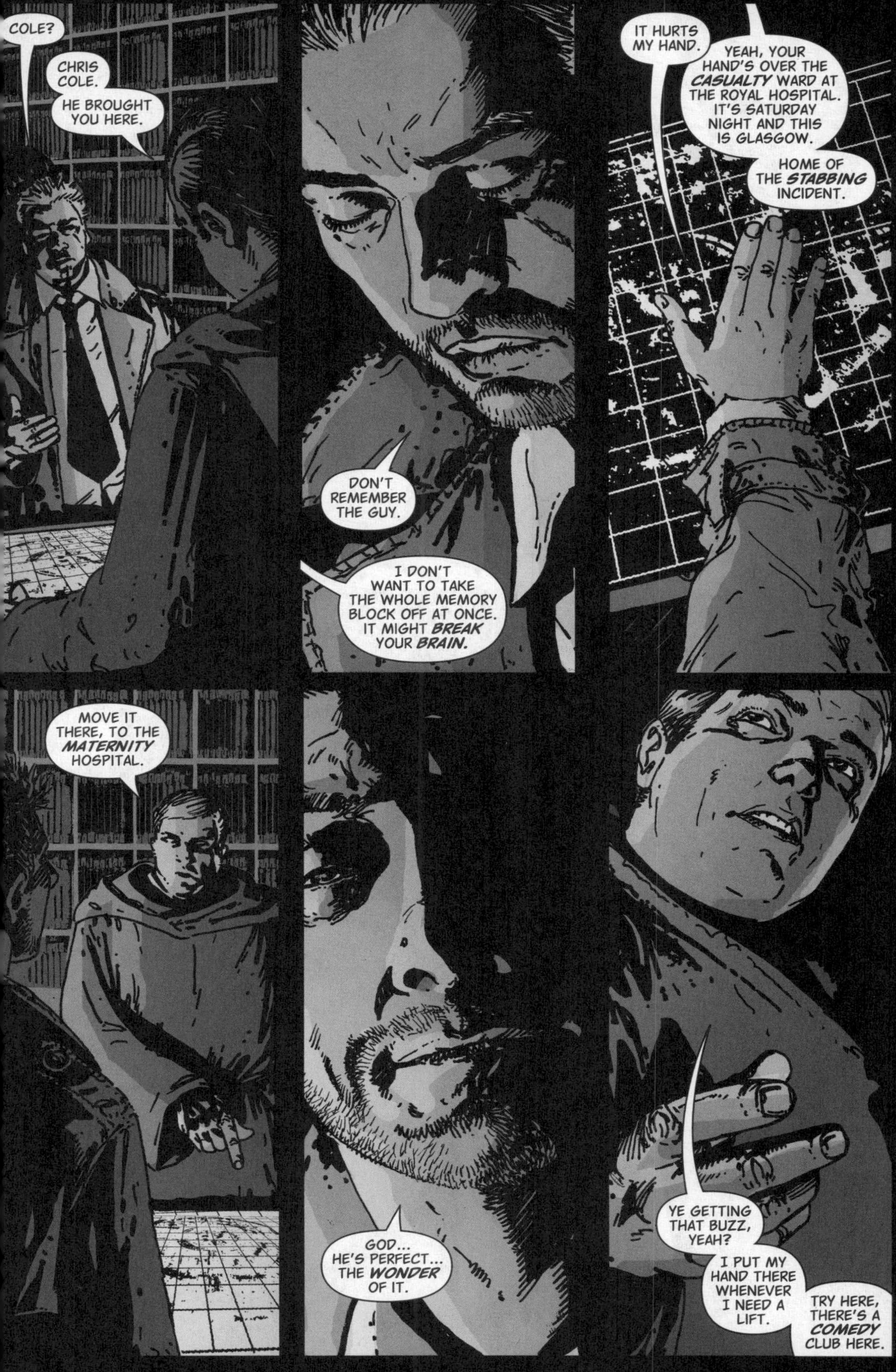
COLE?
CHRIS COLE.
HE BROUGHT YOU HERE.
DON'T REMEMBER THE GUY.
I DON'T WANT TO TAKE THE WHOLE MEMORY BLOCK OFF AT ONCE. IT MIGHT *BREAK* YOUR *BRAIN.*
IT HURTS MY HAND.
YEAH, YOUR HAND'S OVER THE *CASUALTY* WARD AT THE ROYAL HOSPITAL. IT'S SATURDAY NIGHT AND THIS IS GLASGOW.
HOME OF THE *STABBING* INCIDENT.
MOVE IT THERE, TO THE *MATERNITY* HOSPITAL.
GOD... HE'S PERFECT... THE *WONDER* OF IT.
YE GETTING THAT BUZZ, YEAH?
I PUT MY HAND THERE WHENEVER I NEED A LIFT.
TRY HERE, THERE'S A *COMEDY* CLUB HERE.

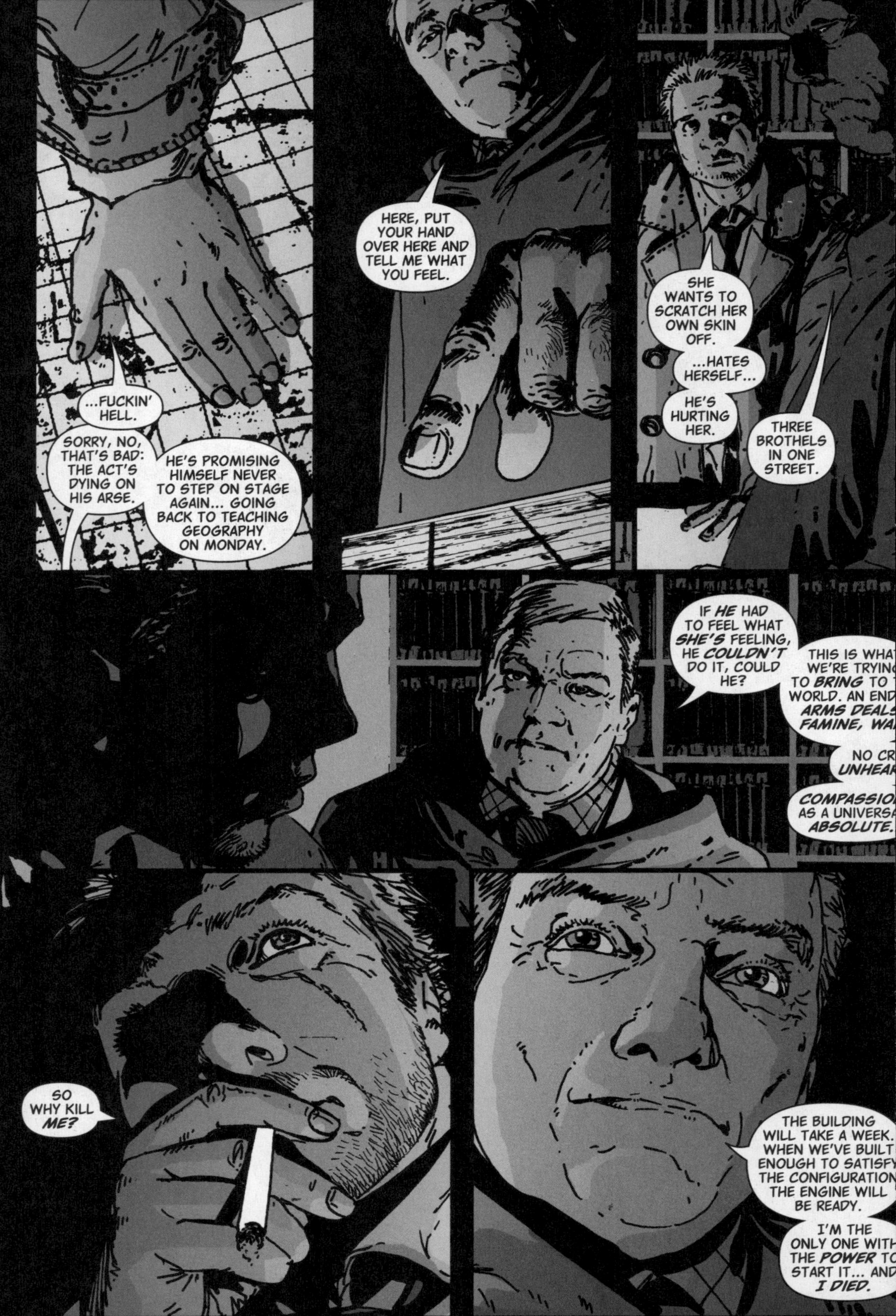
...FUCKIN' HELL.
SORRY, NO, THAT'S BAD: THE ACT'S DYING ON HIS ARSE.
HE'S PROMISING HIMSELF NEVER TO STEP ON STAGE AGAIN... GOING BACK TO TEACHING GEOGRAPHY ON MONDAY.
HERE, PUT YOUR HAND OVER HERE AND TELL ME WHAT YOU FEEL.
SHE WANTS TO SCRATCH HER OWN SKIN OFF.
...HATES HERSELF...
HE'S HURTING HER.
THREE BROTHELS IN ONE STREET.
IF *HE* HAD TO FEEL WHAT *SHE'S* FEELING, HE *COULDN'T* DO IT, COULD HE?
SO WHY KILL *ME?*
THE BUILDING WILL TAKE A WEEK. WHEN WE'VE BUILT ENOUGH TO SATISFY THE CONFIGURATION THE ENGINE WILL BE READY.
I'M THE ONLY ONE WITH THE *POWER* TO START IT... AND *I DIED.*

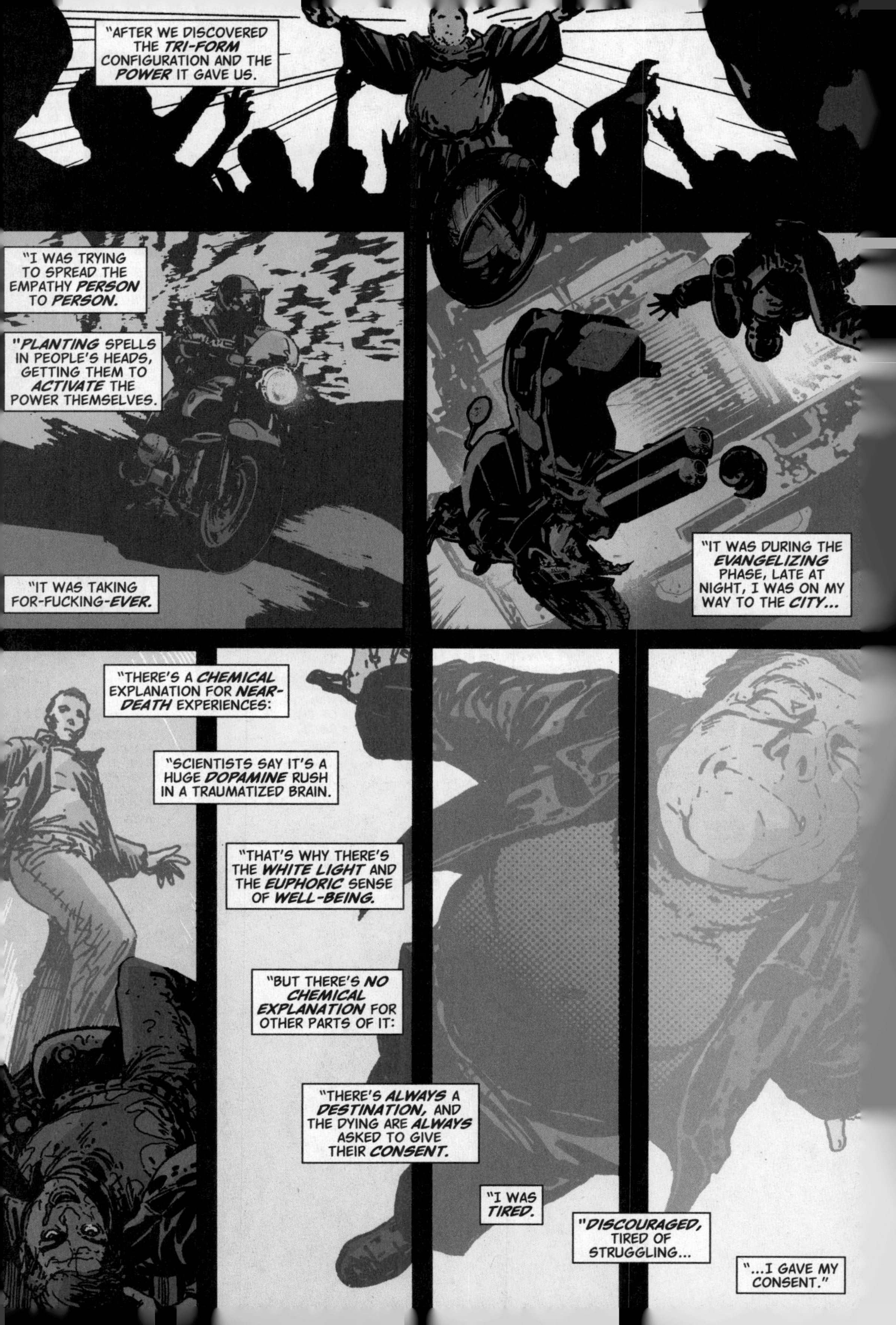
"AFTER WE DISCOVERED THE TRI-FORM CONFIGURATION AND THE POWER IT GAVE US.
"I WAS TRYING TO SPREAD THE EMPATHY PERSON TO PERSON.
"PLANTING SPELLS IN PEOPLE'S HEADS, GETTING THEM TO ACTIVATE THE POWER THEMSELVES.
"IT WAS TAKING FOR-FUCKING-EVER.
"IT WAS DURING THE EVANGELIZING PHASE, LATE AT NIGHT, I WAS ON MY WAY TO THE CITY...
"THERE'S A CHEMICAL EXPLANATION FOR NEAR-DEATH EXPERIENCES:
"SCIENTISTS SAY IT'S A HUGE DOPAMINE RUSH IN A TRAUMATIZED BRAIN.
"THAT'S WHY THERE'S THE WHITE LIGHT AND THE EUPHORIC SENSE OF WELL-BEING.
"BUT THERE'S NO CHEMICAL EXPLANATION FOR OTHER PARTS OF IT:
"THERE'S ALWAYS A DESTINATION, AND THE DYING ARE ALWAYS ASKED TO GIVE THEIR CONSENT.
"I WAS TIRED.
"DISCOURAGED, TIRED OF STRUGGLING...
"...I GAVE MY CONSENT."

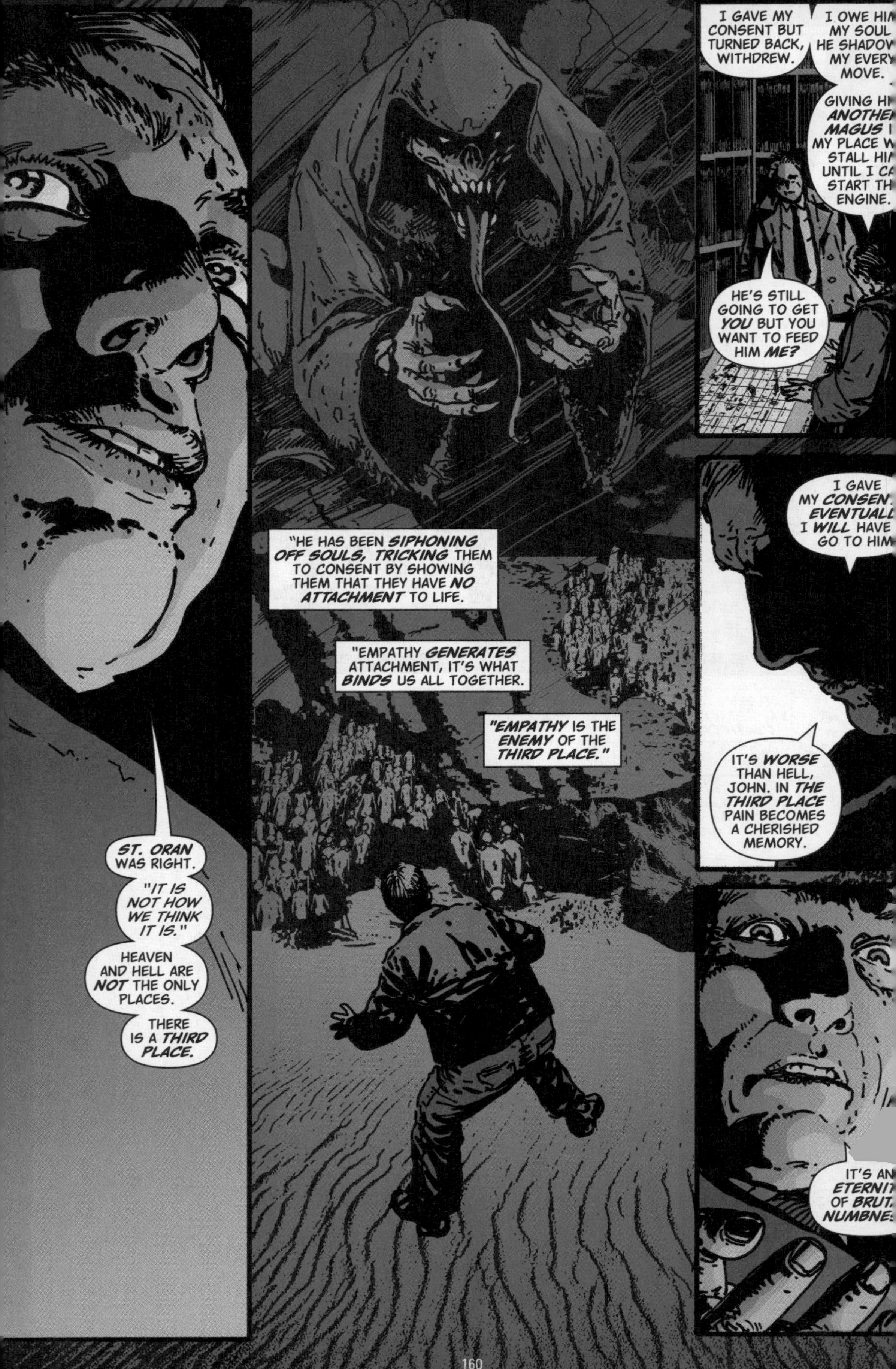
ST. ORAN WAS RIGHT.
"IT IS NOT HOW WE THINK IT IS."
HEAVEN AND HELL ARE NOT THE ONLY PLACES.
THERE IS A THIRD PLACE.
"HE HAS BEEN SIPHONING OFF SOULS, TRICKING THEM TO CONSENT BY SHOWING THEM THAT THEY HAVE NO ATTACHMENT TO LIFE.
"EMPATHY GENERATES ATTACHMENT, IT'S WHAT BINDS US ALL TOGETHER.
"EMPATHY IS THE ENEMY OF THE THIRD PLACE."
I GAVE MY CONSENT BUT TURNED BACK, WITHDREW.
I OWE HI MY SOUL HE SHADOW MY EVERY MOVE.
GIVING HI ANOTHE MAGUS I MY PLACE W STALL HI UNTIL I C START TH ENGINE.
HE'S STILL GOING TO GET YOU BUT YOU WANT TO FEED HIM ME?
I GAVE MY CONSEN EVENTUALL I WILL HAVE GO TO HIM
IT'S WORSE THAN HELL, JOHN. IN THE THIRD PLACE PAIN BECOMES A CHERISHED MEMORY.
IT'S AN ETERNIT OF BRUT NUMBNE

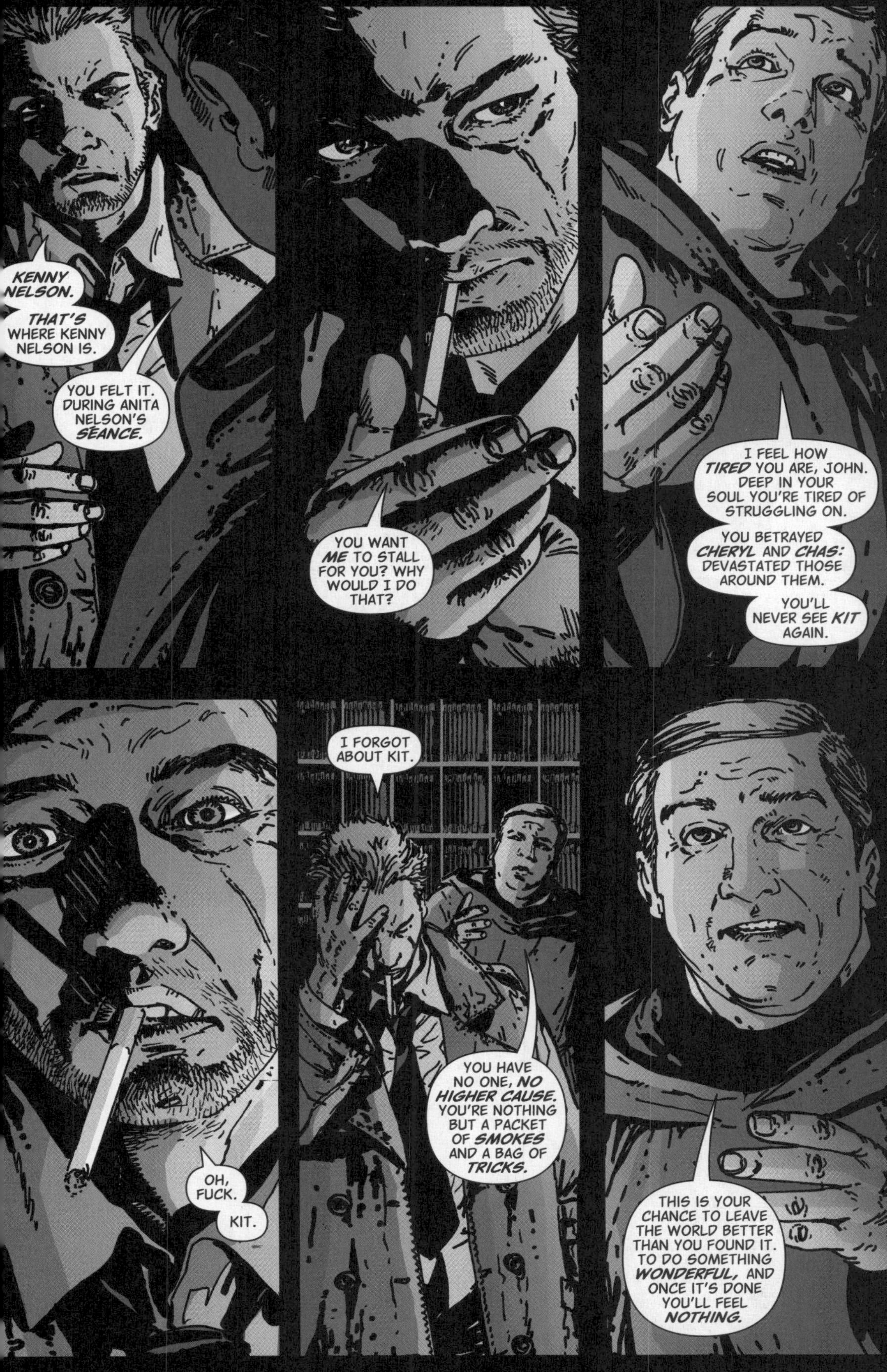
KENNY NELSON.
THAT'S WHERE KENNY NELSON IS.
YOU FELT IT. DURING ANITA NELSON'S SÉANCE.
YOU WANT ME TO STALL FOR YOU? WHY WOULD I DO THAT?
I FEEL HOW TIRED YOU ARE, JOHN. DEEP IN YOUR SOUL YOU'RE TIRED OF STRUGGLING ON.
YOU BETRAYED CHERYL AND CHAS: DEVASTATED THOSE AROUND THEM.
YOU'LL NEVER SEE KIT AGAIN.
OH, FUCK.
KIT.
I FORGOT ABOUT KIT.
YOU HAVE NO ONE, NO HIGHER CAUSE. YOU'RE NOTHING BUT A PACKET OF SMOKES AND A BAG OF TRICKS.
THIS IS YOUR CHANCE TO LEAVE THE WORLD BETTER THAN YOU FOUND IT. TO DO SOMETHING WONDERFUL, AND ONCE IT'S DONE YOU'LL FEEL NOTHING.

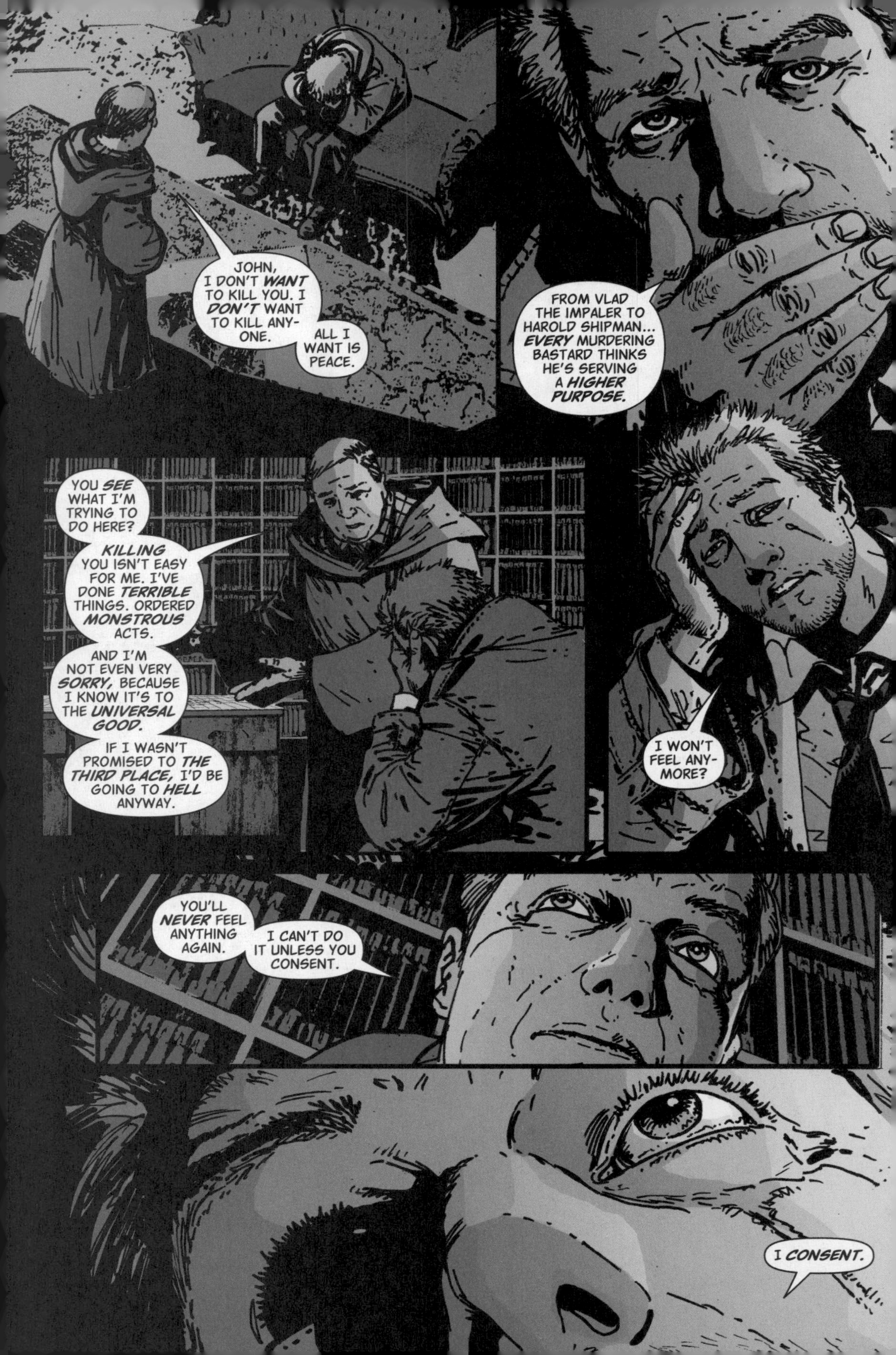
JOHN, I DON'T WANT TO KILL YOU. I DON'T WANT TO KILL ANY-ONE.
ALL I WANT IS PEACE.
FROM VLAD THE IMPALER TO HAROLD SHIPMAN... EVERY MURDERING BASTARD THINKS HE'S SERVING A HIGHER PURPOSE.
YOU SEE WHAT I'M TRYING TO DO HERE?
KILLING YOU ISN'T EASY FOR ME. I'VE DONE TERRIBLE THINGS. ORDERED MONSTROUS ACTS.
AND I'M NOT EVEN VERY SORRY, BECAUSE I KNOW IT'S TO THE UNIVERSAL GOOD.
IF I WASN'T PROMISED TO THE THIRD PLACE, I'D BE GOING TO HELL ANYWAY.
I WON'T FEEL ANY-MORE?
YOU'LL NEVER FEEL ANYTHING AGAIN.
I CAN'T DO IT UNLESS YOU CONSENT.
I CONSENT.

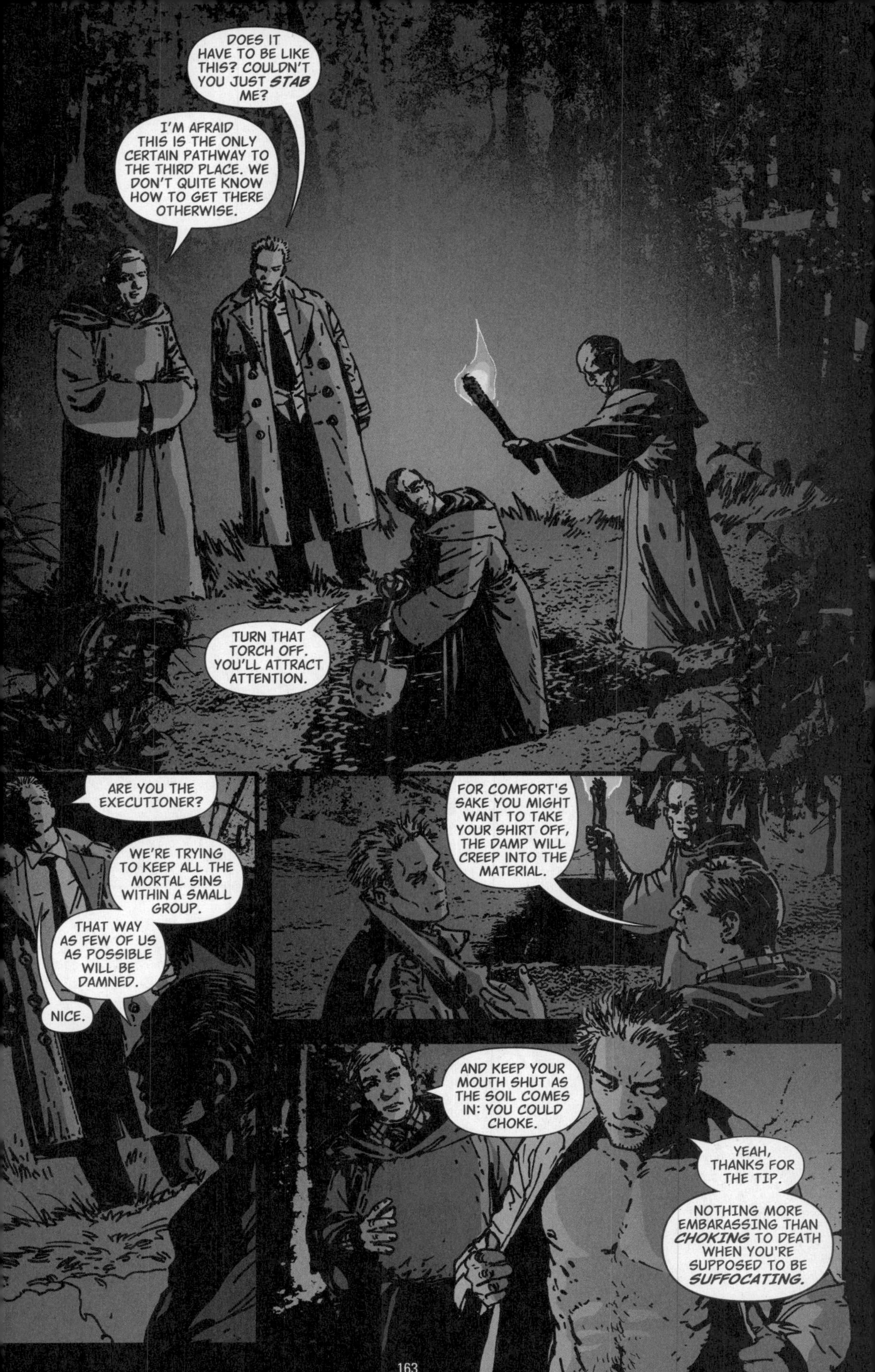
DOES IT HAVE TO BE LIKE THIS? COULDN'T YOU JUST STAB ME?
I'M AFRAID THIS IS THE ONLY CERTAIN PATHWAY TO THE THIRD PLACE. WE DON'T QUITE KNOW HOW TO GET THERE OTHERWISE.
TURN THAT TORCH OFF. YOU'LL ATTRACT ATTENTION.
ARE YOU THE EXECUTIONER?
WE'RE TRYING TO KEEP ALL THE MORTAL SINS WITHIN A SMALL GROUP.
THAT WAY AS FEW OF US AS POSSIBLE WILL BE DAMNED.
NICE.
FOR COMFORT'S SAKE YOU MIGHT WANT TO TAKE YOUR SHIRT OFF, THE DAMP WILL CREEP INTO THE MATERIAL.
AND KEEP YOUR MOUTH SHUT AS THE SOIL COMES IN: YOU COULD CHOKE.
YEAH, THANKS FOR THE TIP.
NOTHING MORE EMBARASSING THAN CHOKING TO DEATH WHEN YOU'RE SUPPOSED TO BE SUFFOCATING.

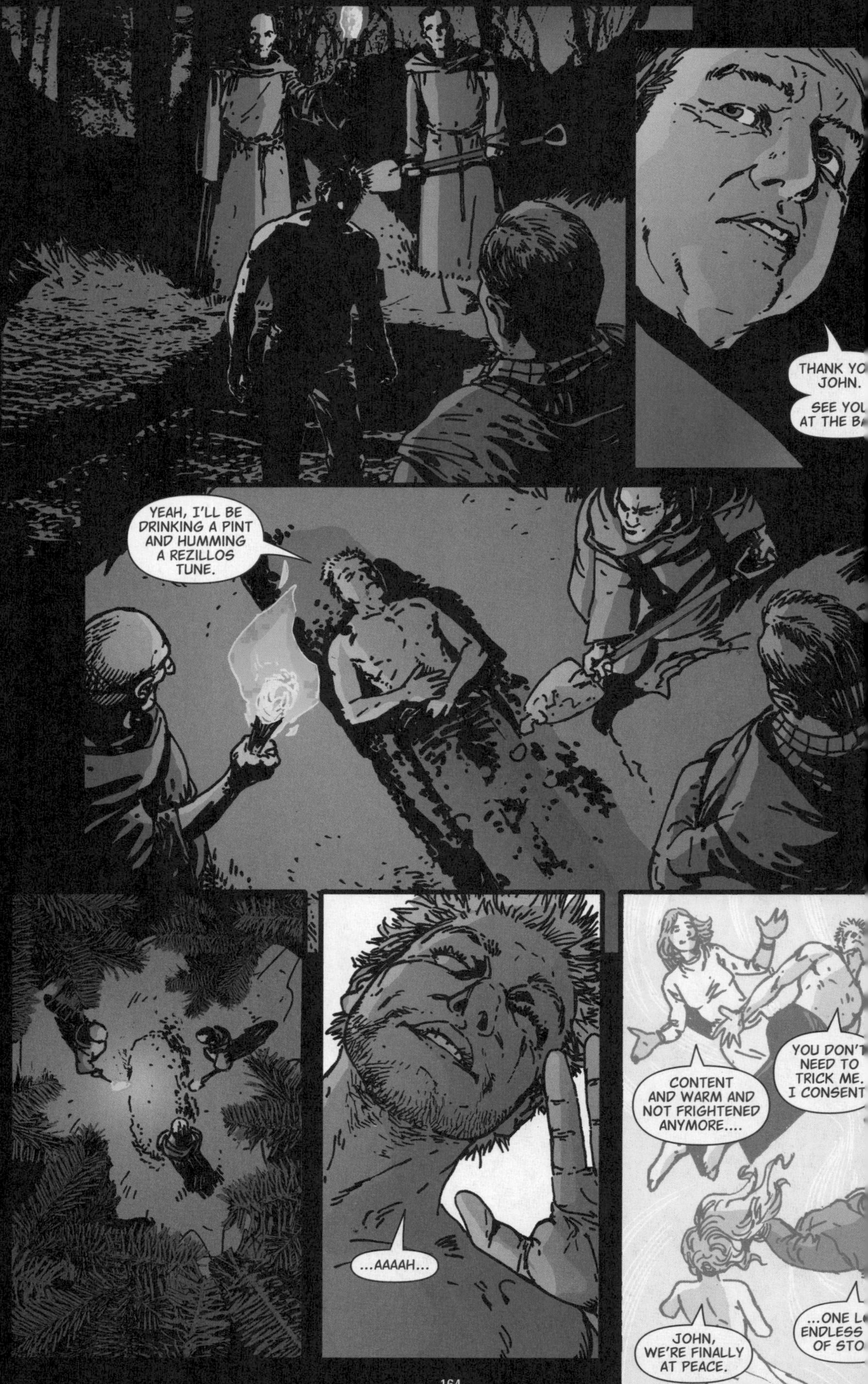
THANK YO JOHN.
SEE YOU AT THE B
YEAH, I'LL BE DRINKING A PINT AND HUMMING A REZILLOS TUNE.
...AAAAH...
CONTENT AND WARM AND NOT FRIGHTENED ANYMORE....
YOU DON'T NEED TO TRICK ME. I CONSENT
JOHN, WE'RE FINALLY AT PEACE.
...ONE L ENDLESS OF STO

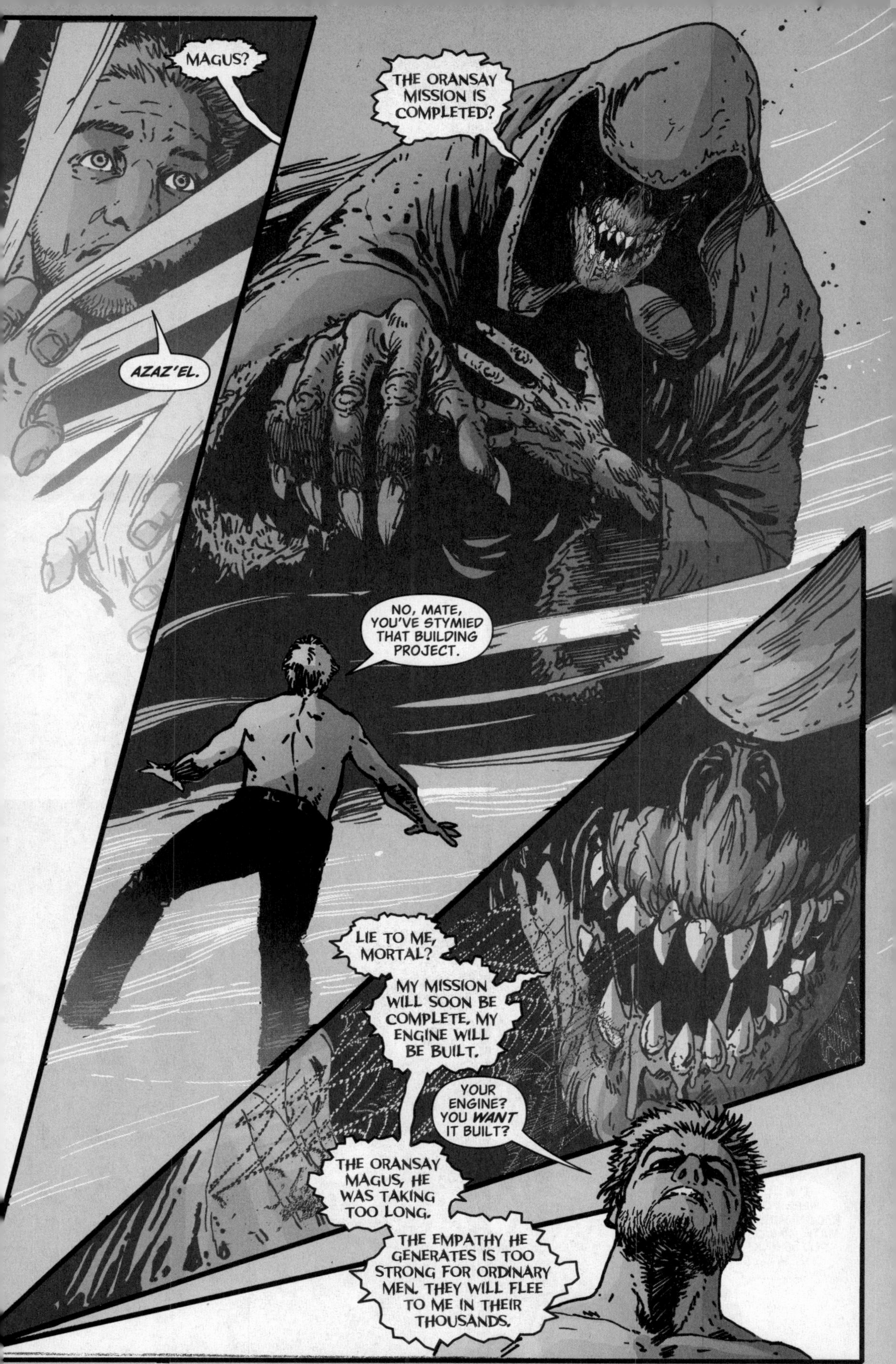
MAGUS?
THE ORANSAY MISSION IS COMPLETED?
AZAZ'EL.
NO, MATE, YOU'VE STYMIED THAT BUILDING PROJECT.
LIE TO ME, MORTAL?
MY MISSION WILL SOON BE COMPLETE. MY ENGINE WILL BE BUILT.
YOUR ENGINE? YOU *WANT* IT BUILT?
THE ORANSAY MAGUS, HE WAS TAKING TOO LONG.
THE EMPATHY HE GENERATES IS TOO STRONG FOR ORDINARY MEN. THEY WILL FLEE TO ME IN THEIR THOUSANDS.

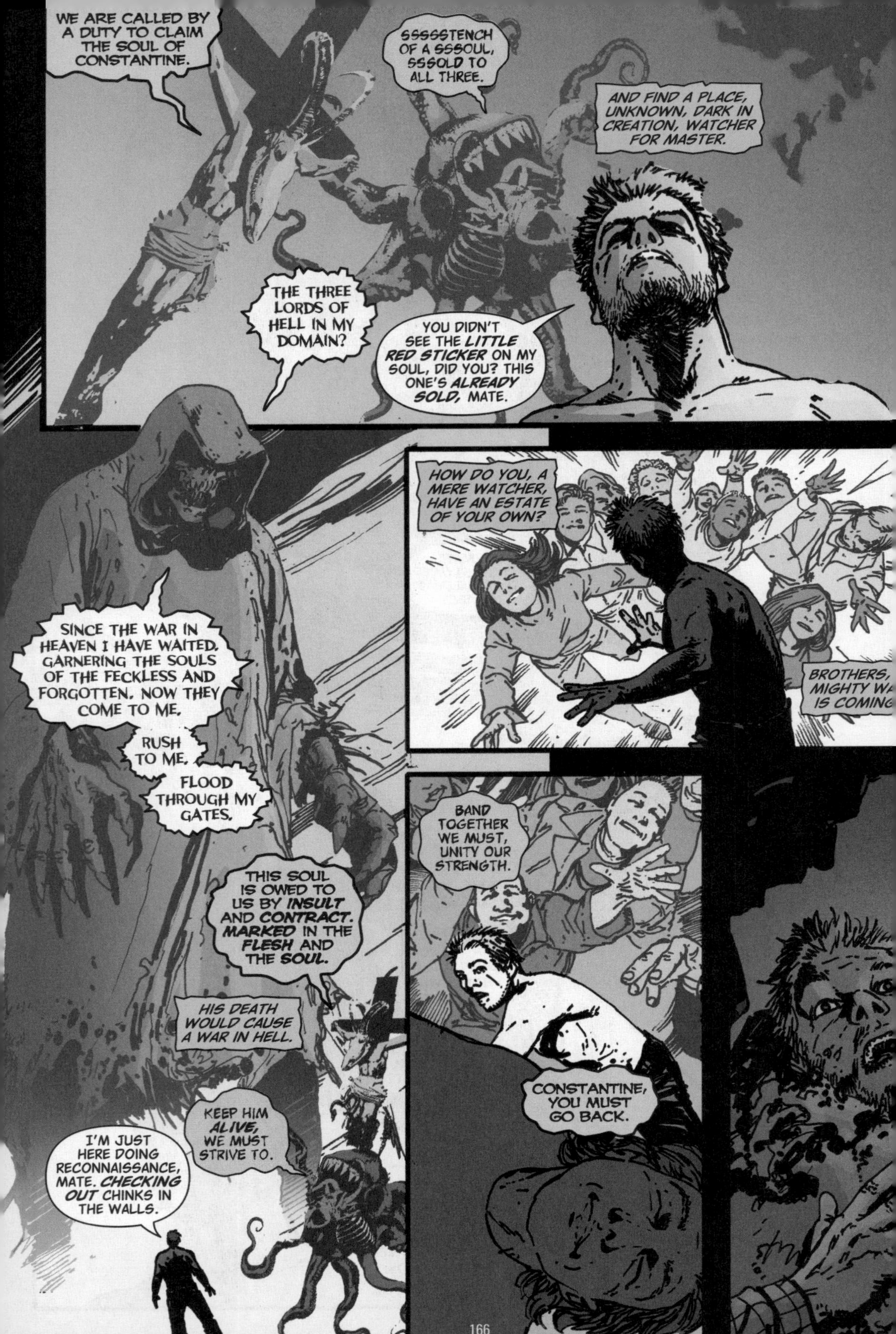
WE ARE CALLED BY A DUTY TO CLAIM THE SOUL OF CONSTANTINE.
SSSSSTENCH OF A SSSOUL, SSSOLD TO ALL THREE.
AND FIND A PLACE, UNKNOWN, DARK IN CREATION, WATCHER FOR MASTER.
THE THREE LORDS OF HELL IN MY DOMAIN?
YOU DIDN'T SEE THE LITTLE RED STICKER ON MY SOUL, DID YOU? THIS ONE'S ALREADY SOLD, MATE.
HOW DO YOU, A MERE WATCHER, HAVE AN ESTATE OF YOUR OWN?
SINCE THE WAR IN HEAVEN I HAVE WAITED. GARNERING THE SOULS OF THE FECKLESS AND FORGOTTEN. NOW THEY COME TO ME.
RUSH TO ME.
FLOOD THROUGH MY GATES.
BROTHERS, MIGHTY WA IS COMING
BAND TOGETHER WE MUST, UNITY OUR STRENGTH.
THIS SOUL IS OWED TO US BY INSULT AND CONTRACT. MARKED IN THE FLESH AND THE SOUL.
HIS DEATH WOULD CAUSE A WAR IN HELL.
KEEP HIM ALIVE, WE MUST STRIVE TO.
I'M JUST HERE DOING RECONNAISSANCE, MATE. CHECKING OUT CHINKS IN THE WALLS.
CONSTANTINE, YOU MUST GO BACK.

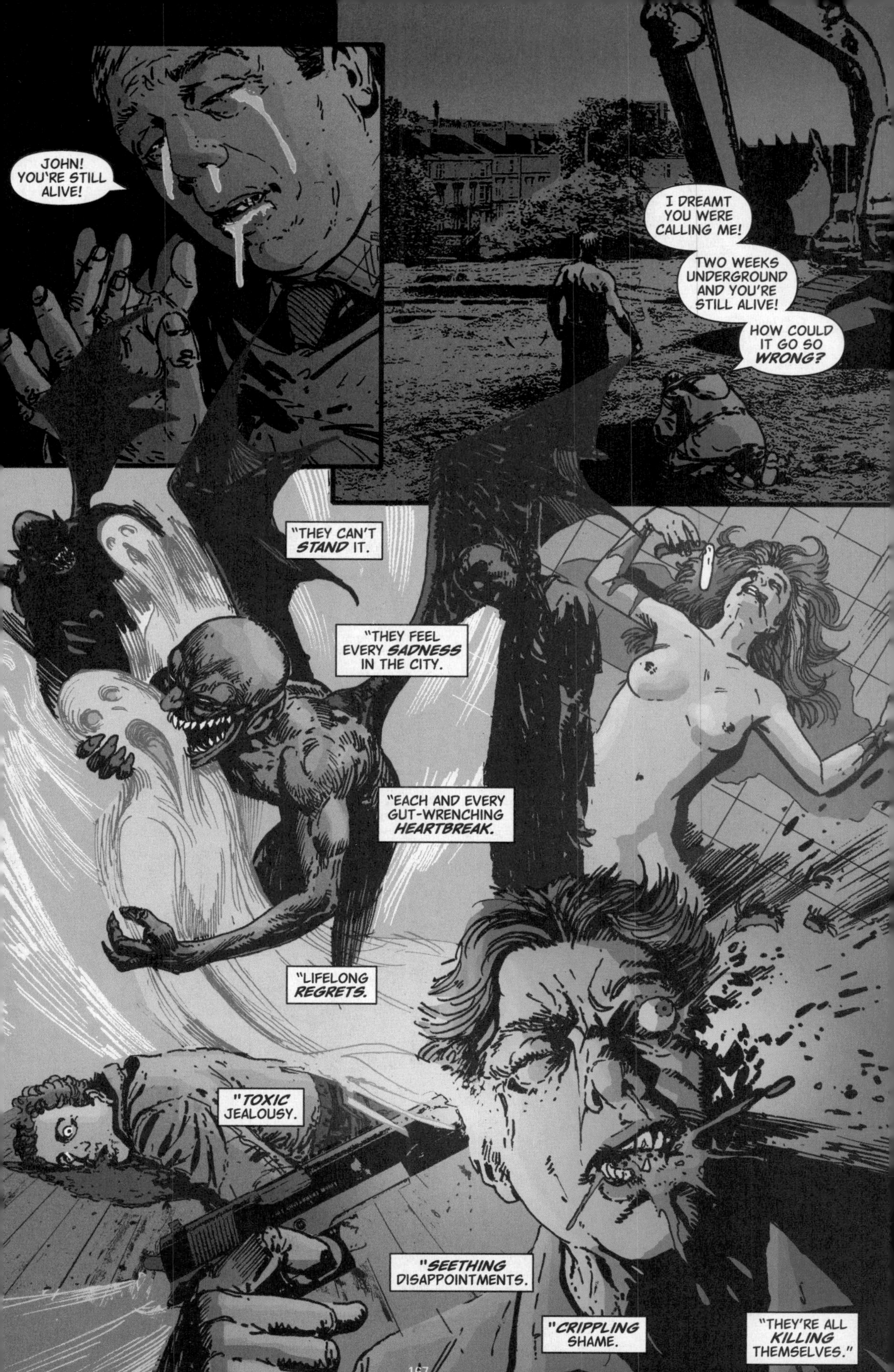
JOHN! YOU'RE STILL ALIVE!
I DREAMT YOU WERE CALLING ME!
TWO WEEKS UNDERGROUND AND YOU'RE STILL ALIVE!
HOW COULD IT GO SO *WRONG?*
"THEY CAN'T *STAND* IT.
"THEY FEEL EVERY *SADNESS* IN THE CITY.
"EACH AND EVERY GUT-WRENCHING *HEARTBREAK.*
"LIFELONG *REGRETS.*
"*TOXIC* JEALOUSY.
"*SEETHING* DISAPPOINTMENTS.
"*CRIPPLING* SHAME.
"THEY'RE ALL *KILLING* THEMSELVES."

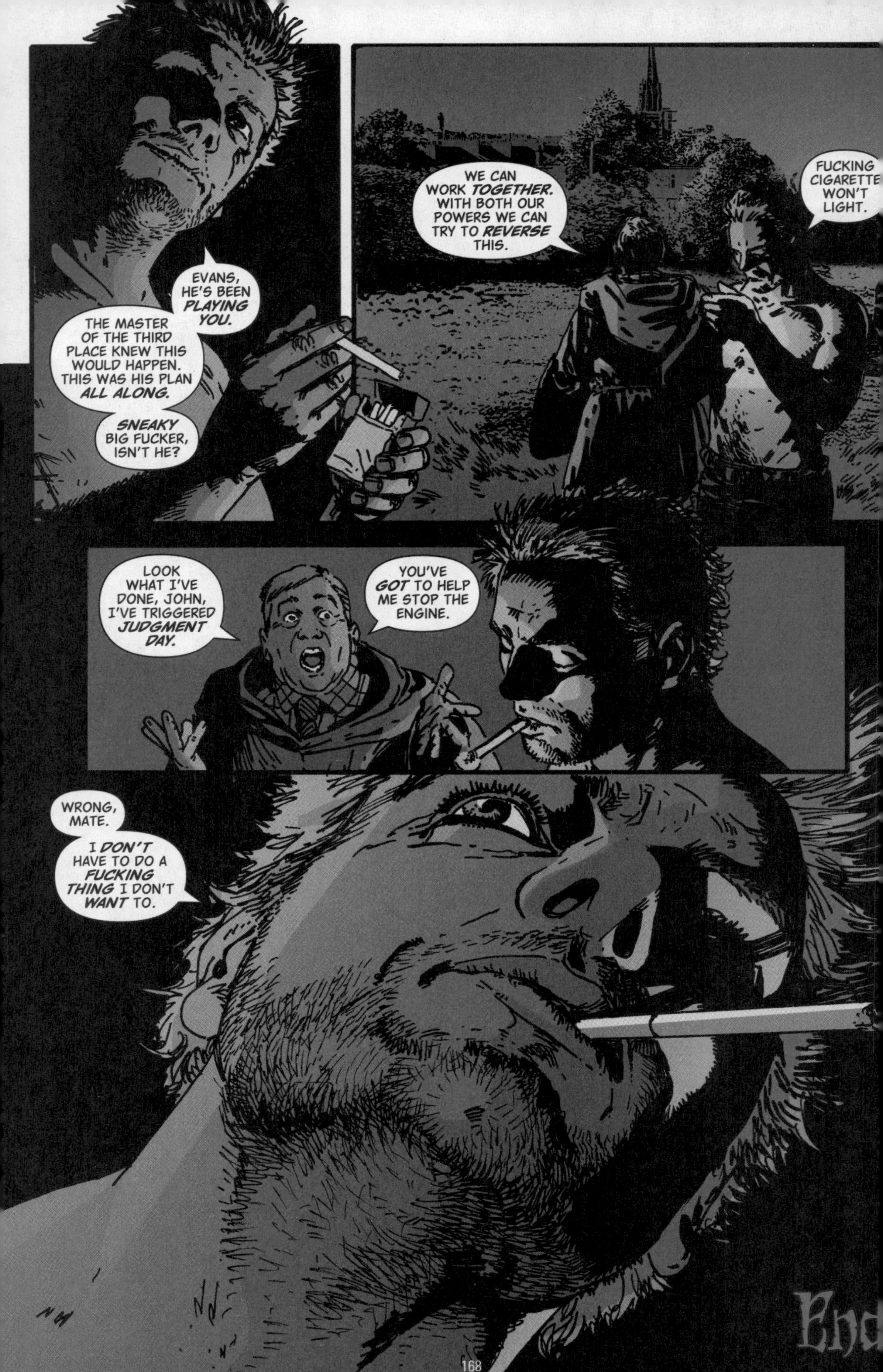
EVANS, HE'S BEEN PLAYING YOU.
THE MASTER OF THE THIRD PLACE KNEW THIS WOULD HAPPEN. THIS WAS HIS PLAN ALL ALONG.
SNEAKY BIG FUCKER, ISN'T HE?
WE CAN WORK TOGETHER. WITH BOTH OUR POWERS WE CAN TRY TO REVERSE THIS.
FUCKING CIGARETTE WON'T LIGHT.
LOOK WHAT I'VE DONE, JOHN, I'VE TRIGGERED JUDGMENT DAY.
YOU'VE GOT TO HELP ME STOP THE ENGINE.
WRONG, MATE.
I DON'T HAVE TO DO A FUCKING THING I DON'T WANT TO.
End